A HISTORY OF
DANISH
LITERATURE

A HISTORY OF

DANISH

LITERATURE

BY

P. M. MITCHELL

WITH AN INTRODUCTORY CHAPTER
BY
MOGENS HAUGSTED

SECOND, AUGMENTED EDITION

KRAUS-THOMSON ORGANIZATION LIMITED
New York
1971

PUBLISHED UNDER THE AUSPICES OF
UDVALGET FOR UDBREDELSE AF KENDSKAB TIL DANSK LITTERATUR I UDLANDET AND
LEKTORATSUDVALGET OF SAMVIRKERÅDET FOR DANSK KULTURARBEJDE I UDLANDET,
WITH DANISH STATE SUPPORT,
AND IN CONJUNCTION WITH THE AMERICAN-SCANDINAVIAN FOUNDATION

Printed in U.S.A.

NOTE TO THE SECOND EDITION

The first edition of this history was published under the auspices of Samvirke-rådet for dansk Kulturarbejde i Udlandet and The American-Scandinavian Foundation. It was issued in Copenhagen in 1957 and in New York in 1958. The present edition incorporates some minor changes in the text of the first fifteen chapters and a new, sixteenth chapter which depicts the development of Danish literature through the year 1970.

I record with gratitude a continuing debt to the staff of the Royal Library in Copenhagen for many privileges, to the Research Board of the University of Illinois for financial support, and to Professor F. J. Billeskov Jansen for encouragement and counsel.

P. M. MITCHELL

ACKNOWLEDGMENTS

The incentive to write this book came from Dr. Henry Goddard Leach of The American-Scandinavian Foundation. The constructive criticism needed for its completion was provided by Professor F. J. Billeskov Jansen of the University of Copenhagen.

My colleagues Professors William D. Paden and Oswald P. Backus read the first draft of the manuscript for style and historical interpretation. Dr. Aage Kabell made numerous suggestions about its factual content. Professor Holger Nygard advised me regarding the Danish folk ballads. Mr. George Herman, M. A., helped prepare the English version of the introductory chapter. Miss Nancy Jamison, M. A., assisted editorially with several chapters. Dr. Svend Dahl has seen the volume through the press.

To the staffs of the Royal Library in Copenhagen and the library of the University of Kansas I am grateful for many kindnesses during a period of several years. I have also been privileged to use the Harvard College Library and the library of the University of Wisconsin.

Financial assistance from the University of Kansas Endowment Association and the University's general research fund enabled me to spend two summers at the Royal Library. A Fulbright grant gave me the opportunity to augment and complete the manuscript in Denmark and, above all, to benefit from the counsels of Professor Billeskov Jansen.

The publication of the book in its present form has been made possible by the coöperation of the Danish Ministry of Education.

P. M. MITCHELL

LIST OF ILLUSTRATIONS

TABLE OF CONTENTS

PREFACE

There is something artificial about limiting one's view to the literature of a single country or a single language. No literature develops in splendid isolation; on the contrary, ideological and formalistic movements cut across national boundaries. The literature of Denmark or of any other Western nation should be seen against a general European background. The literary fashions of France, Germany, England, and Italy have in varying degrees regularly made their way to Denmark.

What is more, Denmark has shared a common heritage with the other Scandinavian countries, a heritage which not only is ethnic, linguistic, and political, but has roots that extend back into an indigenous culture which flourished prior to the introduction of Christianity. Noteworthy is the fact that, since the beginning of the historical era, Denmark, Sweden, and Norway have spoken mutually intelligible dialects or languages.

While the country has enjoyed political independence from the earliest times, the possibilities of an independent cultural development in small, flat, peninsular Denmark have been fewer than in the rougher and more expansive landscapes of Norway and Sweden, not to speak of the insular character of Iceland.

Denmark is nevertheless more than a European state or a part of Scandinavia, and Danish literature is more than a conglomeration of external associations. A small country with a high culture, Denmark constitutes neither an arbitrary political division nor a heterogeneous domain. Its literary record is more than the reflection of intellectual activity on the larger European or Scandinavian scene.

In so far as it is the expression of a distinct and enduring linguistic and political unit, Danish literature, although undeniably dependent on shifting social and economic conditions, has a claim to individual consideration as a singular, organic, cultural phenomenon. It warrants the attention of the outside world at least for those works by Danish authors which transcend local or national demands and interests, by virtue of ethical content and aesthetic excellence.

Not to be left out of consideration is the fact that Denmark, once a great power and now one of the smaller nations of Europe, for centuries a land of agriculturalists and traders and now a closely-knit agricultural, commercial, and industrial state, has persistently had Copenhagen as its cultural font and literary center. Although there has been literature produced outside the Danish capital, the dominant literature of every century has been an adjunct to life in Copenhagen.

While imaginative literature cannot be understood aesthetically if it is approached only on the plane of cultural history, neither can it be grasped in its historical significance if one loses sight of the aesthetic standards by which it is judged. A history of literature tries therefore to combine cultural history with critical interpretation. The present study is consequently an attempt to synthesize an historical presentation with the evaluation of single works which, because of their ethos and literary form, stand as contributions to the enrichment of human existence, the understanding of life, and the comprehension of the possibilities which lie within the realm of the human spirit.

Not all Danish writers have found a place in this history and of those treated many works remain unmentioned. It has seemed pointless to print a compilation of titles which have limited intrinsic value or which are neither historically nor currently significant, which are not living literature and therefore can have little if any meaning outside Denmark. The books which are discussed generally comprise the best known and most highly esteemed works of original or representative writers.

It is trite to complain of the peculiar difficulty in trying to appraise contemporary literature. Even at the risk of failing to give some authors their just due, the literary historian, lacking the perspicacity granted by the passage of time, is wisest in dwelling on works which demonstrate the patterns that he discerns in recent literature, rather than attempting a prognosis of future literary judgment.

The responsibility for the selection of writers and their works which are discussed in the present history rests with the author. Despite the deficiencies and discrepancies which may have resulted, the volume should suffice as evidence that Danish literature has treasures in addition to those suggested by the names of Ludvig Holberg, Hans Christian Andersen, Søren Kierkegaard and the few other Danish writers who already have been accepted into the literature of the world through the medium of translation.

CHAPTER I

Introduction

by

Mogens Haugsted

At the outset of a history of Danish literature, it is fitting to consider the sequence of generations which brought forth the Danish people and which underlie the development of their literature. From as far back as about 10,000 B.C., toward the end of the Ice Age, we have archeological evidence of human activity in the geographical area which is now Denmark, when a tribe of hunters, following reindeer, appear to have penetrated the land from the south. These men were so to speak the first "Danes," but of their ethnic characteristics little is known. We are better informed about the population of the Neolithic Age. These people were agriculturalists with fixed abode. Around 2000 B.C. they faced a great crisis, an invasion from the south of a warrior tribe which fought its way up through Jutland and crossed the Danish Islands. These immigrant warriors, the so-called single-grave people, were doubtless Indo-Europeans. They conquered the indigenous population, and by 1500 B.C., after the beginning of the Bronze Age, the two races were amalgamated in an era of material well-being. We now have evidences of an upper class basing its culture on farming and shipping, and commerce in which Baltic amber plays a notable rôle.

The assimilation of the various races living in Denmark during the Bronze Age seems to have formed the Danish people as we know them in history. Various emigrations and immigrations took place as the centuries passed, but there is no observable major racial change after the second century B.C. Together with other Scandinavians, the Danes are a North Germanic people closely related to the Anglo-Saxons, the Frisians, the Germans, and the Dutch.

It is of course impossible to know anything with certainty about the nature of poetry in prehistoric times. It is not until the Viking Age that we have authentic sources on which to draw; about an earlier poetry we can only guess on the basis of our knowledge of present-day primitive societies.

Of indigenous poetry, the oldest apparent traces are the strange stone engravings which date from the Bronze Age. These inscriptions were presumably of magic import. To understand their possible significance we must bear in mind that man in those times, far more than today, was dependent on nature's grace and sought to placate unknown powers by ritual and sacrifice. The poetic word must have had its mission in the ceremonies which we interpret the inscriptions to represent. Likewise, and by analogy, we may assume that the migrations and wars which took place around the year 2000 B.C. may also have been reflected in heroic poetry; but all evidence of such a hypothesized oral tradition is lacking; the poetry or ritual which they may evince is conjectural, and the inscriptions we have are not the later runes.

So it is that the history of the language itself provides our most reliable evidences from the prehistoric era. Danish, like the other Scandinavian languages—Swedish, Norwegian, Icelandic, and Faeroese—is a branch of the Germanic family, which also embraces English, Frisian, Dutch, Flemish, and Low and High German, as well as the extinct languages Gothic and Burgundian. By 200 A.D., Primitive Scandinavian had separated from the tongue we identify as Common Germanic. It was, therefore, a sister-tongue to Old English and Old High and Low German. Until about 800 A.D., all the Scandinavians spoke a single language which had developed from this Primitive Scandinavian. Then by the beginning of the Viking Age, we notice a division into an East Scandinavian dialect spoken by the Danes and Swedes, and a West Scandinavian dialect spoken by the Norwegians and later by the Icelanders and Faroese. By the year 1000, this dialectal development was completed, but the Scandinavian sense of linguistic unity was so pronounced that as late as 1340 an Icelander identified his mother tongue by the designation that had been used for Common Scandinavian before 800 A.D.: "the Danish language."

RUNIC INSCRIPTIONS

As in the history of all nations, the moment when it became possible to preserve the word by use of symbols was decisive in the history of Scandinavia. The art of writing came to Denmark in the third century through southern Jutland. Knowledge of the runic alphabet probably filtered north from the Saxons, but the exact origin of runes is still in dispute. It is possible that they were an imitation of the Latin or Greek alphabet; it is possible that they had Etruscan models. In Denmark we may distinguish two periods of runic inscription. From the first period, up to about 750 A.D., few inscriptions are preserved, all in the older futharc or runic alphabet, which comprised 24 symbols. During the second period, which lasted into the Middle Ages, a younger futharc of only 16 symbols was employed.

The inscriptions made with the older runes are not literature in the usual sense of the word. They are very short: bits of personal property like combs and amulets often have names scratched on them; just as frequently, series of runes which have no meaning whatsoever are to be found on such items. It is possible that these were formulae of magic power.

Despite the brevity characteristic of the older runic inscriptions, a single inscription bespeaks the possibilities of the language. It is found on one of the two golden horns dating from about 400 A.D., both of which were discovered near Gallehus in the vicinity of Møgeltønder (southern Jutland), respectively in 1639 and in 1734. On the shorter horn is the inscription:

> Ek hlewagastiʀ holtijaʀ horna tawido
> (I, Laegast, son of Holte made this horn.)

We note that three words alliterate with *h*—and that there are resonant vowel endings. One can imagine the poetry of the time to have been recited in a language of which these traits are characteristic.

Toward the seventh century the use of runes decreased, but not before the art had been carried to Norway and Sweden, whence it returned to Denmark in the eighth century, together with the custom of cutting runes in stone. At the same time occurred the above-mentioned simplification of the runic alphabet from 24 to 16 symbols. Several periods can be defined in the history of younger runic literature. Below are some examples from the classical age of runic stones, that is, from about 850 to 1050. The oldest stones bear only a name. Later inscriptions state who erected the stone and in whose memory it was raised, what the deceased had been in society, and who cut the inscription. Some inscriptions conclude with a curse upon him who would misuse or destroy the stone. A complete inscription of this type, incidentally Denmark's longest, is found on the Glavendrup stone, near Odense on the island of Funen, and dates from about 900:

> raknhiltr sati stainþąnsi auft ala sauluakuþa uialiþshaiþuiar þanþia kn ala suniʀ karþu kubl þausi aft faþur sin auk hąns kuna auft uar sin in suti raist runaʀ þasi aft trutin sin þur uiki þasi runaʀ at rita sa uarþi is stain þansi ailti iþa aft ąnąn traki.
>
> (Ragnhild raised this stone in memory of Alli, priest in Salve, the revered servant of the temple. Alli's sons raised this monument in memory of their father, and his wife

in memory of her lord. But Sote hewed these runes in memory of his lord. May Thor hallow these runes! He shall atone his guilt who throws down this stone or removes it elsewhere.)

Not everyone had such a stone raised in his memory: only a few chieftains were so commemorated. It is not surprising that the rune stone sometimes took on the rôle of a public monument representative of the king himself. Best known is King Harald Bluetooth's monument erected near the town of Jellinge in mid-Jutland between 983 and 987 to honor his parents, but likewise also to disseminate his own fame.

> haraltr kunukr baþ kaurua kubl þausi aft kurmfaþursin aukaft þąuri muþur sina sa haraltr ias sąʀ uan tanmaurk ala auk nuruiak auk tani karþi kristną.

(Harald the king ordered this monument to be raised in honor of Gorm his father and Thyra his mother, the Harald who won all Denmark and Norway and made the Danes Christians.)

The stone bears a representation of a haloed Christ on one side and a heathen lion on the other. This monument is historically significant, then, not only in establishing the fact that it was Harald who made Christianity the state religion, but in attesting the meeting of two cultures, the tensions of the times, and an era of transition. Unwittingly the artist who carved the Jellinge stone raised a monument announcing the end of indigenous culture and the advent of a new cultural era in Denmark. With the very runic symbols which immortalized the cultural highpoint of pagan Scandinavia, he spelled the certain triumph of Christian, Judaic, and Roman culture in the North. Here too is the unconscious beginning of the centuries-long domination of ecclesiastical Christian thought in Denmark and the assurance that if a literature was to arise in Denmark, it would be guided by ecclesiastical hands.

Some memorial runic inscriptions have almost a lyrical tone, as for example in the rhythmic formula on the Aarhus stone raised about 1000 A.D. to the memory of a certain Asser by his viking companions; it concludes:

> saʀ tu mana mest uniþikʀ   (He died of men the most noble,
> saʀ ati skib miþ arną   he owned a ship with Arni.)

There is a similar rhythm in the words of Ragnhild honoring her late husband (Tryggevælde stone, about 925):

> faiʀ uar þa nufutiʀ   (few are now born
> þąibatri   better than he.)

It is significant that the only verse fully preserved from the Viking Age is the result of a specific deed which took place about 980, when Toke Gormsson was killed together with his followers. Askel, his companion-in-arms, raised a stone in his memory. The inscription (Hällestad stone in Scania, at that time part of Denmark, about 980) includes these lines:

saʀ flu aigi at	He fled not
ub salum satu	at Uppsala.
trikaʀ iftiʀ	Heroes set up
sin bruþr	after their brother
stin ą biarki	this firm stone,
stuþan runum	with runes on his barrow.
þiʀ kurms tuka	Gorm's son Toke
kiku nistiʀ	sorrowed the most.

If the hypothesis is correct that these lines are but a part of a heroic poem composed in Toke's honor, we have here the beginnings of Danish heroic poetry, to which we next turn our attention. The runic verses suggest the aesthetic form of heroic poetry in the Viking Age—poetry which has been so admirably preserved in Iceland—just as the golden horns of about 400 A.D. gave us an idea, however fragmentary, of prosodic practice during the era of the migration of peoples.

HEROIC POETRY

Although only in the runic inscriptions do we meet with texts as uncorrupted as on the day they were composed, runic inscriptions are not the sole source of literary evidence from olden times in Danish territory. Indirectly, through medieval historians, we know something of the heroic poetry which was cultivated in eastern and western Denmark in those days, poetry which was closely related to Germanic heroic poetry in general.

The background for Germanic heroic poetry as a whole is to be sought in a cultural context common to East, West, and North Germanic tribes, which at the fall of Rome occupied the land all the way from the northern coast of the Black Sea through Central and Northern Europe. The tribes were made up of families or clans whose ideas of life, death, revenge, and loyalty were decisive for the common culture and whose ideals again and again found expression in poetry. Thus verses about revenge, in which the killing of a member of one clan could be expiated only by a comparable killing of a member of another clan, or the pathetic scenes in which warriors fight to the last man around the body of a fallen chieftain, had their counterparts in real life.

The Germanic tribes were characterized by wanderlust and a warrior mentality. Their fateful hour struck when the Roman Empire crumbled and their mighty chieftains could lead militant followers from one victory to another. It was now that the Gothic heroic myths took shape in the stanzas about Attila or Theodoric. The mighty happenings which made contemporary history were treated freely according to the laws of poetry, and reports wandered from people to people as legends, which then were altered and woven into local myths and stories. Finally some gifted skald in a moment of happy inspiration made a stanza which was carried down the centuries by virtue of the phenomenal mnemonic technique of earlier times.

Scholars have not agreed where the heroic poetry had its origins. The problem is still unsolved, but there is good reason to believe that its origin may be sought among the Gothic tribes which dwelt along the coast of the Black Sea and in proximity to the peoples of classical antiquity. Accordingly, it should not be assumed that the Scandinavians borrowed the form of heroic poetry from the Germans. As we have seen, the alliterative language on one of the golden horns of Gallehus is evidence of a poetic potential at a very early date. Again, there is mention of the practice of poetry at the court of Attila. Gothic and Franconian chronicles later attest the recitation of heroic poetry to the accompaniment of strings; and in the lay of *Beowulf* from eighth-century England there is, finally, a clear picture of the poet as a specially gifted warrior who recited his verse in the banquet hall of the chieftain. Just this combination of poet and warrior and an audience of warriors is characteristic, since the heroic poetry of Europe was exclusively the poetry of an upper class. Only the deeds of the warrior caste were immortalized. Of the thrall there is no mention. This is parallel to the evidence furnished by rune stones; they too are concerned almost exclusively with the clan's great men or with the warrior nobility.

Social and political conditions similar to those obtaining in the rest of Europe also prevailed in Denmark. In ancient times the country was divided into areas separated by more or less natural boundaries and inhabited by various tribes or clans. The archeological finds in the bogs of southern Jutland and Funen bear witness that military expeditions and tribal movements took place there as in the larger theater to the south. A high point of internecine warfare occurred in the sixth century when an especially powerful clan with headquarters at Lejre, in mid-

The Jellinge Stone. (Cf. p. 14).

A page of the *Angers fragment* of Gesta Danorum, *with corrections believed to have been dictated by Saxo.*

Zealand, conquered a large part of what is now Denmark. The clan was that of the Skjoldungs, about whose great leaders Roar (Hrodgeir) and Rolf Krake (Hrodulf) many poems seem to have been composed. In any case, the deeds of the Skjoldungs attracted attention outside Denmark as well as at home; in fact, the Skjoldung princes are the chief characters in the English *Beowulf*. The Danes were also mentioned in contemporary international historiography: by the Byzantine Procopius (died about 560); by Jordanes (about 550), the author of the chronicle of the Goths; and by Gregory of Tours (died 594), who wrote the chronicle of the Franks.

For reasons not fully determined, many Scandinavians began to leave their homes on raiding expeditions at the beginning of the ninth century. The raids continued for nearly three hundred years. From Denmark, viking expeditions went mostly to England or Ireland, Frisia or France, but some went as far as Spain and Italy. Subsequently, the advanced culture of western and southern Europe had an increased effect upon Scandinavian thought, especially as friendly commercial relations were established in the wake of the vikings. New impulses also came from another direction. Swedish vikings had early penetrated Russia down to Byzantium, where they in part were merchants and in part entered the imperial Varangian guard. Danes followed, and long before the crusades, poetic motifs of antiquity, which were Greek, Roman, and Oriental in origin and were alive in the east Roman reservoir of culture, began to sift through to the North along the Scandinavian-Russian commercial routes. Inevitably, these new cultural elements made an impression on local traditions and in the course of time entered into folk literature. We may recall at this juncture that the ninth century was pregnant with change in the history of Primitive Scandinavian. It was now that dialects began to develop. What was to become Danish was already at considerable variance from the language of the golden horns. Consequently, the heroic poetry extant before the Viking Age either disappeared or was reformed in a new style: that portion of the older poetry which did live through the linguistic changes was so recast as to incorporate elements from both East and West.

SAXO GRAMMATICUS

It is, in fact, fortunate that we know anything at all of Danish heroic poetry. For its course was strange. Created in the era of the great migrations, it flowered at the time of the Skjoldungs and was reformed by a

2

changing language during the Viking Age. At that time it was preserved merely by oral tradition; runic writing was not for everyday use, but was employed only upon important occasions or ornamentally. The heroic poetry would doubtless have been entirely forgotten had not chance intervened. It happened that from about 1170 to 1240 Denmark reached a high point of political influence, and in order to secure the young and self-conscious nation a reputation in the world of learning, the able statesman and archbishop Absalon commissioned his historian SAXO to write a history of Denmark which, among other things, should tell of the great age of the country. In gathering source material, Saxo came upon the heroic poetry. It was because of his conviction that what he found was historical that important segments of the heroic poetry are preserved to us in his history, albeit in Latin translation—for of course Latin was then the language of the learned. Saxo was a good Latinist, and he therefore painfully translated into Latin the stanzas of the heroic poetry. Had Saxo been satisfied to give a literal translation verse for verse, a reconstruction of the old poetry might still be possible, but Saxo knew classical verse forms well and he endeavored to display his erudition. We must therefore be content to see the old stanzas padded with words to fill the requirements of Latin verse forms. Withal, it was Saxo who preserved the heroic poems many centuries old, some nearly a thousand years old, which had hitherto lived an uncertain oral existence.[1]

Saxo's work is almost a self-contradiction. Written for a Christian bishop, it is nevertheless full of admiration for heathen ideals of valor and physical prowess. Fortunately, Saxo preserved something from the past; but we cannot say that he transmitted a live tradition, for after Saxo evidences of heathen and heroic literature disappear. What is more, Saxo is the only great writer of Latin prose in Denmark before the Reformation. Nominally an historian, Saxo is really a creative writer, for in the first nine books of his *Gesta Danorum (The Deeds of the Danes)* he employs the scattered tales and traditions as raw material from which he creates a whole. We are astounded by the wealth of material which he brings and the number of tales which he weaves into a continuous tapestry of legendary Danish kings, some sixty of them, from Dan to Gorm III.

Saxo's sources were many, but just what they were, whether principally Danish or West Scandinavian, is difficult to determine. He

---

1 There is a translation of *The First Nine Books of the Danish History of Saxo Grammaticus* by Oliver Elton, London, 1894; repr. New York, 1905.

mentions runic inscriptions; Icelandic works; the oral communication of Arnold, an Icelander; lists of Danish kings; and the works of Dudo, Bede, and Paulus Diaconus. We deduce that he also drew on popular tradition, on folk tales and folk songs, on Old Norse mythology and heathen legends, and perhaps also on Icelandic sagas, but the actual sources for his first nine books are far from obvious. His prose is sonorous and ornate. We know him to have had certain Roman writers of the Silver Age as his models, notably Valerius Maximus. He was a brilliant stylist; hence his cognomen (which incidentally was first applied to him in the fourteenth century because of the quality of his style). That we know Saxo's name at all is the result of a chance comment by a contemporary, the historian Sven Aggesen, who in his own history mentioned that his colleague Saxo was writing a Danish history. Of Saxo's original manuscript a few pages have been preserved; otherwise we know his text only from the *editio princeps,* published by Christian Pedersen in Paris in 1514.

Saxo's predilections bear evidence of shifting cultural influences. The migrations, the era of the Skjoldungs, and the Viking Age all helped to form his raw material; but to no small degree Saxo in his time gave to this material a peculiar imprint. Saxo was a master of paraphrase. He was never content to borrow directly. He rewrote in his own style and was generally more wordy than the source upon which he drew, a fact which can be established by comparing certain passages in Saxo with passages in Old Norse which tell the same story, for example the tale of Bothvar Bjarki or the lay of Helgi Hundingsbane.

That Saxo could write as he did, and that he wrote in a fluent Latin full of classical allusions, is indicative of the state of ecclesiastical culture in Denmark in the late twelfth century. For there is nothing of the barbaric about Saxo's language. That Saxo was directed to write what he did tells us that there must have been a society with ambitious leaders who wanted to feel the security of a distinguished past with noble antecedents and who wanted to find support for their own prejudices in the past. The political tenor of the times is reflected in Saxo's *Gesta Danorum* and especially in its outspoken dislike of the Germans to the south.

We do not know in how far Saxo's work was known and read in the decades immediately after it was written. The *Gesta Danorum* is a significant document for the historian, but it may have had very little effect on its own times.

One of the oldest legends in Saxo is the tale of the Anglian chieftain Uffe—a legend which doubtless originated during the migration of peoples. The Saxons presumably moved northward during the fourth century in order to secure themselves the territory around the Ejder River. Here the Saxons met the Angles, and in a duel that, according to the custom of the times, determined which side should be victorious, the Anglian chieftain Uffe won and thereby established the Ejder as a boundary. This dramatic event was the nucleus of the legend which both Saxo and his contemporary Sven Aggesen treated as symbolic of national differences that transcend the single event itself. When King Vermund had grown old and blind, so Saxo tells, the king of the Saxons sent a messenger and demanded his kingdom but offered to let his son duel with whoever dared to meet him. The Danish chieftains were at a loss what to do until an unknown voice offered to fight not only the Saxon prince but the Saxons' mightiest warrior. To everyone's amazement it was Uffe, Vermund's son, who had spoken, he who had been dumb since earliest childhood. Uffe prepared for the holmgang (the island duel), but all byrnies burst and all swords splintered in his grasp because of his strength. King Vermund suggested a last possibility: that his own sword "Skræp" ("Cackle") be dug up. Armed with this weapon from his father's youth, Uffe met the enemy, felled his opponents with two mighty blows and subjected Saxony to Denmark.

That this ancient tale from the fourth century could become a legend about the struggle for the nation's existence must be understood in the light of the differences present along the southern border of Jutland, where first Charlemagne and then the Saxons under Henry I threatened Denmark. The tensions at the border, coupled with Saxo's and his contemporaries' hatred of the Saxon neighbors, kept the legend alive, but in the course of time foreign elements were also absorbed into it almost as a matter of course. The legend was carried to England in the fifth century by the Angles. The Old English poem *Widsith* still bears witness to the Danish origin of the story, although Uffe later came to be looked upon as an English king, Offa, and as such was the subject of a biography written in an English monastery about the year 1200.

Clan warfare in the fifth century is the background for the lay of Hagbard and Signe, known in all of Scandinavia. Hagbard is a chieftain's son who, on a viking expedition, falls in with the two sons of King Sigar, who have a sister Signe. After becoming enamored of Signe, he is obliged to take vengeance on her brothers because they have killed his two brothers. Clad as a maiden, Hagbard comes to King Sigar's hall at nightfall and gains entrance to Signe's chamber. In the night Hagbard and Signe swear eternal faithfulness to one another, despite Hagbard's having killed her brothers; but Hagbard is now to die, for one of Signe's servants has revealed his presence to the king. Doomed to the gallows, he asks that his robe be hanged first. When that boon is fulfilled he sees flames shoot up from Signe's bower. He is then certain of Signe's loyalty and willingly meets his fate, while Signe burns to death. Later, the legend has it, Hagbard's only surviving brother takes bloody and fiery vengeance of King Sigar: the clans have exterminated one another. The leitmotif is clear enough. Of greatest interest was the struggle between Signe's clan which ruled mid-Zealand, and the rival clan that succeeded in destroying the ruling family. Particularly noteworthy is the fact that a secondary motif, the love of Hagbard and Signe, gradually took the center of attention. Of ethically greater importance than the conflict of clans was the troth kept into bitter death, epitomized in the lay. Certain elements in the story, such as Hagbard's gaining entrance to the women's chambers, have parallels in Oriental tales and may even reflect a knowledge of Mediterranean popular literature gained sometime between the historical events of the fifth century and the recording of the lay by Saxo prior to the crusades.

From the standpoint of subject matter, the sixth century seems from Saxo's account to have been the foremost century for Danish heroic poetry. It was at the beginning of this century that the Skjoldungs established the realm which had the approximate size of Denmark today. The poetic masterpiece of the time was the lay of Bjarke, which tells of a clan's demise when internal strife upsets the royal family and threatens to annihilate the Skjoldungs. The lay of Bjarke is mentioned again and again in Scandinavian history and was even used as an incitement to battle for Scandinavian warriors. The Old English lays *Widsith* and *Beowulf* both suggest the historical origins of the lay of Bjarke. At Lejre in mid-Zealand King Roar (Hrodgeir), who succeeded his father Halfdan, lived in his royal hall. Roar's leading warrior was Rolf, his brother's son, while his own son Rørik (Hrodric) and another nephew, Hjarvard, enjoyed less esteem. Roar and Rolf at first kept the peace, according to *Widsith* and *Beowulf,* but internecine warfare broke out when Rolf pushed aside his unqualified cousin and himself took the crown. Rolf's other cousin, Hjarvard, returned in the dark of night at the head of the Goths, seeking revenge. Hjalte and Bjarke, the two leading warriors, roused Rolf's fighters to action and incited one another to battle, but the king's followers were outnumbered. Rolf was slain: his warriors fell one by one and last fell Bjarke and Hjalte, one at Rolf's head, the other at his feet, as the flames of the burning regal hall reddened the nocturnal sky. A great era had come to an end.

The lay of Bjarke is the apotheosis of the warrior caste and of that caste's foremost ideal: loyalty. In the lay there is a wild pathos born of a fanatic belief in the ultimate victory of a man's reputation after death when the deed grants immortality to the hero. A suggestion of the poetry is afforded by a few lines translated from Axel Olrik's reconstruction of the lay:

> Blows of our brands
> Shall back our faith.
>
> The glory of great deeds
> Never is forgotten.[1]

Of the poems pertaining to the Skjoldungs there is finally the lay of Ingjald. The nucleus of the poem is doubtless to be sought in the battle between the realm of the Skjoldungs and the Hadbards, a martial and viking people that dwelt along the north German coast and competed with the Danes for supremacy in the Baltic. An armistice was achieved by a marriage between the son of the Hadbards' king and a daughter of the Skjoldungs, but the connubial festivities were not yet over before the feud broke out anew, and this time the Danes finally crushed the might of the Hadbards. In the course of time, the historical elements were distorted, and in Saxo the legendary figures have changed places. The prince of the Hadbards has become a king of the Skjoldungs named Ingjald, whose father, Frode, was murdered by Sverting, king of the Saxons. The Skjoldung king has nevertheless married a daughter of his father's killer. Still worse, he holds court with the Saxon princes who, with their sister, live in the hall of the Skjoldungs. The scene of the lay is Ingjald's hall, where the young king sits at the table with the queen, the sons of Sverting, and his hird. Unbeknown to all, one of Frode's old warriors enters the hall and is placed among the beggars near the door and ridiculed by the flippant noblemen. Suddenly the old man rises and begins to chastise youthful affrontery. As everyone in the hall becomes more attentive, he ridicules Ingjald to his face not only for having failed to avenge his father but for even having married the daughter of his father's murderer and for holding court with his sons. The climax is reached when Ingjald, egged on by the old man's powerful words, suddenly plunges his sword into the sons of Sverting. Frode's warrior rejoices. With hateful satisfaction he demands that the corpses of the

---

1 Contained in *The Heroic Legends of Denmark* by Axel Olrik. Translated by Lee M. Hollander. New York, The American-Scandinavian Foundation, 1919.

seven princes be cast out to the ravens and wolves of the heath. Frode is avenged.

The poem is a long monologue ascribed to Starkad, Frode's warrior. With great mastery, the skald has been able to create a rising tension that is released in the breathless moment when blood-vengeance is taken. There is no doubt about the spirit of the poem; it is filled with the gruesomeness of blood revenge and contempt for the coward who lets his father lie unavenged.

In the middle of the tenth century the viking spirit was being tamed and more moderate customs were making their way northward, but the spirit of the early Viking Age has left its imprint on the lay of Ingjald. Through Starkad, the poet decried the new generation and expressed his admiration for the life of the warrior-seaman as the best schooling for youth. Rather than tempering the old skald's hatred of the Saxons, Saxo presents these ideas, it would seem, with all their original force.

The most famous of all legends preserved in Saxo is the story of Hamlet, although it may well be that scarcely more than the leitmotif of the legend is of Danish origin. The nucleus of the Hamlet legend is the story of the youth who has but one goal, to avenge his father's murder by an uncle who has married his mother and stolen the crown. In order to protect himself from being suspected of wanting to take vengeance, the youth poses as mad, but when the opportunity arises he takes revenge. The origin of the legend is unknown. The locus of the action however is Jutland. From the contents of the legend one quickly concludes its relation to the heathen ideal of revenge. Around the basic motif there has grown up a wealth of details, some of which suggest Roman or Byzantine literary intermediaries. Hamlet's taking two hollowed sticks filled with gold to England is parallel to the Roman legend of Junius Brutus, founder of the republic, who is sent to the oracle of Delphi by Tarquinius, equipped in a similar fashion. The demonstrations of acumen which Hamlet makes at the English court—he declares that the queen has the manners of a thrall and that the king himself has the eyes of a thrall, whereupon an examination proves that both are the descendents of thralls —have their parallels in Greek-Arabic sources. The foreign motifs, if indeed they are foreign, must have become naturalized very quickly, for Saxo seems to have had no knowledge of their distant origins when he retold the story of the prince-avenger. The legend acquired its international fame when a French version made its way to Renaissance England. But only a name and problem does Shakespeare's brooding figure share with the original Jutland prince.

The *Gesta Danorum* is a remarkable source for legends and lays, for some of which it is the unique source. It is indispensable for a knowledge of the nature of Danish heroic poetry. One might wish that Saxo (or his archbishop) had bid less eagerly for the perpetuity that as a man of his time he could not hope to find in the vernacular. On the other hand, we cannot but feel fortunate that he left us so rich a store that except for his work would be lost to us.

While Saxo is by far the most important source of information about early Danish literature and history, the Old English lays *Widsith* and *Beowulf,* which we have already mentioned, are of interest to the historian of Danish literature. It should be borne in mind that the Angles and Saxons invaded England in the fifth century. They brought their own legends to the strange country and these legends eventually became part and parcel of English poetry. Danish legends also reached England through the medium of the Frisians who occupied the coast between the Weser and the Elbe in the early Middle Ages and who were the most enterprising traders in the North. As usual, legends followed in the path of commerce. *Widsith,* which means "the widely travelled," is from the sixth century and mentions Uffe among the many princes the skald claims to have visited. Half of the story of *Beowulf,* from the eighth century, takes place on Danish soil. The poem tells of a sea monster that terrorized the court of Hrothgar, King of the Skjoldungs. It makes valuable contributions to our knowledge of the history of the Skjoldungs prior to the events related in the lay of Bjarke.

There are, finally, Danish motifs in Old Norse-Icelandic literature. During the Middle Ages, about 1250 A.D., the old heroic poetry again became fashionable, as the Norwegian-Icelandic saga writers exploited ancient material. Lengthy "Fornaldarsögur" (sagas of olden times) tell of the Danish champion Rolf Krake and of the adventures of the Danish viking hero Ragnar Lothbrok.

In retrospect, we note that, aside from runic inscriptions with their indisputable evidence, the early poetry of Denmark is difficult to ascertain and difficult to interpret. It has even been questioned whether there exists a purely Danish tradition in Saxo. Recent scholarship tends to the opinion that the lay of Bjarke, the lay of Hagbard and Signe, and the lay of Ingjald may also be Old Norse-Icelandic in origin. Saxo's however, was the great synthesis of pagan tradition and Latin culture, and he recorded what was being displaced in the memory of a changing society. The culture in which he lived no longer was of the heroic age about which he wrote. Recounting and reshaping the old stories, Saxo is from our standpoint ideally representative of the radical change which took place in medieval Scandinavia.

THE COMING OF CHRISTIANITY

It was the meeting with the universal Church and the subsequent transplanting of Christian culture to Northern soil that made for this change. Scandinavian isolation was broken down and impulses from the Mediterranean no longer followed the circuitous trade routes through Russia and the Baltic. With the Church as a medium, Denmark and the rest of Scandinavia were gradually united with the rest of the European civilized world. New religious, scientific, literary, and above all social influences little by little effected a society and a culture very different from what hitherto had prevailed.

Of course it took some time before the new realm of concepts won firm acceptance, although the Germanic peoples accepted the new faith with remarkable rapidity. The Christian Church meant not only a new faith but an entirely new view of life. It represented a vast complex of cultural phenomena which drew their sustenance from earlier Greek and Roman civilization. Its organization was reminiscent of the Roman state. Its scholastic dogma was the successor to late Hellenistic thought. Much in its rites dated back to the religions of superseded Mediterranean civilizations.

It was a mighty and authoritative church that first entered the Scandinavian portals in the eighth century and completed its conquest in the eleventh. It was a church that kept the tradition of learning alive when the forms of secular life were crumbling, a church that had taken schools and monasteries into its service in order to proclaim, explain, and defend the faith.

The earliest missionaries had come to Scandinavia in the eighth century, but more important was the arrival of the Benedictine monk Ansgar in 826. He accompanied King Harald, who had been baptized in Ingelheim that same year. Ansgar established a school; after numerous difficulties had been overcome, permission was granted for churches to be built in Slesvig and Ribe. The Church in Scandinavia was under the archbishopric of Hamburg-Bremen, and it remained under German sovereignty until 1104, when after many earlier and futile attempts, an archbishopric was established in Lund (now in Sweden). In the interim, the English church, especially under King Canute (1018–1035) had made itself felt in Denmark. The early Middle Ages were an era of transition from indigenous tradition to ecclesiastical culture. The new society which arose in the wake of Denmark's Christianization was at first nearly mute, but from about the year 1100 we can distinguish two groups in society that made contributions to literature: clerics and knights. The former, and more significant, represented internationalism and Latin culture; the latter were more national and local in outlook, although they were also open to foreign influences, above all from France. The key to clerical superiority lay in the church language, Latin. Latin opened the way to all the knowledge which had been of import since ancient times. What is more, the peculiar position of the cleric was enhanced by the medieval differentiation of the spiritual and the secular. As representatives of the kingdom of the Lord, clerics stood above wordly society, recognized only canon law, and partook of a stable cultural entity the members of which spoke the same language, were schooled in the same spirit, and expressed the same ideas throughout Europe.

In contrast to the international clergy, the knights, who were recruited among the well-to-do freeholders descended from the upper class of an earlier age, preserved and carried on indigenous traditions which lived on side by side with the imported Latin culture. The foremost literary contribution of knighthood is the Danish folksong *(folkevise)* which makes its appearance at the end of the twelfth century. It is not until a later era that we hear of the bourgeoisie's literary interests.

The central figures in the newborn literature in Denmark between 1140 and 1240 were the churchmen who occupied the archiepiscopal chair in Lund and the men about them. Eskild (died 1181), Lund's second archbishop, had studied in Hildesheim and later in Paris. He became a friend of Bernard of Clairvaux; and it was he who introduced monasticism into Denmark. He was followed in 1177 by Absalon, who (besides being Saxo's master) was until his death the country's leading statesman under two able kings, Valdemar the Great (died 1182) and Canute VI (died 1202). In 1201 Absalon was succeeded by his nephew ANDERS SUNESON (c. 1160–1228). Like his uncle, Anders had studied in Paris, but he had also studied in Bologna and presumably in Oxford. What he had learned in Paris he put into poetic form in the lengthy didactic poem *Hexaëmeron* ("Six days' task," i.e., the Creation), which, with its 8040 Latin hexameters divided into twelve books, is an impressive example of the influence of early scholasticism in Scandinavia. In concentrated form the learned epic contains, in addition to the story of the Creation, dogma which might serve to instruct priests who themselves could not study theology in Paris. Anders Suneson's work is to a considerable extent based on the *Libri quattuor sententiarum* of the Parisian scholar Petrus Lombardus (died 1160). Many of the dogmatic sentences of the widely-read handbook by Petrus Lombardus were carried over into Anders' epic, clad in the hexameter's pompous form. In the *Hexaëmeron* there are also suggestions of twelfth-century mysticism, of antique poetry, and of the visionary allegorical poetry of Alanus ab insulis (died 1203). Although Anders was not a great or original mind either as a poet or a churchman, he was nevertheless the leading theologian of the North, and his epic was highly esteemed.

The teaching of the medieval church was an expansive one and its expansiveness gave strength. The church could embrace not only a scholastic philosophy of the intellectual elite but also a popular theology which found expression in legends of the saints. Although these legends incorporate many of the myths about the gods and heroes from the pre-Christian era, Denmark's contribution to hagiography is small and not particularly original. As elsewhere, the legends of the saints are didactic. With them a Christian literature treating Danish subjects is begun. The first significant legends are concerned with King Canute the Holy (1080–1086), who was murdered in Odense on July 10, 1086. About 1097 an anonymous cleric of Odense, probably a native of England, wrote an encomium: *Passio sancti Canuti regis*. A second legend, *Gesta Swenomagni regis et filorum eius et passio gloriosissimi Canuti regis et martyris,* was written about 1120 by a certain ÆLNOTH "born in the capital of Kent in the land of the Anglo-Saxons" (i.e., Canterbury). Ælnoth is of interest as a mediator of Anglo-Norman learning. He cites many classical authors and draws parallels with the story of Troy, Hannibal, the history of the Jews, and the history of Rome. He writes a rhythmic Latin and is not far removed from the Breton poets who in the twelfth century evolved the "novels" of Æneas and Alexander the Great. Other members of the ruling house also achieved saintly rank; King Erik Ejegod's son Canute, Duke of Slesvig, murdered by Magnus, son of King Niels, who was the son of Svend Estridsson, is immortalized in the Canute's mass of 1170 (known only in part) and in the legend of Duke Canute written by a Scottish clerk, Robert of Ely, the last named work preserved only in fragments.

A curious mixture of pagan superstition and Christianity is found in the legend of Anders of Slagelse (died about 1205) who after Easter mass in Jerusalem missed the ship on which he was to sail homeward. He throws himself to the ground in prayer and sees an unknown rider who bids him climb on horseback. When he awakens he hears Danish spoken and finds himself on a rise of ground outside Slagelse. It is Easter night; and he is able to attend the evening service at the church in Slagelse after having heard mass in Jerusalem. A cross marking the spot where Anders awakened still stands near Slagelse; but Dean Anders was never canonized.

In the twelfth century another sort of writing, of annals and chronicles, began under the aegis of the church. The origins of these early historical writings, composed in a lapidary style, are associated with the monastery, the cathedral, or the royal chancellery. Examples of early annals are the Kolbazaar book *(Annales Colbazienses)*, written between 1137 and 1170 in Scanian monasteries, and the Valdemar book written from about 1174 to 1219 in the Danish chancellery. The first chronicle which is more than an annalistic compilation is the twelfth-century chronicle of Roskilde, based in part on the ecclesiastical history of Adam of Bremen. The first Danish history, *Brevis historia regum Dacie,* was written about 1185 by a contemporary of Saxo, Archbishop Eskild's nephew SVEND AGGESEN. His paraphrases of heroic legends provide a parallel to Saxo's. The leitmotif in these chronicles is most frequently personal honor and faithfulness to the chieftain-king, just as was the case in the ancient heroic poetry. Both Saxo and Sven Aggesen saw in the heroic legends of the past that high ideal which should inspire their own time. This fact accounts for the artistic freedom which characterized Saxo, and which together with his learning and his pompous and bold Latin, gives his work a lasting place in medieval European literature.

To summarize: Runic inscriptions and heroic poetry were born of the same philosophy of clan and deed. The origins of heroic poetry are to be found in the era of the migration of peoples and shortly thereafter. The heroic poetry is concerned only with free men and the upper class of Germanic society. We are not certain how the early literature was spoken by the skald. He presumably retold prose legends and spoke dramatic and lyric situations in verse. The language of heroic poetry was radically altered at the beginning of the Viking Age. At that time indigenous motifs were exchanged among the Northern peoples and foreign motifs were introduced from distant lands and absorbed into local tradition. The West Germanic legends of the Volsungs, of the Nibelungs, and of Didrik of Bern struck root at this time, and from Byzantium came Greek, Roman, and Oriental material. The last phase in the history of heroic poetry began when it was written down in the twelfth and thirteenth centuries. Norwegian traditions were preserved in distant Iceland, whereas in Sweden the legends were not written down and subsequently all but disappeared. In Denmark, Saxo was the instrument of their perpetuation; he felt the heroic legends to be reliable historical evidence. At about the same time the custom of raising rune stones ceased.

The coming of Christianity to Scandinavia and the incorporation of Denmark into the cultural union of European nations which owed allegiance to the Church meant primarily not an enrichment but a replacement of native culture. As significant as the Classical, Judaic, Christian currents were to become for life in Scandinavia, the new culture and the Latinized literature of the twelfth, thirteenth, and fourteenth centuries in particular were an extension and modification of the culture and literature which held sway to the south. In order to participate in Christian thought and Roman ways, Denmark gave up a goodly part of its patrimony, and most of the earlier indigenous literature was brushed aside or forgotten.

CHAPTER II

The Later Middle Ages.
Folk Songs

Christianity had brought to Denmark the language and literature of
Roman antiquity and a new ethos. While at the beginning of the thirteenth
century Saxo, although nominally a religious, was still imbued with a
feeling for the old Scandinavian literature, by the fourteenth century the
new ethos had triumphed; henceforth the Danes looked to the south for
inspiration. Iceland, distant and isolated in the mid-Atlantic, became the
repository of Germanic antiquity and of indigenous Scandinavian literature. The literature of continental Scandinavia more and more partook
in form and spirit of the common European tradition.

Aside from folk songs, the literature of Denmark in the later Middle
Ages was almost exclusively a Latin literature in the neo-classical tradition; it is stylized and seldom has any emotional appeal. There is perhaps
a single exception: the Latin "Spring Song" *(Carmen vernale)* written at
the end of the fifteenth century by MORTEN BØRUP (1446–1526), which
begins,

In vernalis temporis	Now the happiness of spring;
ortu laetabundo	Gone the frost and cold,
dum recessum frigoris	And the swallows, sweeping, bring
nunciat hirundo	Beauties manifold.
terrae, maris, nemoris	Splendid every outdoor thing;
decus adest deforis	New the earth so old;
renovato mundo	Strength the body makes to sing;
vigor redit corporis	Sorrow from the soul takes wing;
cedit dolor pectoris	Joyous time foretold.
tempori jucundo.	

Latin verses did not often have such a light and fresh lyric quality. The
lyric was not in accord with the spirit of the age; it was not the language,
so to speak, of the times. The late Middle Ages were not an era of original
and inspired writing; authors were keenly conscious of classical models.
Saxo, we recall, strove in his prose to emulate Latin writers and to put
the poetry that he cited into dignified Latin metrical patterns which were
a far cry from the original Scandinavian forms.

Like architecture and painting, sophisticated literature was of little significance in Denmark during the fourteenth and fifteenth centuries. Writing was overwhelmingly ecclesiastical and theological in nature; it consisted mainly of annals and chronicles and legends. There were poems to the Virgin and a few other attempts at Latin verse. Enough fragments of old Danish manuscripts have been preserved to indicate that there was some vernacular writing in the form of translations from the Latin. These fragments are all ecclesiastical. For example, we may mention the legends of Saint Cecilia and Saint Clemens from the *Legenda Aurea,* the revelations of the Swedish Saint Birgitta, a dialogue between a wise man and a disciple, an encomium on the Virgin Mary, and rules for life in a cloister. Few other works in the vernacular are known to have existed. Jean de Mandeville's travels were translated into Danish in the fourteenth century. A rhyming chronicle, unique in medieval Danish literature, was completed at some time in the fifteenth century. In a roundabout way, via Norway and Sweden, chivalric epics which originated in France in the twelfth century came to Denmark in fifteenth-century translations. Finally, an augmented version of the cyclopædic *Lucidarius* was made in Danish in the fifteenth century.

The dearth of written literature cannot be called surprising. The fourteenth and fifteenth centuries were a time of unrest in Denmark. It is as if for 200 years the efforts of the able minds in Denmark were devoted to political machinations rather than to cultural achievement. The late Middle Ages are marked above all by the Union of Kalmar in 1397, which for better or for worse united the Scandinavian countries under Margaret of Denmark. After her death, the union continued nominally to exist until the sixteenth century, but in reality Sweden was independent much of the time and was not infrequently at swords' points with Denmark. What is more, the economic and political structure of Denmark was undergoing far-reaching changes which diminished the importance of the individual, in particular the farmer and the peasant, for the sake first of the monarchy and then of the nobility. Little was immune to the devastating demands of political expediency. The men who held or strove to hold the reins of government did nothing to encourage a cultural revival. In this situation, even the Church was scarcely able to hold its own. Between 1300 and 1500 finally, Denmark was beset by recurrent plagues, which decimated the population.

If the two hundred years preceding the Reformation have little to offer in the way of written literature, we owe to them the Danish folk songs which, according to some scholarly accounts, were composed during that period (or possibly even earlier). The folk song was and is found everywhere in Europe, but nowhere did the folk song come to finer fruition than in Denmark; in late medieval Europe, Denmark was preeminent in that genre. It is an astonishing fact that more than 600 folk songs in many versions have been assembled in the classical edition of Danish folk songs compiled by Svend Grundtvig, Axel Olrik, and H. Grüner Nielsen (1853 ff.).

At the outset of our discussion it must be noted that the great fund of Danish folk songs was recorded not in the Middle Ages but from the end of the fifteenth century onward. Many versions date from the nineteenth century. Danish folk songs are labelled medieval only by circumstantial and internal evidence. We do not possess more than a single fragment of a medieval text, but it is safe to assume that many of the early modern texts are almost identical with their lost medieval precursors.

Danish scholars agree on the antiquity of the folk songs and assign the origins of many ballads to the thirteenth and early fourteenth centuries. Although there is undeniably an element of conjecture involved in dating many Danish ballads so early, the historical incidents which are immortalized in many of the ballads demonstrably date from the twelfth, thirteenth, and fourteenth centuries.[1]

The more closely one examines the historical ballads, the more credible it becomes to assume an early origin for the ballads. That events which otherwise are unknown to the general public could have been given popular form several centuries after the events took place is not plausible. Many of the historical folk songs refer to events of the twelfth and thirteenth centuries, as for example the several ballads about the Danish kings named Valdemar (e.g., "Valdemar and Tove") and the several ballads about "Marsk Stig" (which refer to a regicide committed in 1286 A.D.). At least one historical ballad, "The Death of Erik Emune," pertains to an occurrence as early as the year 1137. "Valdemar and Tove" refers to happenings in 1160. The substance of the ballads about Queen Dagmar dates from about 1205.

Not a few of the ballads are of much later origin, dating from the fifteenth and sixteenth centuries and even later. "Christian I in Frisia" dates itself as of 1472 or later. King Hans's wedding, commemorated in folk song, took place in 1478. A ballad about Christian II in Sweden must

1 An interesting scholarly proof of the age of some of the folk songs has been made by reconstructing the language of the century in which they are presumed to have arisen, and by so doing achieving more perfect rhymes in many verses.

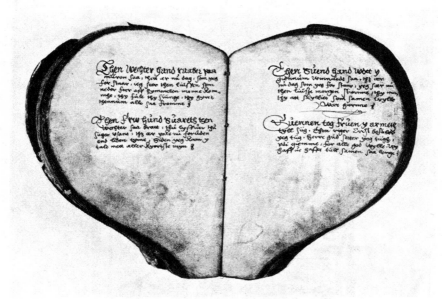

"Hjertebogen"—"The Heart Book", a manuscript collection of Danish folk
ballads, compiled *1553–55*.

Title page of the Rhyming Chronicle, 1495, first book printed in the Danish language. (Cf. p. 46). Actual size.

have arisen after 1520, and a ballad about Frederik II in Ditmarsch after 1559. It may be questioned whether the later ballads belong in the same category as the earlier.

Although the year 1500 may seem a very late date to record a thirteenth-century ballad, the fact remains that the ballads of the Danes were recorded earlier than the ballads of any other people. Despite Humanistic interest in the folk songs around 1500, centuries elapsed before the intrinsic value of the genre was understood either in Denmark or elsewhere. Enthusiastic appreciation of the folk song and other folk literature dates only from the beginning of the nineteenth century.

As a genre, the folk song was neither esteemed nor despised during the Middle Ages. It was a form of entertainment and an aesthetic manifestation which was close to daily life and well removed from the accepted literary models of the time. It had nothing in common with the scholarship and erudition that characterized the formal literature of the fifteenth and sixteenth centuries. It was essentially popular and secular. The folk song may be said to have supplanted the old heroic poetry of the North which had been displaced and made superfluous by the demise of the old mythology subsequent to the influx of Christianity. Though religion tempered daily life during the Middle Ages, folk songs were nevertheless born of material existence, of love and hatred, of war and death, of crime and punishment, of bold exploits and bloody vengeance. The songs did not concern themselves with the lives of saints or with religious subjects, even though here and there a Christian motif or allusion may be recognized. They counterbalanced rather than supplemented the Christian religious thought which permeated all the learning and the writing of the times. They told first and foremost of the nobles—their love affairs, their marriages, and their deeds. On the basis of the folk songs it is possible to construct a picture of life in the upper strata of society during the later Middle Ages. The common man, the peasant, was not commemorated in song.

Since the folk song was and is oral literature, its form and content had to be clear and simple enough to be comprehended by a large audience. Any personal idiosyncrasies that a song contained were sloughed off and its rough edges were made smooth as it passed from person to person without the disciplinary medium of the written or printed word. Who had composed a folk song was of no consequence to its singer or speaker or to his audience, and the poetic integrity of a song did not have to be preserved. The song could be revised at will. A stanza might be added or omitted or altered. A word or phrase or a verse might be changed. Although the songs sometimes preserve archaic expressions, they more often express by newer phraseology the words and ideas which were no longer fully understood. There is abundant evidence of the instability of the folk song in the many versions of the same song collected by Svend Grundtvig, Evald Tang Kristensen, and others. It is nevertheless remarkable how little most early modern Danish texts changed once they acquired the general pattern—and specifically the metrical pattern—of the folk song. It is possible that a ballad created in the fourteenth century may be recognized and recorded as living literature in the twentieth. Some ballads recorded at the beginning of the sixteenth century have been re-recorded from the mouths of rural informants three to four hundred years later, and the modern versions, although linguistically modified, are readily recognizable. Again, the fact must be stressed that the metrical pattern has tended to preserve the text of a ballad. And the metrical pattern was in turn originally dictated by the musical framework into which the text was fitted.

Although it is younger than many of the ballads, "Fair Anna," which is preserved in Swedish, Dutch, German, Scottish, and French, as well as Danish versions, and which is not unsimilar to a romance preserved in several dialects of the Iberian peninsula, may serve as an example of a folk song and its variations. It contains the appealing tale of a kidnapped princess who is sold to a foreign prince and who bears him sons, but is not accepted as his lawful wife or queen until her pedigree is revealed by her sister, whom the prince is preparing to marry. Svend Grundtvig prints eight Danish versions of the ballad, four of which seem to indicate the existence of independent oral traditions, while the remaining variants are dependent on some early printed text or texts. The four significant versions tell substantially the same story; but although certain poignant phrases may be common to several versions, there is independence of diction and phraseology. The shortest version has 32 stanzas, the longest 48 stanzas.

We may suppose unknown ballad composers to have taken the outline of the story, the words and phrases which they remembered, and, employing the same metrical pattern, to have recreated the ballad, expanding or contracting it as they saw fit and substituting new phrases with more connotations for themselves or their audiences. While a single original ballad may be the apparent source of several variants, another ballad on the same theme may sometimes be seen to have affected one or several stanzas of a variant. This is circumstantial evidence that a ballad is modified as it passes from person to person, for each singer has his own knowledge of other versions or variants or of parallel themes and situa-tions contained in still other ballads. That a fictitious tale may become localized is indicated by the mention of a "Graf von Mecklenburg" as the prince who acquired Anna in one version of the song.

The essential nature of the text of a folk song is its combination of epic and lyric qualities. It can usually be classified as a lyrical ballad. In an easy but often dramatic fashion it tells of an event of epic proportions. The form of the folk song is simple; the metrical pattern is not compli-cated. A stanza usually consists either of two verses containing four accented syllables or of four verses containing alternately four and three accented syllables. The verse pattern is repeated from couplet to couplet or from quatrain to quatrain. There is usually a refrain, and the repetition of words and verses is common. In contrast to older Germanic poetry, the folk song is not formally alliterative; if there is alliteration, it is incidental. Rhyme is the rule rather than the exception, although fre-quently only two verses of a quatrain rhyme. The rhyme is not infre-quently assonantal. The fact that rhyme is characteristic of the Danish folk song indicates that the ballad form is not indigenous in Denmark, for the old Scandinavian poetry did not rhyme. The origin of the use of rhyme is hazy; it may have arisen through the influence of ecclesiastical Latin poetry which rhymed.

The folk songs vary greatly in length. Some contain only a few stanzas, although rarely fewer than ten quatrains. Others, like the long version of the ballad about Marsk Stig, contain over one hundred quatrains.

Forthrightness and plainness of expression predominate; complex imagery is rare. The language is unsophisticated, although a folk song may strike modern readers as difficult and possibly affected because of its archaic nature. There are neither nature lyrics *per se* nor any detailed descriptions nor dramatic displays of personal feelings.

At first the folk song was probably cultivated as an accompaniment for dancing, but only in the Færoes has the tradition of dancing to ballads been preserved. When one reflects that the ballads were meant to be sung, one realizes how imperfect our knowledge of the medieval folk song necessarily must be, for little of the ballad music has been preserved. The few melodies which have been preserved are as patently simple as the metrical patterns of the folk songs themselves, and we may assume that the nature of the melodies also influenced the word content of the songs.

While the folk song probably had the French *chanson* as its original model, there was clearly an independent development of the genre in

Scandinavia, and the ballads of Denmark, Norway, Sweden, and the Færoes (but not the younger Icelandic *rímur*) form one group. There are many parallels between Scandinavian and English but (perhaps contrary to expectation) not German ballads.

If adjudged by subject matter, the folk songs may be classified in several ways, but any classification according to content is arbitrary, especially in view of the fact that no exact chronological arrangement of the folk song is possible. Traditionally we speak of historical, chivalric, and mythical folk songs as the most important groups, but this classification, although a practical one, fails to suggest the variety of substance and interest represented by the ballads.

One of the most famous historical folk songs is that about Niels Ebbesen, who killed the German count Gert in Jutland in 1340. The ballad has frequently been taken to be symbolical of Danish resistance to German aggression in the past; and in the Second World War it lent its name to Kaj Munk's wartime drama protesting the German occupation. As the ballad begins, the German Count Gert goes to Denmark despite a forewarning,

> The Count to Denmark took his way,
> And would not be gainsaid,
> What though the spaeman told him true
> That there should he lie dead.[1]

Gert clashes with the outspoken Danish hero Niels Ebbesen and declares,

> Overbold is his speech, Niels Ebbesen,
> That bandies words with me!
> Or thou shalt depart from Denmark,
> Or I'll hang thee to a tree!

Niels plans vengeance and gains access to the count by stealth, seizes and kills him. Although the slaying probably was at night, one version of the lay concludes,

> The goose did cackle, the sheep did bleat,
> And the cock on the high-loft crew,
> 'Twas by daylight and not in darkness
> That Gert the Count they slew.

> God rest thy soul, Niels Ebbesen,
> All for that slaying's sake!
> Full many a German in Denmark
> The selfsame way shall take.

---

[1] The translations of Danish ballads printed here are by E. M. Smith-Dampier and are taken from *A Book of Danish Ballads. Selected and With an Introduction by Axel Olrik.* New York, The American–Scandinavien Foundation, 1939.

Other historical ballads are less explicit in their treatment of events which are more distant and less poignant than the death of Count Gert.

Many of the events of a courtly or martial nature which attracted the popular fancy have been commemorated in ballads, such as the marriage of King Erik Menved (in 1296) and the defeat of the Danes in Ditmarsch (in 1500). Among the chivalric folk songs, the lay about Ebbe Skammelson is a classic. Ebbe's brother deceives his betrothed by telling her that the absent Ebbe is dead. Ebbe dreams that there is trouble at home and returns on the bridal day,

> Now when the dew was falling
> And even was well-nigh sped,
> Up she rose, the beauteous bride,
> To seek the bridal bed.
>
> They followed her, the bridal train,
> Up to the chamber door,
> And first went Ebbe Skammelson
> To bear the torch before.
>
> He led her to door of bridal bower
> That bride so bright of blee:
> "Hast thou forgot, proud Adelus,
> The troth thou didst plight to me?"
>
> "The troth I swore in times of yore
> To thy brother is given away,
> But I'll love thee e'en as a mother mild
> Unto my dying day."

Then Ebbe kills the unfaithful Adelus and cries,

> "Now hearken, Peter Skammelson,
> A laggard art thou to wed!
> The bride is longing after thee
> Now in the bridal bed."

The lay takes a surprising turn and ends in this wise,

> It was Peter Skammelson
> Spake up with mickle spite:
> "My leave thou hast with right good-will
> To sleep by the bride tonight!"
>
> It was Ebbe Skammelson
> That drew his brand so brown,
> It was Peter his brother
> That he to earth struck down.

The chivalric ballad about Holger the Dane which is especially well
known, is of French origin. In it the legendary Didrik of Bern is defeated
by the Jutland king. As the ballad begins,

> Stout Didrik dwells in Berneland
> With brethren eight all told,
> And each of them twelve sons hath got,
> All doughty knights and bold.
> But the battle is raging northward up in Jutland.
>
> Stout Didrik dwells in Berneland
> With fifteen sisters bright,
> And each of them hath twelve fair sons
> That hold their lives full light.

Didrik and his men decide to attack Holger.

> Now all with eighteen thousand steeds
> From Berneland they fare,
> And they've drawn up to Denmark
> To meet King Holger there.

Holger accepts the challenge and,

> They fought for a day, for twain they fought,
> And stiff in stour did stand,
> King Holger and his warriors bold
> Slew many from Berneland.

As a consequence the attackers must flee,

> Oh, stern the stream of red, red blood
> That ran o'er land and lea!
> The reek of it rose up to heaven
> Till the sun was red as blood to see.

There is a plethora of ballads which treat of lovers and their exigencies,
of wooer and bride, and of tragic fates. There are ballads about "Proud
Signild," "Proud Margaret," and "Proud Elselille," about "Bodil's
Revenge," "The Concubine's Revenge," and "Proud Elin's Revenge."
Over a dozen versions of "A Maiden's Morning Dream" have been
recorded, and eight versions of a ballad on "The Test of Faithfulness."
Even humor of a coarse nature finds its place in "Sir Palle's Bridal
Night," in which Sir Palle is tricked into taking the lady's coachman
to bed.

Some of the folk songs do hearken back to the literature of the heathen
era. The most obviously pagan of these is "Thor of Havgard" (a corrup-
tion of "Asgard"), which retells the lay of Thor's lost hammer that is well

known from the Elder Edda *(þrymskviða)*. No other ballad preserves
Eddic poetry. Although it may be termed chivalric, "Havbor and Signelil" is essentially the legend of Hagbard and Signe which was mentioned
in the foregoing chapter as having been preserved in Saxo:

> Havbor the King and Sivord the King
> Have fallen out in strife,
> All for the stately Signelil
> That was so fair a wife.
> Ne'er wilt thou win such a fair one.
>
> Havbor the King hath dreamt a dream,
> And woeful did he wake,
> He went to seek his mother dear
> And of the dream he spake.
>
> "Methought that I was up in Heaven,
> And 'twas so fair a town;
> I held in mine arms proud Signelil,
> And we fell to earth adown."

His mother interprets,

> "Didst dream the maid was in thine arm,
> And thou didst fall from sky
> It bodes that thou her love shalt win,
> And for her sake shalt die."

Havbor declares,

> "When I dream of winning yon maiden
> Such happiness have I,
> That less than nothing I count it
> If I for her sake must die!"
>
> Now Havbor let his locks wax long
> And did don woman's gear
> And so he rode to Denmark
> As though he a maiden were.
>
> Oh his cloak he changed in the castle-garth
> All for the scarlet fair,
> And forth to the ladies' bower he went
> To seek proud Signe there.

Havbor gains entrance to Signe's bower,

> Still sat all the dainty dames
> And sewed their seams aright,
> All save Havbor the Prince, and he
> His needle still did bite.

Up and spake the serving-maid,
So evil a tongue had she:
"Oh, never saw I so poor a seam
Sewn by a fair ladye!"

"Ever her needle is in her mouth,
She sets no stitches fine,
And still she drinketh the goblet out
So fast as they pour the wine.

"Ne'er have I seen a lady's hands
Stiffer than steel, I trow,
Nor ever beheld so bold an eye
Under a lady's brow."

Despite the suspicious maid, Havbor carries out his plan,

Now all were bound to slumber
When as the even was spent
And Havbor with proud Signelil
To the selfsame chamber went.

When Signe is alone with Havbor, whom she has not yet recognized,
she declares,

"Nay, there's never a wight in all the world
That lies my heart within,
Save only Havbor the King's fair son,
And him I ne'er can win."

Discovering Havbor she cries,

"And art thou Havbor the King's fair son,
Why hast thou shamed me?
Why didst not ride to my father's hold
With hawk on hand so free?"

and Havbor explains,

"Oh, how should I ride to your father's hold
With hawk on hand so free?
Hath he not vowed, as well I know,
To hang me on gallows-tree?"

The maid overhears them,

Now she stood nearby to hear and spy,
That evil serving-maid,
And she stole away his byrnie brown,
And stole his trusty blade.

Both trusty blade and byrnie brown
She secretly stole away,
And she hied in haste to the chamber
All where King Sivord lay.

The King is not immediately convinced, but after seeing Havbor's
weapons he acts.

Oh they have knocked at the chamber-door
With glaive and eke with spear:
"Come forth now, Havbor, Havbor,
Come forth and meet us here!"

Up sprang Havbor the King's fair son
Or ever they spake the word,
And gone I ween was his byrnie brown,
All with his trusty sword.

After a valiant struggle the weaponless Havbor is captured.

They've taken him, Havbor the King's fair son,
Fetters on him they draw,
He burst them all asunder
As though they had been of straw.

Now shame be on the serving-maid
That gave them counsel there:
"Never shall ye bind Havbor
Save with proud Signil's hair!"

They took a hair of Signil's head
To bind him foot and hand
His haughty heart would have broken
Before he burst that band.

Havbor secretly makes a last request of Signe,

"Now lithe and listen, Signelil,
Wouldst show thy love to me,
Then burn thy bower and all therein
When they hang me to a tree!"

Then he is led away.

Up spake Havbor the King's fair son,
When first he saw the tree:
"Hang up my cloak of scarlet red,
A sign for all to see!

"Hang up my cloak of scarlet
That is both fair and fine,
The ladies all will weep and wail
When first they see the sign."

It was stately Signelil
To roof and reed set fire,
Both she and all her maidens
Burned in the selfsame pyre.

Long stood doughty Havbor
To look his last on land,
Until he saw proud Signil's bower
That all in flame did stand.

"Take down, take down my cloak of red,
That well its task hath done,
For had I now ten thousand lives,
I would not ask for one!"

Up and spake King Sivord
That looked and needs must speak:
"Oh, what is the bale that burns so red
All with the driving reek?"

Up spake the little foot-page,
And fast his tears did fall:
"'Tis the deed of stately Signelil
That shows her love to all."

Realizing what has happened, the King commands that both lovers be
saved, but it is too late.

When they came to the bower
Signelil's soul was sped,
When they came to the gallows
Havbor was hanged and dead.

"Now had I known but yesternight
How deep in love were they,
Not for all Denmark had I done
What I have done this day!"

Now woe is me for the gallows-tree
And the bower in ashes laid!
They buried her in the earth alive,
The cruel serving-maid.

No folk song embodying a legend is better known than the lay "Aage and Else" which tells of the faithful maiden who pined to follow her beloved even after death.

> It was the knight Sir Aage
> That rode by land and lea,
> He loved the lady Elselil,
> So fair was she.
>
> He wooed the lady Elselil
> With gifts and gold,
> On Monday thereafter
> He lay in the mould.
>
> Sore wept the lady Elselil
> With wellaway,
> That heard the knight Sir Aage,
> Low where he lay.

Aage rises from his grave and visits Else, who declares that she would share his grave, but Aage replies,

> "For every tear thou lettest fall
> In mournful mood,
> Adown into grave doth drip
> A drop of blood.
>
> "Up above my head
> The green grass grows,
> Down about my feet
> The dark worm goes.
>
> "But when a song thou singest
> All in delight,
> Then all my darksome grave is hung
> With roses red and white.
>
> "Now in the darksome entry
> The black cocks crow,
> And all the doors are opening,
> Forth must I go.
>
> "And now the white cock croweth
> In the high hall,
> To earth I now betake me
> With dead men all.

> "Now croweth on the high-loft
> The cock so red,
> And I must be back to earth again
> With all the dead."

So that she cannot follow him, Aage gets Else to look at the stars as he sinks back into his grave, but,

> Home went the lady Elselil
> With care so cold,
> And when a moon was over
> Lay she in the mould.

A few folk songs are allegorical and do not treat directly of persons. An example is "Falk og Smaafugl" ("Falcon and Little Bird") which begins,

> I know where stands a linden
> With many a flower,
> That sheltereth all from frost and snow
> In wintry hour,

and which concludes with an explanation of the symbolism,

> It is no linden-tree so green
> Whereof ye hear.
> It is the courteous maiden
> I love so dear.

To the variegated contents of the scores of Danish folk songs which remain unmentioned here we can only allude.

Parallel to the chivalric folk songs of Denmark was the chivalric literature emanating from France, which made itself felt in Norway and Sweden at the beginning of the thirteenth century and which enjoyed esteem during the reign of King Hakon IV of Norway. Under his aegis a number of French epics, principally by Chrétien de Troyes, were translated into Norwegian. A corresponding interest in chivalric literature is not evidenced in Denmark except by the few folk songs which pertain to characters from the great corpus of medieval secular legends which grew up above all around the figure of King Arthur. Yet even in Norway itself documentary evidence of the interest in thirteenth-century French literature is lacking, for the old Norwegian translations have been preserved only in Icelandic manuscripts. Since chivalric literature did exist in Old Norse-Icelandic in the thirteenth and fourteenth centuries, we can hypothesize some knowledge of the courtly epic in Denmark at that time, but there is no evidence of Danish versions of the courtly literature until about 1500, when Danish translations were made of the three so-called Eufemia lays and of three other chivalric epics.

Chivalric literature and the Arthurian legend in particular seem to have followed a circuituous path to Denmark. The so-called Eufemia lays were apparently translated from French into Swedish at the command of the German queen of Norway, Eufemia, between 1300 and 1312 and later translated into Danish from the Swedish. These are the lays of *Herra Ivan, Hertig Frederik,* and *Flores ok Blankiflur. Herra Ivan* keeps very close to its model, Chrétien's *Yvain. Hertig Frederik,* which resembles *Herra Ivan,* is modeled after a French lay no longer extant. *Flores ok Blankiflur,* a classic love story with an oriental background, is from a twelfth-century French work *(Floire et Blancheflor)* by a learned, unknown author. The Danish versions of the Eufemia lays are different from the Swedish manuscripts which have been preserved, so it would seem that, in addition to condensing the epics, the Danish translator took liberties with the text. It must of course be remembered that medieval translations were generally very free and that there was no obligation on the part of the translator to reproduce his model with any exactness as regards plot or form, language or style. The Danish translator of the Eufemia lays was interested only in the plots. Stylistic niceties and lengthy descriptions in the French originals and Swedish translations are not to be found in the Danish versions. A part of *Hertig Frederik* was apparently missing in the Swedish manuscript used by the translator, for he has tried to fill in several lacunae by his own efforts.

The other courtly epics preserved in Danish are the lays about the Dwarf King Laurin, Persenober and Konstantianobis, and the Chaste Queen. *Dværgekongen Lavrin,* which was translated from the German, belongs to the cycle of romances about Didrik of Bern (i.e., Verona, Italy). *Persenober ok Konstantianobis* is a French love story which resembles *Flores ok Blankiflur.* The finesse of the French original and above all its delight in detailed descriptions have no place in the Danish version, which again is concerned primarily with action. The freedom that the Danish "translator" took with the chivalric epics is indicated by the fact that the eleven thousand verses of the original French *Partonopeus* were cut down to some 1600 verses in the Danish *Persenober.* The original from which the lay about the Chaste Queen was taken is not known.

Like the chivalric ballads, the courtly epics display a penchant for stories of parted lovers, and for tests of endurance, patience, and strength which must be surmounted before the lovers can be reunited. Magic objects play no small part in chivalric romance. For example, Laurin possesses a belt which gives him the strength of twelve men, and Persenober has a sort of pocket lamp which he uses at night to see his lady love. The tournament or the duel is generally a deciding factor in the turn of events. The hero frequently wins because of the intervention of supernatural powers.

That some of the chivalric literature was translated into the Scandinavian tongues indicates the desire of the nobility, and above all of King Hakon IV, to become acquainted with the fashionable literature of Europe from about 1225 onward. That this literature continued to be read and reworked tells us that the literary taste in Scandinavia resembled the common European taste during the later Middle Ages and even later. The courtly epics lived on in popular verse, and some of them are to be found in Danish chapbooks of the sixteenth and seventeenth centuries. *Flores ok Blankiflur, Persenober,* and *Lavrin* continued to be printed until the end of the eighteenth century.

We need not suppose that in the thirteenth century the older indigenous literature was wholly neglected or despised in all of Scandinavia, for at that very time some of the greatest works in Old Norse-Icelandic literature were put into writing. The rise of chivalric literature signified an extension of literary interest; it represented a desire for change and a desire to emulate conditions which obtained in the nation which most closely approached the chivalric ideal, that is, in France.

Although it did not have the broad appeal of chivalric poetry, nor the longevity of the folk song, the Danish rhyming chronicle is a singular monument of the later Middle Ages which deserves special mention. The date of origin of the chronicle has not yet been firmly established, but it was probably written in a monastery at Sorø during the late fifteenth century. The chronicle was the first Danish book to be printed, in 1495. As only one manuscript, with lacunae, has been preserved, the printed version and a sixteenth-century translation of the chronicle into Low German are the principal sources. The chronicle ostensibly tells the history of all the Danish kings from the mythical King Humble to Christian I. It is written in doggerel and seems to be the work of several authors. The text is occasionally reminiscent of the folk song and contains numerous proverbial phrases. Danish scholars have pointed out that the tenor of the chronicle is more popular than that of either the religious poetry of the late Middle Ages or the chivalric lays which were imported into Denmark in the fifteenth century. Incidentally, the Rhyming Chronicle was admired by N. F. S. Grundtvig in the nineteenth century, who undertook to continue it in the same sort of doggerel, although with a more rational and didactic intent than had motivated the medieval authors.

There remains a single work which warrants our attention before we take leave of the Middle Ages, the so-called *Lucidarius,* one of the popular international chapbooks of Europe. The *Lucidarius* has its origins in the *Elucidarium* written by Honoré d'Autun at the beginning of the twelfth century. Basically it is a didactic dialogue between a master and a disciple. Cyclopædic in nature, it treats of the creation, of various points of church dogma, and of geography and astronomy. The first Danish *Lucidarius* was a free version of a German chapbook. Since the *Lucidarius* antedates the Reformation, it is Roman Catholic in conception; but a post-Reformation version of the same chapbook is Protestant in tone. The Catholic version was first printed in Denmark in 1510, the Protestant not until 1558. *Lucidarius* is more nearly a catechism than a literary work; it is without interest when examined for the sake of literary form. Its text and wood-cuts, both of which incline to the fabulous, indicate the degree of general enlightenment in the sixteenth and seventeenth centuries and the wide-spread confusion of Biblical lore, primitive scientific knowledge, and superstition.

CHAPTER III

Humanism, Reformation, and Renaissance

The break with the late medieval culture, its clericalism, its scholasticism, and its traditionalism, came quickly in Denmark. While in Europe to the south the classical revival which was a substantial part of the new movement in learning that we call Renaissance Humanism made itself felt from the fourteenth century onward—first in Italy, then in Germany, the Netherlands, England, and France—it was not until well into the sixteenth century that Humanism became established in Denmark. And when Humanism came to Denmark, it did not come alone. It was very nearly one with the Reformation, which it had fostered elsewhere in Europe. What is more, both Humanists and Reformers took into their services the new art of printing.

While Humanism strengthened and renewed a knowledge of the literature of classical antiquity and aroused a new interest in literature and history, the Reformation effected a new and general use of the vernacular. Consequently, the twenties of the sixteenth century in Denmark may be looked upon as a turning point not only in ecclesiastical and political history, but also in cultural and specifically literary history. From the standpoint of belles-lettres, the Reformation marks above all the use of literary media directed at large segments of population.

Despite the political exigencies of the times and before the impact of Humanism, there had been an increase both in learning and in the use of the vernacular during the fifteenth century. After a false start, the University of Copenhagen had been founded in 1479 under the aegis of the Church and the influence of German scholasticism. Many Danish students attended German universities both before and after the founding of the Danish university. The number of pupils attending church schools increased.

Aside from the vernacular literature (which was discussed in the foregoing chapter), prayers and hymns began to be translated into Danish. The translations were probably made for practical rather than ideological reasons, but they bespeak a growing desire to give the vernacular some of the dignity which the ecclesiastical language had hitherto enjoyed almost alone.

HANS TAUSEN
Painting in the cathedral at Ribe.

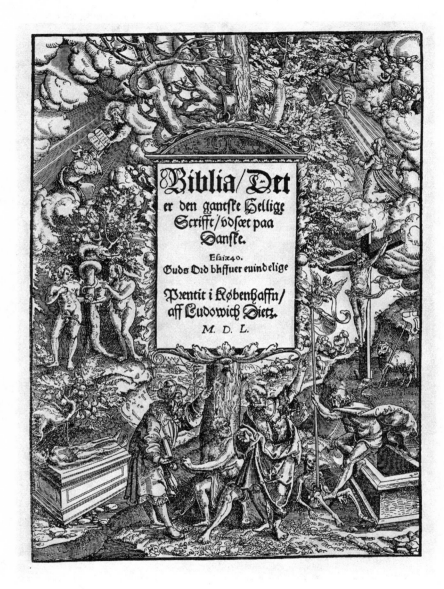

Title page of Christian III's Danish Bible, 1550.

The art of printing was introduced into Denmark in 1482. The earliest printed works were Latin and ecclesiastical, differing in neither subject nor treatment from the manuscripts of the time. The revolutionary element in printing remained latent. Of the eighteen known and fourteen extant Danish incunabula, only one—the rhyming chronicle—was printed in the Danish language.[1] Until 1522, when Erasmus' edition of the Gospel of St. Matthew appeared, books printed in Denmark bore no indication of the new modes of thought that had already burst into expression in Germany.

As early as 1510, however, the Danish scholar CHRISTIAN PEDERSEN (died 1554) had started issuing books in Paris for use in Denmark. The first book which he published was a Latin-Danish glossary. In 1514 he published the *editio princeps* of Saxo's *Gesta Danorum,* under the title *Historia Danica.* The publication of Saxo in 1514 is symbolic of the beginning of Danish Humanism, for Christian Pedersen, although at that time in holy orders, was the first Dane to show an active interest in literature *per se* and in the national past. The publication of Saxo parallels the efforts of other European Humanists and stands in contrast to the absolute domination of theology in the literature of the fifteenth century. It is not surprising therefore that Christian Pedersen was to be found in the Lutheran camp only a decade later.

By the time Humanistic literature was ensconced in Denmark, the political and theological revolt that was the result of mounting tensions had broken out in Germany. Even though there had been some efforts to reform Danish monasteries in the fifteenth century, the ecclesiastical situation in Denmark was not analogous to that in Germany. Nor was the political situation analogous. Denmark had recently stood united against powerful enemies. Although the Lutheran doctrine was to provide an excuse for the Crown to nationalize the Church and for the Crown and the nobles to enrich themselves with the holdings of the Church, there was no schism between Church and State or between king and nobles, as there was in Germany.

The Reformation entered Denmark by absorption, as it were. Its course was less spectacular and less bloody than in Germany, but the religious differences which arose in Denmark do reflect those which obtained in the empire to the south. The eventual success of the Protestant cause in Northern Germany was also mirrored in Denmark.

While it would be erroneous to assume that the literature of the six-

---

1 Incidentally it was printed by a Dutchman, Gottfred of Ghemen.

teenth century was purely theological, the fact remains that the intellectuals of the times bent their efforts primarily in the field of theology. Consequently, what could be called the serious literature of the day is not philosophical or ethical nor is it even philosophically or ethically belletristic but is indeed basically theological. The best efforts of scholars and printers were expended in producing theological or ecclesiastical books. The monument of their work is above all Christian III's Danish Bible, published in 1550.

Like the currents of the Renaissance, the Bible in the vernacular was a relatively late phenomenon in Denmark; it was almost simultaneous with the Reformation. Although some attempts may have been made to translate parts of the Bible into Danish in the late Middle Ages in schools or monasteries, it was not until 1514–15 that parts of the Bible were available in Danish paraphrase in Christian Pedersen's Book of Hours (*Vor Frue Tider*) and Postil (*Epistler og Evangelia,* called *Jærtegnspostil,* i.e., *Miracle Postil*). Curiously enough, the New Testament was made available in Danish translation, through the patronage of King Christian II, only two years after the New Testament appeared in Luther's translation. The Danish version (which was published in Leipzig) was based on the Vulgate and upon Luther's translation. Although generally referred to as the work of HANS MIKKELSEN, it has been demonstrated to have been the work of three translators. The language of the translation was not very idiomatic and there continued to be a demand for a Danish Bible acceptable to a larger number of readers. In 1529, Christian Pedersen published a translation of the New Testament (from the Vulgate) and in 1531 a translation of the Psalms.

In 1535, finally, appeared the translation of the Old Testament by the Danish reformer, Hans Tausen, whose work was based upon a knowledge of the Hebrew text as well as of the Vulgate and of Luther's German translation. The translation was published in Magdeburg, Germany. Like Luther, Tausen endeavored to employ an idiom which was neither stilted nor pedantic and which incorporated many elements from everyday speech. Despite the originality of Tausen's work and the linguistic ability which he displayed as a translator, it is still a matter of historical conjecture whether his translation of the Pentateuch really was influential in his own time. Dr. Bjørn Kornerup, who has written an excellent essay on Tausen's translation, as the introduction to a modern facsimile edition, surmises that the rarity of the book today indicates that it was much read and that most of the copies of Tausen's superior translation disintegrated because of use.

There is a clear-cut relationship between the increase in book production and the Reformation. A cornerstone in the structure of the Reformation in Denmark as in Germany was the translation of the Bible. As in Germany, the leading reformer was himself a translator of the most essential weapon of evangelism, the Bible, although to be sure the Bible issued under the aegis of King Christian III more nearly corresponds to Luther's Bible in its authoritativeness than does Tausen's. As in Germany, the union of reformer and translator had an effect not only on the psyche but also on the language of the times.

HANS TAUSEN (1494–1561), who is called the Danish Luther, was trained in Germany and was inspired by the German reformer. While a number of parallels may be drawn between Tausen and Luther, the Dane was neither the dominant figure nor the prolific writer that Luther was. Hans Tausen represents the man of letters in early sixteenth-century Denmark. His principal concern was theological, and consequently his writings, like the writings of his most significant contemporaries, are first and foremost theological. From the aesthetic standpoint there is little to be said about the works of Tausen and his contemporaries save that they helped to mould a secular language outside the pale of the Church; but this was a prerequisite for the growth of popular literature.

As elsewhere in Europe, the humanistic popularization of the Gospels took place in the sixteenth century, and translations of the Old and New Testaments, and particularly of the Psalms, comprised the elevated reading of the day. There was further a direct relationship between the Bible and the popular or secular literature of the times, for in the last analysis it drew its motifs from Biblical sources. The dramatic quality of many Biblical tales—as, e. g., the story of Susannah—enabled Biblical material readily to become secularized. The Bible in the vernacular was in the sixteenth century a source of inspiration for story and fiction. Biblical tales played a rôle at least somewhat similar to that of fiction in more recent centuries. We can, therefore, not consider the Bible only as a work of theological and historical import when we consider Danish literature—even in the more narrow sense of the word—during and after the Reformation.

In great measure because of the eagerness of the reformers to win over the common man and to make him a party to decisions in matters which hitherto had been the concern of the learned world, the printed word spread more and more widely. The evangelical agitators wanted everyman to be able to see and judge for himself. To be effective, the literary medium had to possess popular appeal. Since belletristic presentation often is a most effective way to make a point clear, the popular song, the woodcut, the anecdote, and the didactic conversation were all made to play a rôle in the great ecclesiastical debate. There were also many polemical and satirical pamphlets which minimized the abstractions of theologians.

The dialectic effort contained in the literature of the Reformation and Counter-reformation was not necessarily an attempt to be original. The reformers had no inhibitions about freely using contemporary German satires if these would be effective, as indeed they were, in Danish versions. Consequently, much of the Danish popular literature of the sixteenth century which has bearing upon the reformatory movement is little more than a pendant to the contemporary German literature of a similar type. As we shall see below, the evangelical hymn stood in a similar relationship of dependency to the German hymn.

Satire was one of the principal weapons in the struggle for a new faith. By it rather than by logic, the reformers could obtain popular support and quickly change popular opinions. One of the most widely read and most effective satires in German-speaking Europe was the "Sick Mass" by a Swiss, Nicolaus Manuel. With considerable humor it ridiculed the mass as a moribund device of the papacy and described the various efforts made to prescribe for it. By 1533 Manuel's satire appeared in a Danish version entitled *Dialogus*. This version, the work of an unknown editor, contains references to local conditions and Danish contemporaries, but is otherwise essentially a translation of a German edition of Manuel's satire.

Perhaps the most effective original Danish piece of satire from the Reformation period is the poem *Om Løgen oc Sandhed (Lie and Truth, 1547)* which is ascribed to Hans Tausen. In the form of a folk ballad, this poem tells of Truth's flight from the court to a town and into the country and from the bishop's palace to a monastery. All the time Truth is persecuted by the triumphant Lie. Even the monks imprison Truth. The poem concludes with the observation that Truth has now escaped its prison and that Papists must beware, for she will reveal the fraud upon which their power is based. The boldness of the piece, its metaphors and personifications, create a lasting impression. It is an effective bit of propaganda.

Another product of the Reformation in Denmark which became popular was the "Dance of Death."[1] Like *Dialogus,* the Danish "Dance of

---

1 The unique copy of the work which is known as *Dødedansen* bears no title.

Death" is unoriginal; it is the revision of a Low German work. Curiously enough, the German original is not a reformatory tract at all; for it ante-dates the Reformation and is medieval in spirit. The Danish version con-tained severe criticism of the Church of Rome, however, and achieved its effect in part by more or less self-explanatory woodcuts, some of which were borrowed from other publications of the time. The ethos in the "Dance of Death" is the same as in *Kortvending (Turnabout,* cf. page 59) by the Danish clergyman Hans Christensen Sthen: that faith in God is the highest good and that worldly possessions are of no lasting value. Death comes to the wealthy as well as the poor, to the mighty as well as the weak.

The sixty-page dramatic conversation entitled *Peder Smed* or *Peder Smed oc Atzer Bonde (Peder Smith and Atzer Farmer,* 1559) is the most nearly original Danish work of its kind, which has been preserved. Strictly didactic and propagandistic, it cannot be considered a drama despite its several speakers and the concluding remarks (by Peder Smith) which imply a stage presentation. In *Peder Smed* the protagonists of the Reformation adduce a number of effective arguments against the Church of Rome, principally on the basis of the ecclesiastical abuses of the day, such as the sale of indulgences. The materialism of the priesthood and the extensive ownership of property by monasteries and cloisters are specifically attacked. The speaker for the Church, Herr Jens, is portrayed as ineffective. As a result of the conversation there are two conversions: the peasant Atzer becomes convinced that the Church is corrupt and a monk gives up his tonsure in order to do something useful in the world.

An enlightening demonstration of the nature of printed literature in the sixteenth century can be had by examining a list of all the books ascribed to a single well-known Copenhagen printer, Hans Vingaard.[1] Vingaard is known to have printed at least 102 books and pamphlets between 1528 and 1559. Predominantly ecclesiastical, they include works of Luther translated by Hans Tausen, Jørgen Jensen Sadolin, Peder Palladius, and Matthæus Parvus. They further include a large number of works by Peder Palladius, only two of which were written in Danish; numerous works of Peder's brother Niels Palladius; two works of Me-lanchthon, translated by Peder Palladius; a translation of the Augsburg confession; translations of works by the German reformers Urbanus Rhegius and Veit Dietrich, by Robert Estienne, and the Dane Albert Giøe; an original work by Hans Tausen; Luther's prayerbook, trans-

1 The examination has been made by Lauritz Nielsen in *Nordisk Tidskrift för Bok- och Biblioteksväsen* III, 1916, pp. 91–111.

lated by Parvus; a catechism for boys; a new songbook; and several Icelandic imprints of a theological nature. Six or eight are on medical subjects, these include Henrik Smith's *Lægebog (Medical Book)* as well as two of Smith's four herbals, and books on the pestilence by three different authors. Only a handful of Vingaard's books may be considered literary in the narrower modern sense of the word. The most important non-ecclesiastical work is the Danish rhyming chronicle *(Den danske Rimkrønike)*, of which Vingaard published two editions. The other non-ecclesiastical, non-medical, and non-learned works issued by Vingaard include the late medieval tale of "Brother Rus" *(Broder Russes Historie)*, the Danish version of the medieval didactic dialogue *Lucidarius,* a rhyming calendar *(Cicio Janus),* a couple of satirical poems, and in addition several accolades to King Christian III, a Danish translation of a German manual of decorum for children, and a translation of Michael Lindener's *Rastbüchlein,* which contained tales taken from the Decameron of Boccaccio. The very lack of works which we would consider literary—lyric, epic or dramatic—is indicative of the lack of interest in and respect for books and pamphlets which did not concern themselves with theological, medical, legal, or purely academic matters. The secular literature of the Renaissance is represented solely by the translation of Lindener's anthology.

Aesthetically, the hymn represents the greatest accomplishment in Danish literature in both the sixteenth and seventeenth centuries, for the best versifiers of the times were clergymen who wrote ecclesiastical poetry with fervor, either after late medieval or more especially contemporary Lutheran models. As a matter of fact, sixteenth-century Danish hymns are to a large extent translations from the German. Some two thirds of the hymns in the so-called "Malmö hymnal" of 1533, for example, were from the German, but like most medieval and early modern translations, they were adaptations of the original German hymns rather than interlinear Danish translations. It is well to keep the older attitude toward translation in mind, for only in the last two centuries have translators generally felt scruples about the exactness of their work or even felt the obligation to state the source of the work which they were rewriting in their own language. Originality of content was not then the basic criterion that it later became in adjudging literature.

A high point in Danish hymnology was reached with the publication in 1569 of HANS THOMISSØN's hymn book, *Den danske Psalmebog,* which achieved an official recognition that Hans Tausen's hymnal had not received a quarter of a century before. Here for the first time was assembled the poetic achievement of the Reformation for use in churches and schools. The evangelical hymn, which is such an important element in Protestantism, was therewith established in Denmark. By royal decree the new hymnal was to be acquired by all churches and schools in the land.

Among Danish writers of hymns HANS CHRISTENSEN STHEN (1544–1610) is worthy of special mention. He wrote in the spirit of the times and his own philosophy was impregnated with the Christian faith, yet insofar as sixteenth-century poetry could be personal, his hymns were personal.

If we consider all the books and pamphlets published during the sixteenth century, the picture remains about the same as that given by a consideration of the books published by Vingaard during three decades. From the period 1482–1550 are preserved some 300 Danish imprints; but in the second half of the sixteenth century there appeared no less than 1374 items large and small (including reissues).[1] Of the nearly 1700 books and pamphlets published by Danes between 1482 and 1600, less than a hundred are literary in the modern sense of the word; and of this number again, half were written not in the vernacular but in Latin or even in Greek; of the remaining works, a few were written in German, so that the number of literary Danish publications *(nota bene,* including translations*)* prior to the seventeenth century, does not exceed half a hundred. Whether in Latin or Danish, these works nevertheless represent a triumph of the Humanistic conviction that literature had aesthetic and ethical values and could, so to speak, exist in its own right. There occurred a distinct change from the literary situation of the first half of the sixteenth century. Under the impact of the non-Christian Roman literature, poets began to write Latin verse addressed to the learned and sophisticated, which was no longer *ad maiorem gloriæ dei.*

The Latin poetry of the sixteenth century is of no great intrinsic value and is all but forgotten today, but it bestowed dignity on belles-lettres. Everyone who could, tried his hand at verse. Even Denmark's great astronomer TYCHO BRAHE (1546–1601) was a Latin poet and his *De nova stella* (1573) commences with a poem to Urania. Of the many neo-Latin poets of the century, the most prolific was the widely traveled ERASMUS LÆTUS (i.e., RASMUS GLAD, 1526–82). His *Bucolica,* published in Wittenberg in 1560, is a series of poems in the style of Virgil's bucolic verse. During his lifetime Lætus was favorably compared with his Latin master and he enjoyed many privileges because of his poetic ability. His later

[1] These figures include books published by Danes in Latin, both at home and abroad.

poems were didactic, historical, and topographical. A clergyman and university professor, he was several times the recipient of royal favor, but presumably because of the occasional poetry which he addressed to members of the ruling house.

Of greater interest today than the Latin literature of the century are those works printed in Danish. Of the scant 50 titles mentioned above (and including the titles already mentioned as having been printed by Vingaard), three are plays: Hegelund's *Susanna* (1578) and *Calumnia* (1579), H. Justesen Ranch's *Kong Salomons Hylding (Allegiance to Salomon,* 1585), and Hans Christensen Sthen's *Lyckens Hiul (The Wheel of Fortune,* 1581). No less than thirteen are chapbooks, several of which went through more than one edition, e.g., *Griselda, Flores ok Blankiflur, Sigismunda,* and the so-called Karl Magnus chronicle. Similar to the chapbooks are two works which clearly antedate the Reformation: the "Story of John the Priest" *(Historie aff Jon Presth,* 1510), a Danish version of the legend about the mythical oriental king Johannes Presbyter; and the rhymed tale of *Brother Rus* (1555), which relates an attempt of the devil to corrupt a monastery. In addition to Anders Sørensen Vedel's influential and pioneer edition of one hundred Danish folk songs (1591), there are finally some eleven imprints of songs of the times. Among the miscellaneous items are Hermann Weigere's translation of the epic of Reynard the Fox (1555); two manuals of decorum for children, one of them translated from the German of Jürg Wickram; a book of fabliaux, also translated from the German; the Danish version of the Dance of Death; and a translation of a didactic dialogue by Sir David Lindsay. We note that the two genres which are best represented, the drama and the chapbook, are at the same time new to Danish literature in the sixteenth century and mark the coming of the Renaissance to Denmark.

As elsewhere in Europe, the beginnings of the modern drama in Denmark were closely related not to folk literature but to the church and the school. The drama of the sixteenth and early seventeenth centuries came to occupy an intermediate position between ecclesiastical and secular literature, and not until the end of the seventeenth century did it finally disassociate itself from ecclesiastical antecedents.

There had been a tradition of dramatization within the churches since the Middle Ages, but the coming of Humanism gave the genre a new birth. Humanism brought a knowledge of Roman comedy, i.e., Plautus and Terence. Latin plays were given at the University of Copenhagen as early as 1521, but it was after the Reformation had passed its zenith that the influence of classical drama really began to make itself felt. By that time dramatic presentations had moved outside the church and it was rare for a dramatization even of Biblical stories to be given in the church proper. The Protestant church was not as liberal as the medieval catholic church when it came to the use of sacred buildings for other than divine service. The school, which of course meant a Latin school, became the foster home of the drama, and during the second half of the sixteenth century the number of plays given at Danish schools seems to have been large. These plays were given in Latin, German, or Danish and provided a link between the school and life outside. We may imagine the audiences to have been made up of the pupils' parents, families, friends, and the general public seeking entertainment, much like the audiences at school plays today. Few of the plays possessed much originality. They were generally the work of the school's director, who could not be expected to be a dramatist by birth. The subject matter of the plays was either Biblical or classical, and on the whole the school plays were reworkings of similar plays which had been given in Germany. This sort of play enjoyed royal favor. Plautus' *Aulularia* was given at the royal castle by students of the University of Copenhagen on the occasion of the betrothal of Princess Anna, daughter of Frederik II and sister of the young King Christian IV, to James I of Scotland in 1589.

There is documentary evidence that public plays were given at some Danish schools in the second half of the fifteenth century, but only three plays and one additional fragment are now extant from Danish drama antedating the Reformation. The texts of most of the later school comedies have also been lost, but we know that at least forty-five different plays were given in Denmark between 1500 and 1610.

The manuscripts of the earliest Danish dramas which are preserved date from the first third of the sixteenth century, although the dramas may conceivably have been written somewhat earlier. Two untitled pieces have been called by a modern editor "The Unfaithful Wife" and "The Judgment of Paris;" the third piece bears the title *Dorotheæ Komedie*. The first of the plays is a farce and is akin to the German *Fastnachtspiel*. The second is a morality play based on the well-known classical allegory. The third is a translation from a Latin play by one Kilian Reuther about the martyrdom of Saint Dorothy. "The Unfaithful Wife" draws on various sources and is anecdotal in content. Its principal character is a woman who remains true to her husband until she is told by a "vetula"—so called because the title and notes of the play are in Latin—that the old woman's dog was once her daughter and that the daughter had been transformed because she refused to let an admirer have his will with her. The farce ends on a comic note and the announcer asks the audience for a pourboire. The aesthetic value of the plays is slight; neither in conception nor in execution do they show any finesse or feeling for dramatic form or poetic language. They seem a very far cry from the elegance of speech, the careful diction, and the florid metaphors of the Latin literature of the time. Crude and coarse as the literature in the vernacular may seem at the beginning of the sixteenth century, it nevertheless eventually won out at the expense of the elegant and learned Latin literature.

A sixteenth-century play which enjoyed particular esteem, PEDER JENSEN HEGELUND's *Susanna,* has been preserved in a printed edition from the year 1578. In a poem prefixed to the original edition of this play a contemporary wrote that, if Danish drama and the Danish language were to become respected, it would be through Hegelund (1542–1614). *Susanna* was presented under Hegelund's supervision at Ribe in 1576. Written in rhyming couplets but with a loose metrical pattern, the play follows the general model of the classical drama. It is in five acts with a prologue and an epilogue. Stage directions and many of the marginal comments are in Latin, but there are also explanatory notes in Danish and appropriate Danish proverbs in the margins. The story of the chaste Susanna, taken from the Book of Daniel, was a favorite subject for the dramatists of the times. Little was left to the imagination of the audience. According to the script, Susanna makes her ablutions on stage, is attacked and repulses her attackers. Her trial is given in great detail. The dramatic realism of the play is suggested by the comment of one character at the end of the play as Susanna's vilifiers are stoned to death: "see how their brains are running down over their eyes." While the didactic intent of the author is obvious, the plot itself is dramatic enough to counterbalance the play's lengthiness and many moralizing monologues.

A more able playwright of the post-Reformation era in Denmark was HIERONYMUS JUSTESEN RANCH (1539–1607). His serious plays, *Kong Salomons Hylding (Allegiance to Salomon,* first printed in 1585), and *Samsons Fængsel (Samson's Prison,* 1599, first printed 1633), are examples of the Biblically inspired drama. Incidentally, *Kong Salomons Hylding* was written at royal command to celebrate the swearing of allegiance to King Frederik II's son, the later Christian IV. From the standpoint of the development of literature, Ranch's farce *Karrig Niding (Stingy Miser,* posthumously published in 1633) is of greater interest. It is a contemporary satire, full of a rough and didactic humor that suggests the farces of Hans Sachs: a niggardly husband, who is so miserly that he scarcely is willing to cut a piece of bread for himself, decides to leave home for a few days, to take the keys to the larder with him, and therewith to save the food that would ordinarily be eaten in his household during his absence. While he is away some beggars arrive and ask for alms. Apprised of the situation, they offer the few provisions they have with them to the miser's wife and servants. The leading beggar is then accepted in husband's stead and an intrigue is devised to make the miser believe that the household is not his own. He returns and finds all locks changed and his wife the spouse of Jep Skald, the beggar. Gradually he becomes convinced that his own wits deceive him and he sits down to enjoy the contents of his own larder before wandering on to find his lost farm and wife. The comedy, written in rhyming couplets, was apparently inspired by a German folk song which tells much same the story about a wealthy miser.

Hans Christensen Sthen's *Kortt Wendingh,* referred to in Danish as *Kortvending (Turnabout,* c. 1570*)*, admonishes the audience and then turns the wheel of fortune so that each character learns a bitter lesson and is moved to humility before God and man. The presentation is rather stereotyped, for there is no development of action but merely a repetition of related situations; but the technique (which occasionally has been employed by modern dramatists) is not mere artlessness.

In contrast to Sthen's *Kortvending,* the anonymous *Thobiæ comoedia* (about 1600) contains dramatic dialogue and a development of plot. It is an original Danish version of the apocryphal legend of Tobias who, unlike Sarah's several earlier husbands, escapes death on the wedding night and whose continence is rewarded by the archangel Raphael. The play is in five acts, each of which is divided into scenes, like the slightly earlier plays of H. J. Ranch. It is a morality play, and preaches the same lesson as Sthen's *Kortvending.*

Another comedy preserved in the same manuscript as *Thobiæ comoedia* is the *Comoedia de Mundo et Paupere,* which was given in Randers in 1607. It is a morality play in three acts divided into scenes with a prologue and an epilogue. There is a didactic interlocutor. The lesson in the comedy is not subtle. A poor man sells himself to the world and becomes emperor. At the height of his power he becomes sick. His friends desert him; his wealth does him no good. He dies and is condemned to Hell. Although the play is fundamentally an allegory and the rôles were meant to present types rather than individuals, the presentation may have been somewhat realistic. There is an almost Shakespearian comic relief in the form of a "rusticus and rustica." With them the drama becomes farcical at times.

Incidentally, English players are known to have come to Denmark around 1600, but what and how they played we unfortunately cannot ascertain. It is just conceivable that Shakespeare may have been played in Denmark at that time.

Aside from the tradition of comedy that bespeaks the innate human desire for amusement and entertainment and vicarious experience in the form of living pictures, the non-ecclesiastical literature of the sixteenth and seventeenth centuries was first and foremost the literature of chapbooks. Literature written purely for entertainment was never held in high esteem by contemporary criticism, and much of what did exist of this sort of literature has now disappeared. The fact that Hieronymous Justesen Ranch's farce *Karrig Niding* was printed several times in chapbook form and that the later satirical farce *Grevens og Friherrens Komoedie (The Comedy of the Count and the Baron)*, from the seventies of the seventeenth century, exists in several copies, is evidence that there was in Denmark a literature of entertainment much nearer to the popular literature of the present day than the more respectable, more demanding works—like Arrebo's *Hexaëmeron*—that possessed the aura of literary prestige.

The Danish chapbooks are all translations, but that does not diminish their historical worth; they were the popular books of the sixteenth and seventeenth centuries. They furnish documentary evidence that Denmark also knew and read the international European popular literature of the sixteenth and seventeenth centuries and that antique and medieval material lived on in the popular mind after it had ceased to be of intrinsic interest to the sophisticated and the learned. The great fund of story and legend that tells of Charlemagne, Griselda, Flores and Blancheflor, Olger the Dane, Doctor Faust, Magelona, Octavian, the Wandering Jew, Till Eulenspiegel, and Melusina provided the raw material for a literature which is a conclusive demonstration for the hypothesis about "sunken culture" *(gesunkenes Kulturgut)*. The entertaining literature of an upper class at the end of the Middle Ages gradually lost its appeal to that class but won new friends among lesser folk. One does not have to look far for parallels in our own day. The so-called comic book containing versions of well-known tales, printed on cheap paper and adorned with gaudy illustrations, is a chapbook of the twentieth century.

In volume 13 of the collection of Danish chapbooks published under the title *Danske Folkebøger fra 16. og 17. Aarhundrede* (1926), Richard Paulli has told the fascinating story of the chapbook in Denmark. Surprisingly enough, the chapbook lived far into the nineteenth century. Most of the earlier chapbooks were reprinted several times during the nineteenth century and two of them, *Uglspil (Eulenspiegel)* and *Judas,* were reprinted during the first decade of the twentieth century. The tremendous and continuing appeal of these books is shown by the small number of changes the texts underwent in the course of four centuries. Some of the woodcuts in the chapbooks were also reproduced and imitated for centuries. Paulli prints several examples of nineteenth-century woodcuts which are but coarse imitations of cuts from the sixteenth and seventeenth centuries.

The plot in the chapbook is regularly of the blood-and-thunder variety, spiced with intrigue and a love story, although the original didactic nature of a number of the chapbooks often excludes a happy ending. The story is one of violent action and strong emotion, so that there can be no doubt about the meaning of the tale or the direction in which it moves.

There is a single monumental work in the genre of the fable which may be compared with the chapbook in early Danish literature: *En Ræffue Bog* (literally *A Fox Book,* i.e., *Reynard the Fox*) printed in 1555. The Reynard-Reineke fable had been popular for a century in French, Flemish, and German-speaking territories. In his Danish version of the Low German Reineke, one HERMANN WEIGERE gave the international fable its Danish form. *En Ræffue Bog* is however more than an ironic fable —unfortunately, one might say. Every chapter is augmented by moralizing prose passages and illustrative didactic material, often in verse, from various German writers, principally Sebastian Brant, Freidank, Johann von Schwarzenberg, and Johannes Morslin. The tale of Reynard is indeed allegorical, but the expositor or expositors who have provided the interspersed commentary and the marginal notes have taken the burden of interpretation upon themselves. It is therefore difficult to read *En Ræffue Bog* for the sake of the story in Weigere's version or in the versions on which his work is based. The book contains the ever-amusing tale of Reynard the Fox who has offended all the other animals in the kingdom but who is able to win favor of the lion-king despite the many complaints which are made about him to the monarch. As in Æsop's Fables, a selection of which was published in Danish in 1556 as the posthumuous work of Christian Pedersen, the intent is fundamentally didactic, but the story itself is really a piece of popular literature of a quality far above that of the moralizing commentary.

The eleven contemporary songs which were among the half a hundred imprints belonging to the second half of the sixteenth century suggest the existence of a popular oral literature, very little of which found its way into print. The large number of poems from the sixteenth and early seventeenth centuries which H. Grüner-Nielsen and others have assembled[1] is evidence enough that the muse was far from stilled in Denmark after the flourishing of the folk song in the late Middle Ages. In part because it is anonymous and undated, the poetry of the sixteenth and seventeenth centuries is little read.

Danish poetry of the early modern era is generally neglected and unknown because sixteenth and seventeenth-century Danish is difficult to read today. The earlier folksongs are, deservedly, better known; but they are read primarily in modern versions, whereas early modern poetry is too close to modern Danish to be translated though at the same time too far removed to be understood by other than scholars.

We are sufficiently historically minded to appreciate folk songs as curiosa rather than as poetry, but our tolerance does not extend to somewhat more sophisticated lyrics; and we want to know the author of a lyrical poem. This prejudice must nevertheless be abandoned if we are to understand and appreciate Danish secular poetry from the Reformation until the eighteenth century. When judged by content the popular songs which arose during that era fall into several categories. Many are historical; some strongly suggest the medieval folk song; there are love songs and comic verses, moral-didactic poems and popular religious hymns, songs which tell stories and even songs which employ classical motifs. Finally, there is a number of personal lyrical poems. Many of the poems have been preserved only in seventeenth-century manuscripts; some are known only from broadsides. Most of the poems have many stanzas. Neither their meters nor rhyme-schemes (when rhyme is present) are complicated. Representative subjects of the poems are the Turks in Persia, reported miracles abroad, Adam and Eve, Androcles and the Lion, marriage, unrequited love, the unfaithful maiden, and various Danish kings from Erik Plovpenning (c. 1250) to Christian IV (1588–1648).

Towards the end of the sixteenth century Renaissance Humanism caused an awakening of interest in the national past. ANDERS SØRENSEN VEDEL (1542–1616), a poet and historian as well as a clergyman at the Danish court, was really the first to break a lance for indigenous literature. He first translated Saxo Grammaticus into Danish (1575) and later he edited the aforementioned collection of one hundred medieval Danish folk songs and ballads (1591). At the same time that Vedel was translating Saxo, the Norwegian PEDER CLAUSSON (1545–1614) was translating Snorri

1 In the seven volumes of *Danske Viser fra Adelsviseboger og Flyveblade 1530–1630*, Copenhagen, 1912–30.

Sturluson's *Heimskringla* and making available one of the major works of medieval Northern history to a forgetful Scandinavia. A century after Vedel had published the first collection of Danish folk songs, Peder Syv republished it in augmented form (1695). The two editions of folk songs are historically of signal importance in the growth of the appreciation of folk literature.

Renaissance currents carried over well into the seventeenth century; in literature they are responsible for the great poetic effort of the early seventeenth century: the epic *Hexaëmeron* of ANDERS CHRISTENSEN ARREBO (1587–1637), a clergyman and one-time bishop of Trondheim, Norway. Arrebo had made a name as a translator of the Psalms—a volume of his free translations was published in 1623—but his magnum opus remained in manuscript until 1661, although it was recognized as a literary achievement in Arrebo's lifetime. After the fashion of the French poet Du Bartas in *La Semaine* (1578), Arrebo undertook to describe the six days of the creation according to the Old Testament. Today we marvel at the assiduity which could produce such a lengthy poem, but we scarcely possess the concentration which is needed to keep our attention fixed on this monumental work. In giving religious tradition wordly form and interpreting for his own time the great mythos of the Bible, Arrebo was a sort of seventeenth-century Klopstock.

Not only did the *Hexaëmeron* represent a fulfillment of the Renaissance longing for an epic of Homeric dimensions in the vernacular; stylistically it heralded a new direction in literature which was to become dominant in Denmark even before Arrebo's death. The events of the first day are told in rhyming hexameters while those of the other five days are in alexandrines. A peculiarity of the epic which is a precursor of the poetry of coming decades is the large number of words which Arrebo himself fabricated. These characteristics of meter and vocabulary are common to the poetry of the seventeenth century from about 1630 onward.

With Arrebo's *Hexaëmeron,* which was produced just a century after the Danish language had replaced Latin in the Danish church service and therewith symbolized a clear break with Rome and its international, medieval culture, we take leave of the era which embraced Humanism, the Reformation and the Renaissance in Denmark.

Chapter IV

An Age of Dualism. Baroque Literature

The era which embraced the Danish Reformation, the subsequent changes in philosophy and theology, and the many reactions which consequently made themselves felt in daily life, lasted about one hundred years. Then, when a new spirit of scientific curiosity already had permeated western Europe and learning had begun to establish itself beyond the bounds of ecclesiastical authority, a new, worldly culture began to make itself felt in Denmark. This culture, although secular in nature, had not actually disassociated itself from the dominant theological thinking of the preceding century. The new worldliness did not engender an wholly secular literature but a literature which, struggling to be self-sufficient, was nevertheless bound to traditional, if reformed, religious convictions. It was almost inevitable that the two great poets of the seventeenth century were religious poets.

The Reformation had taken away the security of existence and instead had stressed the importance of the search for a philosophy of life. That is to say, the Reformation had given secular literature a new ethical function and assignment. As literature gradually was released from ecclesiastical domination, its philosophical importance continued to grow throughout the seventeenth and eighteenth centuries until secular literature finally became more important than ecclesiastical literature in considering the ideas and problems of daily life.

The didactic attitude of litterateurs at the beginning of the century was succinctly expressed by the authoritative and influential German critic Martin Opitz in his *Buch von der deutschen Poeterey* (1624) in which he declared: "Poetry is in the first instance nothing but a hidden theology." Alpha was however not omega. The secularization of literature also produced a literature of words, words artfully and artistically combined, but a literature for which figures of speech were as important as ideas. This literature we term baroque.

For the first time since Christianity had swept away the pagan literature, poetry now existed independently, in the face of the incredible destruction wrought by the Thirty Years' War. And now the number of poets

Title page of the chapbook about "Brother Rus", first printed 1555.
Actual size. (Cf. p. 56).

ANDERS ARREBO
Painting in the church at Vordingborg.

THOMAS KINGO

Etching by Gerard Valck, 1704, after a painting by an unknown artist, c. 1680.

View of Copenhagen at the beginning of the seventeenth century.

Eleonora Christina leaving the Blue Tower, 1685.
Painting (1874) by Kristian Zahrtmann. (Cf. p. 71).

and poetasters became legion. From the thirties of the century onward the flood gates were down and much descriptive, didactic, historical, topographical, and above all occasional poetry was written both in Danish and in Latin. By 1652 HANS LAUREMBERG (1590–1658), a satirist who employed Low German, was moved to make fun of the quantities of verse which were being produced for weddings, baptisms, funerals, and occasions of state. It was as if no man could take a wife and no soul take leave of this earthly life without provoking some versifier to practice his talents. Much of this sort of poetry never found its way into print.

Politically the seventeenth century was an age of absolutism. The Church had lost the authority which it had held up to the Reformation, and religious questions became hopelessly entangled with political questions before and during the Thirty Years' War. Ambitious writers could only hope for reward from men who sat at the political helm and from wealthy and influential patrons. This situation gave rise to much abject verse addressed to the powerful. Although this sort of verse is ethically worthless, it is not without some aesthetic significance when viewed in retrospect. It bespeaks the fact that poetry had come into its own as an art in which linguistic ornamentation existed for its own sake and could be moulded at will by its creator, though the works of which it was a part usually smacked of didacticism.

The aforementioned *Buch von der deutschen Poeterey* (1624, and many times republished) by Martin Opitz was programmatic in fixing literary genres and establishing rules for rhyme and accentuation not only for German but for Danish literature as well. Other German writers—notably Georg Philipp Harsdörffer—were also influential, but Opitz was the supreme arbiter. Danish writers of the century continued to be very sensitive toward the literary tendencies and fashions of Germany. Consequently much that may be said of German literature in the seventeenth century also holds true for its Danish counterpart. The new poetics of Opitz, *et al.,* seem to have been more meaningful to Danish writers and scholars than all the military maneuvers during the wars that plagued Germany from 1618 to 1648.

If Danish poetry continued to be inspired by foreign—and notably German—models, there was nonetheless a sincere and conscious attempt to be original. The essential nature of the so-called baroque poetry is that it tried to find new means of expression. The limitations of subject matter which had been felt for centuries were abandoned and the individual writer was free to be as subjective as he wished. A parallel may be drawn with some of the modern poetry of the twentieth century which similarly has tried to transcend the worn phrases of traditional poetry and to make verse express what it has not expressed before.

The hyperbole, the metaphor, the anaphora—these were elements which delighted the baroque poet. Comparison and contrast and antithesis were favorite devices. Tautology and punning—often without any intention of humor—reflect a pure joy in words and an insistent attempt to be original. The baroque poet had a predilection for adjectives and for description and circumlocution. He believed with S. P. GOTLENDER (in *Synopsis prosodiæ Danicæ,* 1650) that "epitheta" were like "jewels in a ring." And he was convinced of the effectiveness of elevated language.

Some of the devices employed by baroque poets seem futile and ridiculous today. An example is provided by the late baroque poet JØRGEN SORTERUP (1662–1723) in whose *Nye Helte-Sange (New Heroic Ballads, 1716)* dates are to be read by adding up the numerical values of the Roman capital letters contained in his dedicatory verses.

Baroque poetry was however not merely a matter of style. Besides rhetorical devices, the poetry contained a new spirit which sprang from a new attitude toward life: a worldliness which was tense with intimations of the possibilities that lay in the future and which still was concerned with the eternal life. The coarseness of many allusions found in seventeenth-century poetry indicates a different attitude toward bodily functions than prevails in the twentieth century. The so-called dirty story which flourished in the sixteenth and seventeenth century was apparently not the outlawed genre it is today. Despite the baroque love of euphemisms, propriety—or prudery if you will—had not yet come to Scandinavia.

The seventeenth century also evoked an awareness of prosody. Poets were more metrically conscious than before, and by the middle of the century verse patterns had become fixed. Forms, rules, and meter sometimes became more important than inspiration. In this connection ANDERS BORDING (1619–77) is worthy of note as a poet who created stanzas which were reminiscent of the folk song and which appealed to a wider public than did most poetry of the time. Bording's poems were published in collected form in 1735, incidentally the first time a Danish poet's work was published as a whole. Most of Bording's production consists of occasional poetry, which, while showing him to have been a clever writer of verse, lacks lasting aesthetic value. Bording composed both hymns and secular poetry. Such dualism is typical of the baroque poet. Most of Bording's poetry resembles a great stream of words and contains exaggerations, a plethora of metaphors, and a great deal of empty rhetoric. That he is a baroque poet is indicated not only by his vocabulary, style, and syntax, but also by his own literary taste—he is the author of a poem honoring Arrebo's *Hexaëmeron*—and by his pastoral verse about Daphne, Amaryllis, etc. Most of his poems are in many stanzas and favor the set phrases of artificial neo-classicism. Like the other poets of the day, he also tried his hand at Latin and German verse. Bording, who in his lifetime was looked upon as Denmark's foremost elegant poet, was also the author of a monthly rhymed commentary on events and persons in leading European countries. The commentary, entitled *Den Danske Mercurius (The Danish Mercury)*, was published from 1666 to 1677.

The organ-like chords of baroque poetry as it was cultivated in Germany in the seventeenth century were struck by only one Danish poet, the clergyman THOMAS KINGO (1634–1703), in whom Danish baroque poetry reached its zenith. Bording did not equal him as an artist. Although Kingo's verse consists almost entirely of hymns and occasional poetry directed to members of the royal family and great men, he possessed unusual poetic ability, as is borne out by the fact that a number of Kingo's poems still enjoy popularity in Denmark. He was able to fulfill the baroque demand for form and pathos, for the resonant phrase and the hyperbolic comparison; he was at the same time able to breathe into verse his strong Christian faith, a faith that was coupled with a pietistic, almost mystical longing. Like the rest of baroque poetry, Kingo's verse oscillates between worldliness and other-worldliness. His are imperfect pearls. The pictures he suggests spring from a temporal background, but are meant to portray the realm of an awful, supernatural God. Crassly put, Kingo is a theological and didactic versifier, a hymnist, and a laureate. His poetry does not fulfill the demands we usually make of poetry today, for his verse is on the whole elegiac rather than lyric, and descriptive and reflective rather than expressive of personal experience. This does not mean that Kingo was not a great poet. If we judge him before the background of his times, and especially if we compare him with the German baroque poets who were his inspiration, we must pronounce him not wanting in genius. If we undertake to determine how many of his poems are classic—i.e., are alive today—how many, for example, have been reprinted in poetic anthologies of the last half century, and how many are familiar to the Danes today—we are surprised to find that Kingo is better known than the vast majority of more recent Danish poets. Kingo's best-loved hymn, "Far, Verden, Farvel" ("Fare, World, Farewell") from the second part of his *Aandelige Siunge-Koor (Spiritual Chorus*, 1681) is indicative of his ability to strike an individual note with associations for every man. The poem, of which the first stanza is printed in translation below, is philosophical rather than laudatory and possesses a remarkable balance of thought in contrasting "vanity" with the blessings of Abraham's bosom.

> Fare, world, and farewell.
> I'm weary much longer in thralldom to dwell.
> From burdens which long have oppressed me I flee;
> Them will I cast off me and set myself free,
> For weary I am, and I feel but disdain
> For all that is vain,
> For all that is vain.

The first part of the *Aandelige Siunge-Koor,* with the imprint 1674, was intended primarily for private devotions and contains hymns for each day of the week. The collection was carefully organized, with a hymn for each morning and each evening, together with a concluding psalm. The hymns were to be sung to contemporary worldly—and very nearly sprightly—melodies. The same melody was to be used for all the hymns sung on a single day. Later editions of the collection were expanded by additional poems ("sighs," Kingo called them) for each morning and evening.

The success of the "spiritual chorus" made Kingo the obvious person to undertake a revision of the official Danish hymnbook, which was still the compilation made by Hans Thomissøn in 1569 and with which some dissatisfaction had been expressed. Kingo was duly commissioned to compile a new hymnbook, which also was to contain some of his own poems. The resulting collection, in which half the hymns were by Kingo himself, did not win the approval of the crown, and the revision was entrusted to new editors. Finally, in 1699 a new hymnal appeared. It is known by Kingo's name primarily because he was its privileged publisher, but it did contain no less than 85 of Kingo's hymns; it is therefore a monument to Kingo's stellar position as a poet and hymnologist for his own times.

It is the emotional intensity and associative power of certain of Kingo's poems that have insinuated them into the literary consciousness of Denmark. Kingo exists first and foremost in the church hymnal, but the most mundane urbanite is nevertheless aware of Kingo's verse. Kingo was the first of a long line of Danish poets to contribute to the corpus of living hymns which plays a more influential rôle in the history of Danish literature than foreigners are likely to suspect. Up to the twentieth century almost all Danish poets wrote hymns, or poems which have been considered hymns; and the editors of the Danish hymnal are liberal in their definition of a hymn. While the other constituent parts of ecclesiastical

existence are without much significance in Denmark today, many hymns
live on extra-murally, by virtue of their associative and poetic qualities.
Tradition, both ecclesiastical and non-ecclesiastical, has helped to keep
Denmark aware of the treasure buried in its hymnbook, whereas in most
other Protestant countries the hymn has been relegated to the dusty
category of church music.

Of the topographical poetry which flourished in the seventeenth century and to which Kingo among others contributed, only a single work
is alive today: *Nordlands Trompet* (*The Trumpet of Nordland,* not published
until 1739), a description of northern Norway by PETTER DASS (1647–
1708). Dass and DORTHE ENGELBRETSDATTER (1634–1716) are the two
noteworthy representatives of Danish baroque poetry in Norway. Dorthe
Engelbretsdatter, who wrote hymns after the fashion of Kingo, is the
first poetess in Dano-Norwegian literary history. With Petter Dass and
Dorthe Engelbretsdatter, the history of modern Norwegian literature as
a part of continental European literature may be said to have begun.

With regard to the literature which was more widely disseminated than
the learned works of the baroque poets, one must bear in mind that the
chapbooks discussed in the previous chapter enjoyed continual and
probably increasing popularity. Two additional types of popular literature which took a foothold in seventeenth-century Denmark were
pastoral poetry and the pastoral novel. Both are flights of fantastic un-
reality into a realm of decadent chivalry and sentimentality, out of the
crassness and destruction wrought by the Thirty Years' War. Neither
genre is particularly well represented in Danish, but we know that this
sort of literature was widely read by Danes in German and French. The
most famous of the European arcadian, pastoral novels was the *Astrée* of
Honoré d'Urfé, which incidentally also carried on the tradition of the
Spanish "Amadis" novel. D'Urfé's interminable tale of the shepherd
Celadon and the shepherdess Astrea and the many adventures which
grew out of a lovers' quarrel combines bucolic gallantry, eroticism, and
sentimentality. There are numerous lyrical insertions in the prose. Only
the first part of the novel—comprising twelve books—was published in
a Danish translation (based on a German version) as *Dend Hyrdinde
Astrea* (*The Shepherdess Astrea,* 1645–48). The translator was SØREN
TERKELSEN, who also put into Danish the works of Martin Opitz and of
the Dutch poet Jacob Cats.

Indisputable evidence of the popularity of the French and English
pastoral and didactic novels of the seventeenth century is provided by
catalogues of book collections sold at the end of the century. Barclay's

Argenis (originally published in 1621) was to be found in no less than 86 of 126 collections sold between 1700 and 1720, but a Danish translation of this important contribution to pastoral literature did not appear until 1746. That is to say, European baroque novels which had flourished in seventeenth-century France, Germany, and England, still were very much alive far into the eighteenth century in Denmark. This sort of novel had ceased to be of interest to the critical and the sophisticated, but it found less discerning readers. Toward the middle of the century Holberg belittled the baroque novel and the chapbook as empty rhetoric and idle phantasy. The so-called novel of state (in German, the *Staatsroman*) which was popular in Germany in the seventeenth century also found a public in Denmark. A Danish translation of Philipp von Zesen's *Assenat* (originally published in 1670) appeared in 1711 and was republished several times.

Aside from Cervantes' *Don Quixote* (which was not translated into Danish until 1776), the most widely read and long-lived work in novel form produced in seventeenth-century Europe was Fénelon's *Télémaque* (originally published in 1699). It was translated into Danish in 1727–28 and continued to be read in Danish as well as in French (the French version was often used as a textbook) until the end of the nineteenth century. *Télémaque* did not share the fate of the baroque novel, but neither is it representative of baroque culture. Like Boileau, Fénelon was a harbinger of the neo-classicism to which the discriminating of the eighteenth century were to defer.

The transition from baroque literature of the seventeenth century to the neo-classicism which set the tone of the eighteenth century was less abrupt than the shift from Renaissance to baroque literature. In the history of criticism there is however a convenient break with the baroque style in 1701, for in that year TØGER REENBERG (1656–1742) published his *Ars poetica* modelled on the work of Boileau. "Style must be plain and simple," proclaimed Reenberg, but the dominant style of the seventeenth century lived on until well into the eighteenth century and poetry could bear all the earmarks of the baroque as late as the 1770's, in the work of CHRISTIAN FREDERIK WADSKIÆR (1713–79). There is finally the verse of the above-mentioned Jørgen Sorterup, who in 1716 published some occasional poetry about Danish heroes fashioned after the folk songs. His was the first attempt at national historical poetry in Denmark since the Middle Ages. Sorterup founded no school in the eighteenth century; but in the nineteenth century N.F.S.Grundtvig not only admired him but produced a similar sort of historical doggerel.

A pure neo-classical style based on French models can nevertheless be observed as early as about 1675 in the anonymous *Grevens og Friherrens Komoedie (The Comedy of the Count and the Baron)*, generally ascribed to the pen of MOGENS SKEEL (1650–94). This farcical comedy has many of the elements of a play by Holberg and is a forerunner of the works of the master who was permanently to establish Danish dramatic literature half a century later. *Grevens og Friherrens Komoedie* is a satire on the nobility created in Denmark by Christian V. in 1671. The new counts and barons in the comedy are the ridiculous parvenus who, through a farcical intrigue on the part of two servants, get their just due by being duped into letting the new count's daughter marry her real love. After French classical example, the play is in five acts, divided into scenes, and has an intrigue which hinges on the servant-confidantes. The lonely position of this neo-classical play in the seventeenth century emphasizes the lack of baroque drama in Danish literature.

In addition to the conscious literary products which have been described above, seventeenth-century Denmark produced a most unusual autobiographical document which stands isolated from the other writing of the times: the *Jammersminde* (literally "Recollection of Suffering," but translated into English as *Memoirs*) of ELEONORA CHRISTINA of Denmark (1621–1698), a daughter of King Christian IV.[1] The child of a morganatic union, Eleonora Christina was married at an early age to the King's favorite, Corfitz Ulfeld. While her father lived she was the most fêted woman in Copenhagen, but upon the death of Christian her good fortune soon came to an end. Her husband, to whom she was devoted, fled Denmark because of an impending investigation of his conduct as a government official. Subsequently he became involved in a series of intrigues against King Frederik III, his wife's half-brother. After considerable travel abroad and sundry intrigues, Eleonora Christina was seized in England by agents of the Danish crown. Taken to Copenhagen, she was imprisoned in the Blue Tower for over twenty years. Not until she was a sexagenerian was she finally released by King Christian V. While imprisoned she wrote *Jammersminde*, a unique document of historical interest. Her narrative contains not only a defense of her husband but a resumé of the various actions against her and a description in some detail of her existence as a prisoner in the tower. In *Jammersminde* Eleonora Christina shows herself to be the daughter of her famous father; she is quick, observant, intelligent, and conscious of her high birth. Through-

[1] The English translation, by F. E. Bunnett, *Memoirs of Leonora Christina* was first published in London, 1872; a new edition appeared in 1929.

out her imprisonment she never loses the sense of her superior social station nor her pride. She is humble only before God. She is more philosophical than bitter and more concerned with the fate of her children than with her own. She is heroic without being dramatic or sentimental. She is no mere diarist. She has an unusual command of the language and a good sense of style. Incidentally, she tried her hand at verse. For the most part she wrote with an eye to her readers, that is to say the children to whom the manuscript was inscribed. The manuscript remained in the possession of her heirs for generations and was not published until 1869.

An interesting summary of the state of literature in the seventeenth century is to be found in *Nogle Betenkninger om det Cimbriske Sprog (Reflections on the Cimbrian*—i.e., Germanic—*Language,* 1663) by the first Danish grammarian, PEDER SYV (1631–1702). He mentions what he considers to be the foremost extant Danish books. He first lists various translations of the Bible, psalters and postils, law books, herbals, Hvitfeld's Chronicle, Saxo translated into Danish by Anders Sørensen Vedel, various other chronicles, genealogies and topologies, translations (by Birgitte Thott) of Seneca and Epictetus, books on navigation and mathematics, Æsop's Fables, a book of proverbs, and two works by a cyclopaedic printer and amateur poet named H. H. Skonning. Under the heading of "poetical books," he names the following works: the rhymed Danish Chronicle, folk songs, several chapbooks, the epic about Reynard the Fox, the Renaissance plays about Joseph, Samson, Susanna, Absalon and Cleopatra; Ranch's play *Kong Salomons Hylding*; and, in addition, songs and short stories in verse. Farther on, under the heading "poetical writings," he speaks af Arrebo's *Hexaëmeron* (printed in 1661); of d'Urfé's novel *Astrée* in Søren Terkelsen's version; of pastoral poetry and psalms; and of the poetry of three baroque poets, the German Johann Rist and the Danes Anders Bording and Erik Pontoppidan; as well as Lauremberg's satires (translated from the Low German) and Søren Tvilling's satirical poem *Quid Tua.* That he first names the Bible, psalters, and postils is not surprising; it is of greater consequence that the number of non-ecclesiastical books which he lists is greater than the ecclesiastical.

The mention of Seneca and Epictetus suggests the pervasiveness of the classical tradition, but we observe a new conviction in practice, for the classics were being made available in translation. While the sixteenth, seventeenth, and eighteenth centuries carried on the classical tradition, the ideal knowledge of the classics advocated by the Humanists was being altered in part at least by the impact of Protestant thinking. That is to say, the vernacular was becoming accepted as the raw material of poetic art.

Works which can be identified as literary in the usual sense of the word enjoyed a much greater place in Syv's estimation than would have been the case only forty or fifty years previously. Aside from some of the occasional poetry and of the psalms however, belles-lettres are noticeably dependent on foreign models dating from the sixteenth century. The dramas which Syv mentions are Renaissance in spirit and essentially unoriginal. Arrebo's *Hexaëmeron* is a Renaissance epic based on a French model. The nearest thing to a Danish novel is Terkelsen's translation of the French *Astrée*. In short, secular literature was established, but the spark of original genius and the talent which could impart longevity and international significance to Danish literature had not yet been generated.

The law books, genealogies, and the works on navigation and mathematics which Syv lists indicate the erudition of the times. The learned works are however almost exclusively in Latin. To a considerable extent, the poetic language of the learned, and the sophisticated also, continued to be Latin until the eighteenth century. Poetry which was primarily academic employed Latin by preference. Anyone who might claim a place in the literary world had necessarily to be a good Latinist and at least to prove himself in Latin metres. The ability to write in Latin was the sign of the cultured man; and to be a cultured man in the sixteenth and seventeenth centuries usually meant being a clergyman or a scholar. Consequently, much of the neo-Latin poetry was theological or didactic.

Incidentally, Peder Syv, who enjoyed royal privileges as a philologist, also made a collection of Danish proverbs (published 1682–88). There had been but one previous collection of Danish proverbs, made in the fourteenth century by a certain PEDER LAALE. Peder Laale's collection was used in the teaching of Latin in schools for two centuries and was printed as early as 1506. It was a didactic medieval text, whereas Peder Syv's collection was undertaken because of antiquarian and linguistic interests.

The best-known collection of modern Latin verse written by Danes, *Deliciæ quorundam Poetarum Danorum,* was published in Leiden in 1693 and was edited by the young FREDERIK ROSTGAARD (1671–1745), who was later to become a professor at the University of Copenhagen. The distinguished Latinists of the seventeenth century are therein represented, but, like the multitude of other writers of Latin verse in Denmark, they are no more than names today. If one of the anthologized poets should be mentioned it is HENRIK HARDER (1642–83), who at one time was in the Danish diplomatic service in England. Harder was the best writer of epigrams among learned contemporaries in Denmark.

As long as Latin remained the medium of expression and communication, Danish thinkers and scholars—like Tycho Brahe and Niels Steensen (Steno) in the sixteenth century—were readily known and widely read in Europe. As the tendency to use the vernacular grew, the literature of the several European ethnic groups, and more particularly of the smaller countries, became more isolated. The nationalization of literature which came about with the Reformation resulted to be sure in a richer national literature *per se* and in a literature which was closer to native culture, but it also closed many windows to the outside world.

CHAPTER V

The Enlightenment. Holberg and His Successors

Until the eighteenth century, Danish literature, aside from folklore, had little independent national existence. Denmark was the northern outpost of the European literature which was the "world literature" of the times. Men of letters in Denmark, like writers in France, Germany, or the Netherlands, felt themselves to be members of an international republic of letters rather than citizens of their countries of residence. When they wrote—and they wrote primarily in Latin and French—they were addressing an audience of the learned unlimited by national boundaries. In England and France a literature of consequence in the vernacular had been developing since the Reformation, in part because of the political superiority which those two nations enjoyed. Elsewhere however, bellettristic endeavor in the vernacular was slight, though by the turn of the eighteenth century some learned writers in several countries had begun specifically to address their compatriots in the vernacular. Even in the academic world the modern tongues also made some slight inroads, in the wake of Christian Thomasius' revolutionary use of the German language for academic lectures in 1687. The transition to a national literature as we know it today was nevertheless slow. Writers of the first half of the eighteenth century in Denmark reflect the conflict of the vernacular with the languages of learning; they employed Latin or French, as well as Danish, in order to be read in the world. Dependence first on French and English and later on German models continued to be marked until the middle of the nineteenth century.

The new vernacular literature was born of a culture which, by twists and turns, had been disassociating itself from ecclesiastical domination ever since the Reformation. The new culture was a secular culture, but theological and ecclesiastical elements were everywhere to be found in it. Relatively few books published during the first half of the seventeenth century contained imaginative writing and even at the end of the century most books were still of a theological bent. By the end of the eighteenth century the literary scene had noticeably changed.

The new Danish literature reflected the dominant literature of the outside world. Although not all genres flourished in it, Danish literature was a counterpart to that which occupied the fancy of the reading public and the learned world in France and England and the Netherlands. Such dependence was of course not peculiar to Denmark; it was common to the rest of Europe. Indeed, the literary histories of the countries of Europe have more common than separate characteristics during the eighteenth century.

It should be borne in mind that throughout the eighteenth and far into the nineteenth century, Denmark and Norway continued to comprise a cultural unit. Danish literature was, to all intents and purposes, also the literature of Norway from the Reformation until the Norwegian national awakening which is symbolized by the political transfer of Norway from Denmark to Sweden in 1814. As different as the two countries were in their economy and daily life, they were very much one culturally and politically during the seventeenth and eighteenth centuries, although Norway's relation to Denmark was rather that of a stepchild. Copenhagen was the center of a double monarchy. He who sought knowledge or favors, sophistication or privileges, necessarily came to Copenhagen. The cultural currents which emanated from the capital were received in Christiania or Bergen in the same way that they were received in the Danish provinces. Literary activity in particular had Copenhagen as its center. Until the end of the eighteenth century there was simply no conscious difference between Danish and Norwegian literature. The works of Norwegian writers were published in Copenhagen rather than in Norway. It is well to note that some of the foremost writers of the double monarchy were Norwegians by birth; yet despite the asseverations of the twentieth-century patriots, these writers showed no very great predilections for the country of their birth. National feeling as we know it today did not exist.

Although taste in Denmark and Norway was a decade or more behind the literary fashions of France and England, it developed against the same background. What was popular in England in one decade might not achieve popularity in Denmark until ten, fifteen, or even twenty or thirty years later, but the same literary trends and preferences of the eighteenth century may be observed in Denmark as in Great Britain or on the Continent. The great catalysts of the late seventeenth and early eighteenth centuries, Bayle with his skepticism, Locke with his philosophy of experience, Leibnitz with his theodicy, and Newton with his proofs of the laws of nature, eventually had their impact on Denmark-Norway, and there produced similar reactions (though fainter) in the realm of ideas. The works which meant the most to the early eighteenth century—Bayle's dictionary, Fénelon's *Télémaque,* Montesquieu's *Lettres persanes,* Mandeville's *Fable of the Bees,* Defoe's *Robinson Crusoe,* and Swift's *Gulliver's Travels*—all these and numerous other works found readers in Scandinavia. For the transfusion of newer French and English currents in Denmark one man was primarily responsible. He was not only the foremost interpreter of French and English culture in Denmark, but the outstanding Scandinavian writer of the century and the father of modern Scandinavian literature: LUDVIG HOLBERG (1684–1754). Even without Holberg the pattern would probably have been fundamentally the same. Other Danes and Norwegians had studied and traveled abroad, and had read French and English books and periodicals. But if there had been no Holberg, there would be little reason to stress the history of Danish literature during the first half of the eighteenth century, for among his Scandinavian contemporaries Holberg alone is a man of stature and a figure in world literature. Some of the other Dano-Norwegian writers of the eighteenth century are known today; but only Holberg is a classic, that is, is still read as living literature today. Some other eighteenth century authors enjoy the prestige of literary canonization; Holberg lives.

Holberg not only expressed his time; he embodied his time. In him we find the dominant philosophical, literary, and political persuasions of the Age of Reason: he is a rationalist, a neo-classicist, a didacticist, a skeptic, and a monarchist. He represents what might be called the "official" currents of the day. That does not mean that the early eighteenth century did not have other tendencies, some even diametrically opposed to those which Holberg represented; it did. The existence of philosophical rationalism did not preclude the existence of religious irrationalism, nor did literary neo-classicism preclude enthusiasm and sentimentality. Holberg was well aware of irrationalism and sentimentality. He opposed and attacked both. It is, however, of primary importance to ascertain the predominant and positive characteristics of the age rather than those which were incidental and contradictory to the spirit of the times. The literature of an era must be adjudged first by the mode of thought which dominated that era and by the works of writers who enjoyed popularity not only in their own day but who have withstood the test of time and are read today for pleasure and edification. Therefore, the history of Danish literature in the eighteenth century, and more specifically, in the first half of the eighteenth century, is concerned to an overwhelming extent with the works of Ludvig Holberg, while Holberg's contemporaries, whose fate it is to be remembered as such, we see only in a mirror, darkly.

When Ludvig Holberg left Bergen, the city of his birth in Norway, to come to the capital of the double monarchy, he was intellectually alert and ambitious, but was apparently quite uninterested in belles-lettres. Until the year 1717, he was first and foremost a historical and legal scholar intent upon an academic career in the University of Copenhagen. The University was little inclined to encourage original writing; it then preserved the medieval pattern of scholastic disputations—in Latin—and could offer the young Holberg degrees in philosophy and theology only. The University was provincial, medieval, and static. After two years in Copenhagen, Holberg began his early peregrinations across Europe, which were to give him the general education in languages and science that the University of Copenhagen could not provide. A delightful but neither wholly exact nor complete account of Holberg's experiences is contained in his autobiography.[1] This autobiography, written in three parts (1728, 1737, and 1743), is worth special mention as one of the most readable works of its genre by a Danish author.

Holberg's travels abroad have little direct bearing on his later literary activity, although his sojourns in the Netherlands, England, France, Italy, and Germany have given rise to various hypotheses about his literary indebtedness to foreign models. The fact of the matter is that Holberg's foreign travel in the years 1704–16 and 1725–26 widened his horizon, aroused his ambitions, sharpened his wits, and gave him a first-hand acquaintance with foreign thought; but it did not make of him a dramatist, novelist, or essayist. His most fruitful literary experiences were to a very great extent the product of his own study in Copenhagen. He was a scholar and a voracious reader, especially of encyclopædic works. His reading of belles-lettres, on the contrary, seems to have been limited. Although his experiences abroad did not make him the literary figure he later was to become, they certainly did equip him as a critic and an historian to be the intermediary of foreign culture and philosophy and, in particular, to be the harbinger of English and French rationalistic thinking.

There were three centers of learning and intellectual activity at the turn of the eighteenth century: the Netherlands, France, and England. Between 1706 and 1716 Holberg visited all three countries, and Germany and Italy as well. The Netherlands, the bulwark of freedom of speech and of the press, was the twenty-year-old Holberg's first goal, in 1704. Of this first trip we know little. After returning to Norway in 1705, he

1 Published in English translation as *The Memoirs of Lewis Holberg*, London, 1827.

set off for England and Oxford in 1706. While he did not matriculate, he spent two years in and about the University preparing for his career in the academic world, and enjoying life in Queen Anne's England. According to his own testimony, he conceived his first work, an encyclopædic introduction to European history, in the Bodleian Library. After two years in England, he once more returned to Copenhagen, but only to be off again, this time merely to accompany a young man who was to be taken to Germany. After accomplishing his mission, he spent several months in Germany visiting places and persons that interested him. On the whole he found little of great interest in Germany; university life was too nearly like that with which he already was familiar in Copenhagen. Finally, in the spring of 1709, he settled down in Copenhagen to lead the life of a productive scholar who aspired to an appointment to the university faculty. After his first two historical works were published, he became "professor designatus," but it was not until 1717 that he finally was appointed to the first available professorship, in metaphysics, a subject which he thoroughly disliked. In the interim (from 1714 to 1716), he undertook his most extensive foreign journey, to the Netherlands, France, and Italy. While abroad, he was ever a zealous user of libraries and a visitor to sights that were free of charge. He was forced to live very simply, for despite his new title, he had few funds. He rubbed shoulders with the lower classes of society while employing the cheapest means of transportation and living in inexpensive quarters. The trip from Rome back to Paris he made on foot. Here and there he made the acquaintance of distinguished men, like the Danish-French physician Jacob Winsløw.

Holberg was an inept professor of metaphysics, but while he held his chair he discovered he had other talents. Suddenly he began to write satires. Just what prompted him to do so is not clear. The first satire was perhaps written in an academic tiff; in any case, he realized that he had mastered a new medium and he persevered. After producing four shorter satires, he undertook to write a mock-heroic epic poem, which he published during 1719–20 (under the pseudonym Hans Mickelsen) as *Peder Paars*. This comic epic, in part inspired by Boileau's *Le Lutrin*, ridiculed the details and hyperboles of Virgil's and Homer's poetry by relating with exaggerated pathos the journey of one Peder Paars, who was nobody in particular, from Kallundborg, on the Island of Zealand, to Aarhus, on the peninsula of Jutland. While the poem seems crudely amusing to readers today (who would take exception to its great length), the reading public of eighteenth-century Copenhagen was enchanted, except for those few individuals who felt that they were being held up to ridicule. The public bought the book as fast as it could be printed and devoured pirated editions of it as well. Two of Holberg's eminent and learned contemporaries were less than pleased with a satirical book which had been published without being censored and which did not give the place of its publication, as the law required. They formally requested the king that the author be punished, but fortunately for Holberg the Crown found the book amusing and harmless, and the charges were dropped.

Peder Paars was the Danish "best-seller" of the early eighteenth century. Through it Holberg became the most popular writer in Denmark. Quite independently in 1720, his academic career took a turn for the better, when he was appointed professor of Latin literature.

Because of the tremendous success of *Peder Paars,* it was natural, when a Danish theater was about to be established in Copenhagen in 1722, that the theater's manager *in spe* should seek out Holberg and ask him to provide the new company with some Danish comedies. Comedies had either to be translated from the French or written expressly for the theater.

By chance, the right man had been chosen as a collaborator by the new theater. Holberg more than succeeded in fulfilling the promise given by his satires. With apparently no other preparation than a knowledge of Latin and French literature, he was able to write some twenty-six comedies for the new theater in the course of two years. Neither he nor his contemporaries realized it, but he had found a medium of which he was fully master. Holberg is unsurpassed as a writer of eighteenth-century comedy and in the history of European comedy he ranks only below Aristophanes, Plautus, Shakespeare, and Molière.[1]

Of the sixty-odd plays which are known to have been played at the new theater in Copenhagen, 21 were by Holberg and over forty were translations from the French—19 by Molière and six by Regnard. Two comedies were by another Dane, JOACHIM RICHARD PAULLI (1691–1759). Incidentally, Paulli undertook to rewrite Holberg's *Political Tinker* and, as he explained, to make the story seem more plausible. Paulli's version is tolerable but it does not measure up to Holberg's, and it was never played.

---

1 The most recent translations of Holberg's plays into English are to be found in three volumes published by the American-Scandinavian Foundation: *Comedies by Holberg.* Translated by Oscar J. Campbell and Fredrick Schenck, 1914 and several times reprinted (*Jeppe of the Hill, The Political Tinker, Erasmus Montanus*); *Four Plays by Holberg.* Translated by Henry Alexander, 1946 (*The Fussy Man, The Masked Ladies, The Weathercock, Masquerades*); and *Seven One-Act Plays by Holberg.* Translated by Henry Alexander, 1950 (*The Talkative Barber, The Arabian Powder, The Christmas Party, Diderich the Terrible, The Peasant in Pawn, Sganarel's Journey to the Land of the Philosophers, The Changed Bridegroom*).

LUDVIG HOLBERG
Etching by Christian Fritzsch, 1731.

COMOE-
DIER

Sammenskrevne
for
Den nye oprettede
Danske Skue-Plads
Ved
Hans Mickelsen
Borger og Indvaaner i Callundborg.
Med
Just Justesens Fortale
Første Tome.

Tryckt Aar·1723.

Title page of the first edition of Holberg's comedies. (Actual size).

On September 26, 1722, the initial performance of Holberg's *Den politiske Kandestøber (The Political Tinker)* was given in the recently opened theater. This was one of five plays which Holberg furnished the theater by the autumn of 1722; the others were *Den Vægelsindede (The Weathercock), Jean de France, Jeppe paa Bjerget (Jeppe of the Hill)*, and *Mester Gert Westphaler,* all of which were produced in quick succession as Holberg continued to write comedies at the rate of about one a month.

The Political Tinker has remained one of his most successful works, and, together with *Erasmus Montanus* and *Den Stundesløse (The Fussy Man),* among those most frequently played. Like his other comedies, *The Political Tinker* is a satirical and farcical play, from which, if needs be, a moral may be drawn. Holberg liked to think of himself as a moralist and boasted that nearly all of his plays were didactic. The didactic content lies rather in Holberg's intent and in his retrospective epilogues, however, than within the plays themselves. Well-constructed, witty, and pointed, the comedies are absorbing and amusing but—fortunately—fail to convey Holberg's avowed lesson. On the other hand they are really didactic insofar as they hold various human weaknesses and follies up to ridicule. Boastfulness, conceit, affectation, witchcraft, foolish customs, and literary exaggerations are unmercifully exposed and ridiculed.

The Political Tinker and *Jeppe of the Hill* both portray simple and ignorant men suddenly elevated to positions of power and authority. *The Political Tinker,* a satire on armchair politicians, can be fully appreciated by a reader today, despite its allusions to contemporary events and publications. The action is initiated by a love story and an intrigue connected with it. One is soon aware that the servants are often more intelligent than the main characters. This holds especially for the ubiquitous male servant, Henrik. Herman of Bremen, the political amateur, is an avid reader of newspapers and political journals; he pays little attention to the dignity of facts, and is convinced that he could perform tasks of statesmanship much more ably than political leaders. In reality he is a less than mediocre tinker; his political interests conflict with his work. He does not enjoy the respect of his wife, Geske.

Herman is the guiding spirit of a *collegium politicum* whose members are a tavern keeper, a brushmaker, a furrier, a baggage inspector, and half a dozen others, who meet in a nearby tavern to debate the problems of the day and hear Herman's opinions on matters of state. Two men of rank who have overheard Herman's pontifications decide that, for the welfare of society, he must be put in his place; this they decide to do through an involved practical joke, which will take advantage of Herman's weakness for politics. By a clever intrigue, they convince Herman that he has been chosen burgomaster of the city (of Hamburg). Now begins a comedy within a comedy, with the omniscient servant Henrik both enjoying and profiting by the inner-comedy's intrigue. Apparently suddenly thrust into a high station, Herman tries to cope with the mounting problems which the practical jokers have invented to teach him his lesson. He is besieged by petitioners, by a delegation of hatters, by lawyers and others, until he realizes that he is unable to contend with the situation —and breaks down with a call for his wife, who in the interim has demonstrated herself to be just as susceptible as Herman to the temptations of the *nouveaux riches*.

In utter despair and ready to commit suicide, Herman cries: "I don't want to be burgomaster, I never did want to be burgomaster, and I'd rather you killed me. I am a tinker, before God and honor, and a tinker I shall die." He forswears all his political reading, and is only too happy to be a tinker once more and to permit his daughter Engelke to marry the simple but honest young man whose disdain for political matters had previously offended him.

Technically speaking, *The Political Tinker* follows the pattern of the drama of Molière and the classical French comedy of the seventeenth century. The play observes the unities of time, place, and action, possesses a cleverly interwoven plot and sub-plot, and skilfully displays characters who are types rather than individuals.

Although the intrigue in *Jeppe of the Hill* is on the whole similar to that in *The Political Tinker,* Jeppe is a more touching figure than Herman; there are noticeable tragi-comic elements in him. Jeppe's weakness is drink, for only drink gives him the solace that a harsh world and a scolding wife deny him. Consequently he is the laughing-stock of his betters. Found one day lying on a manure pile, Jeppe is carried into a nearby manor house by the lord of the manor, Baron Nilus, and his men, and is laid in the baron's bed. Upon awakening Jeppe finds himself surrounded by luxury and by servants who try to convince him that he is the baron. Jeppe, who at first thinks he is in heaven, is not taken in by the hoax immediately; but, once convinced, he is a coarse and tyrannical master, who nevertheless does not lose his intrinsic good qualities nor the acumen of the downtrodden. Holberg thus permits the audience to get to know Jeppe from all sides. Jeppe's soul is revealed at its worst and at its best as the situation is further complicated. In the face of death—Jeppe is finally condemned by a mock-court for impersonating the baron—he is essentially a good and grateful man. Even though the deacon has made a cuckold of him, Jeppe can speak to his wife without reproach from the gallows. His horse and his dog, his cat, and all his domestic animals he thanks "for good company" before he gulps down the sleeping potion which he thinks is a poison.

When Jeppe is finally restored to life, all is as before. Unlike Herman von Bremen, he remains the same and he undertakes to get drunk right away. Like Herman von Bremen, poor Jeppe is not spared the humiliation of having the hoax revealed.

Jean de France and *Erasmus Montanus* both satirize the sophomoric young man who is the pride and despair of his family and friends. Jean de France—or Hans Frandsen—has become so gallicized after fifteen weeks in Paris that he scarcely understands his native Danish; he is such a snob that he becomes the gullible victim of a hoax devised by the maid, Martha. His coat on backward, his scarf hanging down his back, his mouth smeared with snuff—affectations all, which he believes to be the latest French fashion—Jean turns his back on Denmark for the sake of a non-existent French noblewoman, "Mme. la Fleche," who is no other than the irrepressible Martha in disguise.

Erasmus Montanus, whose real name is Rasmus Berg, flaunts his knowledge of Latin before his fellow villagers and with his newly-acquired logic undertakes to prove that his mother is a stone and Per the Deacon a rooster. He meets an unexpectedly formidable opponent in the person of the deacon, an ignorant but keen man who, in fighting to retain his own reputation as a man of learning, spoils Rasmus's glory. Erasmus has already stretched the credulity of the villagers with his absurd thesis that the earth is round, an assertion which very nearly costs him his betrothal to Lisbeth. After going down to defeat before Per the Deacon in a Latin dispute, because of his inability to answer such nonsensical questions as "Who is the Imprimatur this year?" Erasmus is finally maneuvered into a situation in which, for all his learning, he has no choice but to admit that the earth really is as flat as a pancake—and therewith to reinstate himself in society. Unlike Jean de France, who is just as big a fool at the end of the play as at the beginning, Erasmus, like Herman von Bremen, has learned his lesson.

Holberg's other early comedies have many characteristics in common with those outlined above. They are principally comedies of character, intrigue, and of satire, and they usually employ a love affair as the nucleus for the intrigue about which the comedy revolves. *Jacob von Tyboe* and *Diderich Menschenskræk* (*Diderich the Terrible*) are modern versions of Plautus's *miles gloriosus,* the braggart warrior, between whose words and deeds the discrepancy is great. The title character of *Mester Gert West-phaler* is a talkative barber, who in the original version of the play, in five acts, was so true to life that he bored Holberg's audience. Holberg subsequently transmuted the play into one closely knit act of effective comedy. Like *Den ellefte Juni (The Eleventh of June)*, in which a country bumpkin is swindled out of his possessions in Copenhagen, *Mester Gert Westphaler* must be admitted to defy Holberg's own precept of didacticism, for they are pure comedy.

Den Stundesløse (The Fussy Man) and *Den Vægelsindede (The Weather-cock)* are both caricatures spiritually related to Molière's *Le malade imaginaire*. In the former the busy man seeks a son-in-law who is a book-keeper and who can assist him with his multifarious petty affairs. The busy man is nevertheless tricked into marrying his daughter to the young man of her choice. A complementary female character in the latter play is the unstable Lucretia, the "weathercock", who overexercises a woman's privilege to change her mind.

The machinations of the male servant-confidant are the gist both of the farcical *Kildereisen (Journey to the Spring)*, in which the irrepressible Hein-rich assumes the rôle of a physician in order to unite a loving pair, and of the hastily-written *Pernilles korte Frøikenstand (Pernille's brief Ladyship)*, where Heinrich, disguised as a monk, performs a similar service. In *Henrich og Pernille (Henrich and Pernille)* the intrigue of the two recurrent servants comprises plot and substance of the play as the title characters finally get their just due.

Social ambition was the object of satire not only in the comedy bearing that title *(Den Honnette Ambition)* but also in *Don Ranudo de Coli-brados*. In the former the intolerant snob Jeronimus is cured of his ambitions as a social climber; in the latter (which plays in Spain), the pretense of an impoverished nobility is ridiculed. In both plays the daughters of selfish and ambitious parents resort to trickery to marry their true loves and therewith expose the folly of their parents' vanity. *Barselstuen (The Lying-in Room)* satirized the contemporary custom of paying visits to women in childbed. The slighter *Julestuen (The Christmas Party)* and the more flamboyant *Maskarade* (which were both inspired by an unstaged comedy of Holberg's contemporary Paulli) have their origins in the custom of holding boisterous social gatherings in the Christmas holiday season and in the carnival time before Lent, respectively; they are of interest as evidence of the social usage of the times. A lovers' intrigue provides the plot in each play.

Holberg derided witchcraft and gross superstition in *Hexerie eller blind*

Alarm (Witchcraft or False Alarm) and in *Uden Hoved og Hale (Without Head or Tail)*. In *Det arabiske Pulver (The Arabian Powder)* he ridiculed belief in alchemy.

In *Melampe* and *Ulysses von Ithacia* Holberg made use of literary parody. The former, in which the title character is a lap dog, is a so-called "tragicomedy" in the French style. The latter, subtitled "a German comedy," is a mock-heroic play suggesting the German "Haupt- und Staatsaktion" but conceived in the spirit of Holberg's earlier epic *Peder Paars*.

Den pantsatte Bondedreng (The Peasant in Pawn), like *Jeppe paa Bjerget* and *Det arabiske Pulver,* is the dramatic elaboration of an anecdote Holberg had read in the seventeenth-century German Latinist Jacob Bidermann's *Utopia*: a naïve rustic is tricked by a swindler into playing the part of a count, with unhappy consequences.

Tending more to moral didacticism than the other plays are *Det lykkelige Skibbrud (The Fortunate Shipwreck)* and *De Usynlige (The invisible Lovers)*. In the former Holberg let persons who felt themselves made the object of satire in his earlier comedies accuse him in court. His alter ego in the play, Philemon, is contrasted with a hypocritical *à la mode* poet. In the latter, which comes closest to the *commedia dell'arte* tradition, the unfaithful Harlequin learns the dangers of wooing a masked lady. The first series of plays was concluded by the very brief *Den danske Comoedies Ligbegængelse (The Danish Comedy's Funeral)*, written in 1726, which suggests the economic difficulties the new theater had encountered.

Holberg respected the three unities; and in matters of form he was no innovator. He was aware of his literary indebtedness and knew how to make the best use of his predecessors. He was critical of all comedy except the comedy of Molière and Plautus, whose praises he never ceased to recite in his critical writings. Three plays were adapted from Plautus, but Holberg made no such direct use of Molière. He adapted and localized the style and the dramatic devices employed by both these foreign masters, but in such a way that his own finished comedy seemed a native product. The characters had become members of the Danish bourgeoisie and their speech the everyday Danish of Holberg's own time. It was Holberg's genius to be able to portray people as they are, and each according to his place in society.

As a writer of comedy, Holberg most closely resembles Molière, although the two men must have been fundamentally different at heart. Both ridiculed human vices and eccentricities, the one partially out of philosophical conviction, and the other for dramatic reasons. Both made use of contrast and repetition; both enjoyed farce and punning.

At one time much was made of Holberg's possible indebtedness to the *commedia dell' arte,* with which he apparently became acquainted while he was in Italy. As in the Italian comedy, there is in Holberg a marked use of the stereotyped character and considerable leeway for slapstick, but in the last analysis this does little more than indicate that Holberg was more conscious of the popular literature of the day than he himself was aware.

His poetic rapture came to a sudden end in 1723. In 1725–26 he was again abroad in the Netherlands and in France. At this time German pietism was making inroads in Denmark, particularly at the Danish court. By 1730 the puritanical spirit had made itself so strongly felt that, with the succession of King Christian VI to the throne, the faltering Danish theaters were closed and remained closed during his reign. There was no opportunity for Holberg to devote his energies to comedy. He soon applied himself to other fields of endeavor. Yet, when the theater finally was reëstablished in 1748, he took up where he had left off a quarter of a century before and produced six new comedies: *Plutus, Sganarels Reise (Sganarel's Journey), Abracadabra, Philosophus udi egen Indbilding (The imaginary Philosopher), Republiquen eller det gemene Bedste (The Republic or the Common Good),* and *Den forvandlede Brudgom (The Changed Bridegroom).* These later comedies have not enjoyed the same popularity as the earlier ones.

For a decade after the closing of the theater Professor Holberg applied himself assiduously to the writing of historical and topographical works. He wrote a description of Denmark and Norway, a history of Denmark, a Latin synopsis of universal history, a description of Bergen, a history of the church, a series of biographies of famous men, and in addition began to write his autobiography. His history of Denmark *(Dannemarks Riges Historie I-III,* 1732–35) deserves special mention as the first popular history of Denmark written in the Danish language. It was read as an introduction to Danish history until far into the nineteenth century.

Holberg's love of satire could not be suppressed indefinitely, and in 1740 it found expression once more in a work which combined the elements of an imaginary voyage, a satire, and a utopia: *Niels Klim's Journey to the World Underground* or, to use the book's proper title, *Nicolai Klimii iter subterraneum.* The book was directed at the international audience which Holberg had not been able to reach with his comedies. Written in Latin and published in Leipzig, it was well received and soon translated into German, Dutch, French, Danish, English, and Swedish.

Niels Klim suggests Swift's *Gulliver's Travels,* Defoe's *Robinson Crusoe,* Montesquieu's *Lettres Persanes,* and Thomas More's *Utopia.* It most closely resembles Swift's work; Holberg's intent was much the same as

Swift's, but his end result is more amusing and less bitter, more didactic and less destructive. Niels Klim's visits to a large number of countries in the nether regions permit Holberg to satirize excesses and abuses existing in the real world, and at the same time to champion rational thinking and put many of his own pet ideas into practice.

Because it was written in Latin and because it was and is good reading, *Niels Klim* might be considered to be Holberg's principal contribution to world literature, but the popularity of *Niels Klim* (which makes a book of some three or four hundred pages) has not kept pace with that of the comedies, although it is noteworthy that *Niels Klim* was reissued in French translation as recently as 1949. The last complete English edition was published in London in 1828.[1]

After publishing a history of the Jews and completing the third part of his autobiography, Holberg turned to what was for him a new genre, the moral-philosophical essay, a genre which had received tremendous impetus through the publication of the English *Spectator* and the many periodicals which followed in its wake during the eighteenth century. The *Spectator*, of which there are said to have been no less than two hundred English and five hundred German imitations, attempted "to bring philosophy out of closets and libraries, schools and colleges, to dwell in clubs and assemblies, at tea-tables and coffee-houses." Its stock in trade was the moral-philosophical essay. As early as 1726 Copenhagen had had periodicals which feebly suggested the genre, but the first Spectator-type periodical of note appeared in 1744–45, when Jørgen Riis anonymously published a *Spectator* and at the same time a witty *Anti-Spectator* in verse. At first many readers thought that Holberg, who published his *Moralske Tanker (Moral Thoughts)* in 1744, was the author of the new *Spectator*. He was not, but in his *Moralske Tanker* and the five volumes of his *Epistler* (*Epistles,* i.e., epistolary essays, 1748–54)[2] he is a better representative of Spectator literature in Denmark than the many moral weeklies which sprang up there.[3] That the volume *Moralske Tanker*

1 *Journey to the World Underground; Being the Subterraneous Travels of Niels Klim.* The first English translation appeared in 1742, was several times reprinted and was republished in Edinburgh in 1812. A shortened and revised version, by John Gierlow, appeared in Boston in 1845.

2 A selection of the *Epistler* in English translation was published as *Selected Essays of Ludvig Holberg.* Lawrence, University of Kansas Press, 1955.

3 Among the best-known Spectator periodicals in Denmark in the middle of the eighteenth century one was written in German and the other in French: Johann Elias Schlegel's *Der Fremde* (1745–46) and L. A. de la Beaumelle's *La Spectatrice Danoise* (1748–50).

was to the taste of the times is attested by the three editions of the work which appeared in 1744.

Not until a decade after Holberg's death did a Danish "Spectator" appear which in content and style could measure up to the English original. This was JENS S. SNEEDORFF's *Den patriotiske Tilskuer (The patriotic Spectator,* 1761–63). Like Holberg, Sneedorff was anxious to cultivate Danish as a literary language, and it must be admitted that stylistically his essays are more refined and more sophisticated than are Holberg's; but Sneedorff did not have the breadth or perspicacity of Holberg.

In his essays, Holberg treats almost every subject with which an educated man of the first half of the eighteenth century might have concerned himself. The essays are philosophical and speculative, theological and literary, sociological, metaphysical, historical, and comical; they concern themselves with pedagogical, legal, philological, and even personal problems. Many are satirical. All reflect Holberg's basic rationalism and skepticism, his admiration for the literature of classical antiquity and his extensive reading in French. Holberg's inspiration as an essayist was as much Michel de Montaigne as Addison and Steele. Not a few of the "Epistles" were inspired by Holberg's reading in Bayle's dictionary and other encyclopædic works.

Aside from the late comedies (1750–52), Holberg's last literary effort was a volume of *Moralske Fabler (Moral Fables,* 1751). To the end he deferred to the idea of didacticism and the principle, *utile dulci.*

Viewing his vast production in retrospect, we observe Holberg to have been the apostle of the Age of Enlightenment. He was a consequence of the Reformation in Scandinavia, for he examined every aspect of human existence which he recognized, and armed with the infallible weapon of reason, he undertook historical, theological, philosophical, and literary inquisitions. Holberg attempted the moral and didactic examination of various phenomena, as well as historical presentation, and ventured a satirical and comic interpretation of human existence. It is his satirical humor which has brought him international fame, but we should remember that Holberg became a litterateur almost by accident and that his literary production has more facets than the English-speaking world today is aware of. Like many a great artist, Holberg was not very original in his choice of subject matter or of theme. His significance lies in the form in which he cast the material that he employed. With Holberg aesthetic rather than generic considerations begin to be of primary importance in the history of Danish literature.

Per the Deacon sings for a glass of brandy. Act I, Scene 4, of Holberg's Erasmus Montanus. *Painting by Wilhelm Marstrand.*

View of Copenhagen about the middle of the eighteenth century.

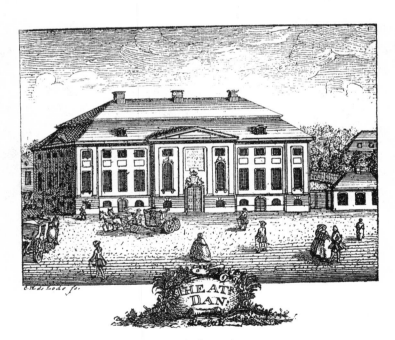

The Royal Theater in 1750.

HANS ADOLPH BRORSON
Painting by Johan Hörner, 1756.

JOHANNES EWALD
Painting by Erik Pauelsen, c. 1780.

Three of Holberg's contemporaries still enjoy a place in Danish literary consciousness. CHRISTIAN FALSTER (1690–1752), was something of a kindred spirit. HANS ADOLF BRORSON (1694–1764), was by nature very nearly Holberg's antithesis; the third, AMBROSIUS STUB (1705–58), was an anomaly.

Falster, pedagogue and classical philologist, had much in common with Holberg. In the same year that Holberg published his first Danish satires, Falster published similar satires in Latin. In these and in the one hundred and twenty-five moral essays that comprise his *Amoenitates philologicae* (I–III, 1729–32) he flayed the same human weaknesses which Holberg satirized in his comedies and in his essays. Although Falster was first and foremost a neo-classicist and devoted most attention to classical philology, his thoughtful and often amusing essays illuminate a myriad of problems which occupied the scholarly European contemporaries at whom the essays were directed. The earlier essays were to a large extent theologically colored, but Falster soon expanded his horizon and wrote on a variety of secular subjects. Some of his *discursus varii* treat of the devil's library, the right way to study physics, a comparison between Greece and modern France, honorable hanging, and a journey to the moon. Because he wrote in Latin, he spoke to a wider audience than did Holberg as an essayist during his lifetime, but for that very reason Christian Falster has all but disappeared from the Danish literary consciousness. His essays were not translated into Danish until 1919; they are not available in English.

Brorson was a clergyman, a pietist, and a writer of hymns. His Danish psalms or hymns were a rare gift of poetry to his fellow-countrymen at a time when the church of Denmark was very much under the influence of German—and particularly German pietistical—theology. Literally and figuratively, Brorson translated German pietism into Danish pietism. From 1732 to 1735 he published a series of a dozen brochures containing in all 190 hymns for his congregation in Southern Jutland. Then in 1739 he published his major contribution, *Troens Rare Klenodie (The rare Jewel of Faith)*, which comprised not only the hymns previously printed but 67 additional hymns. *Troens Rare Klenodie* was in essence a poetic anthology meant for personal use and household devotions. It was not meant as a substitute for the official hymnal. The majority of the hymns which it contained were translations from the German, among others from Gottfried Arnold, Johann Rist, Paul Gerhardt, and, above all from Angelus Silesius, but Brorson's translations possess literary validity in themselves, so well are they reformulated in Danish.

The hymns in the collection are full of longing for the life hereafter. They repeatedly employ mundane and even erotic imagery, and the symbolism of flowers and the mystical marriage between the soul and Jesus. As an example of Brorson's verse may be cited a stanza from one of his original hymns, "Den yndigste Rose er funden" ("The loveliest rose is found"),

> My rose is my gem, my delight
> My rose is my bliss and my light;
> The poisonous lusts he crushes.
> The Cross then sweetness gushes.

Later in life Brorson wrote another series of hymns which was, however, not published until 1765, the year after his death.

Brorson is the second of a series of great hymn-writers—Kingo was the first—who have contributed to Denmark's exceptionally rich store of hymns and who therewith have exerted a positive force in the cultural existence of succeeding generations of Danes.

The popularity of Brorson's hymns, and the appreciation of poetry in Denmark during the first half of the eighteenth century, is attested by the seven editions of *Troens Rare Klenodie* which appeared in the poet's lifetime. Brorson's pietistic hymns fell out of use toward the end of the eighteenth century and were not revived until about 1825. Since then many have enjoyed a place in the Danish "Psalmebog" and on the Danish Parnassus. Brorson's hymns characterize the strongest countercurrent to Holberg's philosophical rationalism, and can be identified with the ascetic pietistic spirit which shut the theaters of Copenhagen in 1730 and which looked askance at the beliefs of Baron Holberg.

Ambrosius Stub, the third, and younger, contemporary of Holberg, was unlike either Brorson or Falster or Holberg. He was Denmark's one secular poet during the early eighteenth century. Stub lived and died without public recognition of his unusual poetic talents; his poems were not printed until many years after his death. He led an unstable life, first as a long-time student in Copenhagen, then as a sort of clerk to a Danish nobleman, and finally as a schoolteacher in Ribe. Secular, witty, and lyric, Stub's poetry gives evidence of an appreciation of natural beauty and a capacity for emotion in the realm of the everyday which his contemporaries lacked. He employed an unaffected, simple, and often humorous style, which may be exemplified by a translation of one of his epicurean and comical poems, "Græm dig aldrig..." ("Never grieve...")

> Never grieve, for grief is woe,
> At your pain will grin your foe.
> Nor a miser should you be;
> That will fill your heirs with glee.
> You in need your foe would see;
> Dead your heir would have you be.
> Be then of good cheer.
> Live both well and dear.
> Live and laugh at both of them.

Stub has had the good fortune to have been made the subject of a popular drama by a later writer, K. F. Molbech. The drama, *Ambrosius* (1877), has served to enhance his name and give him some of the attributes of a mythical figure.

While Holberg was the only Danish writer of the day who was popular, his works had to compete for public favor with the foreign novels which flooded the literary markets of the eighteenth century. The new novel rose in England during the early decades of the century. *Robinson Crusoe, Pamela,* and *Tom Jones* were among the lengthy narratives which were widely read in Denmark in the forties, despite a general critical attitude which deprecated the novel and refused to accept it as an art form. Holberg, for example, declared that most novels seemed to have been written as a pastime by people who had nothing else to do. In the introduction to his *Moralske Tanker,* Holberg wrote about Richardson's *Pamela* and called it "one of the good novels, but no masterpiece." In contrast to most foreign novels, *Pamela,* part one, was translated into Danish almost at once (1743), only three years after the work had originally been published in England. Incidentally, it was imitated in Danish fifteen years later by Carl August Thielo. Fielding's *Joseph Andrews* was translated into Danish in 1749, but Fielding's other novels, like those of Smollett, did not appear in Danish until some thirty years later. Although the English bourgeois novel was popular, it did not evoke Danish imitations until after Holberg's death. *Robinson Crusoe* (originally published in 1719), which had rapidly become one of the most widely imitated and revised books of all times, was not published in Danish translation until 1744–45, although even before that, in 1741, a *Nordischer Robinson* had appeared, in German, in Copenhagen.

The only Danish novelist of any note in the eighteenth century was a woman, CHARLOTTE DOROTHEA BIEHL (1731–88) who published, among other works, a series of *Moralske Fortællinger (Moral Tales,* 1781–82), which are obvious imitations of English and French models. Mlle. Biehl wrote several comedies in the French post-classical style; she is best known not for her original prose works, however, but for her translation into Danish of Cervantes' *Don Quixote,* published 1776–77.

As elsewhere in the Western world, the number of writers in Denmark increased and the market for books increased as the eighteenth century wore on. Many of the new writers enjoyed considerable popularity, though they have long since ceased to lead even a shadowy existence in literature. Consciously or subconsciously, they were content to imitate earlier writers and to reproduce in Denmark the literary styles of England, France, and Germany; they lacked the originality or mastery of form which might have preserved their names for future generations in the annals of world literature.

After the auspicious beginnings of Danish literature under Holberg, the scene changed in 1751, with the arrival in Copenhagen of Germany's leading poet of the day, Friedrich Klopstock. Klopstock's coming meant that Copenhagen was elevated to the position of a European center of belles-lettres, albeit for German and not for Danish literature. It is symptomatic of the times that the leading figure in literary Copenhagen was a German; during the years when Klopstock dominated the literary scene, Danish writing was again in the last analysis imitative.

Holberg's inspiration had stemmed principally from French literature and secondarily from English literature. The great literary inspiration of the second half of the century came from Germany. Klopstock was but the beginning; the golden age of German letters was close at hand. Wieland, Herder, Goethe, and Schiller were soon to equal or surpass Klopstock's name, and Weimar was to vie with London and Paris as a literary center.

Klopstock represented a return to religious and emotional poetry. It was almost inevitable that there should be a reaction against the didactic rationalism of the early eighteenth century. Klopstock had taken Germany by storm with the first cantos of his religious epic *Der Messias.* Through the mediation of the influential diplomat and statesman Count Bernstorff, he was invited to Copenhagen by King Frederik V, and was awarded a generous pension, which carried with it the sole obligation of completing *Der Messias.* Around him there soon assembled the "German Circle" of his friends and disciples. This may seem strange today; the truth was that the court in Copenhagen was German and the king was more concerned with German fashions than with the rude native culture of his subjects. Count Bernstorff himself neither spoke nor wrote Danish and conducted affairs of state in German or French. Such was the disparity between the Danish language and the culture of the court and the

THE ENLIGHTENMENT. HOLBERG AND HIS SUCCESSORS [93]

people. Curiously enough, while King Frederik of Denmark looked to Germany and honored a German poet, Germany's Frederick—Frederick the Great of Prussia—sought his inspiration in French culture, entertained Voltaire, and evinced no interest in Klopstock.

Klopstock spent 19 years in Denmark; during this time the "German Circle" remained the predominant literary force on Parnassus and Danish literature languished. Eventually the great influx of Germans and their rôle in public life aroused considerable resentment among younger Danes; the comparatively slight influence of Klopstock on Danish letters may perhaps be ascribed to this resentment. Only one significant Danish poet chose Klopstock as his model. He is, however, a poet of note: JOHANNES EWALD (1743–81). Though Ewald possessed a great lyric gift, and although he is still acclaimed by some critics as the greatest poet Denmark has produced, he does not today have a large appreciative audience. His emotional yet impersonal style, his pompous verse, and his classical allusions have little appeal in the twentieth century. He lives chiefly as the author of a few poems (with which every Danish schoolchild has struggled): "Til min Moltke" ("To my friend, M."), "Til Sielen. En Ode" ("Ode to the Soul"), the autobiographical "Rungsteds Lyksaligheder" ("The Joys of Rungsted"), and his last poem, the hymn "Udrust dig, Helt fra Golgatha" ("Gird thyself, Hero of Golgotha"). He is also known as the author of the Danish national anthem "King Christian," which originally was contained in the operetta *Fiskerne (The Fishermen)*. The last stanza of "King Christian" (in the translation by Longfellow) gives a taste of Ewald's style:

> Path of the Dane to fame and might!
> Dark-rolling wave!
> Receive thy friend, who, scorning flight,
> Goes to meet danger with despite,
> Proudly as thou the tempest's might,
> Dark-rolling wave!
> And amid pleasures and alarms,
> And war and victory, be thine arms
> My grave!

Eighteenth-century European poetry was only to a limited extent a poetry of lyrical inspiration. Johannes Ewald's time appreciated masterful elegiac verse impregnated with feeling more than light lyric strophes. Being recognized as the leading poet of Denmark, Ewald was expected to produce the best occasional poetry. And so he did. Here is an essential difference between poetry of the eighteenth century (and earlier centuries) on the one hand and poetry since 1800 on the other. The later poetry is overwhelmingly the product of personal experience and inspiration. The eighteenth-century poet, in this case Ewald, produced great poetry because he was a master of form and poetic language. The mood of poetry was set by pathos rather than ethos. For this reason, very little of what many earlier poets have written, and relatively little of Ewald's poetry, has a lasting appeal to succeeding generations of readers. If the reader does not understand the literary situation of Ewald's time, he can scarcely appreciate the grandiose quality of Ewald's poetry, except in the few poems in which the poet transcended the aesthetic bonds set by his time and touched universals in the human soul; these few poems alone, therefore, have become a part of the living Danish literary heritage.

Ewald's life was tragic. Had he lived half a century later, he might have sighed his plight in verse, but he remained the artist and the craftsman, rather than the personal singer and was subsequently read less than Oehlenschläger and members of the generation which followed Oehlenschläger, a generation which stressed personal experiences and personal impressions as of primary importance to poetry.

If we try to dispense with our twentieth-century prejudice that a poem should be an emotional lyric rather than an elegiac and artful expression of ideas, and if we then examine Ewald's poetry critically, we cannot fail to admire his command of the word, his ability to create pictures and to fulfill the formal demands of poetry. There is unmistakable poetic grandeur in verses like those from his cantata on the death of King Frederik:

> Cease, tears, to flow,
> And zither, play thou low!
> Now to his grave is borne
> The king.

There is religious conviction and grandeur in Ewald's ode to the soul ("Til Sielen, En Ode," 1780). Here he is a poet who strives to answer the recurrent questions of human existence.

The twentieth century has little feeling for occasional poetry, and even less for the poetry of state that was produced for official occasions. The eighteenth century had much. Just as we should not complain that Ewald did not produce lyrics, we should not deny that the power of the word was his and that with his German master Klopstock, he ranks among the great poets of the eighteenth century. At the same time, we may note that no one disputes Klopstock's position in the history of German literature; and yet Klopstock is read no more than is his Danish disciple.

Ewald was also a dramatist. He wrote both tragedies and comedies, and was a progenitor of the modern historical drama. *Balders Død (The Death of Balder,* 1774) marks the beginning of a new dramatic literature in Scandinavia, a genre which was to flower in the nineteenth century.[1] In the operetta *Fiskerne (The Fishermen,* 1779), which immortalizes a contemporary event, Ewald treated common men—fishermen of the island of Zealand—as the heroic characters; this choice in the spirit of Rousseau was noteworthy, for it was not in accord with the traditional poetics of the day, which demanded that elevated persons should be the subjects of serious drama.

In fact, Ewald responded to all the literary ideas which were making themselves felt throughout Western Europe. He wrote a religious epic, *Adam og Eva* (1769), after the fashion of Klopstock's *Messias*. He became intensely interested in English literature, revered Shakespeare, and wrote an autobiographical "Life and Opinions" (*Levnet og Meeninger,* posthumously published) in the style of Laurence Sterne. He was attracted first by folk ballads, and then by early Germanic mythology. His interest in Germanic and Celtic antiquities was symptomatic of a new current in European literature, which had been given great impetus by the publication of Macpherson's *Ossian* and Bishop Percy's *Reliques of Ancient English Poetry. Ossian,* fraudulent though it was, fulfilled some of the needs felt by a younger and enthusiastic generation. Seldom have wish and fulfillment so complemented one another as in that work, which unwittingly set a false pattern for primitive poetry that remained a standard for decades. Inspired by *Ossian* and Percy's *Reliques,* Ewald planned to go to Scotland to gather folk songs, but had to abandon the project because of his poor health. Nevertheless, he did turn to earlier Germanic literature for source material. At the suggestion of Klopstock, who by now was himself employing patriotic motifs and writing what (erroneously) was called "bardic poetry," Ewald wrote a prose drama, *Rolf Krage* (1770), on a subject from Saxo Grammaticus. Then he wrote the work which once more brought Scandinavian mythology into the realm of literature: *Balders Død.* Although there had recently been a few spasmodic attempts to revive Scandinavian mythology, namely in Paul Henri Mallet's *Monumens de la mythologie et de la poésie des Celtes* (1756), and H. W. Gerstenberg's *Gedicht eines Skalden* (1766), Ewald's *Balders Død* marks the beginning of what has been called the "Germanic renaissance" in literature.

1 An English translation by George Borrow, *The Death of Balder,* was published in a limited edition, London, 1889.

Even if we disregard Ewald's aesthetic significance, he remains a phenomenon in eighteenth-century Danish literature, for he aspired to be a poet and nothing but a poet. He rashly tried to live exclusively from the proceeds of his pen, and was thus the first Dane who was avowedly a poet by profession. Whether he was successful is a matter of definition. His everyday life was chaotic, fraught with difficulties and frustration. He was often in financial straits; he became addicted to alcohol; much of the time he was an invalid. Although his large quantities of occasional poetry written for weddings and funerals have little interest today, Ewald will not cease to occupy a special position as the leading Danish poet of pathos and the forerunner of the Germanic renaissance in Scandinavia; but he will be little read.

In his own lifetime Ewald was by no means the slighted or misjudged poet. In his later years he was very much the fêted poet of Denmark's capital and the occasional poet whose verses were most highly prized. About his figure grew up a new and enthusiastic literary circle that established itself as the "Danish Literary Society" and which had as its primary function the cultivation of Ewald's work. Thus Ewald, although inspired by the master of the German circle in Copenhagen, came himself to be a point of origin for a society of Danish litterateurs and poets which furthered the rise of a national literature. The literary group about Ewald became the god-parent, as it were, of the new Danish literature that came into being at the turn of the century.

The "Danish Literary Society" of 1775 was not the oldest of such organizations. The first Danish literary society, "for the advancement of the fine and useful arts," had been founded in 1759 (and still exists). The poet who took the first two prizes for poetry set up by this first society was the Norwegian manufacturer CHRISTIAN B. TULLIN (1728–65), who wrote in the style of James Thomson. One of his prize-winning poems dealt with shipping, the other with the perfection of the Creation. Prior to Ewald's literary success, Tullin's *En Maji-Dag,* known as *Maj-dagen* (*May Day,* 1758), was looked upon as the zenith of achievement in Dano-Norwegian literature and was widely read.

Tullin presaged the rôle that Norwegians on Danish soil were soon to play in the double monarchy. Many of Ewald's contemporaries were Norwegians, and in 1772 they established "Det Norske Selskab" (The Norwegian Society) in Copenhagen, an act which bespoke Norwegian national consciousness. It may be noted that there is a direct line of development between the founding of the Norwegian Society and the founding of a university in Norway in 1811.

The "German Circle," which had had an exotic, insular existence in the Danish capital during Klopstock's sojourn, was now replaced by a Norwegian circle, so to speak, for the Norwegians were the most spirited writers in Copenhagen for about a decade. The leading Norwegian literary figures were JOHAN HERMAN WESSEL, JOHAN NORDAHL BRUN, and NIELS KROG BREDAL. Wessel (1742–85), a satirical and witty versifier, partook of the spirit of Holberg and of rationalism. Like his bellettristic contemporaries and fellow countrymen, his source of inspiration was France, but it was nevertheless he who deflated the balloon of the elegant, post-classical French drama, translations of which for many years set the tone on the Copenhagen stage. How this came about is legendary in Danish literary history: Niels Krog Bredal, who was the director of the Danish theater and himself a dramatist and incidentally the author of the first Danish operatic libretto, established a prize for an original Danish tragedy. It was understood that the tragedy would be in the French classical style. The prize was awarded to Brun for the tragedy *Zarine,* which was soon successfully played under Bredal's supervision. No sooner had *Zarine* been given than Wessel wrote a parody on the so-called French tragedies satirizing their exaggerated pathos and declamatory style. The parody, *Kierlighed uden Strømper (Love without Stockings,* 1772) carefully followed the pattern of the French tragedy—and reduced it to absurdity by elevating the trivial to the plane of high-flown tragedy in alexandrine verse. A poor maiden dreams that she must be married a certain day or never, but in order for this to occur, her fiancé must procure a pair of white stockings. This gives rise to an intrigue which eventually brings death to all the main characters in the drama. The devices of the French drama, such as the use of confidants and confidantes by the commonplace hero and heroine, and the absurd concept of honor evoked laughter and made the Copenhagen public realize the artificiality of the dramas which hitherto had been accepted. The heroic French tragedy gradually went out of fashion; but *Love without Stockings* has continued to live as an amusing farce and to perpetuate Wessel's name.

In 1771–73, notable years in the history of the Danish stage, Copenhagen had its first taste of incisive analytical dramatic criticism in the spirit of Lessing's *Hamburgische Dramaturgie.* A young student, PEDER ROSENSTAND-GOISKE (1752–1803) published *Den dramatiske Journal (The Dramatic Journal)* and provided the Danish capital with a commentary on the plays produced at the Royal Theater. Incidentally, the youthful critic gave high praise to the plays of Holberg.

After the death of Ewald in 1781, three very different young men became the leading figures on the Danish literary scene: JENS BAGGESEN, PEDER ANDREAS HEIBERG, and KNUD LYHNE RAHBEK. Baggesen (1764–1826), the poet of the three, was a man whose restless life reflected the restlessness of his own soul. Heiberg (1758–1841), the agitator, first brought socio-political problems into the realm of literature in Denmark. Rahbek (1760–1830), the critic, was the foremost representative of the plodding and self-satisfied bourgeoisie. Baggesen was a Germanophile, Heiberg a Francophile; Baggesen was a friend of the German nobility, Heiberg a friend of Republican France. Baggesen and Heiberg both died as expatriates. Rahbek was content and happy to be a Dane in Denmark.

As a Germanophile, Baggesen was the subject of considerable suspicion because of the prejudice engendered by the recent internal Dano-German conflict that had culminated in the fall of Struensee. Not only had German culture overwhelmed Copenhagen after the middle of the century, but in 1771–72 the insane King Christian VII's German physician, Struensee, who was at the same time the queen's paramour, had through a palace revolution managed to take over the reigns of government. While his brief despotic rule was an enlightened one,[1] Struensee's presence was an affront to native pride. He was intolerant of Danish culture and even went so far as to propose the abolition of the Danish language. Such an attitude could only arouse animosity and evoke a new national consciousness. There was a violent reaction, and Struensee soon met with a sorry end. Political repercussions were felt even on the literary scene.

Despite Baggesen's German predilections, his first work, the versified *Comiske Fortællinger (Humorous Tales,* 1785), enjoyed unprecedented success on the Danish book-market, and the twenty-one-year-old Baggesen became Denmark's leading poet. Five years later he started on the journey abroad which was to result in his principal work, *Labyrinten (The Labyrinth,* 1792–93), a "sentimental journey" *à la* Laurence Sterne through Germany and into Switzerland.[2] *Labyrinten,* although not a very original work, represented a new direction in Danish prose. The picturesque and vivacious descriptive passages scattered through the book are still living literature today. They are free of a certain quaintness of style and expression characteristic of earlier Danish literature and even of Baggesen's

---

1 Under Struensee there was complete freedom of the press and as a consequence Denmark weltered in new journals, papers, pamphlets, and books. After his fall, censorship was again introduced.

2 Translations of several selections from this work are to be found in William and Mary Howitt, *The Literature and Romance of Northern Europe,* II, London 1852, pp. 4–35.

own poetry. Best known are the descriptions of Mannheim, Frankfurt am Main, Strasbourg, and the Luneberg Heath. A continuation of *Labyrinten,* which was not published until much later, relates Baggesen's journey in Paris and his visits to German men of letters—Klopstock, Herder, Wieland, and Schiller.

Although Baggesen was both a clever and prolific writer, he lacked originality and the ability to translate personal experiences into universal symbols. Only a few of his poems and parts of *Labyrinten* therefore belong to living Danish literature.[1] Nevertheless, if anyone gave his stamp to Danish literature at the end of the eighteenth century it was Jens Baggesen. He was however not satisfied to be Denmark's leading poet but tried zealously to play an active rôle on the German literary scene as well. He succeeded only in becoming one of the host of lesser contemporaries of Goethe, Schiller, and the other classical writers of the Golden Age of Weimar. While Vilhelm Andersen devotes over one hundred pages to Baggesen in his monumental history of eighteenth-century Danish literature, German literary histories do little more than mention his name. He is one of several poets who have tried to write both in Danish and German. His two younger contemporaries, Adam Oehlenschläger and A. W. Schack von Staffeldt, also wrote in both languages, and Oehlenschläger was rewarded with some modicum of popular success in Germany. Schack von Staffeldt was unusual in that his mother tongue was German and he chose to write Danish—and was better received as a Danish than as a German poet.

Despite his literary prestige at home, Baggesen left Denmark in 1800, ostensibly for good, but actually for a protracted stay in Paris. For one reason or another his life continued to be without a pattern. He made occasional appearances in Denmark, and continued to receive the Danish patronage which enabled him to live as a writer, but he never settled down to any of the several callings which he from time to time attempted.

Before leaving Copenhagen in 1800, Baggesen performed a symbolic act: at a social gathering of litterateurs, he willed his Danish muse to a young and promising poet by the name of Adam Oehlenschläger, who had recently made his literary debut. It was almost a laying on of hands, for Baggesen had as a young man been hailed by the dying Wessel as the coming poet on the Danish Parnassus. One marvels at Baggesen's per-

---

1 Translations into English of some of Baggesen's poems are scattered in several anthologies. One poem, "Der var en Tid, da jeg var meget lille," ("There was a time when I was very small") has found several translators including H. W. Longfellow, George Borrow, and the Howitts.

spicacity, for Oehlenschläger was to become the greatest poet of his day, the leader of a new school of writing, and, after Holberg, the second great figure in modern Danish literature.

Peter Andreas Heiberg belonged to the extreme left, or republican, wing of the Danish party. Though he considered himself to be thoroughly disillusioned about his native country, he was not without the optimistic zeal of a reformer. The degeneracy of the monarchy in both Denmark and France gave good reason for discontent. The glaring faults of absolutism in France and elsewhere under incompetent rulers fostered political republicanism and intellectual cynicism. When the great crash came in France, it was greeted with widespread sympathy in Denmark, as elsewhere in Europe, although the sympathy rapidly changed to horror at the methods employed by the revolutionists. Only a minority continued to admire the ideas which motivated the French republic and to approve the course of the revolution. The spokesman for that minority of radical republicans in Denmark was Heiberg, who was very free with his criticism of the existing order and whose literary production contains an unmistakable admixture of political agitation. His *Sprog-Granskning* (*Language Study*, 1798) exhibits the cynical humor of a man who has lost faith in existing society and who sees integrity, justice, and honor flaunted everywhere. Here are some of Heiberg's "philological" definitions:

> Arrogance—the mistake of keeping to the truth and sound reason.
> Bizarre—applied to him who cannot be bribed.
> Compliment—the opposite of what one thinks.
> Drinking spree—a test of true friendship.

Heiberg's best-known work, the portmanteau novel *Rigsdalers-Sedlens Hændelser* (*The Adventures of a Banknote*, 1787–93)—which was inspired by an English book, *Chrysal, or the History of a Guinea* (by Charles Johnstone) —is filled with resentment against political and social abuses. Let a single paragraph of the story suffice as an example.

> Political dust, rust, and impurity are so deeply ingrown in the body of the state that at the very least a file or a rasp is needed to scrape it off; but who dares use these instruments when those whose duty it is to use them find it to their advantage to let corrosion get the upper hand. The state is like a sick person who cannot be cured unless a dangerous compound is included in his medicine which the apothecary may not furnish unless directed to do so by the physician. If now the physician is also a clergyman and after due calculation finds that he will earn more from a funeral sermon than by curing the patient, then the patient will die in the peace of the Lord.

Heiberg was also a playwright, but his plays are remarkable for the social criticism from which they sprang rather than their dramatic execution. The best known, *De Vonner og Vanner* (*The "von's" and the "van's,"* played in 1791 and published in 1793), ridicules blind adulation of the nobility. In an overly contrived plot, the von Plagemans (formerly the Petersens) try to make their daughter marry someone with a noble name, but good sense triumphs, in part because of the daughter's governess, who is a true noblewoman; and the girl is permitted to take a bourgeois husband. Popular in its appeal to the uncultivated taste, the play is clumsy and uninspired when compared with a comedy by Holberg.

For lèse-majesté against the English and Russian monarchs, his attacks on the Danish nobility, and his outspoken espousal of republicanism, Heiberg was finally banished from the realm in December 1799. He left Denmark and Danish culture behind him and went to Paris, where he took a position in the French foreign ministry. In Denmark, which he never saw again, he left his wife, who as Countess Gyllembourg was later to become a widely read Danish authoress, and their son, Johan Ludvig Heiberg, who was to become the virtual dictator of Danish literature during the elder Heiberg's own lifetime. Incidentally, the Heibergs are the most notable of the several families who have been represented by more than one member on the Danish parnassus.

Heiberg's political beliefs were shared by another promising writer, MALTE CONRAD BRUUN (1775–1826), who as "Malte-Brun" is well known in the history of geography. Inspired by the revolutionary thinking of the nineties, the youthful Bruun published a series of satirical pieces which brought him into conflict with the law. The witty but bitter *Aristokraternes Catechismus (The Aristocrats' Catechism,* 1796) which satirized both church and state, evoked the displeasure of the authorities. After an interval Bruun again took up his satirical pen and consequently he had to leave Denmark for good. Bruun was officially exiled in December 1800, just a year after Heiberg—and like Heiberg he went to Paris and changed his profession.

There were of course also literary defenders of the status quo. The only one of importance was THOMAS THAARUP (1749–1821), whose one-act play *Høst-Gildet (The Harvest Festival,* 1790) fused idyll and melodrama with royalist sentiment. The plot deals with two sets of lovers who are united despite parental plans to marry each girl to the wrong man. The play was apparently written for a command performance; the author has made literary obeisance to the royal house. In the final scene three characters exemplify the tripartite nature of the contemporary Danish monarchy by singing in their native Danish, Norwegian, and Low German respectively. In short, Thaarup's attitude was nearly antithetical to that of Peter Andreas Heiberg.

Oddly enough, when P.A.Heiberg and Jens Baggesen departed for Paris in 1800, they left Danish literature without any acknowledged leader except for the critic Knud Lyhne Rahbek. It was an anomalous situation. The German circle about Klopstock had long since dissolved and German influence had diminished after the fall of Struensee. The Norwegians were beginning to concern themselves more with Norway and less with Denmark. The turn of the century coincided with a shift in literary scenery. After an interregnum of two years, there was to arise, swiftly, a new literary school.

Knud Lyhne Rahbek was the connecting link between the late eighteenth and early nineteenth centuries. Although Rahbek and Baggesen were personally as dissimilar as water and fire, Rahbek was something of a parallel to Baggesen in criticism. The two men were the most widely read Danish authors in the 1790's and during the first decade of the nineteenth century. They accepted the same aesthetic standards, though they employed them to quite different ends. Rahbek lacked Baggesen's genius, but was accepted as a dramatist and a poet of rank, perhaps in part because of his artistic mediocrity.

Rahbek was everybody's friend, a good fellow, and a gracious host. His home, "Bakkehuset" was the gathering place for Danish literati for many years. This would scarcely have been the case however, were it not for the presence of his gifted wife Kamma Rahbek, née Heger, who quickly gained the confidence of her husband's many literary associates.

Rahbek was not only a critic, but a very prolific writer, translator, and editor. At the age of nineteen he translated Diderot into Danish and wrote his first two original plays. Until his old age he continued to provide the Danish book market with translations from the French, German, and English as well as with his own novels, short stories, and plays. With the Norwegian-born CHRISTEN PRAM (1756–1821) he in 1785 started his first periodical of the *Spectator* type, entitled *Minerva,* which continued to appear until 1808. From 1790 until 1823 he was the editor of a number of other periodicals of a literary nature. With these periodicals, Rahbek firmly established Danish literary criticism. He also made his mark on Danish literature and culture in other ways. For two different periods he served as a professor in the University of Copenhagen. With Rasmus Nyerup he wrote three compendious literary histories that did much to encourage a national Danish literary consciousness. Finally, he was indefatigable as an editor of the works of other Danish writers.

An examination of some of the leading periodicals at the turn of the century gives an insight into the literary state of affairs. In the important but academically inclined *Kiøbenhavns Efterretninger om lærde Sager (Copenhagen Reports on Learned Matters)* the literary traditions of the eighteenth century are upheld. Belles-lettres take their place among theology, history, law, and philosophy. In Rahbek's periodicals, e.g., *Minerva* or *Den danske Tilskuer (The Danish Spectator)*, Danish literature leads a freer existence, but most of the contributions are trivial or ephemeral. In both types of journals there is an acknowledgment of Johannes Ewald's genius and in both, the German poets Wieland, Gellert, Gessner, and Rabener command special respect. It was tacitly assumed that the reader was familiar with German literature. One of the Danish poetical works which was most admired towards the end of the century, Christen Pram's *Stærkodder* (1785) was, for example, but an imitation of Wieland's epic style.

The number of translations into Danish increases and the interval between original publication and translation into Danish is lessened. On the level of August Kotzebue and the *comedie larmoyant,* Danish literature was up-to-date by the end of the century. There are suggestions of the endless stream of popular literature which did not warrant or receive treatment by the critical journals. In *Den danske Spion (The Danish Spy)* for 1772, for example, there is an article on the Spy's lending library, an institution which had been imported into Denmark about 1725 and which was very popular in the late eighteenth century. The "library" consisted almost entirely of chapbooks, baroque novels, and worthless political commentaries. Never had the desire for books been so great nor the number of readers larger. And at this critical juncture most of the literature produced was second-rate, imitative, and *petit-bourgeois.* The one Danish writer of international stature was Jens Baggesen, but even his lyre was silent as the new century began.

"We have poets in quantity, but very little poetry," sighed Rahbek in *Den danske Tilskuer* for October 1800. He mourned the fact that Ewald was dead, that Thaarup no longer was writing, that Heiberg and Bruun were expatriated, and that Baggesen was going to leave Denmark. "Yet at this very moment," he added, "it seems that a new spring is about to burst forth on the Danish Parnassus." There were several young writers who seemed to Rahbek to be full of promise.

An omen of the future course of Danish literature was given in 1800 when the University of Copenhagen established as the subject of an essay contest the question whether it would be feasible to introduce the Old Scandinavian mythology into literature in the place of the traditional classical mythology. The fact that the subject was chosen at all is indicative of a reawakening interest in the Scandinavian past and of the new direction which was making itself felt in German as well as Scandinavian literature at the end of the eighteenth century. Among the factors which contributed to the so-called Préromantisme or early Germanic Renaissance, the publication of Part I of the Arna-Magnæan Commission's edition of the *Elder Edda* in 1787 was particularly significant.

Of the essays submitted in answer to the prize question, one advocating the retention of classical mythology won the first prize, but an essay which made an eloquent plea for the use of Old Norse mythology won a second prize. The author of the second essay was one of the young writers to whom Rahbek referred optimistically in his periodical: Adam Oehlenschläger, the poet in embryo, a vigorous youth only half conscious of his poetic mission and only half daring to be himself. His mind was fertile soil for the seed of a new inspiration.

Manuscript of the Danish national anthem, contained in Ewald's Fiskerne, *written 1778. (Reduced).*

JENS BAGGESEN
Painting by C. A. Jensen, after C. Hornemann, 1806.

*Rahbek's membership plaque in a shooting club portrays his residence, "Bakkehuset",
the gathering place for the literary figures of Copenhagen about 1800.*

ADAM OEHLENSCHLÄGER
Painting by J. L. Lund, 1809.

CHAPTER VI

A Golden Age. Oehlenschläger and His Contemporaries

In the summer of 1802 a young Norwegian mineralogist, geologist, and philosopher named Henrik Steffens, who had spent four years studying in Germany, came to Copenhagen and there preached "natural philosophy" and the doctrine of the so-called German Romantic School. To be sure, Steffens was not the first person on the Scandinavian literary scene to be aware of the new course of German literature. The German-Danish soldier-poet Adolf Wilhelm Schack von Staffeldt had sat at the feet of the same masters as Steffens and had felt the impact of many of the same ideas which Steffens absorbed. But Schack von Staffeldt was unable lucidly to formulate his experiences or to play the rôle of the prophet or demagogue in a Copenhagen that was in need of literary stimulus. During the autumn of 1802, the literati of Copenhagen flocked to hear the new word from the lips of the enthusiastic Steffens, who expounded the philosophy of Fichte and Schelling and awakened his audiences to the fact that Goethe was more than the author of *Werther*. A new literary school subsequently arose in Scandinavia.

Henrik Steffens, who was born in Stavanger, Norway in 1773, had gone to Germany in 1798 in order to study the natural sciences. He soon met the leaders of the new literature and new philosophy—members of a younger generation, who, in reacting to some degree against the neoclassical ideal that had developed in the eighteenth century, came to be known (for better or for worse) as the Romantic School. "The Romantic School," a term which because of its many connotations and manifold applications defies exact definition, may for the present purposes be assumed to mean the members of a younger generation of German writers inspired by contemporary German philosophy, who in the 1790's began to produce a literature which, because of its lyric bent, its radicalism, its desire for universality and brotherhood, its introspection, its interest in the Middle Ages, its love of phantasy, and its insatiable yearning, could ethically be differentiated from the literature which previously had prevailed.

Steffens experienced the great release of emotions which in German literary history dates from the last half-dozen years of the eighteenth century and culminated in the works of Wackenroder, Novalis, Schelling, and the brothers Schlegel. Like most of his contemporaries, Steffens was in addition greatly attracted to Goethe, perhaps especially because of the unity which was an achievement of Goethe's universal genius. Steffens dedicated his first scientific work to Goethe. He nevertheless became increasingly concerned with the younger literature which, with its new philosophy (and new emotionalism), was trying to shake off what were felt to be the shackles of rationalism.

When Steffens returned to Denmark, he was determined to spread the doctrine to which he had been won in Germany. And he was highly successful in winning the public ear in Copenhagen. His lectures were given to audiences that more than filled his auditorium, audiences seeking a new spirit, enthusiasm, and orientation. Yet, despite all that has been written about Steffens' lectures and about the remarkable effects that they produced, we do not know exactly with what they concerned themselves; except for the introductory lectures which are preserved in written form, Steffens spoke without notes, as if inspired. His message seemed to be what intellectual Denmark had been waiting for. He bore the new *Zeitgeist*. The ideas which Steffens disseminated were probably the more effective because some younger Danish intellectuals, and notably the physicist H. C. Ørsted, had also studied in Germany and been impressed by the thinking of Schelling, Friedrich Schlegel, and their German contemporaries.

The young ADAM OEHLENSCHLÄGER (1779–1850), whose slight poetic production hitherto had been imitative, was attracted to Steffens and determined to make his acquaintance. Their meeting is legendary in Danish literary history. The young Danish poet presented himself at Steffens' quarters, and soon the two were deep in a discussion that was to last for some sixteen hours. Although the meeting is mentioned in the autobiographies of both participants, the subjects of their discussion are not known. We may assume that theirs was a meeting of souls and that they conversed about many of the same literary and philosophical matters with which Steffens dealt in his lectures. Just what Steffens told Oehlenschläger that was new is a matter of conjecture, but he did give him the courage to break with the literary traditions of the eighteenth century and to free himself from Rahbek's guiding hand. Steffens said later of his influence on Oehlenschläger, "I gave him to himself." For Oehlenschläger, the immediate result was a poem, "Guldhornene" ("The Golden Horns") which he wrote the morning following the conversation. The poem was significant not only for Oehlenschläger's own production but also for Danish literature; it has become symbolic of a turning point in literary history. Its success convinced Oehlenschläger of his poetic talents and encouraged him to express himself more freely; it clearly marked the beginning of a renaissance in Scandinavian literature.

The young Oehlenschläger had been attracted to Old Scandinavian material even before the meeting with Steffens. He was at the time occupied in writing a tale, "Erik og Roller," which drew upon old Scandinavian literature; in fact, the story was already being printed; but with the decisive action representative of a forceful conviction, Oehlenschläger recalled the proofs and prepared a volume of poetry which more nearly corresponded to his newly acquired and newly clarified and fixed convictions. The keynote in the volume was sounded by "The Golden Horns."

In "The Golden Horns" Oehlenschläger dared to be independent and creative in the realm of myth. The new poem was no longer a synthesis of Ewald and Baggesen, as Oehlenschläger's first works very largely had been, but a synthesis of Oehlenschläger's own feelings with the philosophy which Henrik Steffens was disseminating. It is a great narrative poem which attains the level of Goethe's and Schiller's classical poetry. Although epic in quality, it is the product of lyric inspiration. It is the pure gold of genius.

The facts which Oehlenschläger formed into a new myth are as follows. In 1639 there was accidentally found near Gallehus in Jutland a golden drinking horn, one of the most remarkable archeological discoveries ever made in Denmark. The horn was adorned with illustrations of what scholars assumed to be Northern legends or mythology. In 1734 there was found in the same place a second golden horn which matched the first and which contained a runic inscription. The two solid gold horns were a priceless treasure from a culture which antedated the introduction of Christianity into Scandinavia. They were nevertheless insufficiently guarded after coming into the possession of the Danish crown, and in May, 1802, they were stolen from the royal cabinet—never to be recovered. There was an element of mystery surrounding their origin, their finding, and their disappearance. The disappearance of the horns attracted a great deal of attention; in Oehlenschläger it found an interpreter.

"The Golden Horns," a dramatic ballad written in short, irregular, emphatic stanzas of varying meter, ascribes the finding and the loss of the golden horns to the will of the gods of Scandinavian antiquity. The horns are given modern man as a reward for faithful antiquarian studies and in order to foster a deeper appreciation of the Scandinavian past:

"O, you who fumble blind
Shall find
A timeless trace
Of the vanished race."

The horns are bestowed as a symbol of an earlier, golden age (a concept which Oehlenschläger probably borrowed unwittingly from the philosophy of Schelling):

Ages of gold
Flaming forth
Light from the North,
When heaven was earth.

They are bestowed as a symbol of the infinite and the fleeting and of the union of the past with the present—a fulfillment of the longing for historical unity.

The zenith shakes
With thunder.
All the North wakes
In wonder.

The gods' displeasure is aroused when they find that men look greedily upon the horns simply because they are of gold, and fail to appreciate their deeper significance:

Yet, you only see the graven
Gold, and not the light above it;
Common riches shown for craven
Eyes to estimate and covet.

Consequently the gods decide that it is to no use to unveil a great past to modern man—and the horns disappear:

The hour strikes; the gods have given;
Now the gods have taken back;
Storms crash; the clouds are riven;
The relics vanish in the black.[1]

The entire poem was a translation into dramatic incident of the new German philosophy, which saw in nature and the events of history the revelation of a universal spirit and not merely the teleological world pattern which had been the assumption of rationalists in the eighteenth century. The poem embodied a new attitude and a new psychology.

Oehlenschläger's first volume of poetry, *Digte,* which appeared in December, 1802 (although dated 1803), transplanted to Denmark the

[1] Translation by R. S. Hillyer in *A Book of Danish Verse,* New York, The American-Scandinavian Foundation, 1922. The earlier translation by George Borrow is found in his *The Songs of Scandinavia,* vol. II, London and New York, 1923, pp. 172–77 (=*The Works of George Borrow, Norwich Edition,* vol. VIII).

spirit of the new literature of Germany, of the so-called "Romantic School" of the Schlegels, Schelling, Novalis, and others. The volume is a monument in the history of Danish literature; it marks the conscious beginning of a new literary movement and a break with the dominant tradition of the eighteenth century. While "The Golden Horns" was the most remarkable single item in the collection, we should not assume that the entire volume resulted from Steffens' impact on Oehlenschläger. Some of the poems had been written prior to the meeting with Steffens. The volume represents no real break with Oehlenschläger's previous production, then, but a deepening of Oehlenschläger's original qualities. It includes two other significant contributions: the dramatic idyll *Sanct Hansaften-Spil (Midsummer Night's Play)* and the dramatic poem "Hakon Jarls Død" ("The Death of Hakon Jarl"), the latter of importance as a precursor of the drama *Hakon Jarl* which Oehlenschläger was to write in Halle in 1805.

Like Oehlenschläger's play, the poem suggests the inevitability of conquering Christianity, but, like "The Golden Horns," reminds the reader that a great heroic world has gone down to defeat,

> ...and will never return to the North.
> Eternally, nothing but cloisters and churches;
> Gone are the groves, but he that searches
> May sometimes behold
> In the lonely wold
> An upright stone with a hero's mark
> Still touched with the flames long quenched in dark.[1]

St. Hansaften-Spil, which suggests both Goethe's *Jahrmarktsfest zu Plundersweilern* and the technique of Shakespeare, whose *Midsummernight's Dream* Oehlenschläger later put into Danish, is still a part of living Danish literature, and has been presented on the Danish stage a number of times in the twentieth century. Not a drama in the usual sense of the word, *St. Hansaften-Spil* comprises a series of pictures of contemporary Danish life set in the frame of the great Royal Park *(Dyrehaven)* outside Copenhagen. In an arc-like pattern, the activities of a day from sunrise to nightfall are projected on the stage. One after the other, various characters or activities attract our attention: a poet, a blind man, a marionette theater, a Jewish boy, Harlequin, a glass blower, a drunken man, a pair of lovers, even a firefly and an old oak tree, and Death itself. A pleasing bourgeois idyll on a background of the cultivated hunting park of the eighteenth century, the piece filled the ever-present demand of human

1 Translation by R. S. Hillyer in *A Book of Danish Verse,* 1922, p. 25 f.

beings to see themselves in idealized but everyday situations. On the stage, the success of such an undramatic piece is of course dependent on the histrionic and interpretive talents of the theater's personnel, for it is not borne by any obvious metaphysical or philosophical leitmotif or charged with a profound ethical message.

Oehlenschläger's poems were well received by the critics and reading public. Figuratively speaking, Oehlenschläger did take over the lyre which Baggesen had willed to him two years before. Baggesen was therewith displaced from the first position on Parnassus, a mutation which was to lead to an intermittent literary feud between him and Oehlenschläger a decade later. The literary hopes of the country were pinned on the 24-year-old Adam Oehlenschläger.

Although Oehlenschläger might have been expected to exploit the interest in Old Norse mythology which he had helped to arouse by "The Golden Horns," his next work, *Aladdin* (written in 1804–05, and published in *Poetiske Skrifter,* 1805), was in an entirely different vein.[1] Oehlenschläger now chose dramatically to renew a story from the *Arabian Nights.* He did so with such skill that *Aladdin* must be acknowledged as a literary masterpiece, and, paradoxically enough, a dramatic masterpiece, even though *Aladdin* cannot be presented on the stage quite in the form in which it was written. Treating the Aladdin story with the utmost freedom, Oehlenschläger recreated it in his drama. Although critics have suggested that Oehlenschläger's acquaintance (through Henrik Steffens) with Goethe's *Faust, Ein Fragment* (1790) is perceptible in *Aladdin,* we are probably nearer to the truth in assuming that as a dramatist Oehlenschläger was influenced by Shakespeare through the German translations of A.W. Schlegel. In Shakespearian fashion, Oehlenschläger makes use of the element of suspense by employing the device of misunderstanding and by introducing extraneous material at critical junctures; he employs typical characters, and permits himself puns and willful anachronisms. A taste of Oehlenschläger's less elevated but more individual wit and satire in *Aladdin* is given by this exchange of remarks:

> "He preached magnificently—Oh! what joy
> If he would have the sermon printed."
>
> "What sort of wild imagination is that?
> Do we have printing presses in Asia?"

Oehlenschläger anticipated the surprise of his readers at his treatment of an Oriental and exotic legend, and in a prologue to the play he made

1 Translated by Theodore Martin as *Aladdin; or The Wonderful Lamp,* London, 1857.

Sanguinitas explain the use of Oriental material. Oehlenschläger's public abroad as well as at home was, however, quite satisfied with *Aladdin*. To many it has seemed the culmination of Oehlenschläger's art because of its daring but successful treatment of a well-known if exotic motif, its light-hearted and optimistic point of view, and its exuberant theatrical qualities. Indicative of the attitude of German as well as Danish contemporaries is the fact that Goethe's inscription in Oehlenschläger's autograph book was simply "dem Dichter des Aladdin." Jean Paul, writing in 1808, said that if Oehlenschläger chose to versify all the *Thousand and One Nights,* he for one would be willing to read them all.

Oehlenschläger attempted in an epilogue to expound *Aladdin* symbolically, and various older critics have sought to interpret the drama symbolically or allegorically, but modern criticism opines that the drama as a whole is essentially neither a symbol nor an allegory; it is a delightful phantasy. The poet Aladdin is a child of nature and a lucky fellow—like Oehlenschläger. Oehlenschläger himself suggested the parallel. For Oehlenschläger as for Aladdin, the guiding principle seems to be good fortune rather than some basic philosophical idea. Neither Oehlenschläger nor his Aladdin delve into aberrations of the psyche or concern themselves with social and political problems. Oehlenschläger's exposure to the philosophy of German Romanticism afforded him an emotional release, but did not deeply affect him intellectually, a fact which has served to diminish his reputation outside Denmark in the course of years.

In addition to *Aladdin,* Oehlenschläger's *Poetiske Skrifter* contained *Vaulundurs Saga,* and two lyrical cycles, *Langelandsrejsen (Langeland Journey)* and *Jesu Christi gientagne Liv i den aarlige Natur (The Life of Jesus Christ symbolized in the Seasons)*. In the first of these works Oehlenschläger again drew on old Scandinavian literature. If he now wrote without as much genius as he had shown in *Aladdin,* the works were nevertheless well-received. As we consider Oehlenschläger in retrospect and view the many plays and poems which he produced after the first few years of youthful inspiration, we favor those works which gave Old Norse literature and mythology new life and new form: *Hakon Jarl, Baldur,* and the *Helge* trilogy. Many of the historical dramas seem to be *tours de force.* A few works such as the sentimental *Axel og Valborg (Axel and Valborg,* 1810) at one time enjoyed great popularity; they still find readers, but are rarely played today.[1] *Correggio,* which Oehlenschläger originally wrote in German, was widely read in Germany during the first half of the nineteenth

---

[1] English translations appeared in London in 1851 (by Jane Chapman), 1873 (H. W. Freeland), 1874 (Pierce Butler), and in New York in 1906 (F. S. Kolle).

century but is no longer a part of living German literature.[1] Had Oehlenschläger not written so much, many of his lesser works might possibly be
more appreciated and still read today, but since he surpassed himself in
a few works, most of his production has fallen into the obscurity of
literary history. Curiously enough, Oehlenschläger wrote his historical
plays according to the didactic principle (explained in the foreword to
Nordiske Digte, 1807), that "every nation... ought to have its own peculiarly national dramas. The peculiarly national is the finest flower of poetry."
Oehlenschläger's attitude, easily misinterpreted in the politically nationalistic twentieth century, does not mean that he confined his attentions to
the literature of his mother tongue; he himself zealously tried to become
a German as well as a Danish poet, and he called Shakespeare the colossus
who should be the model for every modern dramatist, even though
Shakespeare, as Oehlenschläger noted disparagingly, paid little attention
to the unities.

Oehlenschläger was probably attracted to Schiller even more than to
Shakespeare. The late classical German drama of Schiller is the key to the
form and technique of *Hakon Jarl,*[2] although not to the spirit in which
the subject was chosen. The carefully constructed rise and fall of the
action in *Hakon Jarl* reminds one of Schiller's eminently playable drama
Maria Stuart with its stirring conflict between Elizabeth and Mary, Queen
of Scots. But for once Oehlenschläger does more than represent a stirring
event in history and the clash of two great historical figures; *Hakon Jarl*
also symbolizes the turning point in Scandinavian history: the introduction of Christianity. Jarl Hakon is the last great heathen, and when he
falls, with him falls the heathendom of the North.

While Oehlenschläger, as a Christian, must sympathize with the ideals
of Hakon's antagonist, the Christian King Olaf, he passes a mild judgment on the tragic figure of Hakon. Despite Olaf's victory, Hakon in
defeat—like Schiller's Maria Stuart in defeat—remains in the eyes of the
audience the principal character in the play.

Hakon Jarl is the expression of poetical convictions. The attraction of
the theme for Oehlenschläger is clear; he could not rest until he had
exploited the dramatic possibilities which were suggested to him by his
poem of the same title in *Digte,* 1803. *Hakon Jarl* is dramatically the most
trenchant of Oehlenschläger's plays, although it is not as widely read as the

1 Translated by E. B. Lee, Boston, 1846, and Theodore Martin, London, 1854.

2 Translated by Jane Chapman as *Hakon Jarl,* London, 1857; by Frank C. Lascelles as *Earl
Hakon the Mighty,* London, 1874; by J. C. Lindberg as *An English Version of Oehlenschlæger's
Hakon Jarl,* Lincoln, Nebraska, 1905 (= *University studies,* Vol. V., no. 1.)

Digte

af

Adam Ohlenslæger

Was ich irrte, was ich strebte
was ich litt und was ich lebte -
sind hier Blumen nur im Strauß!

Göthe

Kiöbenhavn
Trykt paa Universitetsboghandler Fr: Brummers
Forlag hos Andreas Seidelin
1803

Title page of Oehlenschläger's first volume of poems. (*Cf. p. 108*). *Actual size.*

Steen Steensen Blicher talking to gypsies on the heath.
Painting (1866), by Christen Dalsgaard.

anomalous and idyllic *St. Hansaften-Spil.* In contrast to *Aladdin, Hakon Jarl* is well-suited to presentation on the stage. It is worth mention that Goethe at one time contemplated presenting *Hakon Jarl* in Weimar. So near was the drama to fulfilling the classical ideal of Weimar, even though it drew its theme from the Scandinavian past and in some ways represented a reaction against Weimarian classicism.

In *Baldur hin Gode (Baldur the Good)* Oehlenschläger turned to Scandinavian mythology and gave an explanatory portrayal of the decline of Mithgarth—the realm of the Scandinavian gods. The choice of subject was not capricious or without a philosophical overtone; to an adverse critic of the drama (Abrahamson), Oehlenschläger stated that a mythological fable was more real to him than an historical deed, since mythology is based "in eternal nature," whereas historical events are of the time past. Mythology, Oehlenschläger said, in accord with the philosophy of the times, "is the product of an entire nation's character and way of thinking and feeling." Here is a key not only to Oehlenschläger's outlook but also to the emotional and philosophical attitude of the times.

Baldur himself plays no rôle in Oehlenschläger's drama, although the action hinges on his fate. Oehlenschläger tries to give a poetical and psychological explanation for Baldur's death. Loki's hatred of Baldur is a result of jealousy, which is in turn caused by a craving for love. Oehlenschläger makes us feel that Baldur is the spirit of good and that Loki, in his own words, "... is the power which, if it will, can destroy Valhalla." In contrast to *Hakon Jarl, Baldur* does not follow the pattern of the German classical drama when adjudged from the standpoint of form. Like *St. Hansaften-Spil* and even more like the German dramatist Heinrich von Kleist's tragedy *Penthisilea,* which was written only a year later, *Baldur* is a series of scenes comprising a single act. It employs several types of neo-classical verse. The action is so rapid that the reader or spectator hardly has time to draw his breath. Baldur dreams. Loki meditates. Suddenly Baldur is dead. All the gods except Loki try to retrieve Baldur from death by showing their sorrow; but Loki cannot show any sorrow about Baldur's death and Baldur must therefore remain in the realm of the dead. Consequently, the golden age of Mithgarth has abruptly found an end. Although *Baldur* lacks the limpid beauty of *St. Hansaften-Spil* and the geometrical pattern of *Hakon Jarl,* Oehlenschläger was still at his best in this dramatic treatment of a myth from the Old Norse. He evinced mastery of content and form; he created plastically, with an unerring hand.

Helge (1814) is made up of three parts: *Frodes Drapa, Helges Eventyr,* and *Yrsa.* Only *Yrsa* is in a dramatic form; the first two parts consist of cycles of interrelated poems. These poems nevertheless seem almost to be scenes from a drama. One might speak of a drama disintegrated into poems and by using twentieth-century terminology identify the style as impressionistic. The three parts are stylistically different and are only loosely connected, but taken together they are Oehlenschläger's greatest original dramatic achievement. In *Helge* he was no longer imitating Schiller but was for once creating his own form. *Frodes Drapa (Frode's Dirge)* is a poetical re-working of the Volsung legend and bears the mark both of Danish folk songs and Eddic poetry. The poems of the cycle are in various meters, as the mood requires. *Helges Eventyr (Helge's Adventure)* tells of Helge's experiences, of his union with Queen Oluf, and of the birth of their daughter Yrsa. Oluf, in order to revenge herself on Helge, lets him marry their daughter in ignorance of their relationship. After the truth of the situation has been explained to the lovers, they both consider suicide, but the goddess of love, Freya, convinces Yrsa she should live to give birth to Hrolf, who is to inherit Helge's crown and become the greatest hero of the North. This fantastic ending is a bond between Oehlenschläger's trilogy and its prose sequel, *Hroars Saga* (1817). Incidentally, in *Hroars Saga* Oehlenschläger made some use of "Erik og Roller," the very story which he had suppressed in the tumultous autumn of 1802. It would seem therefore, that Oehlenschläger finally had achieved a synthesis of the old and the new, or so to speak, of Ewald and Steffens. The fiery partisanship kindled by German philosophy through Henrik Steffens was replaced by a less discriminating and more benevolent attitude. Perhaps it would be more exact to say that Oehlenschläger's youthful exuberance was replaced by mellow maturity. But Oehlenschläger himself remained an Aladdin. Oehlenschläger is therefore practically unknown today in the world of literature outside Denmark, despite his undisputed genius and his eminent position in the history of Danish literature. He charms us with his lyric virtuosity in *St. Hansaften-Spil,* and moves us by his dramatic power in the "Golden Horns" and *Hakon Jarl* but he seldom engages the inner man who is searching for eternal verities. Thus Oehlenschläger is now outshone by many lesser poets, i.e., writers whose lyric gift was not as great as his, but with whom the reader more frequently and more thoroughly can identify himself in the realm of ideas.

Not only did Oehlenschläger employ Old Norse material and subjects in dramas, he also wrote in *Nordens Guder (The Gods of the North,* 1819) a sort of modern Edda.[1] In a series of poems he summarized Scandinavian

1 Translated by William Edward Frye, London and Paris, 1845.

mythology. The poems are indicative of Oehlenschläger's familiarity with his source material, although they are neither translations nor paraphrases of the Icelandic originals. The book was immediately accepted as a surrogate for the old mythology. When Johan Ludvig Heiberg wrote a Scandinavian mythology in 1827 he drew not only on the Old Norse source material, but, curiously enough, also on Oehlenschläger's revitalization of the mythology, so much did Oehlenschläger's work represent the ideal of the past for his contemporaries.

As an older man, Oehlenschläger continued to enjoy great prestige until his death in 1850. He was an academic as well as a literary figure, for he had been appointed professor of aesthetics in 1810. He remained the nominal Olympian of Danish literature while his later work underwent several phases, but the reins of leadership had slipped from his hands in the 1820's, when another literary school under the aegis of Johan Ludvig Heiberg, and subsequently other philosophies, especially as embodied in the thought of Grundtvig and Søren Kierkegaard, arose and occupied the minds of men. Oehlenschläger's popularity nevertheless reached its zenith in 1829, when he was crowned with laurel leaves in the cathedral of Lund by Sweden's poet-primate Esaias Tegnér, while cannon boomed through the Scanian university town and Danish and Swedish students paid him homage.

Among Oehlenschläger's literary contemporaries the aesthetically most significant was a poet who had been moulded by many of the same forces as Oehlenschläger but who otherwise stood in almost pitiable contrast to him: the aforementioned AUGUST WILHELM SCHACK VON STAFFELDT (1769–1826). Whereas Oehlenschläger was cheerful, uninhibited, and honored, Schack Staffeldt (as he is known) was introspective, hypochondriac, and little-read. The contrast between Oehlenschläger and Schack Staffeldt is so sharp that it almost seems ridiculous: Oehlenschläger's native tongue was Danish and he adopted German as a means of poetic expression; Schack Staffeldt's native language was German and he chose to write chiefly in Danish. Oehlenschläger lived and died as a poet; Schack Staffeldt spent a hapless life, first as an army officer and then as a government official. Oehlenschläger had a wife and children; Schack Staffeldt was unmarried.

Except for two years at the University of Göttingen, 1791–93, and five years of travel in Germany, Italy, and France in 1795–1800, Schack Staffeldt lived a life of gloomy meditation. If Oehlenschläger was Aladdin, Schack Staffeldt never advanced beyond Faust's *Studierzimmer*. Oehlenschläger never entered the plane of introspective reflection, but Schack Staffeldt shared Faust's eternal dissatisfaction; he found peace neither in worldly attainments nor in his own soul. Nevertheless, in the realm of poetry Schack Staffeldt and Oehlenschläger are two sides of the same coin. Both felt the impact of the so-called Romantic School in Germany at the turn of the nineteenth century, Schack Staffeldt directly and Oehlenschläger through Steffens. Oehlenschläger was inspired by the Germans—by Schelling and by the Schlegels—while Schack Staffeldt tried to give the new German thought poetic form in Danish. Consequently, Schack Staffeldt's poetry is more demanding and more heavy-handed than Oehlenschläger's, for he tried not only to write verse which would reflect the new philosophy but to imbue much of his poetry with the abstractions and principles of that philosophy. It has been Oehlenschläger's good fortune to find many translators, but no more than a handful of Schack Staffeldt's poems have ever been put into a foreign language.

The publication of Oehlenschläger's *Digte* in December, 1802, was apparently fateful for Schack Staffeldt, who had had a far better opportunity to absorb the new literature and the new philosophy in Germany than had Oehlenschläger and who himself had been planning to assemble and publish his poems and therewith to arouse the Danish Parnassus. Suddenly the deed, his deed, was done—a *fait accompli*. Attention was drawn not to the melancholy army officer who had studied in Germany at the very feet of the masters, but to a harbinger's harbinger: the ten-year-younger Oehlenschläger. It was a bitter pill, and Schack Staffeldt set about to rectify the situation and to obtain his just due by publishing his own poems. They appeared just one year after Oehlenschläger's. Unfortunately for Schack Staffeldt, he chose the same title, *Digte,* as had Oehlenschläger, published his volume in the same month as had Oehlenschläger, and gave it a similar typographical appearance. There seemed to be as many parallels between the two collections as there were differences between the two men. Contemporary criticism saw the parallels and overlooked the differences, despite Schack Staffeldt's valiant protest that he was no mere imitator of Oehlenschläger. The sincere philosophical conviction which pulsed in Schack Staffeldt's poems was not felt and probably not understood. The poems were too dull, too classical—perhaps despite some similarity of phrase and form too unlike Oehlenschläger's? A second volume of poems *(Nye Digte)* was published in Kiel in 1808. Schack Staffeldt's muse spoke less and less with the years and then ceased almost entirely. Half of Schack Staffeldt's production dates from the last few years of the eighteenth century.

There have been spasmodic attempts to revive Schack Staffeldt's poetry—the first was made during the poet's lifetime—and to obtain for it a wide audience, but he has remained an enigmatic if respected figure in Danish literary history.

While Schack Staffeldt remained isolated in Danish literature, assembled no clique, and won no disciples, a number of Danish writers were greatly impressed with Oehlenschläger's early works and were sympathetic to his person and his muse. In some ways they followed his style of writing and, consciously or unconsciously, accepted his theory and practice of literature. Most closely identified with Oehlenschläger are B.S.Ingemann, Carsten Hauch, and Christian Winther. It is tempting but erroneous to include N.F.S.Grundtvig. To be sure, Grundtvig was early attracted to and associated with Oehlenschläger, but he so quickly outgrew the limited world of Oehlenschläger's experiences and identified himself with so many ideas foreign to Oehlenschläger that he may best be considered by himself (cf. Chapter VII).

BERNHARD SEVERIN INGEMANN (1789–1862) enjoys a special place in the literary consciousness of Denmark. Every Dane knows Ingemann's hymns and his historical novels. Aesthetically speaking, his poetry has greater lasting value than his prose.[1] The poems are full of naïve and grandiose pictures such as "The Castle in the West" in Ingemann's most famous hymn ("Der staar et Slot i Vesterled"), of which this is the first stanza, in R.S.Hillyer's translation,[2]

> There stands a castle in the west
> Sheath'd with shields of gold;
> There seeks the sun his nightly rest
> Within the bright stronghold.
> No mortal hand has raised those high
> Flame-towers richly gilded,
> That portal stretched from earth to sky—
> These God himself has builded.

As a young man Ingemann was fêted because of his first volumes of poetry in 1811–12 and his *Procne* (1813). In these works Ingemann, more than Oehlenschläger, is the representative of a new sentimental, allegorical, and dramatic school, which stood indebted to the German poet Ludwig Tieck (whom Ingemann greatly admired). In the twenties Ingemann turned to the prose narrative and in this genre also won a large audience.

Like the novels of Sir Walter Scott, his novels have been standard reading for generations of adolescents. Although Ingemann is frequently

1 Of the several poems by Ingemann which have been translated by various hands, the best known is "Through the Night of Doubt and Sorrow" (in S. Baring-Gould's translation) which is to be found in hymn-book of the Church of England.

2 In *A Book of Danish Verse*, 1922, p. 59f.

compared with Scott, his novels contain more blood and thunder than Scott's. Only the naïve reader can today enjoy Ingemann's medieval revival, as for example in the most famous of his novels, *Erik Menveds Barndom* (*The Childhood of Erik Menved*, 1828).[1] Whether he produced great literature or not, Ingemann at least made the Danish past come to life for many a Danish reader. His books were read and acclaimed by his contemporaries and he enjoyed almost universal respect.[2] Ingemann is something of a combination of Oehlenschläger and Grundtvig. Indeed, he enjoyed a peculiar position in being a friend of both men. Although Ingemann usually is felt to be a sort of homely Oehlenschläger, it is worth noting that it was Grundtvig who originally suggested that Ingemann write his historical novels.

Like Oehlenschläger and Ingemann, CARSTEN HAUCH (1790–1872) was a pedagogue as well as a poet, but he was more catholic in his interest and more academic than his mentor Oehlenschläger, whom he succeeded as professor of aesthetics in the University of Copenhagen. He was a serious author devoted to the ideas of the natural philosophy propounded by German thinkers and by Hans Christian Ørsted. Hauch was interested both in natural sciences and belles-lettres; he wrote his doctoral dissertation on a zoological subject. His own evolution from natural science to aesthetics was contemporaneous with a shift in genres; he first concentrated on verse, then on the drama, and finally on the novel. While most critics agree that Hauch reached the height of his powers in some of his serious lyric poetry, Hauch's contemporaries and the reading public today have agreed in admiring him almost exclusively as a novelist.

Hauch's most important novels are *En Polsk Familie* (*A Polish Family*, 1839) and *Robert Fulton* (1853). The second, based on the life of the American inventor of the steamboat, has been the most widely read.

In the foreword to *En Polsk Familie* and within the framework of a melodramatic story sympathetically portraying the Polish people's struggle for independence in the years 1829–30, Hauch debates the issue whether questions of the day should be treated belletristically. Apparently trying to justify his use of contemporary material, he asserts that the poet must not be isolated from the times. A modern reader is puzzled by Hauch's apology until he learns that Hauch had been attacked by Henrik Hertz in the satirical *Gjengangerbreve* (*Letters of a Ghost*, 1830) as being

---

1 Translated by J. Kesson, London, 1846.

2 Two other novels appeared in English translations by Jane Frances Chapman: *Waldemar, surnamed Seir, or the Victorious*, London, 1841, and *King Eric and the Outlaws*, London, 1843; title edition, 1850: *The Outlaws and King Eric*.

"stone deaf to the voice of the times" and as being of the opinion that the poet has "no obligations towards the times in which he lives." The novel is thus a rebuttal by the older literary school of Oehlenschläger and his followers addressed to the new criticism of Johan Ludvig Heiberg and his coterie, whom Hauch previously had been so bold as to satirize.

From the standpoint of style and content the reader still finds in Hauch's novels the crystal world of the late eighteenth century, and the general pattern of Goethe's *Wilhelm Meister*. Hauch requires from the reader no aesthetic response or appreciation. The tale is told clearly and masterfully, but the reader is ever aware of Hauch's guiding hand and is conscious of the author's idealistic motivation. The denouement is not realistic in the usual sense of the word; nor does Hauch demonstrate himself to have been a particularly keen observer. A novel by Hauch is nevertheless absorbing reading. Following the example of many novelists around 1800, Hauch interspersed his story with poems or tales tangential to the plot. As *En Polsk Familie* developed in Hauch's hands, it became more and more a receptacle for tangential material after the fashion of the German novels on which it was patterned, with first this, then that life story or bit of high adventure inserted into the novel in a most unrealistic manner.

Robert Fulton,[1] which is more artistically composed than the other novels, was written with considerable historical license: Benjamin Franklin and Joel Barlow are two of the novel's major characters. The other figures are stock personalities of the novelist: a beautiful songstress, a faithful and god-fearing wife, a crafty villain and his despicable helpers, an embittered father, a wealthy miser, and both helpful and doubting friends. It is particularly significant that Hauch wilfully chose a hero from the realm of the practical. In that respect Hauch is to be differentiated from his late eighteenth-century predecessors. Like Hans Christian Andersen, Hauch evinced admiration for technology and the resolution of practical problems by the human mind. This materialistic attitude is not a trait of what generally is called "the Romantic School."

CHRISTIAN WINTHER (1796–1876) is by Danish critics often classified with Oehlenschläger and Ingemann as a "Romanticist." There is much to be said for this identification, but Christian Winther was also a connecting link between the poetic renaissance of the first decade of the century and a later generation of lyrists, between Oehlenschläger on the one hand and the eclectic poets of the forties and fifties on the other. His major work,

---

1 A translation by Paul C. Sinding was published in New York in 1868.

Hjortens Flugt (*The Flight of the Hart,* 1855) appeals to the lover of the exotic, the national, and the medieval, despite the fact that Winther had made his debut in the twenties with erotic poems and ballads which gave new life to the lyrical muse in Denmark and which afforded some parallels to the works of Byron, Victor Hugo, and Heinrich Heine abroad. Like Byron's *Mazeppa* and Sir Walter Scott's *Lady of the Lake, Hjortens Flugt* is a romance that engages and satisfies the fantasy of an adolescent; it enjoyed tremendous popularity during Winther's own lifetime and has remained a classic. It is a tale of breathless adventure, of love and hatred, of bold knights, treacherous adversaries, and hearty peasants, who move before the background of the pleasant landscape of Zealand which the poet himself so loved. While the poem may be considered a poetic parallel to Ingemann's historical novels, it was written with greater feeling and sensitivity, with greater understanding of form and content, and at the same time with less concern with historical events than was Ingemann's prose.

Christian Winther was a master of the romance and the idyll. Many of his romances employ motifs from folk-ballads; perhaps the most widely read is, however, an original humorous romance, "Flugten til Amerika" ("The Flight to America"), in which the youthful hero "drowns his sorrow and finds his solace at the bottom of his soup plate" (namely, the raisins in Danish sago soup). The idylls entitled *Træsnit (Woodcuts,* 1828) are reminiscent of the German poet Voss' earlier bourgeois romances.

While Adam Oehlenschläger and his elegant companions dominated the Danish literary scene from Copenhagen, and subsequently gave way to the elegant Johan Ludvig Heiberg as the ruler of the Danish Parnassus, another writer, who was a lowly clergyman in Jutland, was suffering a miserable provincial existence, an unhappy marriage, and pressing debts. He was at the same time composing the verse and prose which were to make him one of the best loved of Danish poets and a writer near to the heart of Denmark. STEEN STEENSEN BLICHER (1782–1848) did not contradict the times, nor was he one with the times or the literary schools of his day. He cut an isolated figure. During his lifetime he was looked upon as an unsuccessful clergyman, a hapless husband, and an incompetent businessman. He was nevertheless rather widely read in his later years, and he did have patrons who occasionally heeded his pleas to help diminish his debts.

That Blicher is a thoroughly tragic figure is a fact which cannot be deduced from his literary production and a fact of which Blicher himself was not conscious. His life was too careless and disorganized to allow

him to sense in it a tragic pattern. Blicher was by nature a poet and a
hunter. He loved the moors of Jutland, he loved to walk, to shoot, to
talk with the common people. Although these traits helped make him an
interpreter of common folk, they fitted him ill as a pastor of the established church. One wonders how Blicher could have chosen such an
incongruous profession. The answer is probably that the cloth was the
easiest life he could choose and the only profession that he, a clergyman's
son, might select and still retain a goodly quantity of freedom. Too, the
clerical tradition was strong in his family.

For succeeding generations of Danes, Blicher at his best has been an
incomparable storyteller with a genius for pictures, for portraying local
conditions, and for making words come to life. Some of his works were
potboilers however, stories written to fill the columns of a local publication merely for the shillings they brought their author. Blicher was uncomplicated; his was a homely philosophy. There is nothing one cannot
understand, no abstract thinking, just a story that holds the reader's
attention to the end and possesses a most remarkable attribute: that of
making the reader want to read the story again. In some of Blicher's
stories Danes find themselves portrayed so delightfully that reading a
story by Blicher becomes on certain occasions almost as mandatory as
the annual reading of Dickens' *Christmas Carol* over the American radio.
Perhaps it is not too much to say that Blicher's stories are to Danish
literature what Dickens' *Christmas Carol* is to English literature. Who
does not know the *Christmas Carol*? Who, in Denmark, does not know
Blicher? Many a Dane to whom Oehlenschläger is only a name has read
stories by Steen Steensen Blicher. A recent translation into English of
twelve of Blicher's tales was well received and has as it were turned the
tables on the more eminent figures of the Golden Age of Danish literature,
as far as the English-speaking world is concerned.[1]

Blicher can be called a "romantic" or a "realist" as you will. His own
literary taste would be defined as "romantic," but what he himself wrote
was often a portrayal of existing conditions in the Jutland which he knew
from personal experience. Oddly enough he made his first essay into
literature with a translation of Ossian into Danish in 1807–09, thirty
years after the Ossianic rage had been at its height. A volume of Blicher's
own poems was published—in Aarhus, not in Copenhagen—in 1814, and
his first play appeared in 1819. It was not until about 1824, when Blicher

---

1 *Twelve Stories. Translated from the Danish by Hanna Astrup Larsen with an Introduction by Sigrid
Undset*. Princeton University Press for the American-Scandinavian Foundation. New York,
1945.

was over forty years of age, that he really found his medium, the short story. His tragedy *Johanne Gray* (1825) was played at the Royal Theater in Copenhagen, but was unsuccessful. By 1833 he had won enough of an audience with his short stories to ensure the publication of a five-volume set of the tales in Copenhagen. Some of these tales won the favorable comment of the eminent philologist J. N. Madvig, whose judgment is valid even today:

> "The pictures which are painted here at once attract our attention by their national tone and appeal to us through the feeling which makes us want to keep to the cosy homestead; but this tone takes on a more specific, more individual, and therewith more forceful character by being not only Danish in general but provincial in particular."

The "national tone" is the more noticeable if the reader is made aware of Blicher's attempts to arouse the Danes to an appreciation of their country, somewhat after the fashion of N. F. S. Grundtvig, by arranging annual gatherings at Himmelbjerget, a hill in Jutland. But such peripheral information distracts us from an aesthetic appreciation of Blicher as a writer. Suffice it to say that a parallel may be drawn between some of the ideas of Grundtvig and Blicher, although the two contemporaries were independent of one another and as individuals were worlds apart.

Blicher's best known tale is *En Landsbydegns Dagbog* (*The Journal of a Parish Clerk,* 1824) which freely employs the story of an enigmatic seventeenth-century woman, Marie Grubbe, who was later to become the principal character in J. P. Jacobsen's novel *Marie Grubbe.* (Blicher nevertheless lets the action take place in the eighteenth century). In its fragmentary way, the "Journal" calls up some vivid pictures while telling of the degeneration of "Miss Sophie," of whom the clerk, a good man, once was enamored, and who, by mistake, was his for a brief moment. He sees her again after thirty years, an old crone with a yellowed, sullen face. The story is typical of Blicher's weakness for effects as well as of his literary genius. *Præsten i Vejlby (The Clergyman of Vejlby),* one of Blicher's well known works, although based on fact, is a mystery story of an improbable sort, made very nearly credible by being told much in the same fashion as the *Journal of a Parish Clerk.* Although nominally a *novelle,* one of Blicher's most famous stories, *E Bindstouw (In the Spinning Room),* which, like some of his poetry, he wrote in the Jutland dialect, is more description than fiction.

Blicher's technique may be observed best in *Røverstuen (The Robber's Den,* 1827) or in *Hosekræmmeren (The Hosier,* 1829), stories which exhibit pathos, subjectivity, and a reflective, almost didactic tendency. They are a mixture of the exotic and the provincial, the commonplace-didactic and the dramatic, the wistfully pathetic and the entertaining. Blicher is everywhere humane and full of sympathy for his fellow men. "Sorrow," he wrote in "The Family at Avnsbjerg," "is the birthright of man."

The charm of Steen Steensen Blicher's tales is somewhat difficult to explain. Nor can a comparison with any Anglo-American writer do him justice, for to make comparisons is not always to the advantage of the lesser known writer. Perhaps a paragraph—in this case the beginning of "The Robber's Den"—will suffice to give an idea of the mood which Blicher creates.

The islands of Denmark wear such a charming, friendly, peaceful aspect that when we try to imagine their origin, our thoughts are never carried back to any violent convulsion of nature; they do not seem to have been cast up by earthquakes or furrowed by mighty floods, but rather to have risen gently from the falling waters of the sea. The plains are level and wide; the hills are few, small, and gently rounded. No steep bluffs, no deep hollows remind us of the labor pangs of the earth. The forests do not cling wildly to sky-high mountains, but range themselves as hedgerows around the fruitful fields. The brooks do not dash down as frothing waterfalls through deep, dark clefts, but glide along, clear and tranquil, between reeds and bushes.[1]

The counter-currents to the prevailing literature of the first two or three decades of the nineteenth century come to expression not only in Blicher, the Jutland poet of the heath, but in a younger and more urbane contemporary as well, POUL MARTIN MØLLER (1794–1838).

Oehlenschläger's generation had been attracted by the exotic and the distant but had traveled only in Europe; the student-poet Poul Møller felt the same attraction and set off as a ship's clergyman to the Orient after he had taken his theological examination and spent two years in teaching. His finest contributions to literature are the poems he wrote on his journey to China from 1819 to 1821; of these, "Hjemve" ("Nostalgia"), also called "Glæde over Danmark," ("Joy over Denmark"), is the best known.[2] After contrasting the pleasures of the East with those of the North, it concludes:

> If such things be poverty's true measure,
> Silk-clad eastern prince, I understand;
> Then I break my Danish bread at leisure,
> Thanking God, I too exclaim with pleasure,
> "Denmark is a little, beggar land."

Also among the verse written halfway round the world from Denmark are the realistic poems which comprise the little cycle "Scener i Rosenborg Have" ("Scenes in Rosenborg Garden") and which attest not only Møller's

1 From the translation by Hanna Astrup Larsen.
2 Translated by R. S. Hillyer in *A Book of Danish Verse*, 1922, pp. 63–5.

poetic genius and love for Denmark but also the beginnings of a bour-geois realism in Danish poetry. The journey to the Orient instilled in Poul Martin Møller a greater appreciation and understanding of life and conditions in Denmark and burst for him the attractive bubble of the exotic. After his return from China he undertook to write an historical novel after the model of Sir Walter Scott's, but the fragmentary product, the result of several revisions, *En dansk Students Eventyr (The Tale of a Danish Student)* is not an historical novel at all. It is rather a humorous and imaginative conglomeration of personal experiences, ideas, and aphorisms in the guise of prose fiction. Møller wrote little. A successful schoolteacher and later a professor of philosophy, he was probably more influential as an inspiring friend of writers than as an author.

Reflecting on the development of Danish literature in the works of Oehlenschläger and Steffens, Ingemann, Blicher and Poul Martin Møller, we observe a gradual revulsion from the radical theories of the German philosophers of the beginning of the century, a lessening of interest in the Middle Ages and in Scandinavian antiquities, an apparent remission of the turbulence of the Napoleonic era, and at the same time a rise of the bourgeois mentality. Although Danish culture as a whole may to be sure be said to have been moving towards the realization of bourgeois ideals, Oehlenschläger and the writers associated with him are only one factor in the Danish literature of the first half of the nineteenth century, a half century which is deservedly called the Golden Age of Danish literature. These fifty years produced not only Adam Oehlenschläger but the seer, prophet, and poet N. F. S. Grundtvig, the critic and dramatist J. L. Hei-berg, the philosopher Søren Kierkegaard, and the writer who has become Denmark's most famous son: Hans Christian Andersen. Although they were not all popular or influential at exactly the same time, these men were all contemporaries. It should be borne in mind that no matter how much validity the concept of the generation seems to have in the study of literature, writers born within a few years of one another may or may not reach their maturity and years of meaningful literary productivity at the same time. Hans Christian Andersen's first book was published when he was only seventeen, in 1822; while Steen Steensen Blicher was unknown in literature until he was over forty. Christian Winther was born two years before Henrik Hertz, who belongs not to Oehlenschläger's school but to Heiberg's, yet Winther did not produce his best known work until 1855, whereas Hertz wrote his best plays in the thirties.

A golden age of Danish literature! But against what a background of social, political, and economic turmoil it arose! The twentieth-century reader is somewhat taken aback to find how little awareness early nineteenth-century men of literature had of events that seem world-shaking in the eyes of the present-day historian. The first half of the century saw the rise and fall of Napoleon, Denmark's defeat at the hands of the allies, a Danish state bankruptcy (in 1813), the ceding of Norway to Sweden in the following year, revolutions elsewhere in Europe (in 1830 and 1848), the arrival of constitutional government in Denmark (1848), and the Danish-Prussian War (1848–50). To our times it seems strange that wars and economic crises failed to put their indelible mark on the literature produced from 1800 to 1850, and that the principal concern of Danish literature, far from being political, was, if not philosophical, at least spiritual.

CHAPTER VII

Grundtvig

NICOLAI FREDERIK SEVERIN GRUNDTVIG (1783–1872) is a gigantic and unwieldly figure in the history of Danish literature—and of Danish theology, history, politics, and education as well. He is the one figure in the history of nineteenth-century Denmark that it is impossible to avoid and much less to overlook. Whether we consider the men inspired by Henrik Steffens in 1802 and the renaissance of interest in Scandinavian antiquities, or the contemporary theological and philosophical debates, or the periodicals of the time, or the Danish hymnbook, or the Danish constitution, the Danish educational system, or Danish historiography— in every case we meet with the name of Grundtvig. Although Søren Kierkegaard is far better known abroad, Grundtvig exceeds Kierkegaard as an influence on daily life and thought in Denmark. It is however an extremely difficult task to distill the essence of Grundtvig's life and works for the purposes of historical interpretation and to assess his contributions to Danish life. He does not fit into any ready-made category. The young Grundtvig might be considered together with the young Oehlenschläger, but their paths separated at an early date, and they had almost nothing in common after about 1815. In the several fields of intellectual activity where he made his influence felt, Grundtvig was fundamentally dynamic, whereas Oehlenschläger was philosophically and aesthetically static. What is more, Grundtvig remained a living force and an irritant in Danish life and letters until his death in 1872; while it was Oehlenschläger's fate to have a younger contemporary succeed him as the central figure of belletristic endeavor.

Grundtvig was a volatile, explosive person, a voluminous and enthusiastic writer, and a critic vitally interested in many aspects of human existence. For decades he has been a dividing line in Danish intellectual life. He has had vigorous partisans and equally vigorous opponents. Few Danes have been indifferent toward Grundtvig and Grundtvigianism. His thought has brought about a schism in the church and a new direction in education. More than any other man, he aroused national consciousness in Denmark. His provocative religious argumentation has made Danes affirm their own religious convictions either in conformity or non-conformity with his ideas. In a way, he has been to Denmark what Herder has been to Germany, although his influence is more pervasive and more obvious in Denmark than Herder's in Germany.

It is only now, in the middle of the twentieth century, that men are beginning to look with more objectivity upon Grundtvig and to evaluate his life and achievements. Yet an objective evaluation cannot label Grundtvig by genus and species. He was a source of endless energy and ideas, a man of fearless words, and an unbelievably prolific writer, although it cannot be denied that much of what he wrote was impetuously and even carelessly produced.

Within the scope of literary history, Grundtvig, like his younger contemporary Søren Kierkegaard, assumes the rôle of a semi-literary figure. Grundtvig's chief concern was not belletristic, but he did use literature as a medium to express his ideas, and he was an eminent writer of hymns. His hymns, which number about 1400, comprise his poetic contribution to Danish literature; many of them have achieved a lasting place among the songs of Denmark. There is no Dane who does not know such a hymn as "De Levendes Land," of which this is the first stanza:

> I know a land
> Where hair grayeth not, time palsies no hand;
> Where temperate the wave, where burns not the sun;
> Where harvest and springtime are happily one;
> Where evening and morning, in gayest festoon,
> Share the brightness of noon.

Though Grundtvig's *forte* was not imaginative writing, he is not unimportant in the history of literature. He has been an important background figure for many writers who have followed him, and indirectly he has influenced the ethos of many a work in Danish literature through his interpretations of history, his translations from the Latin, Old Norse, Old English, and Old Danish, his encouragement of national and regional sentiments, and above all through his idea of the folk high school.

Grundtvig was one of the young men who heard Steffens' lectures in the autumn of 1802; as he was Steffens' cousin he had an added reason to listen to Steffens' expositions. In his later years, Grundtvig ascribed to Steffens a great influence in moulding his life, but from documentary evidence provided by Grundtvig's letters and early works, we deduce that Oehlenschläger actually meant more to Grundtvig than did Steffens, whose lectures Grundtvig, according to his own testimony, did not fully comprehend. In the foreword to his *Verdens Krønike (World Chronicle,*

1812) Grundtvig retrospectively analyzed his own literary origins; he wrote:

> It was Steffens who first made me realize that history had a meaning. I did not believe a word he said... but the idea of the unity of various eras with Christ as a central point nevertheless made its way into my soul—and was revived after several years when I found similar thoughts in my beloved Schiller.

Although Grundtvig may err in ascribing the awakening of his historical consciousness to Steffens, he has come close to giving a key to the central ideas of his own thought by stressing his awareness of the meaning of history and at the same time suggesting his almost mystical reverence for the Saviour. If we attempted diagramatically to represent the origins of Grundtvig's philosophy, we could draw a connecting line from the German philosopher Schelling to Grundtvig. The line would transect Steffens, for it was to a considerable extent the philosophy of Schelling that Steffens was trying to interpret. Grundtvig regularly argued on a basis of historical justification. For him history taught the supreme lesson and was the arbiter of human action in the present and future. Since history is not merely a body of facts but a matter of interpretation, however, Grundtvig's arguments, which to him seemed historically incontrovertible, were often subjective.

Time and again Grundtvig paid his deep respects to Adam Oehlenschläger, prizing in particular Oehlenschläger's poetic insight into the past. Not Oehlenschläger's poems *(Digte)* of 1803, but the collected works *(Poetiske Skrifter)* of 1805, and especially the drama *Hakon Jarl,* aroused Grundtvig's enthusiastic admiration. In Grundtvig's estimation these works were written with divine inspiration. Oehlenschläger had, opined Grundtvig, "done more for Christianity than the apologetic works of all time." In considering his own possible abilities as a dramatist, Grundtvig stated in *Danne-Virke* for 1816: "if I were to write a Scandinavian tragedy it would at best be a copy of *Hakon.*"

The inspiration for Grundtvig's first significant work, *Nordens Mytologi (Scandinavian Mythology,* 1808), was Oehlenschläger's *Poetiske Skrifter,* but Grundtvig's predilection for Old Norse literature antedated Steffens' lectures, as he noted in his diary in December, 1806. His interest had been aroused by reading P.F. Suhm's history of Denmark; what Steffens said about the *Nibelungenlied* excited his imagination still more. By 1806 Grundtvig was seriously interested in Old Norse antiquities and he had become increasingly aware of the treasures preserved in the Old Icelandic manuscripts. In that year he wrote his first article on the

Oehlenschläger reading from his own works. Drawing by Wilhelm Marstrand.
Grundtvig is supporting his head on his hand. Hans Christian Andersen is taking snuff.
Carsten Hauch is wearing a skullcap. Bertel Thorvaldsen, the sculptor, is asleep.

N. F. S. GRUNDTVIG
Painting by C. A. Jensen, 1831.

Edda and planned a series of poems on Scandinavian mythology, while he was reading Fichte, Schelling, and Schiller. "I want to transform the entire North into historical tales," he wrote in his diary. He felt that he had been called to be an interpreter of the North and of Northern antiquities. Grundtvig was aware of the conflict which the introduction of Christianity had caused and of the lost values in the old indigenous culture. He was eager to revive what had been lost, without compromising the Christian faith which was a part of his concept of life. He was more than an antiquarian and more than a writer seeking a new source of material in the past. For him there was usefulness and importance in awakening his people to what he felt to be original and Danish. In a way, the old struggle between paganism and Christianity was revived in Grundtvig.

Nordens Mytologi is an enthusiastic retelling of Old Norse mythology with an eye to the dramatic possibilities of the material. It is, however, difficult for the reader to extricate Grundtvig himself from the myths, for the retelling is often subjective. The myth was Grundtvig's element. Here as elsewhere, he was convinced of the practical application of a myth. For him the myth was no mere ornamental or poetic device but a profound symbol through which it was possible to approach universal truths and to transcend the limitations of logic and uninspired human thinking. In the myth there was at least a spark of the divine. He who comprehended the myth therefore saw a facet of the divine. Not a clear logical structure but a myth was for Grundtvig the supreme achievement of the creative mind. Because Scandinavian antiquity possessed a wealth of myths, an insight into the divine and the infinite might, he argued, also be obtained through a comprehension of Scandinavian mythology. Myth permitted man to understand what otherwise could not be understood, and myth gave to the past and to traditions a plastic reality and provided a defensible basis for what otherwise might be considered an irrational and emotional epistemology. This was Grundtvig's attitude as a poet, and as a translator, mythologist, and historian. Grundtvig's continual use of the myth and its handmaiden, the metaphor, make him anything but a man of simple ideas or an author who is easily interpreted. Like the great myths of the Bible or the Elder Edda, Grundtvig's writings from *Nordens Mytologi* onward incite his readers again and again to a reinterpretation and discussion of the substance of his words. In the introduction to the second *Nordens Mythologi,* which he issued in 1832, Grundtvig explained that, in contradistinction to many contemporary students of mythology, who were interpreting the old mythology as symbolical of natural phenomena or physical elements, he took the myth to be a symbol of life.

Despite the quantity of doggerel which it contained, the first version of *Nordens Mytologi* was well received. It was followed less than two years later by *Optrin af Kæmpelivets Undergang i Nord (Scenes from the Decline of Heroism in Scandinavia)*, dramatic conversations which suggest Oehlenschläger's style. The work was introduced by a dedicatory poem to Oehlenschläger and the foreword bore the date of Oehlenschläger's thirtieth birthday. Grundtvig was no Oehlenschläger, however, and the book was not very successful. As one of Grundtvig's biographers, F. Rønning, writes, "when Palnatoke speaks, we hear Grundtvig." As an antiquarian Grundtvig henceforth was a more critical and synthetic writer. He became a guide to the realm of the Scandinavian past, whereas Oehlenschläger had been a herald who helped to awaken his countrymen to a consciousness of that past.

Grundtvig was always more concerned with content than form, with ethos than expression, and with myth than logic. His attitude is indicated by an early entry in his diary: "whatever bears the stamp of the eternal is poetry." This is fundamentally an unaesthetic standpoint and serves to explain the fact that Grundtvig showed remarkably little interest in the poets and poetry of his own time.

Grundtvig bespeaks a reaction against the predominant literary taste of the late eighteenth century. As early as 1816, in the periodical *Danne-Virke,* Grundtvig pronounced himself antagonistic not only to the literature of the eighteenth century but to the century as a whole. He was, he wrote, "opposed to the eighteenth century on every count except technology." He rejected novels and *à la mode* plays and was particularly annoyed by the works of Christoph Martin Wieland, who (as we already have noted) commanded great respect in the Danish periodical literature of the late eighteenth century. The works of Sterne, Fielding, and Smollett, which Ewald, Baggesen, and Rahbek had admired, he called ludicrous and dirty. He spoke with admiration of Schiller, who (it is of interest to recall) was not only an able author of historical dramas but himself a professional historian. He had praise for Goethe—"the brightest mind in Germany"—but in 1827 he was to pronounce Goethe an enigma. He lauded Kant, Lessing, and Herder. He sympathized with Fichte, but despite his early attraction to the so-called Romantic philosophers, he came to despise Schelling, Schleiermacher, and their "natural philosophy." Grundtvig admired Rousseau because Rousseau had started the battle which he himself was to continue against intellectualism and, at least nominally, the university, a battle which eventually was to engender the folk high school.

Despite his many dislikes in the realm of literature, Grundtvig was keenly aware of the power of poetry and he debated with himself the possibility of experimenting with various literary genres. Besides his essay into dramatic conversations (the *Optrin*), he planned a series of mythological poems and a history of Scandinavia. He soon became aware of his facility in writing poetry and he subsequently produced vast amounts of verse, not only hymns but also didactic epic poetry and occasional verse. In later life Grundtvig put not only Scandinavian but also ancient and Biblical history into verse, so that it is possible to acquaint oneself with the rudiments of world history through the medium of his didactic poetry.

Stylistically considered, Grundtvig may be called baroque. His resonant metaphorical language reminds one of the sonorous Baroque poetry of Thomas Kingo, and as a matter of fact Grundtvig undertook to rewrite a number of Kingo's hymns. Figures of speech abound in Grundtvig to the point of confusion. He did not try to be subtle, and in the first instance he was frequently emotional rather than lucid. Many of his poems are unpolished and many of his rhymes slipshod. He sometimes gives the impression of an irrepressible poetic machine. The urgency of his poetic rapture nevertheless did not preclude the production of forceful poetry which found, and still finds, readers and admirers. Grundtvig also undertook to translate Saxo and Snorri Sturluson into Danish. His translations occupied him for about eight years; they were begun in 1813 and were published between 1818 and 1822. They are in a popular, colloquial tone; Grundtvig often took considerable freedom with the text. While he may be adversely criticized for not having translated exactly, the fact remains that Grundtvig's translations made the works of Saxo and Snorri come to life and thereby contributed to the renewed appreciation of medieval Scandinavian literature. Of especial interest to the English-speaking world is Grundtvig's translation of *Beowulf*, in 1820. Grundtvig was the first scholar to call attention to the significance of the Old English poem, and the revival of *Beowulf* can be ascribed directly to his concern with it. He visited England several times. The summers of the years 1829, 1830, and 1831 he spent examining Old English manuscripts. In 1830 he published in London the plan of a "Bibliotheca Anglo-Saxonica" "for the publication of the most valuable Anglo-Saxon manuscripts," but the proposed series did not appear.

At the same time that Grundtvig was translating from the Icelandic of

Snorri, the Latin of Saxo, and the Old English of *Beowulf,* he continued to be prolific in other fields. His production of hymns, although uneven in quality and quantity, was continuous, and he wrote numerous poems, articles, sermons, and polemics. From 1816 to 1819 he wrote and edited the periodical *Danne-Virke,* which became a repository for his opinions on literature, the church, the state, and the school. In 1832 he published what ostensibly was a second edition of *Nordens Mytologi,* but which in reality was a new work that endeavored by means of symbolic interpretation to emasculate Old Norse mythology and make it compatible with the ecclesiastical point of view.

Although evidence of Grundtvig's Christian convictions is discernible in all his writings, including the early works pertaining to Old Norse mythology, it was not until about 1810 that he himself became painfully conscious of the religious convictions which were to throw him into a theological maelstrom from which he never emerged. After 1810 Grundtvig was less the writer and poet than he was the theologian and thinker; but despite his inward struggle to answer the ultimate questions of human existence through the application of Christian faith, he never abandoned his interest in Germanic antiquities. While Grundtvig's interest in both Christianity and Old Norse mythology at times may seem incompatible, for Grundtvig the two religions possessed a mystical unity or a common mystical root which permitted logical conclusions to be transcended. For Grundtvig, Christianity in the North was great and positive for the very reason that it had been preceded by an indigenous mythology and by the life and culture of the Viking Age. The relation between Christianity and paganism is now hazily, now clearly expressed in his thought.

Both the weakness and the strength of much of what Grundtvig wrote depended upon his originality and his independence. If he had confidence in an opinion, he expressed it vociferously. If he were in doubt, he expressed his doubts so that discussion might ensue. His readiness to speak and criticise others led him into polemics against some of his leading contemporaries. A seemingly endless series of pamphlets came from his pen. In contrast to so many of his literary contemporaries, Grundtvig was also concerned with political problems, with current events, and with the burning issues of the day. In 1815, for example, Grundtvig wrote a book of 184 pages against Napoleon (who had been Denmark's ally). In 1848 he issued a flurry of anti-German publications, evoked by the war with Prussia. If Grundtvig was in many ways a reactionary, he was nevertheless not behind the times. In his own way, he was "Denmark's mirror," to use a Grundtvigian metaphor.

He was a consistent nationalist. His national pride was great. He was convinced that "none of the peoples of modern Europe are so rich in the realm of the spirit" as the Danes (*Danne-Virke,* 1816). In his so-called literary testament, which he wrote in 1827, after he had been sentenced to censorship for life,[1] he declared: "to be a Danish and at the same time a Scandinavian writer and nothing else in the world, that was my burning wish when I came of age." He characterized his own efforts as a fight against "that which was without spirit" and "that which was anti-Scandinavian." "I serve," he wrote in 1827, "the spirit of the Bible, of History, and of the North."

The Bible, history, and the North were also inherent in the pedagogical ideas of the older Grundtvig, ideas which have made his name most widely known both at home and abroad. His first essay into pedagogy was an address (in 1837) to the Norwegians on the desirability of a Norwegian people's college and the possibility of a Scandinavian university. It was soon followed by his plan to erect a "school for life" in Sorø. Grundtvig wanted to abandon the program of the classical *gymnasium* and establish a school of "the living word" that would do more to fill the needs of young people in daily life. He believed that the mother tongue should be stressed rather than Latin, and that a knowledge of Danish history and literature was more significant for a Dane than a knowledge of mathematics and other abstract subjects. When he first made public mention of it, he stated that he had nurtured the idea of a "folk high school" for many years. In the introduction to the revised *Nordens Mythologi* of 1832, he elucidated his concept of popular enlightenment, a concept which was pretty much at cross-purposes with what generally had been called enlightenment. By 1840 his ideas had become more explicit and the direction of his thought more pronounced, as he pleaded for what he identified as the historic-poetic school. Here as elsewhere, Grundtvig remained the prophet and the seer rather than the initiator of practical reform. His ideas lay fallow for a decade before they were tested by Christian Flor and Kristen Kold, the educational pioneers who established the first "folk high schools" along the lines suggested by Grundtvig, and who therewith became the progenitors of the folk high school movement which has been influential in Scandinavia and especially in Denmark during the last hundred years.

Whereas the older Grundtvig's theological ideas, with their stress on the sacraments of baptism and communion, have cleft the Danish state church, so that one branch within the church is known as the Grundtvig-

1 A result of having been convicted and fined for not respecting the law of the freedom of the press. Grundtvig was released from the strictures of censorship in 1838.

ian, his philosophical and practical ideas are the heritage of the folk high school. Not that Grundtvig ever developed any sort of formal or systematic philosophy. In fact, some of his ideas, expressed at different times, are incompatible with one another, but his opinions are a source of inspiration for Danes who accept his synthesis of Christianity and nationalism. At the folk high schools thousands of young Danes have learned to appreciate their country's culture, its history and its literature, so that, in the long run, Grundtvig's contribution has been a substantial one in making Denmark the highly literate nation it is today.

Grundtvig's ideas of education stand in contradistinction to his own life, for although he decried the "black school," i.e., the university with its scholarship and its books, he was himself an academically trained scholar devoted to his studies and his books. This paradox he himself recognized, at least to some extent, for he aptly characterized himself as "half skald and half bookworm." Throughout his life, in his hymns, in his mythology, and in his pedagogical thinking, he tried to synthesize the national and the Christian. It was his intent to arouse national consciousness and to reawaken to vital Christianity. He was given to the didactic principle.

Since content was more important to him than form, a discussion of Danish literature by genres might not make clear his stature in Danish literary history. For Grundtvig, the delineation of an ideal and the way to the ideal were important. He was a visionary poet, but he was not an esthete. His point of view was diametrically opposed to that of his contemporary Johan Ludvig Heiberg, who was the moderator of Danish literature during Grundtvig's middle years.

CHAPTER VIII

Aesthetic Irony. Heiberg and His School. Søren Kierkegaard

While Oehlenschläger continued to bear his poet's laurels until his death at mid-century, JOHAN LUDVIG HEIBERG (1791–1860), taking his bearings by the work of his slightly older contemporary, started off in a different direction and soon assembled about his person many of the younger writers who could not find satisfaction in the literature Oehlenschläger and Ingemann represented and who were aloof from the sort of thinking that engaged Grundtvig. A versatile aesthetician in Danish literary history, and himself both a poet and a critic, Johan Ludvig Heiberg overcame the so-called Romantic School and reëstablished a literature which was aesthetic rather than enthusiastic, topical rather than retrospective, and satirical rather than sentimental. He came to represent the triumph of irony over enthusiasm and of sophistication over naïveté, and to assume in Danish literature the position of a literary *pontifex maximus*.

The son of Peter Andreas Heiberg and Thomasine Buntzen (later the Countess Gyllembourg) and for two years a foster child of the Rahbeks at "Bakkehuset," Heiberg had early come to know the literary circles in Copenhagen. He chose an academic career, and when still in his twenties wrote a doctoral dissertation on Calderon.

Although Heiberg, like the other young writers of the early nineteenth century, at first accepted the works of the older generation as models, it was soon eminently clear that Heiberg had an original mind which followed its own course. The shift is clearly seen in his *Julespøg og Nytaarsløjer* (*Christmas Fun and New Year's Jesting*, 1817) which ostensibly was a continuation of Oehlenschläger's *St. Hansaften-Spil*, but which evolved from a parody into a satirical phantasy and an ironic comedy that suggests Oehlenschläger's German contemporary Ludwig Tieck's *Der gestiefelte Kater*. The play is in three parts. In part one, Heiberg parodies Oehlenschläger and satirizes B. S. Ingemann. In the second part, called the "Intermezzo," Heiberg unleashes a dramatic irony which breaks down the pattern of the traditional drama. The poet appears on the stage, and as the action progresses, it becomes more and more difficult to distinguish between what is happening on the stage, and what is happening off-stage within and without the theater. Harlequin himself produces a comedy within the comedy in which a boot, a glove, and other fantastic characters play the leading rôles. The high point of confusion is achieved by a fire said to be off-stage—a fire which actually is only a scene in Harlequin's play, but which is differently interpreted by the audience, the on-stage audience, and the players in the play within the play. *Julespøg og Nytaarsløjer* is a literary satire and a literary drama, too ambitious for presentation on the stage in the form in which it was written. Besides including a parody of Ingemann's early production, it includes a very clever pastiche of Holberg.

Heiberg's ridicule of Ingemann offended N. F. S. Grundtvig, who therefore criticised Heiberg. As a rebuttal, Heiberg published a ruthlessly satirical *ABC,* in which he called Grundtvig a boor, and a priest whom Satire could make the most of. The lines were becoming drawn between the critical camps, and it was clear that Heiberg stood for certain theoretical principles which he was not afraid to defend. He ridiculed Grundtvig and Ingemann; he defended the classical German and French drama; and he admired Holberg. Heiberg was no mere litterateur who, like Rahbek, conquered by quantity rather than quality, or who wanted to embrace and support all the products of the Danish muse. On the contrary, he was oriented in contemporary French and German literature and philosophy and he judged severely the products of other men's pens. That he may be said to have had a right to do, for his own work was a significant contribution to the literature of the times. Heiberg was self-contained and certain of his judgments. Though he was far from being an eighteenth-century rationalist, he had nothing of the mystic in him. He possessed rather some of the phantasy and the irony of an E. T. A. Hoffmann.

After visiting his exiled father in Paris 1819–21, the young Dr. Heiberg became lecturer in Danish at the University of Kiel. At first unattracted to German philosophy, he became a convinced Hegelian while in Kiel in 1824—according to his own testimony, suddenly and by intuition—and he returned to his homeland filled with some of the zeal of a reformer. "My taste," he wrote in 1826, "is correct."

After an essay into Hegelian speculative philosophy, Heiberg again turned his attention to belles-lettres. He became the central figure in Danish literature and criticism from about 1825 until about 1840, by virtue of his ability as a publicist, the reliability of his judgments, and his advocacy of new genres, coupled with an ironic attitude fostered by Hegel's philosophy. Under his aegis, several prominent Danish writers entered the lists of literature. Among them were two authors who subsequently achieved world renown: Søren Kierkegaard and Hans Christian Andersen.

Although Heiberg's interests were by no means limited to the stage—he was at one time or another a philologist, an historian, and a student of astronomy—the stage was and remained his principal concern. He introduced into Danish literature a new type of musical drama or comedy, the so-called vaudeville, which at first met with a great deal of adverse criticism. Heiberg felt called upon to defend his position as a progenitor of the new genre; to this end he published a critical essay entitled *Om Vaudevillen som dramatisk Digtart* (*On the musical comedy as a dramatic genre,* 1826). This essay, his most significant theoretical exposition, vigorously attacked dilettantism and took great pains to establish the so-called vaudeville as a genre separate from the opera bouffe or the play. In so doing he expressed his admiration for Kleist, Schiller, and Goethe, and cited Holberg at great length, but was contemptuous of the newest German literature (incidentally, including the Austrian dramatist Grillparzer's *Die Ahnfrau*). As the most dangerous bunglers of all he labeled those writers who put arbitrariness in the place of reason and replace objective necessity with subjective fancies. Heiberg's arguments were convincing to many contemporaries and, as a consequence, the new type of comedy which hitherto had seemed to many to be a profanation of the Royal Theater, came to be accepted. As a result of Heiberg's success, both dramatically and dialectically, the genre of the "vaudeville" was subsequently employed by many other poets, including even Adam Oehlenschläger. Heiberg's musical comedies, i.e., "vaudevilles," were very well received by Copenhagen audiences, a fact to which Heiberg pointed with pride; for, said he, to be effective, literature must have a public; a play without a public would be like a shoemaker without customers. Although he himself often seemed preoccupied with German literature and German thought, he complained that the Germans had been mimics of other nations and that in imitating the Germans the Danes therefore were only the mimics of mimics.

Heiberg's concern with dramatic theory found pungent expression in an exchange of ideas with the German poet and dramatist Friedrich Hebbel in 1843. The clash with Hebbel showed Heiberg to have passed the high point of his influence. He underrated the new drama and its spokesman, who was himself a vigorous playwright and who, far more than Heiberg, was to make a lasting impression in the history of the stage. Heiberg's zenith was reached about 1828, when he was editing the critical periodical *Kjøbenhavns flyvende Post.* It was in 1828 that his work

Elverhøj (Elfinhill) was chosen in preference to a work by Oehlenschläger to be performed on the occasion of a wedding in the Danish royal family. Although it lacked the prevailing irony and satire that most of Heiberg's other works possessed, *Elverhøj* represented a victory of the new aestheticism over the "Romantic school." Heiberg was subsequently a figure to be reckoned with in the administration of the Royal Theater (where he held a series of positions), but in the popular mind his prestige did not equal Oehlenschläger's.

Despite the fact that *Elverhøj* was produced on command and written in a hurry, it was not only an immediate but a lasting success. For over a century it has remained the most popular piece on the Danish stage. *Elverhøj* is a skillful blending of elements which have intrinsic and lasting popular appeal: the figure of the most inspiring of the Danish kings, Christian IV, a simple but dignified and touching plot, a ballet and appealing music (by Kuhlau). Its charming union of phantasy and reality continues to delight audiences in Denmark today. It should be seen on the stage to be appreciated; merely reading *Elverhøj* is as unsatisfactory as reading an opera libretto.

Heiberg's literary position was made secure by *Elverhøj,* but he achieved greater literary success by the satirical drama *En Sjæl efter Døden (A Soul After Death)* which was published in *Nye Digte (New Poems,* 1841), on the occasion of the author's fiftieth birthday. Despite many allusions to local conditions, the ethos of the drama is universal, and it is worthy of being considered a Danish contribution to world literature.[1] The deceased, who, according to the chorus of the bereaved, was a worthy man, a faithful husband, a loving father, an upright friend, and a citizen of virtue, actually represents the essence of mediocrity. In life, he chose the line of least resistance, and never made any real contribution. He has, as he explains to St. Peter, always honestly made his way; he has never coveted his neighbor's goods, and he has made money perseveringly. But this is not enough to admit him to Heaven, for he has never grasped the essential idea of Christian doctrine nor tried to practice a Christian way of life, and St. Peter sends him on to the classical heaven to try his luck. There the soul converses with Aristophanes, whom he tells of his interest in the freedom of the press and of the anonymous letters he has sent to Copenhagen newspapers. To the soul's query where he should make himself at home in the realm of the blessed, the Greek poet replies curtly, "Soul, you go to Hell." Continuing his wandering, the soul meets

---

1 It has been translated only into Swedish.

a very pleasant gentleman with whom he is favorably impressed. The stranger—it is Mephistopheles—bids him welcome to a realm which has no prerequisites for entry, and gives him a description of the realm—or, rather, a description of contemporary Copenhagen. The soul is charmed, although Mephisto warns that it is the "realm of tediousness; one yawns a lot down here." When the soul finds out to whom he has been speaking and in what realm he is, he is shocked, and it takes some persuasion to overcome his prejudice against Hell. At the suggestion of Mephistopheles, the soul looks around Hell; not only is he pleased with what he sees, but he comes to feel that he has found his rightful place. He is proud to devote eternity to helping the Danaïdes fill a bottomless vessel; it is inspiring "to be able to coöperate toward a common goal" and "to lend a hand to such an endless, mighty task." Heiberg's condemnation of the soul is spoken indirectly by Death, who quotes St. Peter to a dying actor:

> You disgraced your specialty, your office;
> Were a poor poet, a poor carpenter,
> A poor minister or chimney sweep.

Heiberg's periodical *Kjøbenhavns flyvende Post (Copenhagen's Flying Mail,* 1827–28, 1830; continued under the title *Interimsblade,* 1834–37) was primarily a literary journal concerned with the theater. It may be viewed as a connecting link between the historical-exotic direction in Danish literature—the school of Oehlenschläger and his followers—and the aesthetic-ironic direction with its penchant for Hoffmannesque phantasy. The periodical, that is to say Heiberg, engaged in feuds with Oehlenschläger and Carsten Hauch, but also published numerous contributions from hands as different as Hans Christian Andersen and Christian Winther. The paper bears the imprint of Heiberg's critical and aesthetic spirit, but at the same time admits its indebtedness to August Wilhelm Schlegel, Ludwig Tieck, Schiller, and Goethe, who were some of the very writers who had inspired Steffens and Oehlenschläger.

It was in *Kjøbenhavns flyvende Post* that the new popular literature which we shall view as representative Danish bourgeois eclecticism made its appearance, with the anonymous *En Hverdagshistorie (An Everyday Story)* by Heiberg's mother, then the Countess GYLLEMBOURG (1773–1856). This and succeeding tales from her pen, all published under the aegis of her son, made her one of the most widely-read writers of the day. Charming without being sentimental, realistic and evidencing considerable psychological insight, her novels delighted her son's contemporaries. They can still be read as good entertainment, as well as a picture of the times. For all their deference to the seriousness and the rights of passion, they epitomize a stolid early Victorian view of life, which accepted existence within the limitations of conventional society.

Heiberg's place in literary history is also closely identified with that of his wife JOHANNE LUISE, née PÄTGES, (1812–90), the most celebrated actress the Danish stage has ever had. Not a little of Heiberg's dramatic success may be ascribed to the talents of his wife, for whom he created many rôles both before and after their marriage in 1831, when she was only 19. Incidentally, Johanne Luise Heiberg also wrote for the theater; her best known work is the light vaudeville *En Søndag paa Amager* (*A Sunday at Amager*, 1848), but her original efforts are otherwise of no consequence. She is better remembered as the author of a long memoir, *Et Liv gjenoplevet i Erindringen* (*A Life Relived in Memory*, 1891–92).

In the last analysis, Heiberg was a transitional figure. In contrast to Hebbel, he was not a harbinger of the direction literature was to take in the nineteenth century. Although several of his plays—notably, *Elverhøj, En Sjæl efter Døden*, and the farce *Aprilsnarrene* (*April Fools*, 1826)—still live on the Danish stage, Heiberg's principles have long since been superseded. It is almost as if his aesthetics were a foil for the new generation of 1870, which, with its successful plea for the treatment of social problems in literature, gave to literature a new intellectual content. During his heyday, however, Heiberg's influence was pervasive. With the vaudeville he conquered the Danish stage and forced both his older and younger contemporaries to acknowledge the genre.

No author was more closely identified with Heiberg than Heiberg's friend and fellow dramatist HENRIK HERTZ (1798–1870), known in the English-speaking world of the nineteenth century as the author of *King René's Daughter*. Hertz had an elective affinity with Jens Baggesen, even to the extent of writing in Baggesen's style and using Baggesen's name as a pseudonym in the elegant, satirical, and witty *Gjengangerbreve* (*Letters of a Ghost*, 1830), but Hertz out-Baggesened Baggesen, who never wrote quite as wittily or with quite such a light hand. These satirical letters, which purported to carry on the Baggesen-Oehlenschläger feud of the previous literary generation, were a sensation; they were read by everyone, while their authorship remained a secret for two years. They were directed to Heiberg and Carsten Hauch as representatives of the new and the old, respectively, on the Danish literary scene. Hertz here broke a lance for Heiberg and his aesthetics, and served to make literary partisanship more distinct.

Hertz wrote half a hundred plays, many of them expressly for Heiberg's wife. Aside from *Kong Renés Datter* (written in 1843, first played in 1845), only two of his plays still live: *Sparekassen* (*The Savings Bank,* 1836, published 1840) and *Svend Dyrings Hus* (*Sven Dyring's House,* 1837). In content, these plays are very different from one another. Together, they have made Hertz the third most frequently played Danish dramatist. *Sparekassen,* which is in prose, suggests some of the situations in Holberg's *Political Tinker.* The family Skaarup inherits a small sum and is cajoled into buying a lottery ticket with part of the money. Through a misunderstanding the Skaarups are given to believe that their ticket has won the grand prize of fifty thousand crowns. The world now seems to fall in at their door until the mistake is rectified and the new friends show their true colors; whereupon a foster son, home from America, saves the day. There are all the ingredients of a popular, exciting comedy, and Hertz knew how to make most effective dramatic use of them. As a curiosity, it can be noted that *Sparekassen* was not an immediate success, although it soon won a fixed place in the repertoire of the Royal Theater and has been played regularly ever since.

Hertz was not bound to a single type of drama. Whereas *Sparekassen* plays against a background of daily life in Copenhagen, *Svend Dyrings Hus* is based on medieval folk songs, and *Kong Renés Datter* is identified with knighthood.[1] *Kong Renés Datter,* which is in iambic pentameter, is set in fifteenth-century Provence but contains no more than a suggestion of historical fact. King René's daughter, Iolanthe, who is blind, lives a secluded existence, unaware of her terrible affliction. René finds himself in the impossible situation of having betrothed his daughter to Tristan of Vaudemont, who has never seen Iolanthe and does not know of her blindness. By chance, Tristan comes into Iolanthe's secluded valley, speaks with her, falls in love with her, and, incidentally, gives her an inkling that she is blind. By virtue of love that is requited and because of the guidance of a Moorish physician, Iolanthe regains the vision she had lost in infancy. The highly sentimental plot complied perfectly with mid-nineteenth-century taste. With Fru Heiberg in the title rôle, *Kong Renés Datter* was a great success on the stage. It was revived at intervals of about ten years until the middle of the 1920's.

When one considers the pervading sentimentality of *Kong Renés Datter,* and the medieval setting of the play, it may seem a little puzzling that Hertz was such a faithful henchman of Heiberg rather than a member of Oehlenschläger's school. There are however essential differences between

---

1 There are at least three translations into English, some published several times, of *Kong Renés Datter.* The first translation, by Jane Frances Chapman, appeared in London in 1845. The last edition of Edmund Phipps' translation (first published in 1848) appeared in 1922.

Oehlenschläger and Hertz. Oehlenschläger is more virile than Hertz; consider, for example, the dramatic power of *Hakon Jarl*. Despite his Aladdin-nature, Oehlenschläger gave some of his plays a moral substance that Hertz's totally lack. Hertz was above all a playwright and a versifier rather than a dramatist and a poet. The easy, lilting rhythm of some of Hertz's poetry has fixed his name on the roster of Danish poets. His verse is varied in nature, sometimes lyrical, sometimes reflective, and sometimes imitative of the Danish folk-song. No comprehensive anthology of Danish poetry would be acceptable without his "Posthuset i Hirschholm" ("The Post-Office in Hirschholm"), written after the fashion of the immortal Swedish singer Carl Michael Bellman and dedicated to Heiberg's wife.

While in the world of letters outside Denmark Johan Ludvig Heiberg is little known except for his criticism of the eminent German dramatist Friedrich Hebbel, he remains a key figure in the history of Danish literature. What is more, both Søren Kierkegaard's and Hans Christian Andersen's literary origins are closely identified with Heiberg. Just as a sharp critical faculty and an ironical bent were predominant characteristics in Heiberg, criticism and irony set the tone in the early works of Kierkegaard (1813–55), and Andersen (1805–75). Both men were keenly aware of Heiberg's dogmas and doctrines; both entered the literary arena in Copenhagen as contributors to Heiberg's journal *Kjøbenhavns flyvende Post,* Andersen with several poems and a fragment of the *Fodrejse,* his most ironically humorous work, and Kierkegaard with an anonymous article on woman's place in society. Andersen later imitated Heiberg's vaudevilles and continually sought Heiberg's favor. One volume of the *Eventyr (Fairy Tales)* he dedicated to Heiberg's wife, and another to Mme. Gyllembourg, Heiberg's mother. Kierkegaard's magisterial thesis treated the concept of irony while *Enten-Eller (Either-Or)* debated the question of the aesthetic versus the ethical.

The interrelationship of Heiberg, Andersen, and Kierkegaard is the more striking when we note that Kierkegaard's first book, *Af en endnu Levendes Papirer (From the Papers of a Person still Alive,* 1838) was a criticism of Andersen's novel *Kun en Spillemand (Only a Fiddler,* 1837) and that in 1846 Kierkegaard published a lengthy review *(En literair Anmeldelse)* of a story edited by Heiberg but written "by the author of *En Hverdags Historie,*" i.e., Mme. Gyllembourg. Kierkegaard's *Krisen og en Krise i en Skuespillerindes Liv (The Crisis and a Crisis in an Actress's Life),* which appeared anonymously in 1848, alluded to Heiberg's wife.

From the standpoint of the organic development of Danish literature,

Kierkegaard and Andersen may be considered as having evolved from Heiberg's school. Andersen is however so significant and versatile an imaginative writer that he warrants treatment in a separate chapter. Without trying to diminish the reputation of Kierkegaard in the history of theology and philosophy, we shall here briefly review the writings of Søren Kierkegaard insofar as they made literary history.[1]

In his magisterial disputation, in *Enten-Eller,* and in his criticism of Hans Christian Andersen and Mme. Gyllembourg, Kierkegaard was directly concerned with belles-lettres, but he was not primarily a literary figure. Judged by the contents of his works, Kierkegaard was a thinker, a philosopher, a theologian, and an ecclesiastic. He nevertheless enjoys a place in literary history because of his consciousness of form, his style, and his aesthetic interests. Although theological and philosophical in character, much of what he wrote can be read as imaginative literature. *Enten-Eller,* his principal work, is in the form of a novel, and specifically the novel of the late eighteenth century; it has been called an offspring of Goethe's *Wilhelm Meister.* As different as Goethe's view of life was from Kierkegaard's, *Wilhelm Meister,* like *Enten-Eller,* is ostensibly a novel, represents the search for a philosophy of life and culminates in a positive philosophical conviction, which to be sure may be termed more pragmatic than religious. Aside from the fact that Goethe's novel was not primarily a didactic work, there is however an essential difference between Goethe and Kierkegaard as writers. Goethe gave ethos aesthetic, literary form; Kierkegaard used literary form to carry on philosophical and religious arguments. Because of his form and his style, Kierkegaard not only enjoys a special position among philosophers but has been able to appeal to a wider audience than the professional theologian and systematic philosopher.

Kierkegaard's life was as anomalous as his writing. After taking his degree at the University, he never made practical use of his academic training in theology. Whereas his brother, P. C. Kierkegaard, also a theologian, entered the service of the state church and rose to be a bishop, Søren Kierkegaard lived on the means he had inherited from their wealthy father. He was early beset by ethical and religious problems to which he found no satisfactory solutions. In him a docile believer became a fiercely searching theologian who strove to know what is truth and what it is to

---

1 Translations and editions of Kierkegaard's work in English are so numerous that no attempt is made to enumerate them here. It was not until 1935/36, however, that the stream of translations began. Prior to that there existed only one volume of selections from Kierkegaard in English, translated by L. M. Hollander, and published at Austin, Texas, in 1923.

be a Christian. His reflective, intellectual existence, which was a life in a state of tension, made him unable to compromise with bourgeois conventionality and soon led him to withdraw into himself, and to seek a personal relationship with God rather than a social solution of man's existence. His break with the world was symbolized and epitomized by the breaking of his engagement to the young Regine Olsen. The moral justification for this act caused him concern for years afterwards, and he told the story of his engagement with variations many times in his works. Was he guilty or not guilty in acting as he did? The question was perhaps an odd one to be so vital to a philosopher, but it provided an example which his readers could understand. The engagement was the second important moment in Kierkegaard's life. About the first—the "earthquake" of adolescence to which Kierkegaard refers without explanation—we can only guess.

A third moment of great importance was the affair with *Corsaren*—"The Corsair"—Meïr Goldschmidt's critical weekly. The youthful, brilliant, satirical Goldschmidt respected Kierkegaard's works, and consequently spared Kierkegaard alone among the authors in Copenhagen from his critical barbs. Kierkegaard came to feel his position to be intolerable, and, writing under a pseudonym in another journal, he requested criticism by the "Corsair." Goldschmidt promptly replied by ridiculing Kierkegaard in such a way that Kierkegaard could not help but be hurt and driven to rebuttal. Subsequently the "Corsair" went out of existence, as Goldschmidt himself turned to more serious literary expression.

The fourth moment of great consequence in Kierkegaard's life was his break with the state church, occasioned by a funeral sermon in which a deceased bishop who upheld the *status quo* was called a witness of the truth. At this hypocrisy Kierkegaard revolted and broke with organized religion. If the Bishop Mynster had been a witness, then anyone could be a witness; then Christianity had no meaning, and to be a Christian meant only to accept given forms and to say idle words. Kierkegaard's later serious theological publications mark a turn away from literary expression and, while important to an understanding of Kierkegaard, are of little interest to the student of literature. After a flurry of polemics in 1854–55, Kierkegaard died, his life-work completed, at the age of 42. His production had been enormous. His collected works fill 14 thick volumes and his posthumous papers 20 more. The quantity of printed matter which bears Kierkegaard's name is however not as significant as the anomalous nature, the profundity, and the abstruseness of Kierkegaard's work. He who would know and understand Kierkegaard must be prepared to

Thomasine Gyllembourg reading to her son Johan Ludvig Heiberg and his wife Johanne Luise Heiberg. Painting by Wilhelm Marstrand. The painting on the wall is of Fru Gyllembourg as a young woman.

1827.   Nº 66.

Kjøbenhavns

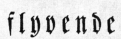

flyvende   Post.

Fredagen den 17de August.

Redigeret af J. L. Heiberg.   Udgiven af Ferdinand Prinzlau.

Aftenen.

(Et Træsnit).

En Aften deilig, som i en Roman!
(For Rimets Skyld, som een i Hindostan).
O Alnaturen til mit Hjerte taler!
Det maa herud: "Ja, ogsaa jeg er Maler."
See, Solen synker i sit røde Blod,
Og Xander suse gjennem Skovens Toppe.
Her slumrer Uskyld født ved Bøgens Rod,
See hvilke fede Bønderdrenge-Kroppe!
Violer dufte fra det unge Græs,
Og hisset vandre Præstens hvide Gjæs.

See hist en gammel Bonde paa sit Øg,
En Fuglestræmme paa en Rocinante!
Nu holder han hist ved den flakke Bøg,
Og tæller Penge af en gammel Vante;
Endnu engang han ret beseer sin Stat,
Og derpaa griber atter Tøilen fat.
Ham Længsel driver mod det elskte Hjem,
Hvor Hytten staaer imellem Rødbehække,
Men ikkun langsomt, langsomt gaaer det frem;
See, hvor han seer mod Skyens Bjergerække.
Dog Phantasus ham følger i hans Rød,
Og viser i det Fjerne et Fad Grød.

Hvor malerisk staaer Fiskerhytten der!
See, Vindvet kneiser med halvtredje Rude.
Hvor gløde dog i Aftensolens Skjær
De halve tre imellem gamle Klude!

Og rundt om Hytten Tjørnehække staae,
Broderede med Strømper og med Sokker,
Og Himlen favner Alt saa klar og blaa,
Mens Fiskerkonen hjem fra Stranden sjokker.

See, hist paa Skrænten staaer en lang Person
Med Ansigtet saa blegt, som salig Werther,
Og med en Næse, stor som en Kanon,
Og Øine bitte smaa, som gule Ærter.
Han synger noget Tydsk med et: "woher?"
Og stirrer derpaa ud i Vesterlide.
Hvorfor mon vel han staaer saalænge der?
Ja Herre Gud! hvor kan man Alting vide?
Dog er det sikkert, har jeg rigtig seet,
En Gal, en Elsker, eller en Poet.

h — —

Den rædselfulde Time.

(Phantasiestück in Callots Manier).

Kom ei Rundetaarn for nær. er det Midnatstide;
Hvad mig nylig hændte der, skal I faae at vide.
Paa Bibliotheket hist er et rart saa silde,
Thi ved Midnat holde der Xander Dands og Gilde.
Jeg om Dagen gik derop for en Bog at laane,
Gik en Smule der omkring, og kom til at baane.
Ingen savned mig; be gik, jeg blev der allene,
Ak, ved selve Tanken end ryste mine Bene!
Længe laae jeg i en Krog uden mindste Spratten;
Da jeg til mig selv nu kom, var det ud paa Natten.

---

*Issue of Heiberg's "Flying Mail" with the first contributions by
Hans Christian Andersen.*

SØREN KIERKEGAARD
Idealized sketch by N. C. Kierkegaard, 1838.

Manuscript title page of Kierkegaard's Either-Or. *(Reduced).*

devote years of study to the products of his pen. We can here but suggest the content and nature of his work.

In recent years Kierkegaard has attracted international attention, especially because of his influence on that direction in modern philosophy called Existentialism. Whether Kierkegaard can be brought into harmony with the thinking of a Heidegger or a Sartre is a question we are not prepared to answer here. Kierkegaard has been studied in Denmark intensely since the last decade of the nineteenth century. Both before and after the first World War he became the object of attention in German philosophical and theological circles, and shortly before the second World War his thought began to penetrate the English-speaking world. There is no doubt that he has achieved a permanent place among philosophers of world stature, but his present popularity is not to be explained as the result of an organic growth of interest in his works. On the contrary, interest in Kierkegaard has been sudden and spasmodic. He himself is perhaps a "stage on life's way" that must be overcome in the progress of the human spirit. His pervading irrationalism, the culmination of philosophical reaction against the rationalism of eighteenth-century enlightenment, finds sympathetic readers in the twentieth century, as men turn bewildered from the destruction of war and the apparent defeat of a rational and social faith, in search of an eternal verity.

Since Kierkegaard is above all the author of *Enten-Eller,* we shall center our attention on that philosophical work, which he wrote in the form of a novel. The book is composite and contains A's papers, B's papers, and "The Diary of a Seducer." The reader is immediately struck by the abundance of pseudonyms, incidentally a characteristic of most of Kierkegaard's writing. *Enten-Eller* is edited by "Victor Eremita," who is publishing "A's" and "B's" papers which he has ostensibly found by accident in an old secretary. "A" has made a copy of papers written by "Johannes," who in turn draws on "Cordelia's" letters. We almost forget —as Kierkegaard wants us to—that Kierkegaard is the author of all this material, that he himself is Victor, A, B, Johannes, and Cordelia. "A's" papers are in a state of chaos; "B's" papers are in perfect order. The papers themselves are thus indicative of two ways of life. "The Diary of a Seducer" is often read independently of *Enten-Eller*. It is a *novelle* in letter and diary form, after the best eighteenth-century models; the story which evolves from the documents is gripping. There was more than the makings of a novelist in Søren Kierkegaard. Of all that he wrote nothing is easier to read than "The Diary of a Seducer," but read by itself it distorts the idea which he was expressing in his indirect and non-rationalistic way in *Enten-Eller,* for the seducer's story is only part of a complex whole. The philosophical question that is put in *Enten-Eller* is this: Should one choose the ethical (B) or the aesthetic (A) way of life? The answer which Kierkegaard gives is: Neither. The only solution, according to Kierkegaard, is to make a "leap" into the religious way of life. This is a paradoxical answer, a begging of the question—but that is characteristic of Kierkegaard. Kierkegaard is a paradox, and the results of his thinking are paradoxical, original, and profound. The reader must not expect a prosaically rational answer to a philosophical question from Kierkegaard. Whether we agree with Kierkegaard or not, or whether we even admire him, he remains provocative.

In the rest of Kierkegaard's production he is frequently concerned with aesthetic as well as philosophical and religious problems, but it is well to remember that in his own "literary testament," *Synspunktet for min Forfatter-Virksomhed (My Point of View as an Author,* written in 1848 but not published until 1859), he characterized himself as a religious writer. His aesthetic concern caused him repeatedly to employ a novelistic form of expression and to synthesize belletristic and philosophical elements.

The consideration of three stages of human development, or three levels of existence, the aesthetic, the ethical(-philosophical), and the religious, lies at the basis of his work; and the most aesthetically inclined of his works *(e.g., Krisen...)* is not unphilosophical. Similarly, profoundly religio-philosophical works from his pen *(e.g., Frygt og Bæven)* are not entirely without narrative qualities; they can at least make use of the parable and therewith touch upon the literary sphere subject to aesthetic criticism. A dash of the ironically humorous is frequently present, as is indicated by many of the titles and pseudonyms which Kierkegaard chose even for serious and essentially religio-philosophical works.

Just as there were three ways of life suggested in *Either-Or,* there are three stages in *Stadier paa Livets Vej (Stages on Life's Way,* 1845) which is a counterpart to *Enten-Eller.* Both books are in the form of novels and both books make use of tales within a tale to a degree of complexity reminiscent of the Chinese puzzle. Ostensibly, *Stages on Life's Way* is a collection of papers gathered and published by one "Hilarius Bookbinder." The fact that the book is divided into three parts serves only to remind us of Kierkegaard's unending debate about aesthetic *vs.* ethical *vs.* religious existence. Part one, "In vino veritas" is noteworthy as a modern symposium that is a willful parallel to Plato's *Symposium.* In it Kierkegaard lets his characters discuss Eros and the nature of woman. The second part of the book—one hesitates to call it a novel—comprises a lengthy statement on marriage and some objections which can be made thereto; while the third part, "Guilty—Not Guilty," ascribed to one "Frater Taciturnus," but consisting principally of a diary written by an hypothetical character, contains a series of tales that present the problem of guilt or lack of guilt under varying circumstances. All in all, this section of the book is symbolical of individual introspection in the abstract, but is incidentally one of the several places where Kierkegaard suggests his relationship to his one-time fiancée.

Of the other, progressively more philosophical, works, at least four should be mentioned as having aroused a good deal of critical attention in the twentieth century. *Gjentagelsen (Repetition)* and *Frygt og Bæven (Fear and Trembling)* were written contemporaneously and were published the same day in October 1843, only nine months after the lengthy *Enten-Eller. Gjentagelsen*'s pseudonymous author is "Constantin Constantius." The ethos of the book is suggested by the title: what is the possibility that there may be repetition? The reader is forced to conclude that aesthetic and ethical repetition is not possible, but is lead to the assumption that repetition in the realm of the religious is possible. Whatever repetition there may be, Kierkegaard believes, takes place within the individual and is not to be ascertained in external occurrences. Kierkegaard's concept and treatment of repetition is brilliant, if not judged from the rationalistic standpoint; he must be given credit for having introduced a new principle into modern thought: that all apparent and attempted repetition is nonetheless not repetition. Although the book itself is difficult reading, it possesses narrative form and is not *prima facie* speculatively abstract. "Constantin Constantius" takes a trip to Berlin in order to seek a repetition of earlier experiences and subsequently invents a "young man" who is caught up in the impossible task of attempting to achieve repetition in a human relationship.

Whereas the young man in *Repetition* finds inspiration in the Book of Job, "Johannes de Silentio," the pseudonymous author of *Frygt og Bæven (Fear and Trembling)* takes as his point of orientation the story of Abraham and Isaac from the Book of Genesis. Here it is the peculiar nature or quality of faith as demonstrated by Abraham which interests Kierkegaard, who undertakes to tell the story of Abraham several ways, as a musician might compose variations on a theme.

Begrebet Angest (The Concept of Dread), which appeared within a few days of *Philosophiske Smuler (Philosophical Fragments)* in 1844, also took up a Biblical theme: original sin. Kierkegaard's point is that the fear of sin, which is essentially irrational, itself causes sin, and the dread of sin is transmitted from generation to generation. Here Kierkegaard assumes the rôle of an experimental psychologist, and if his theological position may be called reactionary, his argument does not fail to find resonance in modern psychological thought.

The *Afsluttende uvidenskabelig Efterskrift (Concluding Unscientific Post-script),* which appeared early in 1846, is of more importance than the work *(Philosophiske Smuler)* to which it nominally is an appendage. Although the book also was published under a pseudonym, "Johannes Climacus," it is entirely a product of speculative religious thought. Kierkegaard champions the idea that truth is subjective and that subjectivity is truth; and he dismisses the various objections which might limit the truth of divine revelation for the individual. Objective and rationalistic considerations no longer have validity or importance. Kierkegaard shows himself to be the asocial anti-rationalist; truth is subjective, and religious truth is a matter for the individual to decide for himself.

Kierkegaard's position was now antithetical to that of Hegel's with regard to the position of the individual *vis-a-vis* the community. These speculative ideas were communicated directly in the *Postscript*; Kierkegaard had therefore moved outside the sphere of belletristic writing.

Although the lives of Grundtvig and Kierkegaard were dedicated to other disciplines than literature, Grundtvig, Kierkegaard, and Hans Christian Andersen outshine the other Danish writers of the nineteenth century. Lesser contemporaries, important as they may have seemed and as important as they intrinsically may be, fade into relative obscurity as the stature of these great and original writers becomes more clearly delineated with the passing of time. Grundtvig, Kierkegaard, and Andersen are read. Consequently, they have become the subjects of scholarly research, as well as central figures in living Danish letters. Even people who do not read Grundtvig and Kierkegaard have opinions about those two iconoclastic and controversial writers. We observe that Grundtvig and Kierkegaard are living agents, who can stir up dissension today, whereas most of their contemporaries have in time become fossils rather than catalysts. Both Grundtvig and Kierkegaard were independent thinkers; neither was affiliated with an established school or party in philosophy or theology. Both were concerned about the course which Christianity had taken within the state church and both tried to create vast patterns of thought. Otherwise they had little in common. They were unlike and shared few ideas. Grundtvig was unstable and dynamic, a man whose attitudes changed radically during his lifetime. Kierkegaard was static and highly charged, and was not ready to give up a philosophical position which he had once taken.

It may seem a far cry from the light vaudeville of Johan Ludvig Heiberg to the profundity of Kierkegaard's writings, but seen from the standpoint both of philosophical and literary history Heiberg and Kierkegaard had common roots. It is significant that Heiberg once encouraged Kierkegaard to be a writer. In the last analysis Kierkegaard rejected the aesthetic way of life; but that he knew it and understood it may indubitably be ascribed to Heiberg.

Søren Kierkegaard was the one of Heiberg's protégés who achieved lasting world fame. Hans Christian Andersen was the other.

CHAPTER IX

Hans Christian Andersen

HANS CHRISTIAN ANDERSEN (1805–75) is known throughout the world today almost exclusively as the author of fairy tales (or *Eventyr,* to use the Danish term), but during his lifetime he was by no means principally concerned with writing tales and still less with writing for children. There could scarcely be a less accurate picture of Hans Christian Andersen than that of a kindly gentleman who devoted himself to writing fairy tales. On the contrary, Andersen was an irascible, ambitious, high-strung, egocentric poet whose life was a series of never-ending crises, and whose foremost literary concern during the first half of his career as a writer was his novels and plays. At first the *Eventyr* were but a minor phase of his writing, and for years they were given little or no attention by Danish critics.

Only in Denmark are his novels, plays, and travel books now read at all. There has been no English edition of any of Andersen's novels for fifty years, although they were early translated into English and fairly widely read in both England and America from 1845 until about 1885. None of Andersen's plays has been translated into English. The last English edition of a travel book by Hans Christian Andersen, *A Poet's Bazaar,* was published in 1881. Contrariwise, the number of editions of translations and versions of the *Eventyr* is legion. Scarcely a single year since 1900 has failed to bring one or more editions of Andersen's tales in English alone.[1]

No critic today doubts that the tales comprise Andersen's great contribution to literature, but in order to understand Andersen, his times, and the literary scene in Denmark while he lived, and in order to make a just evaluation of Andersen's contribution to Danish literature, it is necessary to consider all his works.

Intent upon becoming an actor, Hans Christian Andersen, who had been born into the simplest of homes in Odense, on the island of Funen, came to the Danish capital when in his teens. He managed to appear only a few times as a supernumerary on the stage, but his combination of

---

1 A sixty-page list of Andersen's works in English translation is included in Elias Breds-dorff's *Danish Literature in English Translation. A Bibliography.* Copenhagen, 1950. All but five pages are given to translations of the tales.

helplessness and aggressiveness, clumsiness and poetic promise won for him the favor of several well-to-do and influential citizens, and subsequently the young Andersen was sent to a secondary school in order to make up for some of the worst gaps in his education. He had early been attracted to literature; indeed, when he was seventeen his first literary efforts were printed under the pseudonym of Villiam (for William Shakespeare) Christian (for Andersen himself) Walter (for Walter Scott). The pseudonym was indicative of Andersen's literary inclination and predisposition. At school he now read Goethe and Schiller, Schlegel and Novalis, Hoffmann and Jean Paul, and other German writers, as well as Shakespeare, Scott, and Smollett. His acquaintance with German literature, and especially with the German master of phantasy, E. T. A. Hoffmann, is evident in the work which was Andersen's real literary debut: *Fodrejse fra Holmens Kanal til Østpynten af Amager i Aarene 1828 og 1829 (A Walk from Holmens Canal to the East Point of the Island of Amager in the Years 1828 and 1829)*, a tale which immediately won for Andersen the attention of litterateurs. In substance, the work is a fantastic narrative similar to E. T. A. Hoffmann's *Der goldene Topf*; it may be read with amusement today. In the book, Andersen is openly conscious of Hoffmann, and undertakes his walk armed with a copy of Hoffmann's *Die Elixiere des Teufels*. He also quotes or cites Tieck, Jean Paul, Hölty, Jung-Stilling, Iffland, Kotzebue, Chamisso, Goethe—and even Washington Irving. As different as the *Fodrejse* seems at first glance from Andersen's later tales, one can perceive that here Andersen had without realizing it found his true medium. Yet he was not to return to it until 1835, after seven years' labor at novels, plays, and poems. As in all of Andersen's early works, there are in the *Fodrejse* motifs that again appear in the *Eventyr*.

Johan Ludvig Heiberg was kindly disposed towards the *Fodrejse*. He published a selection from it in *Kjøbenhavns flyvende Post* and reviewed the book when it appeared. Andersen's ironic-fantastic spirit was quite to his taste. Heiberg was later to be very critical of Andersen's plays however, and in his *En Sjæl efter Døden (A Soul after Death)* he let two of the plays be given in Hell.

The early plays, *Kjærlighed paa Nikolai Taarn (Love in St. Nicolai Church Tower*, 1829) and *Agnete og Havmanden (Agnete and the Merman*, 1834) were scarcely meant for the stage; they were only moderately successful. It was not until Andersen wrote *Mulatten (The Mulatto*, 1840) that he was acclaimed as a playwright. A melodramatic work which has some of the pathos of *Uncle Tom's Cabin*, *Mulatten* portrays the evils of slavery, and

pleads for the rights of the mulatto. Andersen voiced the political liberalism of the day and attracted considerable attention and respect,
especially in Sweden. Despite its humanitarian idea, the play drags for
the modern reader, and the plot seems very unlikely indeed. Among his
later plays should be mentioned *Ole Lukøje* (*The Sandman,* 1850); *Liden
Kirsten* (*Little Kirsten,* 1846), a sentimental operetta which lives by virtue
of its having been set to music by one of Denmark's foremost composers,
J. P. E. Hartmann; the comedy *Den Nye Barselstue* (*The New Lying-in
Room,* 1845, published 1850), a parallel to Holberg's comedy *Barselstuen* ;
and finally Andersen's most popular play, *Fuglen i Pæretræet* (*The Bird in
the Pear Tree,* 1842, printed 1854). Andersen's relation to the theater was
not a happy one. He was in constant fear of having his plays rejected by
the theater's directors or booed by the audience, as indeed they sometimes were.

With his novels Andersen won an audience in both Denmark and Germany, and the novels were considered his chief genre. As late as 1843,
seven years after he had begun publishing the tales, a German edition of
Andersen's complete works, so-called, did not include the tales. In the
twentieth century this seems strange indeed, because the novels have lost
much of their interest for modern readers. We still can enjoy the remarkable descriptive passages with which Andersen's prose abounds, but the
sentimentality which pervades the novels, the looseness in their structure,
and the improbability of their plots demand a certain tolerance of a reader
used to the European novel since Zola and Galsworthy.

Improvisatoren (*The Improvisator,* 1835), Andersen's first novel, has been
compared with Mme. de Staël's *Corinne,* and justly so. Not only did
Andersen read Mme. de Staël while he was writing *Improvisatoren* in
Munich, but his novel might, like *Corinne,* also have born the subtitle
"Ou l'Italie." The plot is subordinate to lengthy descriptions of the
Italian landscape, of Rome and its festivals, and of life in Italy as Andersen
had observed it. Similarly, the two novels *O. T.* (1836) and *Kun en Spillemand* (*Only a Fiddler,* 1837) are predominantly descriptive of life in Denmark, despite the rudimentary and overdramatic plots by which he tried
to unify each of them. All three novels have numerous explanatory foot-
notes of an historical-cultural nature. It was not unreasonable that *O. T.*
and *Only a Fiddler* should have been published in English under the
common title "Life in Denmark."

The factualism and sentimentalism of the novels stand in sharp contrast to the Hoffmannesque fictions in the *Fodrejse* of 1829. For one who
is familar with the details of Andersen's life, the novels are full of auto-

biographical material. But their metaphors and pictures also often suggest the later tales. From a comparison of the novels with the *Eventyr,* it is evident that Andersen's *Eventyr*-style was developing even while he was writing novels. Motifs later found in the *Eventyr* can be observed in embryo in the novels, especially in *Improvisatoren.*

Improvisatoren is autobiographical in two ways; it reflects Andersen's own experiences in Italy as well as his own life and personal problems in Denmark. This fact is not essential to the understanding and appreciation of the novel—perhaps it is detrimental—but it gives the novels some historical validity and therewith an added interest for modern readers. Parallels to Andersen's relations with the Collin family in Copenhagen, the family in which he was almost an adopted son, are unmistakable in his portrayal of the relation of the hero of *Improvisatoren* to the family of an Italian patron in Rome. The feelings engendered in the hero, Antonius, when his poetry is adversely criticized are the same which Andersen had had under similar circumstances, and which he expressed first in his diary and later in his autobiography.

That Andersen identified himself with his leading characters or that he portrayed in them the mental struggles and tortures which plagued him is both understandable and defensible, but he himself was always on guard against such a critical identification, and he spoke disdainfully of the fact that critics probably would find a prose work he had written autobiographical. Actually, the urge to portray his own life was very strong in Andersen. In fact, he wrote not one but several autobiographies. Unfortunately the most widely circulated autobiography in English translation is *The True Story of My Life* (first published 1847), translated by Mary Howitt from an incomplete, intermediary autobiography which originally appeared in German. The complete autobiography (to the year 1855) is, however, available in an older edition (several printings, 1871–80) and in a new edition published in 1954.[1] The autobiographies and the various prose works all tell of Andersen's anxious search for security and certainty, and of his belief that he was being mistreated and persecuted by his friends as well as by the critics. He was so concerned with slights, imaginary and real, and was so sensitive, that in his letters and autobiographies he created a myth of himself as the unrecognized poet, in short the myth of "the ugly duckling," that has come in the popular mind to be symbolical of his life. In reality Andersen was not treated more severely by the critics than were other contemporary poets; he

---

1 *The Fairy Tale of My Life* [Transl. W. Glyn Jones] with Illustrations in Colour by Niels Larsen Stevns, New York, London, Copenhagen.

received more than his share of fame and recognition during his lifetime, and from a very early age he was the recipient of largesse from the hands of patrons and from the Danish crown. Yet his thirst for praise and fame could not be satisfied. He basked in the friendship of German noblemen and later of monarchs and great men. He was partial to Germany because his works first enjoyed unusual popularity there and because German princes bestowed attention and decorations on him. "And I leaned forward, like a sick person, towards the sunshine, happy and thankful—" he wrote metaphorically in his autobiography.

Andersen's remarkable powers of observation and his genius to make others see what he had seen and to make his experiences live for his read-ers—characteristics already noted in considering his novels—found an outlet in his travel books, *En Digters Bazar* (*A Poet's Bazaar,* 1842), *I Sverrig* (*In Sweden,* 1851), and *I Spanien* (*In Spain,* 1863). These works are among the classics of their genre in Danish and still enjoy some popular-ity in Denmark. *En Digters Bazar,* the most significant of the travel books, describes a journey through Germany, Italy and Greece, Turkey, and up the Danube to Vienna, but is no mere travelogue. *I Sverrig* ends with a curious chapter entitled "Poetry's California," which strongly suggests the tales and which prophetically proclaims that the future belongs to the sciences. Here Andersen shows himself to have held a progressive point of view and to have been no reactionary, in contrast to his older contem-porary Ingemann, for example, who wrote critically to Andersen in May of 1851 that Andersen was far too deeply influenced by the Empiricists and by the physicist Hans Christian Ørsted.

The common denominator of all of Andersen's works is phantasy. Phantasy is both his strength and his weakness. It evoked humor in the *Fodrejse* and enabled, yes forced, Andersen to elaborate on the improbable in his novels and plays. Andersen had simply failed at first to recognize the genre into which his literary efforts might best be channeled and the genre which would benefit rather than suffer from a massive and ebullient phantasy. This does not mean that Andersen's plays and novels did not enjoy success during his lifetime. They did; but they were addressed to the spirit of the times, whereas the tales have a universal and lasting appeal.

The *Eventyr*—the tales—were at first, as we have said, incidental to Andersen's other literary activity. The first tales "told for children," were published in 1835, but it was not until 1843, with the publication of *Nye Eventyr* (*New Tales,* dated 1844), that the genre was acclaimed; the first Dane to praise them intelligently was the incisive critic P. L. Møller. Thereafter, Andersen's works in this genre rapidly achieved popularity.

In talking to English and American acquaintances, Danes are frequently taken aback to discover that in the Anglo-American world Hans Christian Andersen's tales are considered to be only for children. It can be stated without exaggeration that Andersen's *Eventyr* are the common spiritual property of all Danes, young and old. Furthermore, adults in Denmark do not read Hans Christian Andersen merely out of piety or sentiment. Andersen has as much to say to adults as does Lewis Carroll in *Alice in Wonderland*. Like *Alice in Wonderland,* most of Andersen's tales have a double meaning which only the adult perceives. The comparison is however imperfect, for while *Alice in Wonderland* is an homogenous work, Andersen's eight score or more tales have many facets. He who thinks that Andersen's tales are only for children should read "The Bell," "The New Century's Goddess," or "The Most Incredible Thing." These involve abstractions which have no place in the nursery. It is no simple task to explain Andersen's intent or meaning in such tales; the "Snow Queen" for example, employs symbolism that the learned are still debating. Readers who are not familiar with Andersen's tales in the original Danish or in accurate unaltered versions, may be advised to examine a selection of the tales other than the well-known "Ugly Duckling" or "The Constant Tin-Soldier" in order that they may pass a more accurate judgment on Denmark's most famous son.[1]

The fable, the folk tales, and similar stories had all been cultivated for centuries before Andersen wrote his *Eventyr*.[2] *Märchen* directed at an adult public had been a favorite genre of the German Romantic school. Even Adam Oehlenschläger had in 1816 edited a collection of *Eventyr*. But as a genre, this kind of tale was not meant for children. Just as the political rhymes of yesteryear have disappeared into "Mother Goose," similarly the folk tale had withdrawn into the nursery by the nineteenth century, especially among the sophisticated. The so-called Romantic schools in European literature at the beginning of the nineteenth century evinced great interest in the folk tale as naïve literature and as a model for fantastic stories. Although they were not the first, the Grimm brothers were the most notable collectors of folk tales in Germany. Their work gave the German tales new literary life, and scholars in other countries followed the example of the Grimms. Incidentally the next best-known

1 The only complete edition of Andersen's tales in English is the translation by Jean Hersholt: *The Complete Tales of Hans Christian Andersen, I-III,* New York, 1947. Repr. with varying title, 1948–49, 1952.

2 The equivalent of German *Märchen*. There is no exact English term for the genre. "Fairy tale" is misleading; "folk tale" is vague and does not include the works of known authors.

collection of folk tales is probably that made by Andersen's Norwegian contemporaries Asbjørnsen and Moe.

The reborn consciousness of the folk tale which is a part of the beginnings of modern folklore, also engendered a new literary genre which, like the *Eventyr,* has no name in English and is often identified by the German term *Kunstmärchen,* that is to say, a synthetic folk tale. The great master of this sort of tale was E. T. A. Hoffmann; and the best-known of his tales is *Der goldene Topf (The Golden Pot)* to which Andersen referred in his *Fodrejse.* Andersen's tales are also *Kunstmärchen,* but differ essentially from most *Kunstmärchen* in that many of them were written ostensibly for children and that most although not all of them can be appreciated naïvely by children. Andersen was in fact the first to address works in the genre to children. Stylistically Andersen's tales differ from both the true folk tale and the *Kunstmärchen* of earlier writers. The true folk tale when reproduced in written form usually seems a bit artless and dull; the *Kunstmärchen* of the so-called Romanticists is often adjudged grotesque. Andersen's tales are neither artless, dull, nor grotesque.

Although the tales vary considerably in length—one is some fifty pages long—on the average they cover only a few pages. This does not mean, however, that they are simple in their origins, allusions, and psychological content. Andersen's tales, optimistic and pessimistic, humorous and sad, fantastic and philosophical, are not the resolutions of homely ideas or single experiences. Some, like *Sommerfugle (The Butterflies),* are fables; a few, and foremost among them *Big Claus and Little Claus,* are folk tales retold; others, like *Hun duede ikke (She was Good for Nothing),* are more or less autobiographical. Some pertain to other individuals: *Børnesnak (Childish Talk)* is about Thorvaldsen, and *De to Brødre (The Two Brothers)* about H. C. and A. S. Ørsted. A number of the tales may be classified in other traditional categories, as myths, allegories, and even as parables, but the majority, with their wealth of common and uncommon characteristics, must be considered to comprise their own genre.[1] Some tales bespeak a belief in the supernatural and in divine providence, whereas *Vanddraaben (The Drop of Water)* expresses H. C. Ørsted's progressive natural philosophy. Some contain a mystical element; others are rationalistic. *Gudfaders Billedbog (Godfather's Picture Book)* is essentially a history of Copenhagen; *Laserne (The Rags)* is a satire on Danish and Norwegian

---

1 A brilliant analysis of the tales has been made by Paul V. Rubow in his *H. C. Andersens Eventyr* (2nd ed., Copenhagen 1943). An introduction to the tales, by Rubow, is "Idea and Form in Hans Christian Andersen's Fairy Tales" in *A Book on the Danish Writer Hans Christian Andersen. His Life and Work,* Copenhagen, 1955, pp. 97–135.

differences with special reference to the new Norwegian nationalism in language and literature. A number of the tales are admittedly didactic; a few, and notably *Det Utroligste (The Most Incredible Thing)*, have hitherto defied exact identification.

Andersen himself accounted for the origins of many of his tales in some remarks that he appended to an edition of the *Eventyr* in 1862. He was no pedant, and his statements about the *Eventyr*, like much in his autobiography, cannot be accepted unconditionally; but these critical remarks are invaluable, also as a conclusive demonstration that the tales are not the work of a naïve poet. Andersen shows himself to have been a conscious artist who took great pains to put the tales into the form in which we now know them. He affirmed that he first employed the genre when he wrote *Dødningen (The Spectre)* contained in his *Digte*, 1830, but that it was not until *Skyggebilleder af en Reise til Harzen (Silhouettes from a Journey to the Harz Mountains, 1831)*[1] that "the right melody was found, with the story of the old king who thought he never had heard a lie." Andersen stated that some tales were borrowed from Danish folk tales, that the *Emperor's New Clothes* was of Spanish origin, and that *The Naughty Boy* was taken from Anakreon. He admitted a didactic purpose in some of the later tales like *Anne Lisbeth*. He noted that he knew many of the persons who appeared in the tales, and added that while some were contemporaries, others had "long rested in their graves."

Of the incentive to write most of the tales Andersen said, "They lay in my mind like seed that needed but a gentle breeze, a ray of sunshine, a drop of wormwood, in order to flower." But he could not account for *The Story of a Mother*. "It came without incentive; while I was walking on the street the thought came to me." A small number of tales were written at the suggestion of friends; *Skarnbassen (The Beetle)*, for example, was written at the suggestion of Charles Dickens. A few of the tales had their roots in one or more of the earlier tales, as for example, *Isjomfruen (The Ice Maiden)* in *Snedronningen (The Snow Queen)*.

Andersen's style or technique as a story teller and a residual element from his personal experiences are the salt that in the last analysis gives his tales a flavor different from that of similar stories by other authors. Andersen tapped many sources and blended several sub-genres of the prose narrative; an exact determination of all his motifs would be a very complicated and perhaps not very rewarding task. An examination of Andersen's letters and diaries provides many details about the writing of

1 First translated into English (by Charles Beckwith) as *Rambles in the Romantic Regions of the Hartz Mountains, Saxon Switzerland, etc.* London, 1848.

the tales, but such details are scarcely of aesthetic significance, although they contribute much to an understanding of Andersen as an individual. In particular, some of the tales, and notably *Skyggen (The Shadow)*, seem to reflect Andersen's relations with the Collin family.

Common to the majority of the tales is Andersen's individual mode of telling a story: his apparent stylistic naïveté; his peculiar relation to the reader or listener; his use of metaphors, similes, symbols, and other figures of speech; his personifications; his social pathos; and his irony. Insight into his way of composing the tales may be obtained by examining one of them in some detail. For our purpose we select one of the later tales, representative neither of Andersen's best nor worst, *Portnerens Søn (The Porter's Son,* 1866), which may run the risk of being "spoiled" by an analysis.

The Porter's Son is in essence a story of snobbery overcome through the good will of a nobleman and the guiding hand of Providence: a poor boy overcomes all obstacles and is recognized as a great man and artist. The autobiographical element is evident to anyone who is familar with Hans Christian Andersen's own life; Andersen himself said that this tale contained "many characteristics taken from real life." While there is a certain amount of tension built up as the story progresses, the reader is certain from the beginning that there will be a "happy ending." The story is told in short and simple sentences. Abstractions are made tangible. The childish listener is attracted by the story's apparent lucidity and the adult reader by its graceful charm and magnetic irony.

Irony and social pathos set the tone in the very first sentence, in which Andersen employs an unusual figure of speech: "the general's family lived on the second floor and the porter's family lived in the cellar; there was a vast distance between them, the entire first floor and the entire ordinance of rank and precedence." Satirical and ironical comments made in an innocent, naïve tone crop up throughout the narrative. We learn, for example, that the general's wife has a "costly coat of arms, bought by her father for shiny dollars," a fact which many people remember but which she and her family have forgotten. The general and his wife are presented in caricature. The general is a stuffed shirt on whose bosom there were so many decorations that it was unbelievable—but "it was not his fault; as a young man he had been in the army." But the general had never been to war "and when war came he became a diplomat and visited foreign courts." Both he and his wife repeat fixed phrases; everything that pleases the general he finds "charmant" and everything that displeases his wife gives her "a terrible headache."

Andersen makes the difference between the social climber and the true nobleman eminently clear. The born nobleman, in this case both the count and the king, recognizes and rewards genius where it is to be found. As the porter's wife remarks, "the more distinguished people really are, the less they make of it." Andersen's own preoccupation with royalty is reflected in the remark that the hero at last enjoyed "the grace of the court, the grace of God"—and was made honorary counsellor of state *(Etatsraad)*. The guiding hand that shapes men's fates is suggested several times. "Our Lord has bestowed many gifts upon you," says the old count; "how much more our Lord has bestowed upon you than upon the rest of us," says Emilie.

Once Andersen breaks into the story with a didactic remark: that the worthy suitor whom the general sought for his daughter "stood right outside the door—people don't see very far beyond their own thresholds." Just as the satire is clothed in apparent naïveté, explanations are made in a naïve manner which children accept unquestioningly: if the poor tailor had been better off and had had a number of helpers, he might have been court tailor; George's watch gained, but that was better than had it lost. There are such simple phrases as "a blooming locust tree, when it bloom-ed;" and "the old count, for there was an old count." Remarks like "he was born the day after his daughter, but of course before she was" are meant to be witty for the adult reader. The double meaning is clear when Emilie's mother tells her she is too big to throw kisses to George.

Stylistically considered, the tale contains numerous examples of some of Andersen's favorite devices. Such are the similes "a boy, who looked like a fresh tulip," or "Emilie, who looked like a blossoming rose tree;" such, the hyperbole "if she were to be sketched it would have to be on a soap bubble;" the non-sequitur "I know you; you sent me the saddle;" the play on a popular saying, "the general on his high horse;" the appeal to superstition—the hymn book is used for divination—; and a pun (which does not carry over into English). Many expressions are taken from the spoken rather than the written language.

Two other outstanding characteristics of Andersen's prose fiction are to be found in *The Porter's Son,* to wit, the "leap" in time and the preoccupation with description. Andersen frequently relieves the reader or listener of a tiresome sequence of events by springing over them without a word of explanation. The intermediate action can easily be deduced, however, as for example in the paragraph that begins "George is to be confirmed at Easter," or in his mother's complaint, "What will he do in Rome?"—a query pregnant with meaning for the reader. Andersen's love for description results in an eloquent portrayal of the count's garden. Similarly, his penchant for the exotic and for travel is reflected in the subjects which George draws for little Emilie: the Kremlin in Moscow, a Chinese house, and a Norwegian church.

While not all the tales share all the characteristics outlined above, the majority of them do have a good deal in common with *The Porter's Son*.

There is much more that could be said about the tales of Hans Christian Andersen, and many penetrating books and articles have been written about them (unfortunately almost none of this criticism is available in English). The reader who overcomes his prejudiced belief that Andersen is only for children, and who undertakes to read the tales, will find a never-ending source of pleasure, for the tales have the attributes of classic literature. When a reader starts a tale, he will finish it; he wants to turn the page and read on. When he has finished one tale he wants to read another, and when he has read them all, he marvels the more at Andersen's genius, and turns to read the tales again and again. With each reading he finds some new idea, some hidden wit or satire, or nicety of expression that had escaped him before. Although many of the tales are laid in Denmark, the popularity of the tales in such distant lands as Japan and India is evidence enough that the reader needs no special topographical or historical knowledge in order to appreciate them.

Andersen inspired no disciples and he has had no successful imitators. From the time that the tales won critical acclaim, his was an anomalous development. As a writer of tales he stands alone, although to be sure a parallel may be drawn with Carl Ewald, whose nature stories are suggestive of some of the tales, and with Johannes V. Jensen, whose "myths" comprise as flexible a private and informal genre as do Andersen's *Eventyr*.

Andersen's life more than spanned the Golden Age of Danish literature. Born in 1805, the year Oehlenschläger published his *Poetiske Skrifter,* he saw the demise of the Romantic school, the supremacy of Heiberg, the ascendancy of bourgeois taste, and finally, before his death in 1875, a new awareness of foreign literature and social problems. Although from the standpoint of literary history Andersen can be viewed as associated with Heiberg, it seems almost presumptuous today to stress Andersen's literary origins and affinities, the more so since the English-speaking world has yet to rediscover his autobiography, his novels, and his travel books.

HANS CHRISTIAN ANDERSEN
Painting by C. A. Jensen, 1836.

Eventyr,

fortalte for Børn

af

H. C. Andersen.

Første Hefte.

Kjøbenhavn.

Forlagt af Universitets-Boghandler C. A. Reitzel.

Trykt hos Bianco Luno & Schneider.

1835.

Title page of the first volume of Andersen's tales.
(Actual size).

FREDERIK PALUDAN-MÜLLER
Painting by Constantin Hansen, 1849.

MEÏR GOLDSCHMIDT
Painting by Elisabeth Jerichau-Baumann, 1852.

CHAPTER X

Bourgeois Eclecticism

There is no compelling means of identification for the forties, fifties, and sixties of the nineteenth century, decades which comprise an era of eclecticism and are bounded on the one side by Oehlenschläger's national Romanticism and on the other by Brandes' radicalism. The period is not without great names, for much of the work of Grundtvig, Andersen, and Kierkegaard appeared between 1840 and 1870, but there is an important aspect of the Danish literature of the times which those names ordinarily do not suggest: the ascendancy of bourgeois culture and the ultimate triumph of a literature of resignation which sometimes has been identified by the uncertain appellation "Biedermeier"—a term borrowed from the history of art. The tenor of the times was echoed in three genres. An epic that satirized bourgeois values was the final achievement of Heiberg's school. There was a lyric harvest in the work of a few "Biedermeier" poets. Finally, the early realistic novel began to accept and portray middle-class society. In each of the genres bourgeois culture produced a significant Danish writer: in the epic, Frederik Paludan-Müller; in the lyric, Emil Aarestrup; and in the novel, Meïr Goldschmidt.

Because of his inimitable style and the mastery of one prose genre, Hans Christian Andersen has become the most widely known of all Danish writers. Because of the originality of his thinking and the peculiarity of his presentation, Søren Kierkegaard has become the best-known Danish philosopher. FREDERIK PALUDAN-MÜLLER (1809–76), the third great writer who received encouragement from Heiberg and his circle, whom a Danish critic might well put on a plane with Andersen and Kierkegaard, is, however, almost unknown outside Scandinavia. This fact ironically reminds us that Paludan-Müller held the conviction that the poet writes for his own time and his own people. Nevertheless, he produced a classic work which is deserving of a place among the monuments of not only Danish literature but world literature: the lengthy satirical epic *Adam Homo*. In laying bare human frailty as he saw it, and in castigating the emptiness of a good burgher's life in Denmark during the early nineteenth century, he touched the sensitive nerve of all human existence. His portrayal of the hollowness of the ambitious man, although directed at his own times, certainly has as enduring validity as the philosophy of Kierkegaard or the tales of Andersen.

The skeptical, somewhat pessimistic spirit evident in *Adam Homo* pervades all that Paludan-Müller wrote. His several works, different in subject matter, bespeak the same convictions. It was, however, the elegance and poetic form rather than the ethical content of his early works which won for Paludan-Müller the approbation of Johan Ludvig Heiberg. His first work, the short epic *Danserinden* (*The Danseuse*, 1833)[1] suggested Byron and at once made clear his poetic virtuosity. The mythological drama *Amor og Psyche* (1834) again made evident not only his facility as a writer of verse but also his conservatism in the choice of subject matter. It was therefore with some bewilderment that the critics and the reading public received the first part of *Adam Homo* in 1841, for the plot of the epic was taken from everyday life and might even be considered trivial. It was not until the publication of the rest of the poem in 1848 that its satirical intent became unmistakable. The work has since won unqualified acceptance.

Adam Homo is an epic poem in three parts, with lyrical intercalations. The predominant verse is the easily read ottava rima (the verse form of Byron's *Don Juan*). Content and form are so perfectly fused that the work can be read almost like prose, without any concessions to the usual demands of metrical form. It is a matter of literary history that the poem was written with exacting patience, and that Paludan-Müller weighed and polished every verse; the reader finds the verses unusually smooth and readily comprehensible, and not without humor and wit.

Adam Homo, son of a Jutland clergyman, is in a way a self-contradiction. He wastes his life, makes the wrong decision whenever given the opportunity, and sacrifices every ideal to expediency. At the same time, he rises on the social ladder—although not without vicissitudes—and ends in possession of all the civic titles and honors which an ambitious man might want. He has gained the world and lost his own soul. We are aware of his fate from the first, for it is clear that even his clergyman-father is essentially materialistic, without any deeper understanding of spiritual or ethical values.

Young Adam is sent to the University of Copenhagen with lengthy paternal admonitions which are indicative of the father's spiritual degeneration. After yielding to a series of temptations, Adam attempts suicide—and fails. This act is really the turning point in his life. He sub-

---

1 An English version by Robert S. Hillyer of the last nine stanzas of the first canto of *Danserinden* are included in *A Book of Danish Verse*, 1922, pp. 110–12.

sequently finds a pure requited love and selfless affection in Alma Stjerne, the daughter of a gardener. It would now seem that he is about to achieve a stable bourgeois existence, but Adam sacrifices Alma as the first step toward social distinction and outward success, by marrying a young noblewoman. Adam eventually becomes a clubman, a royal chamberlain, a baron, and a counsellor of state, while Alma lives a selfless life externally impoverished but inwardly rich. The epic closes with an apocalyptic scene in which Adam is saved from perdition through the intercession of Alma, who still loves him. More unequivocally than Gretchen in *Faust,* she saves the man she loves and the man who has deceived her, by virtue of her forgiveness and her boundless love.

There are elements in *Adam Homo* which remind one not only of Goethe's *Faust,* but also of Byron's *Don Juan* and Heiberg's *En Sjæl efter Døden (A Soul after Death)*. Paludan-Müller was demonstrably conscious of Goethe's poem when he wrote *Adam Homo,* but *Adam Homo* is by no means an imitation or a descendent of *Faust,* even though the concluding situation, where Alma resembles Gretchen, seems to be a conscious parallel. Adam Homo himself is more a Danish Don Juan, given to sensuous enjoyment of the moment, than a Faust. Paludan-Müller himself nevertheless objected to the parallel with Byron's *Don Juan,* which was drawn by contemporary critics, since he felt that the two poems and their respective characters were differently conceived. The theme of Paludan-Müller's epic may best be compared with that of Heiberg's satirical *En Sjæl efter Døden*. Both authors were satirizing similar weaknesses among their own contemporaries, although Heiberg dealt primarily with a bourgeois lack of aesthetic appreciation, whereas Paludan-Müller was decrying a lack of nobility of character in his fellow men, and a lack of moral and ethical values in modern society. Heiberg was the cultured critic of his immediate contemporaries; Paludan-Müller was an introspective satirist writing a commentary on life and depicting the tragedy of ideals sacrificed to expediency and for the sake of external and ephemeral values. As a critic, Heiberg was, in the last analysis, concerned with Copenhagen; Paludan-Müller was concerned with man.

Adam Homo has been called realistic, and didactic, theological, and idealistic. Each of these labels has something to be said for it, although it may be debated whether the poem is theological. Essentially it represents Paludan-Müller's effort to create a philosophy in the sphere of everyday life and of everyday ethics. It stands in contrast to Kierkegaard's religio-philosophic contemplation. Had Paludan-Müller lived three decades later, he, who later in life was to be on good terms with Georg

Brandes, would probably have hearkened to the latter's demand that literature make social problems a matter of literary debate. As it was, Paludan-Müller's work rests on a foundation of Heiberg's criticism and practical aesthetics. In a naïve tone but with cutting wit, he composed a great modern epic which is both didactic and realistic.

A far cry from the satirical admonitions of Frederik Paludan-Müller, the philosophical profundity of Grundtvig and Kierkegaard, and the imaginative and fanciful writing of Hans Christian Andersen, was the poetry of two of their contemporaries, Emil Aarestrup and Ludvig Bødtcher, who are the hidden blossoms of anacreontic poetry in mid-nineteenth-century Danish bourgeois culture. Of the provincial physician-poet EMIL AARESTRUP (1800–56), the unorthodox critic P. L. Møller wrote concisely and accurately in 1847: "Aarestrup moves between two diametrically opposite poles, Oehlenschläger and Heine...in addition he is something of an Anakreon." Except for praise from Møller, Aarestrup was as good as unrecognized as a poet during his lifetime. Only one volume of his verse, *Digte* (1838), was published while he lived and of it only a handful of copies were sold. Yet Aarestrup is the most facile of erotic poets and one of the most direct and comprehensible poets on the Danish Parnassus, although to be sure the full meaning of many of his poems is evident only after reflection. Since his death, Aarestrup's star has risen higher and higher.

Aarestrup's lyrical ability developed with the years. A ballad quality predominates in the poems which he wrote while translating Goethe, Fouqué, Blumenhagen, and the earlier Götz into Danish. His later verse exhibits a light touch of the humorous and the ironic, as for example in his "Erkjendelse" ("Recognition"). The "Erotiske Situationer" ("Erotic Situations") of 1838 remind one of the anacreontic poetry which had blossomed almost a century before in French and German literature. Incidentally, Aarestrup translated Thomas Moore's anacreontic poems into Danish. Later in life Aarestrup translated works of Béranger, Byron, Heine, Victor Hugo, and Friedrich Rückert into Danish.

The number of Aarestrup's short lyric poems which tell of a specific emotional experience is small, but these are his most poignant. The poem "Til en Veninde" ("To a Friend") shows Aarestrup at his lyrical best:

> There's a magic on your lip,
> An abyss is in your glance,
> In the echo of your voice
> Is a dream's ethereal dance.

There's a clearness to your brow,
And a darkness to your hair,
There's a flow of flowers' genii
About you, where you fare.

There's a hoard of treasured wisdom
In the dimple in your cheek,
There's a clear and healthful fountain
In your soul for hearts to seek.

There's a whole world within you
A spring's chaos in the land,
Which I never shall forget,
Which I love and understand.

LUDVIG BØDTCHER (1793–1874) was quiet of nature and content to let the world go by, apparently unconcerned with the tribulations of his fellow men. He did not play a significant rôle in contemporary literature; his first collection of poems was published in 1856, when he was 63. It is as if he distilled from the fruits of life a few rare juices in his elegiac poems. In Italy between 1824 and 1835, he found inspiration and tranquility. He was one of many Danish poets, painters, and sculptors who visited Italy during the early part of the century, among them Oehlenschläger, Ingemann, Carsten Hauch, Christian Winther, Hans Christian Andersen, Frederik Paludan-Müller, and, above all, the immortal sculptor Thorvaldsen. These poets and artists forged a strong cultural link between Italy (above all, the city of Rome) and Denmark. The classical longing for Italy, the desire to follow Winckelmann and Goethe, and especially Goethe in his *Italienische Reise,* is a common characteristic of European literature during the first half of the nineteenth century; one thinks of Byron, Keats, and Shelley. Nor did the attraction of Italy and Rome diminish after the middle of the century. Goldschmidt, Vilhelm Bergsøe, Henrik Ibsen, Bjørnstjerne Bjørnson, and P. A. Munch were among the Danes and Norwegians who visited Italy during the second half of the century. Of all the Danish poets who were enthusiasts for Italy however, Ludvig Bødtcher resided longest on the Mediterranean peninsula and found the greatest personal satisfaction in the land and its people, and later in his memories of the country. His Italian experiences are perhaps best expressed in the two poems "Aften ved Ariccia" ("Evening at Ariccia") and "Mødet med Bacchus" ("Meeting with Bacchus").[1]

1 "Meeting with Bacchus" in a translation by S. Foster Damon is found in *A Book of Danish Verse,* 1922, pp. 86–98.

VILHELM KAALUND (1818–85) was a third mid-century poet who may be put in the same category as Bødtcher and Aarestrup. Of his few works, his versified *Fabler for Børn* (*Fables for Children*, 1845) with illustrations by Lundbye, has become familiar to every Dane.

Realism, when defined as the portrayal of everyday life coupled with psychological penetration into human character and a concern with social and economic problems, is usually applied in Denmark to the literature produced especially by authors who were influenced by the critic Georg Brandes from 1871 onward. The beginnings of a literature which complied to such a definition of realism nevertheless antedated the so-called "Breakthrough" of modern literature in the seventies. There were elements of a realistic art in the stories of Steen Steensen Blicher and the work of Poul Martin Møller in the twenties, and Heiberg had chosen realistic subjects at least, if not a realistic form, for his vaudevilles. Social criticism was implicit in Paludan-Müller's *Adam Homo* (1841–48), in Heiberg's allegorical play *En Sjæl efter Døden* (*A Soul after Death*, 1841), and even in Carl Bagger's novel *Min Broders Levned* (*The Life of my Brother*) which had been published as early as 1835 and had enjoyed considerable popularity.

The most significant forerunner of modern realism was however MEÏR ARON GOLDSCHMIDT (1819–87), who has been mentioned above as the satirical editor of *Corsaren* (*The Corsair*), the periodical which played such a crucial rôle in the life of Søren Kierkegaard. Despite his feud with the "Corsair" even Kierkegaard recognized that Goldschmidt's *En Jøde* (*A Jew*), published under the pseudonym Adolph Meyer in 1845, was a remarkable novel, and that Goldschmidt was no mere sharp-tongued journalist.[1] A quarter of a century before the advent of Georg Brandes, Goldschmidt attempted to portray the position of a Jew in contemporary Danish society, to explain his psyche, and delineate the cultural and religious environment in which he, in contrast to other Danes, grew up. Goldschmidt drew heavily on his own experiences and those of his own family; the book is consequently pervaded with an air of actuality. Often it reads like a memoir rather than a novel. It does not achieve its effects by means of sentimentality. The novel was something of a sensation in its day, for most Danes knew little if anything of the life and culture of the few Jews in early nineteenth-century Denmark. Goldschmidt's Hebraic brethren were far from happy about the book, perhaps in part because they felt themselves suddenly brought before the public eye; but

1 Two English translations were published in London in 1852, one by Mrs. Bushby, the other by Mary Howitt. The former was republished in 1864.

the anti-Semite could scarcely find cause to rejoice. There is no doubt that Goldschmidt has in the long run contributed to the better understanding of Jew and Gentile in Denmark because of his success in portraying his people impartially and realistically.

Goldschmidt wrote a number of other novels, of which the most important is the amorphous *Hjemløs* (*Homeless*, 1853–57),[1] and also several dramas. As an artist he is best in his short stories, which are, however, far less realistic than his novels. They were produced over a period of many years; the first volume of *Fortællinger* (*Tales*, 1846) contains most of the best-loved stories, humorous, sentimental, and exciting.[2] *Slaget ved Marengo* (*The Battle of Marengo*), which Goldschmidt later identified as one of the earliest of his stories, has an ironic charm that we do not meet again until half a century later in Henrik Pontoppidan's *Skyer* (*Clouds*) in 1890. Like his more famous disciple, Pontoppidan, Goldschmidt was a master of the Danish language. He is always lucid and careful in his diction. He excels in exposition and description and avoids the fanciful or the fantastic. His sentences are precise, with many modifying clauses and limiting phrases. He makes no effort to portray spectacular outward events. His characters are affected by particular situations and occurrences, the significance of which is revealed only through the intuition of the author. Incidentally, Goldschmidt's later works also reflect his philosophical belief in nemesis.

Another forerunner of the literary realism or "naturalism" that was to prevail later in the century was HANS EGEDE SCHACK (1820–59), a writer very different from Goldschmidt. An erstwhile student of Poul Martin Møller, Schack is known in Danish literature for a single work, the semi-autobiographical psychological novel *Phantasterne* (*The Fantasts*, 1857). While Poul Møller achieved an equilibrium and was satisfied to employ humorous satire in the fragmentary *En dansk Students Eventyr* (*The Tale of a Danish Student*), Schack, who tried to capture the spirit of Don Quixote, was himself too little of a humorist and too little of a philosopher to accomplish his ends. *Phantasterne* is a psychological document from which Schack's own inner world may be deduced. It verges on the classic in Danish literature because Schack, in indirectly portraying his own soul, his dependence on daydreams, and his preoccupation with the erotic, has described psychic conditions to which all human beings are subject to a

---

1 Published in English as *Homeless; or A Poet's inner Life*, I–III, London, 1861.

2 "Avromche Nightingale," translated by Lida Siboni Hanson, is contained in *Denmark's Best Stories*, New York, 1928, pp. 71–116.

greater or lesser extent. His book is a forerunner of the psychological analyses in the literature of the last decades of the nineteenth century. Schack's novel is no lucid narrative; it is, rather, the desperate reaction of a fanciful hypochondriac against a host of the literary models of the times. The novel was meant to be a condemnation of phantasy, which had been the lode-star of poetry from Oehlenschläger to Heiberg. It was to settle accounts with phantasy by means of an ironic realism; but Schack himself resolved his plot by means of phantasy. His work echoes a tragic life of depression and disillusionment. Schack, who evinced neurotic traits, suggests the above-mentioned introspective CARL BAGGER (1807–46), although the parallel between Bagger and his schizophrenic self, as portrayed by the two brothers who are the principal characters in *Min Broders Levned (The Life of my Brother)*, is more striking than the parallel between Schack and either of the two disillusioned fantasts in *Phantasterne*. Despite the practical cut of Schack's life as a politican and government official, he was a dreamer, a fantast, and an hypochondriac. It was his own tragedy as well as the tragedy of two of his leading characters that, in reacting to the existing conditions and to traditional ways, they expended all their vigor. It is as if the characters were dependent on the very forms and conditions they would destroy. The story is narrated by one of the three young men who as youths find satisfaction in flights of imagination into a make-believe existence. Although they meet very different fates, the two characters who continue to tread the path of phantasy find only unhappiness, while the third, who has his feet on the ground, achieves more concrete results in life than his two hapless friends.

One of the few young talents in Danish prose literature of the sixties, finally, was VILHELM BERGSØE (1835–1911), whose rambling novel of life in and about Rome, *Fra Piazza del Popolo (From Piazza del Popolo, 1867)* is still widely read in Denmark. Although the ideas of his generation were superseded by those of Brandes and the younger generation of writers about Brandes, Bergsøe was able to make his voice heard in contrast and in opposition to the Brandesian movement. Bergsøe represented a literature which for all practical purposes left out of consideration the natural sciences that Brandes stressed. This is curious, for Bergsøe was himself a zoölogist by training. From origins similar to those of his contemporary Sophus Schandorph, he went a very different way. He cultivated the traditions of the earlier nineteenth-century novel, and may be said to represent the narrative ability of the older school at its best. *Fra Piazza del Popolo,* although written most nearly in the spirit of Meïr Goldschmidt, suggests Hans Christian Andersen's *Improvisatoren,* with its pictures of life in Italy. Modeled on a work by Alfred de Vigny, Bergsøe's novel is conglomerate; it comprises a cycle of short stories which involve the Scandinavian colony in Rome. Its popularity may be perhaps ascribed to Bergsøe's ability to tell a good story free of the ubiquitous social and psychological problems which entered literature with the "Breakthrough." At the verge of the Brandesian era, Bergsøe published his second most important work, *Fra den gamle Fabrik* (*From the Old Factory*, 1869), a cycle of tales reminiscent of Meïr Goldschmidt's *Erindringer fra min Onkels Hus* (*Recollections from my Uncle's House*), contained in *Fortællinger* (*Tales*, 1846).

About the middle of the nineteenth century CARL PLOUG (1813–94) and JENS CHRISTIAN HOSTRUP (1818–92) developed pleasing literary individuality on the bourgeois level in their poems and plays. Both writers are best known for the informal tone of their works, which played on the idyllic and nationalistic aspects in Danish student life. During his best years Ploug was a popular national figure, and many of his poems were set to music and became part and parcel of student life and national consciousness in Denmark. As a politician and journalist, Ploug was one of the leading men of his time. Ploug was originally a young radical, enthusiastic about the French revolution of 1830. He remained true to the liberalism of the thirties and forties which, as the years passed, seemed liberal in name only. Subsequently, his opposition to the new ideas of the seventies and eighties caused him to be ridiculed by Schandorph, Drachmann, and others of a rising school, who saw in Ploug, who was the editor of the conservative newspaper *Fædrelandet,* an arch-reactionary and consequently an arch-enemy of the so-called "Breakthrough" of modern European literature in Denmark. His poetry is an expression, often pompous, of his outward life. Aesthetically, Ploug means little to literature, but as the leading representative of patriotic poetry and nineteenth-century Scandinavianism, he cannot be overlooked.

In his own student days, Ploug wrote a series of plays which were the immediate forerunners of the "student comedies" by his contemporary Hostrup, who became the master of this special and popular genre which was rooted in bourgeois morality. Hostrup learned from Oehlenschläger, Johan Ludvig Heiberg, and Hertz, but the spirit which he instilled into the plays that he produced during the forties was his own. His dramatic ability was first successfully displayed in *Gjenboerne* (*The Neighbors,* 1844). The innocent charm and bouyancy in his plays is at its best in the lyrical comedy *Eventyr paa Fodrejsen* (*Adventures on Foot,* 1848). Both these dramas are still played in Denmark; in fact, among the Danish dramatists whose works have been played most frequently at the Royal Theater in Copenhagen, Hostrup ranks just below the other great "H's": Heiberg, Holberg, and Hertz.

In the earlier work of Ploug and Hostrup are to be sought the literary origins of the epigonic CHRISTIAN RICHARDT (1831–92). As a young man, Richardt also wrote student comedies and shared Ploug's Scandinavianism. Richardt was however a more gifted poet than either Ploug or Hostrup, and his ability developed with the years. His verse, which has its own elegance, echoes the tones of the first half of the nineteenth century, the ethos of Oehlenschläger and Ingemann, and the aesthetic of Heiberg. It is above all melodious, and many of his poems, in musical settings, have insinuated themselves into the store of living Danish lyrics. An outstanding example is "Lær mig, Nattens Stjerne" ("Teach me, star of the night") from the collection *Smaadigte* (*Shorter Poems,* 1860) which was exquisitely set to music by J. P. E. Hartmann.[1] Incidentally, Richardt wrote the libretto to P. A. Heise's opera *Drot og Marsk* (*King and Constable,* 1878), one of the few Danish operas of consequence. Although sometimes didactic in tendency and pious in mood, Richardt's poetry bespeaks no philosophical or social convictions. He was content to accept the traditional and give it polished poetic expression.

If we view the literature of the first seventy years of the nineteenth century chronologically, we discern three periods of remarkable literary activity which constitute the era often referred to as the Golden Age of Danish literature. The first falls in the years 1802–08, when Oehlenschläger published his early works, Schack Staffeldt his poems, and Grundtvig his *Nordens Mytologi.* The second, around 1824, brought the works of Steen Steensen Blicher and Poul Martin Møller, the novels of Ingemann, and the vaudevilles of Johan Ludvig Heiberg. The third includes the years between 1835 and 1850, when there were published the fairy tales of Hans Christian Andersen, Paludan-Müller's *Adam Homo,* the novels of Carsten Hauch and Meïr Goldschmidt, the plays of Henrik Hertz, and most of the works of Kierkegaard.

As we have noted, a more or less steady stream of literature continued to be produced in the fifties and sixties, but to many critics these two decades have seemed to be a quiescent or even stagnant era of lesser imitators. True enough, the times evolved no radical or vitally new idea. The reverence for what had been was greater than the curiosity about

1 An English version of the poem is contained in *A Second Book of Danish Verse.* Translated by Charles Wharton Stork, New York, 1947, p. 53 f.

what might come. Not so however among Norwegian writers; in these very decades, literature written by Norwegians and published in Denmark was of as much or more importance than literature written by Danes. It is not possible in retrospect to differentiate the impact of Danish and Norwegian literature, at least in the Danish capital. The dramas of Ibsen, and the works of Bjørnson, Jonas Lie, and Alexander Kielland were all published in Copenhagen by the Gyldendal publishing company, and Norwegians were not then looked upon as foreigners in Denmark. A differentiation between Norwegian and purely Danish literature in Denmark of the seventies and eighties is therefore artificial and arbitrary. Ibsen and his compatriots wrote in a Danish with insignificant national variations; for all intents and purposes Norway's written language remained Danish until into the twentieth century. Despite the political differences of Norway and Denmark, Copenhagen remained the literary center of both countries, and, curiously enough, from the publication of Ibsen's *Brand* in 1866 until nearly the end of the nineteenth century, the Norwegians played a dominant rôle in Danish letters. For traditional reasons presentation on the stage in Copenhagen and literary acceptance by critics in Copenhagen remained the ultimate goals of the Norwegian writers. When Ibsen was living in voluntary exile in Italy, Austria, and Germany, it was to Copenhagen and the Gyldendal publishing company that he sent his works for publication. It was the Danish Royal Theater that produced Ibsen's momentous *Pillars of Society* only a month after the drama had been published in 1877.

Since detailed analyses of the works of Ibsen, Bjørnson, *et al.,* are to be found in histories of Norwegian literature, our concern here is first and foremost to point out the place which those writers have in Danish literary history.[1] Between 1870 and 1890, the greatest single rôle in Danish literature was played by Henrik Ibsen. It was he who captured men's minds and made them think.

That the Norwegian authors were so influential is in part to be ascribed to the benevolent efforts of FREDERIK V. HEGEL (1817–87), the head of the house of Gyldendal, at that time Scandinavia's most eminent and powerful publishing firm. Hegel was ever ready to encourage Norwegian as well as Danish writers with both words and monetary advances. It was the ambition of Norwegian as well as Danish authors in the late nineteenth century to be accepted by "Gyldendal." The paternal Hegel, was,

1 Reference is made to *A History of Norwegian Literature* by Harald Beyer. Translated and Edited by Einar Haugen. New York University Press for The American-Scandinavian Foundation, 1956.

to quote Bjørnson, the home port and anchorage of the young and promising writers of the day. Hegel was modest himself, respectful of talent wherever it might be found, and a good business man as well. He was willing to publish an author's serious work, even though the author was a target of attack by the powers that were. The first Norwegian to turn to Hegel for help was a woman, Camilla Collett, authoress of *Amtmandens Døttre (The Governor's Daughters)* which had first been published anonymously in Norway in 1854–55. The second edition was published by Gyldendal in 1860. Other Norwegians quickly followed her example: Asbjørnsen, Welhaven, Jonas Lie, Magdalene Thoresen, Kristian Elster, Alexander Kielland, and Kristofer Janson among others. The fact that the majority of important Norwegian books were published in Denmark by Gyldendal made for a continued close interrelationship of literature in Denmark and Norway, despite the cultural nationalism which was otherwise making itself felt in Norway and which eventually was to lead to a complete break with Copenhagen and to an independent Norwegian literary existence.

If Danish letters tended to be static in the sixties, Denmark nevertheless had its spate of promising young literature from its sister state, literature which contained the seed of what was to come, in the regionalism of Bjørnson, the social philosophy of Ibsen, and the realism of Jonas Lie and Alexander Kielland. When the scales inevitably tipped against a jejune bourgeois culture in Denmark, the new Danish literature found an ally in young Norway.

CHAPTER XI

The "Breakthrough"

We may speculate whether the European currents identified by the term Naturalism and the new socio-psychological view of literature which was finding widespread acceptance in France, England, and Russia would not have made inroads in Denmark in the early seventies if there had been no GEORG BRANDES (1842–1927); but the fact remains that Brandes projected these issues on the Danish cultural landscape and aroused his countrymen to a new consciousness of foreign literature and to the European demand for a new literature. Analogously, the new currents of the early eighteenth century would have had their effect in Denmark without Holberg; German philosophy and the new literature of the 1790's would have made themselves felt without Henrik Steffens; but in each case the change wrought would have been less swift and thorough. In order that there can be a radical change there must be an articulate leader with new ideas. Georg Brandes was one of the distinguished company of articulate leaders who have interpreted European literature for Denmark and for Scandinavia.

There is no denying it. Georg Brandes' lectures at the University of Copenhagen in 1871 and the new literary interests of the seventies in Copenhagen are epochal and pivotal in Danish literary history. From Brandes the lines are clearly drawn down until the 1930's. Late nineteenth and early twentieth-century Danish literary criticism has Brandes as a point of orientation. Most modern critics, foremost among them Valdemar Vedel, Hans Brix, and Paul V. Rubow, are Brandes' pupils or admirers; a few critics, chief among them Harald Nielsen, are his adversaries; but it is Brandes who has remained the central figure in literary discussions in Denmark during the past eighty years.

Brandes came to be a line of demarcation in the development of Danish letters for three reasons. He was by nature an unusually gifted speaker and writer; the literary situation of the fifties and sixties in Denmark had been static; and the new criticism which Brandes brought from the outside world gave Danish letters the new ideas which it needed to experience a rejuvenation. Brandes is not important as an original or systematic thinker, for much of what he wrote and said was drawn from or based on the works of French and German critics. Like Steffens before him, with whom he frequently is compared, he was an apostle, a prophet, and a mediator who succeeded in making new ideas live in Denmark and in inspiring his contemporaries to a new and enthusiastic literature. In contrast to Steffens, Brandes by no means met with general respect and approbation. Conservative Denmark was skeptical, and the young Jewish agitator soon had his enemies among good churchmen and others who wanted to preserve the *status quo*. Judging by the number of important writers who at some time were under the influence of Brandes, it is easy to jump to the false conclusion that Brandes soon had the majority with him in Copenhagen in the seventies. To be sure, Brandes did attract the young and searching minds of his generation, but if we examine the books and periodicals of the day quantitatively, we find that the Brandesian wing was small and that the anti-Brandesians were vociferous. Nor did Brandes find grace in the eyes of the university authorities; he was not appointed to the chair of aesthetics left vacant at the death of Carsten Hauch, despite a public statement by Hauch, written a few weeks before his death, to the effect that Brandes was by far the best candidate for the position. The prejudice against Brandes was so strong that none of the leading Copenhagen newspapers *(Berlingske Tidende, Dagbladet, Fædrelandet)* would even print Hauch's statement. Brandes subsequently emigrated to Berlin in 1877, where he lived for five years, until a group of his partisans and admirers performed the unique service of inviting him back to Denmark on the condition that he accept a yearly salary equivalent to that of a university professor.

Brandes had published some significant literary and aesthetic essays in the late sixties, essays which are among his finest. After taking his doctor's degree in 1870 with a dissertation on modern French aesthetics, he travelled abroad for a year and made the acquaintance of many leading minds in Europe. The men who had made the greatest impression on him were Hippolyte Taine, Ernest Renan, and John Stuart Mill, and in accordance with their ideas he undertook to delineate the "main currents of European literature" in the sensational lectures which he delivered upon his return to Denmark in 1871. It was Brandes' thesis that Denmark had not kept pace with the rest of Europe, and that while the ideas of the great revolution were bearing cultural fruit elsewhere, Danish literature was becoming more and more inbred and self-satisfied. These principles were parallel to ideas which Henrik Ibsen was expressing; and indeed Ibsen and Brandes found in each other related spirits.

In discussing the new literature of the seventies which was associated with Brandes, it is impossible to overlook the rôle which HENRIK IBSEN played in Danish, as well as Norwegian—and for that matter also German—literature. The ferment of a new literature was contained in some of Ibsen's early dramas to such an extent that critics and the public were not satisfied to discuss the merits of Ibsen's works as dramas. On the contrary, the ethical values at stake aroused heated discussion, and the fact was often all but overlooked that Ibsen was able to create the furor he did with his plays because of his mastery of the dramatic form. His ability to fulfill the demands made on the drama by contemporary criticism, to wit, that it be realistic and that it debate problems, cannot be denied; yet the fulfillment of those demands was tangential to Ibsen's essential intentions.

The reaction to Ibsen's philosophical drama *Brand* (1866) had been cataclysmic. Pastor Brand, with his unequivocal demand of "everything or nothing," stirred moral consciences, while the apparent final repudiation of Brand's own philosophy—which knew not *caritas*—necessarily evoked strong differences of opinion. The drama was read and discussed, primarily from the standpoint of ethics, and Ibsen was looked upon as a new Savonarola rather than as a gifted younger dramatist. His *Brand* was received much as Kierkegaard had wished his works to be received. There are in fact several parallels which may be drawn between Ibsen as the author of *Brand* and Kierkegaard, for the figure of the fiery Norwegian pastor suggests the stern "either-or" of the Danish thinker. What is more, the conclusion of Brand's life suggests a possible "leap" to the religious as a radical solution of the problem of human existence with its unreconciled aesthetic and ethical demands. But in the last analysis Kierkegaard remains a poetic philosopher and Ibsen a philosophical poet. The question of the direct influence of Kierkegaard upon Ibsen has never been and presumably never will be answered unequivocally. It is probably near the truth to say that both men held some tenets in common and were the products of much the same intellectual and social environment, and shared an intensity of literary personality and imagination.

The Danish critics were by no means of one mind about Ibsen's plays, although the forceful impact of the plays upon the times is indisputable. The leading critics and even the young Georg Brandes were skeptical about *Peer Gynt* (1867) and *De unges Forbund* (*The League of Youth*, 1869). Yet the latter play found favor in the eyes of Johanne Luise Heiberg and was successfully produced at the Royal Theater in 1870. The so-called social dramas, i.e., the dramas beginning with *Samfundets Støtter (The*

Pillars of Society) in 1877, soon had a thunderous effect. *The Pillars of Society* took the critics off guard, but *Et Dukkehjem* (*A Doll's House,* 1879) called forth a crescendo of many voices in Denmark as elsewhere. One edition followed another and the play drew packed houses at the Royal Theatre, audiences that went home heatedly debating whether Nora had a right to leave her husband and children. Suddenly Ibsen seemed to be much different from what Copenhagen had taken to be the Christian moralist who was the author of *Brand*. Ibsen had apparently been misunderstood and *Brand* misinterpreted before the radicalism of the younger generation had been revealed by Georg Brandes. Readers and audiences in Copenhagen as elsewhere saw only the problem suggested by the drama but neither Ibsen's philosophical motivation in the later plays nor his dramatic prowess. *Gjengangere* (*Ghosts,* 1881) was understood only too well. That is to say, the external problem seemed neither abstract nor poetic, while again the basic idea of the play, its skillful technique, and Ibsen's psychological analyses were not appreciated. *Ghosts* was looked upon by many simply as a bold and immoral play. It was felt to be more than presumptuous of Ibsen to indicate the problem of venereal disease from the stage. The conservative critics saw in the drama only destruction.

Whether or not Ibsen had any social doctrine in mind when he wrote his later dramas, the times nevertheless chose to see in him an arbiter of social problems and an author who fulfilled Brandes' demand that literature debate the problems of the day. Whether with the will of the author or against it, Ibsen's dramas encouraged the production of much literature concerned with social and contemporary problems. Denmark looked askance at Ibsen, just as it looked askance at Brandes, and consequently party lines became drawn; Brandes, Ibsen, and the new writers who were inspired by them were on the one side as the literary Left; and the writers who subscribed to bourgeois, post-Hegelian aestheticism were on the other as the literary Right. The new generation which was engendered by the so-called cultural struggle of the seventies and eighties—the generation of the "Breakthrough"—became predominantly socially conscious and politically and philosophically radical. Its members very soon tended to associate themselves either with the proletarian Left, e.g., Holger Drachmann, or with the Grundtvigians, e.g., the young Henrik Pontoppidan.

Brandes raised a cry for realism and for a criticism which first and foremost took the origins of literary works into consideration, and specifically a criticism that was more concerned with heredity and milieu than

*Georg Brandes, lecturing at the University of Copenhagen.
Painting by H. Slott-Møller, 1890.*

A meeting of the society "Bogstaveligheden" ("Literalness"). Painting by Erik Henningsen, 1882. Georg Brandes, left foreground, is facing Jens Peter Jacobsen, who is reading from his own works. Seated at Brandes' left are Sophus Schandorph and Holger Drachmann.

HOLGER DRACHMANN
Painting by P. S. Krøyer, 1895.

JENS PETER JACOBSEN
Painting by Ernst Josephson, 1879.

with the formal demands of the older school of aesthetics. That Brandes' method was a step on the way which could lead to a barren biographical literary history that only now, in the middle of the twentieth century, is being supplanted by a criticism particularly sensitive to form, is another matter.

The new character of Danish literature in the early nineteenth century, the trend identified with Henrik Steffens, had been philosophical and poetic. The mid-century had been an era of religious speculation. Grundtvig and Kierkegaard were the new theologians; but Kierkegaard's attitude was individualistic and intense, whereas Grundtvig's was social and expansive. In many ways the two thinkers seem to have been antithetical. Kierkegaard could be accepted by the cosmopolitan intellectual Brandes; Grundtvig could not. The new trends identified with Georg Brandes were aesthetic, ethical, and scientific.

"My ideas are the ideas of the intelligent in Europe," the young Brandes proclaimed—scarcely in a diplomatic way. Literature, he continued, should "make problems a matter of debate." The phrase became the catchword of the new literature which sprang up about him. Brandes' social doctrine was incorrectly interpreted by his adversaries as socialistic, and (like many great men since the late seventeenth century) he was subsequently accused of atheism. It is interesting to note that, far from being either a socialist or a democrat, Brandes was an intellectual aristocrat with a predilection for the Caesars of history.

While Brandes' essays on Scandinavian writers are perhaps the most lasting of all his works, the first four volumes of the *Main Currents in Nineteenth Century Literature, (Hovedstrømninger i det nittende Aarhundredes Litteratur,* 1872–75) were looked upon as his principal contribution during his lifetime.[1] They contained brilliant criticism as well as programmatic and polemic judgments in favor of an enlightened Europe and against a Biedermeier and a Grundtvigian Denmark. The volumes of *Main Currents* were translated into several languages including English, as were a number of Brandes' later works, notably his volumes on Nietzsche, Lassalle, Voltaire, and Goethe.

As Steffens had inspired a new generation and spurred Oehlenschläger to poetic action 69 years before, Brandes now had a positive and electrifying effect upon a number of young writers in Copenhagen. The deep and lasting impression Brandes made upon his time is recorded not only in literary history but in literature itself by some of the men who had

1 An English translation of all six volumes appeared in London, 1901–05. Repr. New York, London, 1923.

12

sensed his influence. Three writers, two of whom had not set out to be poets at all, came to represent the first Brandesian triumph in literary Denmark: Sophus Schandorph, who already was an established author in 1871, Holger Drachmann, who originally was a painter, and Jens Peter Jacobsen, who was a natural scientist.

In the works of SOPHUS SCHANDORPH (1836–1901), the transition from eclectic bourgeois to naturalistic literature is realized. Schandorph is the most telling example of the young writer who came under the influence of Georg Brandes. His position in Danish literature was axial because of the essentially shifting nature of his work rather than by virtue of any great talent or outstanding originality that he possessed. His early work was part and parcel of the literature of entertainment of the fifties and sixties. Through Brandes, Schandorph acquired an entirely new attitude, which came to expression in his novel *Uden Midtpunkt* (*Without a Center,* 1878). The theme of *Uden Midtpunkt* is the conflict of the new and the old, which is delineated in an objective although somewhat overbearing fashion. The leading figure in the novel, Karl Albrecht, is an opportunistic champion of the new philosophy and of political national-liberalism, but he is "without a center." He is a man who, in the words of Pastor Jespersen, another character in the novel, has nothing to believe in and whose fate consequently sets no shining example for the new times. "There had always been," writes Schandorph of Albrecht, "an unusual discrepancy between his fantasy and his real life... He had never known what it was... to complete a task." He is at best a representative of the embryonic ideas of the sixties, ideas which were to be clearly formulated and methodically applied by Brandes. Albrecht's unstable world of ideas is overwhelmed by the strong personality of one Otto Holm, who, like Brandes, was conscious of his goals in life.

Critically speaking, a number of objections might be raised against Schandorph's novel. Albrecht's penchant for citing poetry seems most improbable; the delineation of character leaves much to be desired; the descriptions of the nobility are to a large extent caricatures. Such objections were not raised by the reading public of the day, however, and Schandorph remained popular during his lifetime, although he is little read today. His popularity may in part be ascribed to his gift of describing life in rural Denmark with accuracy and feeling.

From the standpoint of literary rather than cultural history, Schandorph's principal work is *Thomas Friis' Historie* (*The Story of Thomas Friis*; 2 vols., 1881), a novel of development (i.e., in German, *Entwicklungsroman*), in the tradition of Goethe's *Wilhelm Meister*. After spending a fantastic youth, Thomas Friis, "the son of a courtesan and a bourgeois," decides to be an aesthetician, meets up with the bourgeois world of compromise, and returns to his childhood home, there to find peace of mind at last as an agriculturalist and to acquaint himself with natural science, politics, and the theories of Feuerbach, Darwin, and Spencer. He returns to Copenhagen in the seventies, not as a leader of a new movement, but as a "well-trained soldier in the phalanx of the young," who, we infer, have been inspired by Georg Brandes. Despite the novel's tendency toward the exotic, it has a serious ethical content; with Jacobsen's *Niels Lyhne,* Pontoppidan's *Lykke-Per,* and Jacob Paludan's *Jørgen Stein,* it is one of the more important works which has been produced in Denmark in the sub-genre of the novel to which it belongs.

The relation of Brandes to HOLGER DRACHMANN (1846–1908) and JENS PETER JACOBSEN (1847–85) was different than to Schandorph. It is a curious fact that Drachmann misunderstood Brandes and that Brandes, like most of his contemporaries, misunderstood Jacobsen. The young Drachmann embraced the political radicalism of which Brandes was accused, and Jacobsen's prose was looked upon as the ultimate in scientific realism. Nevertheless, Drachmann broke with Brandes after a few years; and Jacobsen, who died before reaching forty, looked askance upon a programme which would make literature a floor for socio-political debate.

Holger Drachmann's *Digte (Poems)* of 1872 reflects both his travels abroad and his meeting with Brandes. The volume is dedicated to "my friend Georg Brandes." In the poem "Ude og Hjemme" ("Abroad and At Home"), Drachmann expressed in verse the same thesis that Brandes was propounding in the university auditorium:

> At home it was so cozy and pleasant,
> The teakettle purred its song.
>
> Abroad there was a devilish storm,
> Birches thrashed like flags in the wind.

A more poignant result of Drachmann's experience in England in 1870–71 and the subsequent influence of Brandes was the poem "Engelske Socialister ("English Socialists"), first published in the autumn of 1871 in the periodical *Nyt Dansk Maanedsskrift.* Here Drachmann's sympathy with political radicalism and for the Paris Commune and its ideals found powerful expression.

Despite the agitating nature of the poem, it demonstrates Drachmann's lyric ability and impressionistic style. And in the last analysis, Drachmann was here as elsewhere more a poet than an agitator or didacticist; he was moved to verse by the emotional and picturesque situation rather than by political conviction or doctrine. "Clenched fists, thirteen, fourteen" are raised by men who cry out against "Church and state and the tyranny of gold," and who orate upon the Commune amidst the applause of an audience of workmen until "the pub is cleared by the police." The same spirit informs the poem "King Mob." For a few years Drachmann was the programmatic poet of Brandesian naturalism. His social consciousness still had the upper hand in the second important collection of his verse, *Dæmpede Melodier* (*Muted Melodies,* 1875), as for example in the poem "Misericordia," but new tones—artistic, dramatic, historical—sounded here at the same time. From now on Drachmann was as unstable in his writing as he was in his daily life. In life and in poetry he was much concerned with the erotic, cf. especially *Ranker og Roser* (*Vines and Roses,* 1879). Drachmann was always contemptuous of *petit-bourgeois* morals and the Biedermeier culture of Denmark:

> Come to me, my sunburned maid!
> On the greensward our wedding we'll hold soon.
> We've no more use for the gossiping staid
> Than we have for the man in the moon.

Drachmann was then, and long remained, scandalous to middle-class society. He often shocked his contemporaries by his love affairs and his outspokenness, but he remained a free spirit through the several phases of his authorship. His attitude he expressed in these verses in *Ranker og Roser*:

> I wear the hat I want to.
> I sing the songs I want to
> And can.

It was to Drachmann's credit, wrote the youthful Herman Bang (in *Realisme og Realister,* 1879) that he arose "in an era when men said there was no room for a lyrical poet, an era of the psychological novel." Although Drachmann's major achievement is as a lyrist he employed several genres. His travel books enjoyed considerable popularity. He wrote exotic tales in verse (for example, *Østen for Solen og Vesten for Maanen— East of the Sun and West of the Moon,* 1880), novels, and plays. His two-volume novel *Forskrevet* (*Mortgaged,* 1890), although of interest as a "key" both to Drachmann's life and to conditions in contemporary Copenhagen, is an amorphous monstrosity, if judged from a formalistic standpoint. Of Drachmann's operettas, the most successful is *Der var en Gang* (*Once upon a Time,* 1885), with music by P. E. Lange-Müller; it is a charming dramatic piece which still enjoys great popularity on the Danish stage. The "Midsummer Song" which it contains has become one of the best-known modern Danish songs.

Drachmann is a good example of how ill a literary-historical label fits a poet. If we attempt to apply the traditional categories, he is at once a Naturalist, a Romanticist, and an Impressionist.

Sophus Schandorph is unknown outside Denmark; Drachmann's tremendous production means nothing outside Scandinavia today; but Jens Peter Jacobsen is standard reading for the student of comparative literature in the Western world; his works have been translated into many languages. Among the writers who were closely associated with Brandes, Jacobsen is the author whose place is most secure in literature. Even though he was not interested in Brandes' programme for "portraying problems in literature," it was nevertheless Jacobsen who fulfilled Brandes' demand for a psychological novel. One seeks in vain his prototype in Brandes' gallery of foreign models. Far from being the Danish equivalent of some foreign model, Jacobsen was himself an original writer, although he was by no means a naïve writer and was familiar with the modern literature which Brandes was discussing. Jacobsen's canon is small; it consists of two novels, some short stories, and a few poems. His biography is short and tragic. As a young man his interests were divided between natural science and poetry. Subsequently he demonstrated himself to be talented both as a scientist and a creative writer. He became Darwin's disciple in Denmark and translated the *Origin of Species* and the *Descent of Man* into Danish. For twelve years he struggled with tuberculosis, until he was overcome by the disease in 1885. During these twelve years he produced almost all of his prose fiction. He wrote slowly, painfully slowly, a few sentences, a page perhaps in a day. He was the most conscientious of stylists, the most exacting master of description.

Despite Brandes' demand for a literature that made problems a matter of debate, and in the face of Brandes' enthusiasm for Jacobsen's prose, neither of Jacobsen's two novels, *Marie Grubbe* and *Niels Lyhne,* can be said to be problem literature in the usual sense of the term.[1] *Marie Grubbe* is a study of spiritual degeneration, and therewith a facet of life which interested many European writers toward the end of the century. *Niels Lyhne* is the story of a man's vain struggle to acquire a philosophy of life.

---

1 *Marie Grubbe. A Lady of the Seventeenth Century.* Translated by Hanna Astrup Larsen. New York, 1917, and several times reprinted.—*Niels Lyhne.* Translated by Hanna Astrup Larsen. New York, 1919; repr., 1921, 1947. Both published by The American-Scandinavian Foundation.

It is hard for us to understand that *Marie Grubbe,* Jacobsen's first novel (1876), could have caused offence, but it was nevertheless attacked by conservative critics for its crass realism. Realism indeed, but today we judge it to be not crass but sensitively human with its psychological penetration into the soul of the main character, Marie Grubbe, who from being a viceroy's consort descends to the lowest of social stations, and becomes the wife of a ferryman. As mentioned above, Marie Grubbe's fate has attracted the attention of a number of writers. Holberg mentioned her in his Epistle 89; Blicher adapted her story in *En Landsbydegns Dagbog (The Journal of a Parish Clerk)*; and Hans Christian Andersen made use of her in *Hønse-Grethes Familie (Chicken Grethe's Family)*. Incidentally, Jacobsen had become acquainted with the historical figure of Marie Grubbe through Holberg and Andersen. The subtitle of the novel is significant: "interiors from the seventeenth century." This subtitle should have been enough to indicate to critics of the seventies that Jacobsen was not attempting naturalistic effects. He wrote his psychological-historical novel with the care of a scholar and an historian and went to great pains to verify all historical details. The book may therefore rightfully be called interiors—i.e., pictures, descriptions. To say that the book is rich in description is to do it an injustice. It abounds with details and reflects especially Jacobsen's awareness of color, yet these aspects of the novel neither obstruct the development of the story nor make the characters in the book seem any less genuine. One may read *Marie Grubbe* for the plot alone and find it exciting and full of tension. Such is Jacobsen's art that, despite his exacting attitude towards detail and minutiae, the result of his efforts does not try the reader's patience. His descriptions of nature, and particularly of the heath, are masterful. Similarly, considerable attention is given to meteorological conditions. The beginning of Jacobsen's story *Mogens* (1872)[1] is frequently cited as an example of his style and his descriptions of nature, but the beginning of *Marie Grubbe* is equally characteristic:

> The air beneath the linden crowns had flown in across brown heath and parched meadow. It brought the heat of the sun and was laden with dust from the road, but in the cool, thick foliage it had been cleansed and freshened, while the yellow linden flowers had given it moisture and fragrance. In the blissful haven of the green vault it lay quivering in light waves, caressed by the softly stirring leaves and the flutter of white-gold butterfly wings.

---

1 *Mogens and other stories.* Translated by Anna Grabow. New York, 1921. Jacobsen's story "Fru Fönss," translated by Carl Christian Jensen, is contained in *Denmark's Best Stories,* New York, 1928, pp. 119–145.

The feeling for color is apparent on almost every page. Compare for example this passage from Chapter XI[1]:

A row of flambeaux cast a fiery sheen over the red wall, made the yew and box glow like bronze, and lent all faces the ruddy glow of vigorous health. See, scarlet-clothed halberdiers are standing in double rows, holding flower-wreathed tapers high against the dark sky. Cunningly wrought lanterns and candles in sconces and candelabra send their rays low along the ground and high among the yellowing leaves, forcing the darkness back, and opening a shining path for the resplendent train. The light glitters on gold and gilded tissue, beams brightly on silver and steel, glides in shimmering stripes down silks and sweeping satins. Softly as a reddish dew, it is breathed over dusky velvet, and flashing white, it falls like stars among rubies and diamonds. Reds make a brave show with the yellows; clear sky-blue closes over brown; streaks of lustrous sea-green cut their way through white and violet-blue; coral sinks between black and lavender; golden brown and rose, steel-gray and purple are whirled about, light and dark, tint upon tint, in eddying pools of color.

Jacobsen achieved unusual effects by his handling of paragraph and sentence structure. Long descriptive sentences are broken off by curt, momentous remarks. Important events are reported briefly, and in a matter-of-fact way. Compare for example, this passage that pertains to one of Marie's admirers in Nürnberg:

Thus Marie little by little grew reconciled to herself, but then it happened one day, when Remigius was out riding, that his horse shied, threw him from the saddle, and dragged him to death by the stirrups.   (Chapter XV)

Jacobsen also employs the sudden shift of attention or action, as in the beginning of *Mogens*: "It was summer;" or at a critical juncture in *Marie Grubbe*: "Marie Grubbe was now seventeen years old."

Jacobsen's was a different art than Zola's or Dosteyevski's, for the realism of Zola and his followers stressed intellectual content rather than technique and was wont to treat contemporary problems. Jacobsen was a stylist, a word-magician. That he at the time was considered the great naturalistic writer of the "Breakthrough" may be ascribed to the *Zeitgeist*, or, more precisely expressed, to the fact that Jacobsen was a natural scientist, a Darwinian, and a friend of Georg Brandes. That there is a certain lack of organic development in *Marie Grubbe* reflects Jacobsen's view of the rôle of change in human life. Here again he is more "naturalistic" than many more recent writers who have acknowledged the naturalistic program; he portrays a series of events without forcing them into any neat or artificial pattern of interrelationship.

1 From the translation by Hanna Astrup Larsen, p. 151f.

Marie Grubbe is a woman without principle, without a personal philosophy, and the end result of her life is resignation. Jacobsen does not debate the question of milieu or heredity with his readers. We are left to decide for ourselves just what the forces of the past and present are of which Marie Grubbe is the resultant. Nor does Jacobsen condemn or praise Marie Grubbe for what she does. She is to be forgiven, because we understand all and because her actions are not caused by any evil premeditation. Without knowing it, she is struggling to be herself and rejecting the falsity of the society in which she grew to maturity. The life of a lady of her time was essentially pointless and bereft of the satisfaction of much intellectual or personal achievement. Marie Grubbe longs for an experience that will give a meaning to her life; this is the key to her actions. She says, "I wish that life would overwhelm me and either crush me to earth or elevate me so that there was no room in my soul for anything but the force that had lifted me up or crushed me." And this is what she finally experiences in her life. At least in the eyes of her contemporaries, and adjudged by the values of the society from which she went forth, she is crushed. Perhaps her accomplishing of a goal, her satisfaction of being as nearly the person outwardly as she is inwardly, counterbalances the degeneration that the course of her life otherwise would indicate.

Jacobsen's ability to hold an international audience for decades is more readily apparent in *Niels Lyhne* (1880) than in *Marie Grubbe,* for the philosophical problem which embodies the ethos of *Niels Lyhne* has a validity that transcends the appeal of the book either as the work of a great stylist or as the work of a naturalistic writer. Although it is a story from the nineteenth century and is scarcely to be defined as a historical novel, *Niels Lyhne* has much in common with *Marie Grubbe* besides stylistic similarities. It too is a psychological novel. *Marie Grubbe* is the delineation of a human being who exists without a philosophy of life and who degenerates; *Niels Lyhne* exhibits a human being who struggles to find a philosophy of life and fails—who never advances beyond the first step, the negation of the patent philosophies which would force themselves upon him. The hero is a dreamer by nature and an atheist by conviction. He can find no firm ground to stand on; he falls in love and love makes of him a dreamy poet. Like Mogens and Marie Grubbe, he seeks salvation in the consolations of bourgeois existence: "No home on earth, no God in heaven, no goal out in the future! He wanted to have a home at least; he would win it by love...."

A brief happy marriage is Niels' lot; then his wife dies—but not before she has abandoned the negative faith Niels had taught her. Their child dies and Niels is again alone. Niels enters the army and falls in combat, true to his own convictions His physician mumbles, "If I were God... I would rather save them who were not converted on their death bed." Niels dies without having achieved Mogens' bourgeois peace of mind or Marie Grubbe's resignation. He represents the searching mind of the nineteenth century. He is the modern man who would find a substitute for the antiquated concept of a deity, a concept that had been destroyed for him by philosophy and the natural sciences. Since, in Jacobsen's opinion, there is no divine pattern to be found and no satisfactory conclusion regarding the reasons for existence to be deduced from the many premises which the enquiring mind finds in the natural world, Niels Lyhne's end can only be meaningless and chaotic.

Jacobsen's few poems, which have several facets, mark the advent of a modern spirit into Danish verse.[1] The poems are a synthesis of many currents, rationalistic, classical, and naturalistic. Some poems, for example "Stemninger I" ("Moods I", 1868) are characteristic of the agnostic in Jacobsen. Others, like "Saa standsed'—" ("Then Stopped," 1884) seem to reflect a teleological optimism which is lacking in *Niels Lyhne*. On the whole, the philosophical idea rather than the picture dominates in Jacobsen's verse; the situation is nearly the reverse of that in Jacobsen's prose. While much of his verse is rather pedestrian, at least one poem, "Irmelin Rose" (c. 1875), a ballad of haunting rhythm, is a lyrical masterpiece.

The theme of degeneracy which Jacobsen had used in *Marie Grubbe*, was magnified by HERMAN BANG (1857–1912), whose works, at least stylistically, were the ultimate in the attempt to write photographically. Bang was at once the poet of decadence and an iconoclast with regard to form. His general subject was the "hopeless generations," which provided the title of his first novel (*Haabløse Slægter*, 1880). His realistic descriptions verge on both the photographic and the phonographic, and in his later works his technique suggests the snapshot and the tape-recorder.

In the preface to the second, revised edition of *Haabløse Slægter*, published in 1884, Bang wrote with unusually incisive self-criticism:

"This book was written when I was 22. It bore all the marks thereof. It was broad, unclear, impassioned, a child of all the longings of 'Weltschmerz,' unfinished in its form, disquieted, bold in its description. But in the chaotic work, despite its weaknesses, there were characteristics of something definite in the life of my contemporaries."

1 Of the several poems translated into English, the most accessible are contained in *A Book of Danish Verse*, New York, 1922, and *A Second Book of Danish Verse*. Translated by Charles Wharton Stork, New York, 1947.

Insofar, Bang was but living up to the definition he had himself set as a critic in his first publication, *Realisme og Realister (Realism and Realists)* in 1879, in which he declared:

"A man does not become a poet because he is above his times but because he is a full and living expression of the times, because he has suffered with it, fought with it and understood it."

Bang felt that his times were approaching a degenerate *fin de siècle*. He was content to be a "degenerate" with it and to be a protagonist of the realism which has a predilection for the abnormal, for it was his conviction that realism, although the "current that has brought life into our literature," would later be supplanted by a new synthesis.

The immediate reaction to Bang's first novel was shock. After many copies had been sold, the original edition of the book was confiscated. Actually, there is nothing particularly daring or sensational in the original edition; it is unpolished rather than coarse or distasteful. The story does not contradict the title. William Høg, a young man of unstable mind, overrefined, lacking a strong will, is the scion of a fine and proud family and the culmination of its degeneracy. As Bang's leading figure, he is the opposite of what Ibsen might have considered an ideal. William could, if he would. He need only believe in himself; but that he can never do. William is an anti-Aladdin—a contrast which was implied by Bang himself in the novel. William has other literary kin; he is spiritually related to the leading characters in Thomas Mann's *Buddenbrooks* (1901) and Rilke's *Malte Laurids Brigge* (1910). Even the death of William's grandfather, the "Excellency," suggests the death of Christoph Detlev Brigge in Rilke's novel. In his choice of subject matter, Bang represents a stage in the development of the novel from Jens Peter Jacobsen to the Danish novelist Harald Kidde (*Aage og Else,* 1902), and the German writers Mann and Rilke.

In *Haabløse Slægter* there are also the beginnings of the impressionistic style which Bang was to cultivate more and more during his life and to bring almost to the point of incomprehensibility in the novel *Stuk (Stucco,* 1887). In contrast to Jens Peter Jacobsen and his imitators, Bang broke with the tradition of well-organized prose description and resolved his story into non-expository dialogue. He possessed an unusual ability to make the reader feel that several conversations are going on in the same place at the same time. No writer prior to Bang had undertaken to reproduce in prose a situation in which several characters talk at once. That Bang not only could interweave several laconic and cryptic conversations which both give the reader the feeling of simultaneous speech and convey an understanding of what essentially was being said, demonstrates his peculiar artistry. Without being formally dramatic, the conversations are like those in a drama. In his later novels, the technique which makes a very short or epigrammatic remark imply much is highly developed. A novel like *Det graa Hus* (*The Grey House*, 1901) consists chiefly of cryptic dialogue coupled with brief but pregnant descriptions. Impression is joined to impression without any attempt to agitate the reader either by plot or description, yet the result is devastating enough as a sadly satirical reflection on the emptiness and degeneracy of contemporary society. Human beings live in their own passions without finding one another and without performing actions of consequence. Although he is not agitating for any particular philosophy, Bang describes human relationships in such a way that his readers necessarily question a social order responsible for such conditions.

In Bang's autobiographically colored and nostalgic *De uden Fædreland* (*Denied a Country*, 1906),[1] scene follows scene in which stilted conversations are cryptic, and facial expressions are of importance for understanding the course of events. "Nor do I know of a realistic novel," Bang had written in 1879, "that is not a collection of pictures, loose leaves from the great book of the human soul." Bang's comparisons often seem forced. One reflects that, although he is classified as a realist, he can be remarkably unrealistic. For example, the exposition frequently proceeds by means of a character's train of thought. Here Bang may be considered a precursor of the more recent "stream of consciousness" technique. His use of this type of exposition is especially effective in *Ved Vejen* (*By the Wayside*, 1886). His most mature work in regard both to ethos and language, *Ved Vejen* depicts the grey hopelessness of everyday life. While it is possible to point out a rise and fall in the action, there is no plot in the novel and the course of events could as justifiably be represented diagrammatically by a straight line as by a curved line. Man and woman can live and die "while the railroad train is covered by the winter's fog across the fields"—by the wayside. The picture Bang suggests at the end of the book is the same as at the beginning—the colorlessness and essential meaninglessness of life by the wayside.

Bang once tried without success to become an actor; he was subsequently a well-known elocutionist, and in his later years an inveterate traveller—he died while in the United States on a speaking tour. His own

---

1 Translated by Marie Busch and A. G. Chater. New York and London, 1927.

longing, his homelessness, and his unhappy and abnormal life are reg-
istered in *De uden Fædreland.*

A curious parallel to the self-styled realistic literature of the Brandesian
"Breakthrough" is the work of the gifted journalist VILHELM TOPSØE
(1840–81), in whose prose there is a suggestion of the style which Herman
Bang employed. At the same time that Topsøe, an editor of the Copenhagen newspaper *Dagbladet,* was looked upon with animosity by Brandes
and his circle (members of which were soon to found the radical newspaper *Politiken*), the moderate, conservative Topsøe produced as realistic
a novel as any of the revolutionary minds: *Jason med det gyldne Skind (Jason
with the Golden Fleece,* published anonymously in 1875). *Jason* is a psychological study akin to the novels of Jens Peter Jacobsen, Herman
Bang, and the later Viggo Stuckenberg and Harald Kidde. While Topsøe
did not undertake to make a conscious break with the literature of earlier
decades, the intellectual content of *Jason* was nevertheless new. The hero
is a man of indecision, just as Stuckenberg's main figure in the much
younger novel *I Gennembrud* is a youth of indecision. Time and again
the engineer-physician Anton Hasting is in a position to win the affections
of a woman who might quiet his restless soul—but he hesitates and is lost.
Topsøe had a deep understanding of people, which he had acquired from
his experiences as a journalist, traveller, and a politician rather than from
contemplation; he knew how to exploit his understanding in vivid
portrayals of city and country life both in *Jason* and in *Nutidsbilleder*
(*Pictures of the Times,* 1878). A promising literary career was terminated
by his death at the age of 41.

Topsøe made stylistic innovations and excelled in the lifelike presentation of everyday existence. There is a discernible line of development
from Sophus Schandorph, who was one of Brandes' first and most outspoken disciples, to Vilhelm Topsøe and Herman Bang, yet neither
Topsøe nor Bang was ever personally close to Brandes. The affinity
between Topsøe and Bang is however historically documented; Bang
dedicated his first work of prose fiction to Topsøe.

If Topsøe was a parallel to the "Breakthrough," then SOPHUS BAUDITZ
(1850–1915) was a conscious counterpart who spoke for the conservative
opposition. His cycle of tales entitled *Historier fra Skovridergaarden*
(*Stories from the Forester's House,* 1889), with their rural idyll and naïvely
positive attitude toward life, seem anachronistic when compared with
the more experimental modern literature of the eighties and nineties.
Centering about the idealized life of a forester, the tales may be considered
representative of a kind of dream world for bourgeois and patricians who

were well satisfied with the *status quo*. There are no abstract social problems for Bauditz; the individual of the upper middle class is the person who counts. The single characters in the stories are nearly caricatures, because of Bauditz's attempt to make them distinct in the mind of the reader. His forester is a hearty man with the traditional rough exterior and heart of gold, a gentleman and a patriot—certainly not the kind of man who would have any truck with Brandes and his followers. In the novel *Hjortholm* (1896), Bauditz's second most widely read book, the young heroine makes a few essays into the radical and modern currents of the times (the dangerous Dr. Brandes is mentioned *en passant*), but soon inclines to believe with her elderly aunt, that the world, although not quite as good as depicted in older literature, nevertheless is "much better than it is in the new books."

The stories "from a forester's house" which won considerable popularity for Bauditz were for a long time a model for a lengthy series of books that are identified in Danish as "Herregaardsromaner," i.e., novels about life on a country estate. Such novels provide unsophisticated readers with a surrogate for a problem-free life in which people exist without having to soil their hands and, despite some thrilling tribulations, false accusations, and dire predicaments, nevertheless manage to live happily ever after. This kind of novel is still widely read in Denmark today, albeit less in Copenhagen than elsewhere.

Another, related type of novel and short story constitutes what in Danish is called "schoolmaster literature," that is, imaginative works of a didactic and pious cast written by teachers or their ilk for popular consumption. Representative of this kind of writing is the work of ZAKARIAS NIELSEN (1844–1922), whose literary proclivity was determined by an older generation of authors and who carried on a faded bourgeois literary tradition. Like the younger Naturalists, Nielsen's general subject was the struggle between the old and the new, especially in the realm of religion, toward the end of the century. His *Maagen (The Gull,* 1889) sounded a warning against the radical new morality. *Kulsviere (The Charcoal Burners,* 1893) was an attempt to depict the seriousness of life as it is lived by simple and common folk in Northern Zealand. Crassly put, the book is the story of lovers who are beset by self-imposed obstacles which they finally surmount. While the novel (which is considered his best work) contains a credible picture of rural Danish life, the substance of the narrative is not profound and the psychological delineation of the characters is weak.

The dogma of naturalism, and specifically the Darwinian doctrine, found unusual literary expression in the writings of CARL EWALD (1856–

1908). Beginning as a novelist, Ewald turned to a genre which had been without a master since the death of Hans Christian Andersen: the tale, i.e., the *Eventyr* or *Märchen*. Ewald became a kind of naturalistic Hans Christian Andersen. If his fame has not equalled that of the great virtuoso of the fairy tale, it is nevertheless considerable and international. Ewald's tales have been published many times over in Denmark and have been widely translated.[1] With the tales of Andersen, Christian Winther's *Flugten til Amerika*, and a few other books, they make up the core of any collection of children's books in Denmark.

Ewald not only gave to the tale a dash of Darwinian theory but demonstrated a unique ability to make the forces of nature and the animal world on land and in the water comprehensible, real, and alive. In a foreword to the first collection of tales, *I det Fri* (*Outdoors,* 1892), the author's father, H. F. Ewald, himself a popular Danish novelist of the time, stated that Carl Ewald was of the opinion that "nature with its complex and variegated life contained new material from which children could profit in their own way..."

In short: *utile dulce*. And Ewald's tales are more than a little didactic. Indeed, they disseminate a large amount of fundamentally correct information about plants, animals, and natural phenomena. Yet they are entertaining and are dramatically told. An example of one of the most engaging tales, which was included in the above-mentioned first collection, is "The Queen-Bee." The most ambitious tale, "The Quiet Pond," is in no less than twelve parts. The reader's attention is led in turn to the plant louse, the grasshopper, the eel and the cabbage worm, the beech and the oak tree, to coral, to the wind, the ocean, and the animals of the night, as Ewald depicts by implication and suggestion the struggle for existence in nature and the everlasting motion and interdependence in the infinitely complex world outside man's limited realm of immediate experience.

Ewald wrote in an easy and prepossessing style, but he did not affect naïveté as had Hans Christian Andersen. Nevertheless, he reminds us of Andersen in his enthusiastic manner of telling a tale and in his extensive use of personification and anthropopathism. Nor is it too much to contend that Hans Christian Andersen, had he been born half a century later than he was, would have incorporated the theory of evolution in his philosophy. Andersen was ever the friend of scientific and technological progress, as we have seen in the discussion of "Poetry's California," above.

1 Twelve volumes of Ewald's tales appeared in English translation and several were reprinted, between 1907 and 1934.

With the work of Carl Ewald, the principles of the New Literature espoused by Brandes may be said to have permeated Danish literature, for Ewald's tales became household reading matter in Denmark.

A picture of the times, and specifically a representation of the effect of Brandes and the "Breakthrough" and of Grundtvigianism in Denmark, is to be found in works by KARL GJELLERUP (1857–1919) and HENRIK PONTOPPIDAN (1857–1943), who shared the Nobel Prize in 1917. Therewith the similarity of the two writers ends, however. Although Gjellerup was widely read in his own lifetime—two of his novels were translated into English—he has now sunk very nearly into literary oblivion, while Henrik Pontoppidan has become a Danish classic.

In a rather sensational and hyper-dramatic fashion, Gjellerup was able to embody the tensions of the "Breakthrough," to caricature the narrowness of the Danish bourgeoisie, and in addition to record the impact of the higher Biblical criticism that was essentially German in origin, in his most influential book, *Germanernes Lærling* (*The Teutons' Apprentice,* 1882). Having been trained as a theologian at the University of Copenhagen, Gjellerup had before this made an unusual start in Danish literature with his emotional novel *En Idealist (An Idealist),* which had been published under the pseudonym "Epigonus" in 1878. *Germanernes Lærling,* which is generally considered as having been inspired by Schandorph's *Thomas Friis' Historie,* was his farewell to theology. Though the novel is a far cry from Henrik Pontoppidan's *Lykke-Per,* the two works have some common characteristics. Both are pictures of the times and in each the main figure, who may be identified with the author, is struggling to achieve a philosophy of life. Gjellerup was strongly attracted by German intellectual life and classical German literature, indeed, he spent much of his later life in Germany. His early novels bear the impression of European naturalism, especially the French and Russian schools, although in a German interpretation. Like Holger Drachmann, Gjellerup broke with Brandes in the eighties. His later works bear witness to his restless search for religious satisfaction. At one time he was strongly attracted to Buddhism and Indian thought. His interest in the Near East bore fruit in *Pilgrimmen Kamanita* (*The Pilgrim Kamanita,* 1906),[1] but in his last works he turned back to Christianity. He may be summed up as a phenomenon of the times and an example of the intellectual unrest towards the end of the nineteenth century, of the atheological search for God, and of the impact of foreign currents on Danish and German literature.

1 Translated by John E. Logie. London 1911; New York, 1912. The earlier novel *Minna* also appeared in English translation, by C. L. Nielsen. London, 1913.

The "Breakthrough" found its critic and chronicler in Henrik Pont-oppidan. While it is no hyperbole to state that Pontoppidan was indebted to Brandes and the men about Brandes, it is similarly no exaggeration to state that he was able to preserve his originality and critical independence when confronted with the radicalism of Brandes and his followers. That is to say, Pontoppidan felt the impact of Brandes without being dominated by him. The ideas which emanated from Brandes were but some of many currents late in the nineteenth century which seemed to converge in the person of Pontoppidan, whose works express the nineteenth century's dream of the exotic, the Grundtvigian idea of enlightenment, the Kierkegaardian inclination to introspection, the political radicalism of the seventies, the clerical tradition of the Danish manse, the new faith in technology, and the new social consciousness.

Henrik Pontoppidan's first works primarily depicted social injustice and contemporary conditions. They stood in contrast to the early idyllic tales of his older Norwegian contemporary Bjørnstjerne Bjørnson. They therewith placed Pontoppidan in the ranks of the Brandesians, who fol-lowed the dictum of debating problems of the day. Aside from social in-dignation, there are two motifs which recur throughout Pontoppidan's works and are subtly developed in the later works: the crippling effect of environment upon the individual, and the rôle played by the ghosts of the past. The former motif is suggested by the symbolic title of Pontoppidan's first book, *Stækkede Vinger* (*Clipped Wings*, 1881), and is best known from his allegorical tale "Ørneflugt" ("The Flight of the Eagle" 1894; 1897), a conscious counterpart of Hans Christian Andersen's optimistic "Ugly Duckling." The latter motif is suggested by the title *Spøgelser* (*Ghosts*, 1888). Pontoppidan's frequent concern with clergymen and parsonages is a result of his own origin; he was the son of a Jutland pastor who belonged to one of Denmark's best-known and traditionally clerical families.

Pontoppidan developed rapidly as a thinker and a stylist. From the somewhat clumsy and sentimental author of *Stækkede Vinger* and of *Sandinge Menighed* (*Sandinge Parish*, 1883), he became a master of the effec-tive phrase in *Skyer* (*Clouds*, 1890), a work that boils with political indigna-tion about conditions to which Denmark was subjected by the provisional governments of J. B. S. Estrup, prime minister 1875–94, who in the eighties all but circumvented democratic processes by means of provi-sional laws.

Pontoppidan was a prolific writer; between 1881 and 1890 he published thirteen books; four of them were published in 1890 alone. His earlier works form a group by themselves and culminate in *Skyer*. Although he

HERMAN BANG
Sketch by P. S. Krøyer, 1899.

HENRIK PONTOPPIDAN
c. 1915.

continued to produce shorter novels, short stories, and even plays for the next thirty years, Pontoppidan's great literary achievement after 1890 is the series of socio-philosophical novels which, taken together, give a penetrating and thorough exposition of life in Denmark between 1875 and 1910: *Det forjættede Land (The Promised Land), Lykke-Per (Lucky Per)*, and *De Dødes Rige (The Realm of the Dead)*. Of these novels the second, originally published in eight volumes (1898–1904), is his *magnum opus* and his great confession. Together with Paludan-Müller's *Adam Homo*, Hans Christian Andersen's fairy tales, Jens Peter Jacobsen's novels, Martin Andersen Nexø's *Pelle Erobreren,* and Johannes V. Jensen's short stories, *Lykke-Per* is one of the works in recent Danish literature that seems to have the best claim to lasting fame in the annals of world literature.

The interrelation of *Det forjættede Land* and *Lykke-Per* is similar to that of Ibsen's *Brand* and *Peer Gynt*. Like Ibsen's Brand, Pontoppidan's Emmanuel Hansted is the fanatical believer who sacrifices all, knows not love, and is rewarded with hallucinations, while Per Sidenius—Lucky Per—is like Peer Gynt, a phantast who does not know good fortune when he sees it, who possesses no philosophy of life, and who must above all learn the lesson to "be himself."

Det forjættede Land (The Promised Land, 1891–95), like much of Pontoppidan's writing, is ironic in nature.[1] The object of castigation is the Grundtvigian party, the compromises which that party had made, and the religious enthusiasts which it produced. Pontoppidan had deserted the Grundtvigians in 1881 after he had for some time lived close to Grundtvigianism, of which he had gradually become critical, although in a different way than Georg Brandes. The first two volumes of the trilogy *Det forjættede Land* parallel Pontoppidan's own experiences, whereas the third volume, "The Day of Judgment" (*Dommens Dag,* 1895)— incidentally less effective both in conception and execution than the other parts of the trilogy—is more speculative. The principal character is a young theologian who is attracted to the Grundtvigian doctrines and who, like Pontoppidan himself, marries a peasant girl from Grundtvigian circles, but who gradually and against his will becomes more sophisticated, and who finally deserts his family in order to become a new Messiah. But Emmanuel Hansted is neither a great mind nor a prophet; at the zenith of his religious enthusiasm his mind gives way and shortly thereafter he dies, leaving a legacy of pious myth amongst the simple folk. Pontoppidan condemns his protagonist in the words of another

---

1 The first two volumes, translated by Mrs. E. V. Lucas, were published in London, 1896, as *Emanuel, or Children of the Soil,* and *The Promised Land.*

character, Pater Rüdesheimer, who says that on Emmanuel's tombstone there should stand: "Here lies Don Quixote's ghost, Emmanuel Hansted by name, who was born to be a good chaplain, but thought himself a prophet and a saint; who therefore took on the costume of a shepherd and felt every inspiration to be a special call from heaven; who bungled everything that came into his hands, left his wife, and mistreated his children; but who nevertheless felt himself to be chosen by Providence to prepare the second coming and to preach God's judgment upon man."

The descriptions of Danish society in *Lykke-Per* are more all-embracing than in *Det forjættede Land,* for Per Sidenius—"Lucky Per"—succeeds in moving in many spheres of Danish life. Whereas in *Det forjættede Land* Pontoppidan portrayed only the rural milieu, much of the action in *Lykke-Per* takes place in the Danish capital. One of the remarkable aspects of *Lykke-Per* is that the exposition is nearly complete as a picture of the times, that is, of Denmark in the nineties. Although Pontoppidan did succeed in giving a picture of the times and wrote on the basis of his own experience, *Lykke-Per* is, however, in the last analysis, a philosophical novel.

It is both a philosophical novel and a psychological novel; at the same time it represents a culmination of all the forces which met in the person of an author who assumed the complex heritage of nineteenth-century Danish literature. Pontoppidan was keenly aware of those ideas which are historically identified as romantic. He fought against them, but many of them persevered, being encouraged by the nationalism that made itself felt more and more after the disastrous wars with Germany in the middle of the nineteenth century. Pontoppidan and his leading character Per Sidenius revolt against Biedermeier bourgeois culture, the *status quo,* and rural Grundtvigianism. Pontoppidan's introspective and critical thinking, suggesting as it does the philosophical ideals which Henrik Ibsen embraced, is spiritually related to Kierkegaard's brooding. The rise of natural science and Darwinism and the cultural currents espoused by Brandes provide the intellectual background for *Lykke-Per.* Industrialisation and the subsequent social consciousness which it fostered inspired Per Sidenius to dream that he could change the face of Denmark.

Lykke-Per originally appeared in eight small volumes between 1898 and 1904. It was revised for publication in a second edition of 1905. A third edition was published in 1907; and a fourth, revised edition in 1918. The novel is therefore available in three versions which differ slightly from one another. In introductions to volumes three through eight of the original edition, Pontoppidan summarized the narrative. This is his own summary of the story in volume eight:

Per Sidenius, son of a Jutland clergyman, is a poor young engineer who has not taken his degree; he nurtures a vast project of a combined canal and free harbor as well as plans for wind and wave motors. He has tried to arouse public interest in his ideas by publishing a booklet about them. He has at the same time been introduced to the extremely wealthy Jewish merchant Philip Salomon, whose daughter Jakobe he wins after a brief struggle. Because of his engagement to Jakobe, his plans come to be looked upon with favor by certain capitalists and speculators. Just as he returns from a long tour of study abroad and there seems to be some possibility of establishing company to carry out some of his ideas, he receives word of his mother's death. In part because of his irreligious views, his relationship to his home had always been poor and finally had been broken altogether. Nevertheless, and as previously had happened under similar circumstances, he is seized with religious fervor. He suddenly leaves Copenhagen and goes to Jutland to seek a reckoning with himself while visiting the estate of two elderly women whom he had met abroad and who are very much interested in him. Here he meets a Pastor Blomberg, under whose influence his craving for religion is further aroused, and he is attracted to the pastor's daughter Inger. He finally breaks with Jakobe and her circle. Then, in order to open the way to a secure bourgeois existence and to the possibility of marrying Inger, he decides to take the state surveyor's examination. On his way back to Copenhagen he visits the city of his childhood in order to consecrate himself to a new life at the grave of his parents.

In the final volume Per becomes a surveyor and marries Inger; for a time they lead a bourgeois existence, but Per leaves his family, fearful that he may pass on to his children the curse which he feels to lie upon him. He lives very nearly a hermit's life on the west coast of Jutland; there at last he achieves a philosophy. At his death it is found not only that he has made Jakobe Salomon's school for underprivileged children his heir, but that he has left in writing some reflections which show him to have reached a worthy goal: to have recognized himself and to have conquered the universe within him.

The psychological and philosophical problem in *Lykke-Per* is so real and so gripping that the sensitive reader may overlook the fact that *Lykke-Per* also was meant by its author critically to portray and interpret the times. Reflecting upon the book today, we see it as a meaningful novel of development about an individual who gradually achieves a philosophy of life. This explains the novel's wide appeal in German, Swedish, Russian, Dutch, Hungarian, and Polish translations.[1]

Pontoppidan's basic sociological assumption in writing *Lykke-Per* was

1 One half of the novel has appeared in French translation.

13*

the same as in his famous "Ørneflugt" ("The Flight of the Eagle," 1894), which ended by reversing Hans Christian Andersen's optimistic formula and stating that, "It doesn't help to have lain in an eagle's egg, if one has to grow up in the barnyard."[1] While this rather depressing view of the influence of environment and heredity was certainly long held by Pontoppidan, he nevertheless came to conclusions that represent a more highly developed stage of his own thinking; his message is Ibsen's message: Know thyself.

In *De Dødes Rige* (*The Realm of the Dead,* five volumes, 1912–16), Pontoppidan wrote more as a social novelist than as a thinker.

De Dødes Rige is less personal than *Lykke-Per* and less of a psychological caricature than *Det forjættede Land.* Nor does it have a leading character in the same way as the other two cycles of novels by Pontoppidan. Far more than the earlier works, *De Dødes Rige* is an interpretive picture of the times—in this case the first years of the twentieth century. Rather than exposing a leading character to the many strata of society, Pontoppidan now describes a number of related and interdependent figures who represent the political, ecclesiastical, economic, and social life of the times. The predominant note is one of failure—not always failure in outward achievement but rather the failure to realize the ideas which had motivated society in a previous decade and had set a course for the new century. Such failure, the reader concludes, is ultimately to be ascribed to weaknesses in human character: the spirit of compromise, insincerity, and a lack of personal integrity. It is not so much that society is rotten (as Ibsen put it) but that the realm which men were striving to maintain was not an organic and living thing, because they were themselves afraid of life and were not fully up to taking the consequences of their own actions and own decisions. Pontoppidan was particularly sharp in his attitude toward the church in *De Dødes Rige.* The agent of salvation on this earth seems if anything to be the medical profession. It is the wonder of modern medical science that permits Torben Dihmer—who is most nearly the central character of the novel—to overcome a physical ailment which otherwise would be fatal. And yet, after his return to the everyday world, Torben finds that life is not really worth living.

The novel, which is Pontoppidan's most ambitious attempt to weave a historical tapestry, as it were, strikes no optimistic note and is morose in its implied criticism of human institutions as they existed in Denmark around 1900.

1 Translated as "Eagle's Flight" by Lida Siboni Hanson in *The American-Scandinavian Review,* 1929, pp. 556–8.

Pontoppidan deals with the problems of decadence which attracted many writers at the turn of the twentieth century. A comparison with some of the novels of Thomas Mann *(Buddenbrooks, Der Zauberberg)* is not out of the question.

Pontoppidan's last novel, *Mands Himmerig* (*Man's Heaven*, 1927) is laid at the beginning of World War I. A searching picture of the times centered about a main character, it is critical of the power of the press. As a literary work it scarcely bears comparison with Pontoppidan's earlier novels, however.

Pontoppidan's prestige is derived from a number of his short stories quite as much as from the longer novels. His stories fulfilled the demands of the Brandesian school, for they have as their themes a number of intellectual, social, and philosophical problems. Stylistically they suggest Meïr Goldschmidt. As Pontoppidan matured as a writer, he became less concerned with social and political questions and paid more attention to the search for ultimate human values. The later stories—from *Skyer* (1890) onward—are more penetrating in their analyses of human character and are on a higher aesthetic plane. Pontoppidan is wont to ferret out hidden weaknesses and falsehoods, to castigate the day-dreamer and the man afraid to be true to his own convictions. He expresses great admiration for the individual who can accept the consequences of his convictions. Several stories, e.g., *Kirkeskuden* (*The Ship Model*, 1881, one of Pontoppidan's earliest works), depict the revolt against the parsonage, and in so doing presage *Lykke-Per*. Other stories are concerned with the artistic temperament and the artist's clash with society. The foremost example of this type is *Nattevagt* (*Night Watch*, 1894), an angry tale of a naturalistic painter who crassly but valiantly fights against reactionary and unrealistic art, and who loses his wife and his fortune in the attempt to throttle the "lie of life" *(livsløgn)* against which Henrik Ibsen had so fervently written. In Pontoppidan's short stories he frequently makes a point dramatically. Indeed, some of the earlier tales may be criticised as overly dramatic.

Although he wrote not without a didactic impulse and was merciless in his sarcasm and criticism, Pontoppidan reached the peak of his artistry in the stories which make up the collection *Skyer* (*Clouds*, 1890) which, as aforementioned, are a condemnation of the suppression of civil liberties under the provisional government of late nineteenth-century Denmark. To read the first story in the collection, "Ilum Galgebakke," is to become acquainted with Pontoppidan's mastery of metaphor and exposition. An example of an inimitable introductory descriptive passage will suffice:

Heavy rich waves of soil press down to the shore, and the land bears woods, villages, churches, and mills on its broad back... If one comes up here on a still summer evening when the setting sun lays a sheen as of melted butter on every puddle, when the churches round about on the rises begin to cackle like the hens that have just laid eggs... one can imagine oneself transported to a wonderland where everything breathes peace and eternal happiness. Just below lies Ilum Lake, hidden among the round hills, as peaceful and cozy as a spot of butter in a dish of porridge.

Such an overture provides a foil for the acrid sarcasm that is to come.

Other stories reflect Pontoppidan's admiration for the non-conformist and individualist, be that person only sincere in his philosophy. Pontoppidan has set a semi-humorous monument to the unfeigned individualist in the whimsical *Isbjørnen* (*The Polar Bear*, 1887), a tale of the struggle between a straightforward, virile, realistic clergyman and his stubborn, reactionary, and hypocritical congregation. The clergyman—"the polar bear"—finally leaves his congregation in rage and writes in chalk on the church door, "You have the tyrants you deserve." We may assume this sentiment to have been Pontoppidan's own in moments of despair. Another exemplary tale is *Den kongelige Gæst* (*The Royal Guest,* 1908), a study of a middle-aged couple whose lives are altered by a visit from a stranger who calls himself Prince Carneval and who for one brief evening takes them, and first and foremost the wife, out of grey, humdrum, daily existence. The one evening is enough to spoil the pattern of the pair's bourgeois life.

At the end of his life Pontoppidan gave to Danish literature an unexpected treasure in his memoirs, which were published in five volumes 1933–43.[1] These small books are the crystal-clear distillation of a long and productive life and demonstrate that, even as an octogenarian, Pontoppidan was the master of Danish prose. He is no sensationalist; he is a chaste, meticulous, and lucid autobiographer. "As an author," he concluded in his final paragraph, written in the midst of World War II, when he was 86,

"I was something of a fighter, but that was a time when the pen was a weapon... I served for a number of years as a common soldier in the eternal war to free the human spirit."

To the last, Pontoppidan was a rationalist and a philosophical optimist. "There must come a time when reason again rules in the world and creates an existence one need not be ashamed of," he wrote in 1943. These were Pontoppidan's last words to the reading public which he had been addressing since 1881.

---

1 The fifth volume is a summary of the four preceding volumes.

These were also the last words of a generation of naturalistic writers, a generation which had been oriented in European literature, which had been admonished that literature should concern itself with social problems, but which had shown itself to be more deeply concerned with the psychological problem of the individual's place in a society dominated by technology, and in his struggle for a philosophy of life.

CHAPTER XII

The Road to Materialism

In Danish literary history, the beginning of the nineteenth century is clearly defined by the influence which German philosophy and literature exerted in Denmark from 1802 onward. There is no such disjuncture at the end of the century. In fact, the years from 1870 through 1914 can be taken to constitute a single era. Until the First World War the leading names of the eighties and nineties continued to dominate Danish literature. Brandes remained the best known critic, and Henrik Pontoppidan was generally recognized as the foremost writer of fiction. There were nevertheless several trends which first made themselves felt at the turn of the twentieth century.

Beginning in the nineties there was a lyrical reaction against the naturalism of prose espoused by Brandes. There followed a critical and national reaction against Brandes and his cosmopolitanism; and there arose a vigorous regional literature nurtured by Grundtvigian thinking and bolstered by the emancipation of Danish smallholders. There developed an insistent social criticism at first coupled with the regional literature but later separate from it. Finally there was a counter-reaction against the lyrical aestheticism of the nineties, in the form of a new materialism. Furthermore, at the beginning of the century, Danish literature also suffered a loss: Norwegian literature rapidly declined in significance for Denmark, as Norway became increasingly independent in its culture.

The lyrical reaction was expressed above all in the poetry of Johannes Jørgensen, Viggo Stuckenberg, and Sophus Claussen. The less renowned and unorganized critical reaction was actuated by figures as different as Helge Rode and Harald Nielsen. The national reaction found expression in the regional literature that went hand in hand with a revivified social criticism which found eloquent spokesmen in Jeppe Aakjær and Martin Andersen Nexø.

These various trends may be considered chronologically in the order named, for the lyrical reaction received its impetus in the nineties, the critical and national reaction began in the first decade of the twentieth century, and the social criticism and materialism were spurred in the second decade of the century.

The nineteenth century had begun by cultivating first the historical, the national, the exotic, and then the fantastic and the sentimental. The seventies and eighties had reacted against the literature of the preceding decades and struggled to portray life as it was, and had rejected the self-satisfied bourgeois or "Biedermeier" spirit of the fifties and sixties. The key word of the then-new literature was "realism"; the authors who followed Brandes were convinced that they were portraying life realistically. It is therefore not a little ironic that by some retrospective thinkers, and notably the neo-Catholic poet and critic JOHANNES JØRGENSEN (1866–1956)—writing in his *Essays,* 1906—, Brandes and his realism were labeled merely as a new form of romanticism.

The younger writers were not actually rejecting realism but disputing the meaning and the application of the term, for realism became a desirable appellation from about 1860 onward. Realism was to be sure not as abstruse a term as "romanticism," but it generally meant whatever the speaker himself stood for. In 1904 Johannes Jørgensen wrote that "true realism was to be found not in the works of Brandes and Co. but in the works of Bjørnson, Lie, Strindberg, and Selma Lagerlöf," because their writing expressed "the true realistic concept of guilt and punishment, the idea which is the *leitmotif* of all honest poetry from Shakespeare on." The emotions which the Naturalists had repressed since Georg Brandes' heyday were again to be unfettered. During the last decade of the century, a new generation of writers who looked upon the treatment of social, familial, and economic problems in literature as an undesirable "grey romanticism" brought about a poetic renaissance.

The all-conquering prose novel suddenly had a competitor in the verse forms of a younger generation—a generation of poets rather than thinkers, a generation of God-seekers, symbolists, and aesthetes, who (unlike Pontoppidan's Per Sidenius in *Lykke-Per*) were willing to let themselves be carried away by their emotions; who did not pin their faith to reason; and who sought, sometimes painfully, a new way of art. Theirs was a reaction against the prevailing naturalistic technique in prose description. The lyric, which for some time had had only Drachmann as a champion, came into its own once more.

Although the ultimate fates of the three principal representatives of the *fin-de-siècle* lyrical movement in Danish literature were very different, Johannes Jørgensen, Viggo Stuckenberg, and Sophus Claussen originally had much in common. They were intimate friends, as is evidenced by poems they addressed to one another and to Stuckenberg's wife; "she was our muse," Johannes Jørgensen was later to write. All three began in the eighties as disciples of Georg Brandes but very soon became dissatisfied with what seemed to them to be the sterility of materialistic, naturalistic philosophy and this philosophy they left behind them. In founding the periodical *Taarnet (The Tower)* in 1893, Johannes Jørgensen established himself as an outspoken critic of materialistic realism, and for the time being became an advocate of a poetic symbolism which aimed to express the nuances of the spirit and not merely to describe photographically or to narrate. The turn to symbolism seems to have been almost a direct result of the lectures on French symbolism which had been delivered in Copenhagen during the previous year by the French Catholic writer Léon Bloy. An interest in symbolism coupled with his own philosophical uncertainty encouraged Johannes Jørgensen to acquaint himself with mystical and religious literature. Then, gradually, he was won over to Roman Catholicism. His conversion in 1896 meant a break with Stuckenberg, who could neither follow Jørgensen's example nor reconcile himself to the thought of finding solace in the arms of the Church. Precisely because of his conversion, an experience which he has described in great and agonizing detail in the seven-volume *Mit Livs Legende (The Legend of My Life,* 1916–28),[1] Johannes Jørgensen is the best known of the three authors from the turn of the century. During and since his conversion, he spent much of his time in Italy. He is known abroad for those of his prose works which have been translated—principally the autobiography, and his biographies of Saint Francis of Assisi (1907)[2] and Saint Catherine of Siena (1915)[3]. Although his prose was rich in moods, he was more gifted as a lyrist than as a prose writer. Only in his work in the early nineties was Jørgensen a symbolist, however. His poetry is often reminiscent of the work of the German Friedrich von Eichendorff and other writers from the beginning of the nineteenth century. Much of his verse is the poetry of yearning, as for example the poem "Sne" ("Snow") and the introspective "Bekendelse" ("Confession") written two years prior to his formal conversion. The latter ends with the cry:

Eternity, I am in your hands.

Jørgensen's published work spans six decades, for the old poet published a number of poems since the end of World War II. For sixty years he

1 Translated by Ingeborg Lund as *Jorgensen,* London; New York, 1928–29.

2 Translated by T.O'Conor Sloane, New York; London, 1912.

3 Translated by Ingeborg Lund. New York, London, and Toronto, 1938, and several times reprinted.

found an audience of faithful readers, in part no doubt because Jørgensen was long Denmark's leading Catholic layman.

VIGGO STUCKENBERG (1863–1905), Jørgensen's erstwhile friend, was a gifted lyrist and a less volatile man. Unable to understand his friend's interest in Catholicism, he addressed him in "Bekendelse," an answer to Jørgensen's poem of the same title, and sadly noted that Jørgensen would have him rue and renounce his youth—something which he, Stuckenberg, by no means could or would do.[1] Although there are several phases in his work, Stuckenberg remained true to his youthful ideals and true to his early self during a short and outwardly colorless life. While Jørgensen may be criticized as egocentric, Stuckenberg must be acknowledged to have been a judge of men. His lyrics have more than a single facet. The collections of verse entitled *Flyvende Sommer* (*Gossamer*, 1898) and *Sne* (*Snow*, 1901), give abundant evidence that he could write delicate and moving love poetry as well as expressionistic prose or reflective verse like the above-mentioned "Bekendelse" and the contemplative "Aarhundred-skifte" ("At the Turn of the Century").

As a prose writer Stuckenberg was Jens Peter Jacobsen's successor. There is no doubt that Stuckenberg himself was aware of his debt to Jacobsen both as a descriptive precious stylist and as a psychologist. *I Gennembrud* (*Breaking Through*, 1888) is remarkable for its penetration into the mind of the weak-willed average youth and in particular for its sympathetic understanding of a boy's world during adolescence. Like Jacobsen in *Niels Lyhne* before him and Harald Kidde in *Aage og Else* after him, Stuckenberg realistically depicts human beings who cannot make up their minds to be true to themselves and therewith to achieve the happiness and tranquility which a positive philosophy of life can grant. Stuckenberg does not portray unusual people in his early prose; on the contrary the average reader can probably find a score of scenes from his own life depicted with amazing accuracy in *I Gennembrud*. That Stuckenberg's writing is autobiographical in nature goes almost without saying. *Messias* (1889) is a counterpart to *I Gennembrud*; in the lyrical prose of *Valravn* (1896) and above all in *Sol* (*Sunshine*, 1897) Stuckenberg gives a different solution to the problem of despair engendered by yearning. In *Sol*, Stuckenberg lets his hero ruthlessly break the bonds of everyday life and set off into the great unknown world; but Stuckenberg, it is to be noted, did not follow his hero's example.

If Johannes Jørgensen was a religious, then SOPHUS CLAUSSEN (1865–

1 Translations of both poets' poems entitled "Confession" are to be found in *A Book of Danish Verse*, 1922.

1931) was a satyr, as indeed he was wont to characterize himself. Claussen was clearly international in his literary tastes; his affinities were with the French symbolists; he himself was a friend of Paul Verlaine. His earlier poetry, especially the second volume of his verse, *Pilefløjter* (*Willow Pipes,* 1899), shows him to be an original artist with a command of erotic, lyrical, and satirical wit. His later production lacks the bounding spirit and enthusiasm of the early verse. Many of his metaphors are indistinct to the point of being incomprehensible, and his poetry, like his life, is indicative of the fact that Claussen, in contrast to Jørgensen, achieved neither a philosophy of life nor peace of mind. As a poet Claussen was Denmark's master symbolist; he perpetuated and extended the French symbolist movement which otherwise made but a passing impression. Claussen continued to employ and create symbols of a highly personal nature, as some of the French symbolists had done. He was wittier than the other European writers who were affected by the symbolist doctrine. His attempts in prose, his tales and travel books, emphasize the fact that he was an artist without any overwhelming message, but one whose command of metaphor and simile give him a peculiar position in Danish literature. Incidentally, Claussen's own literary tastes are suggested by his able translations into Danish of Shelley's "The Sensitive Plant," Heine's "Atta Troll," and several poems by Baudelaire.

With remarkable metrical facility, HELGE RODE (1870–1937), a friend of Jørgensen, Stuckenberg, and Claussen, translated abstract concepts of existence into easy lyrics which, although spiritually related to the poetry of Stuckenberg and of the Norwegian Sigbjørn Obstfelder, frequently suggest the verse of Holger Drachmann. Some of Rode's poems, first and foremost "Sne" ("Snow"), enjoy unusual popularity, despite an attenuated literary attitude which pervades his verse. As a lyrist, Rode seemed almost completely removed from problems of the day and was a communicant in nature's temple. Rode was also a prolific dramatist.

The critical reaction to Brandesianism was not uniform in character. It was characterized first by a revulsion against materialism and rationalism, and then by a nationalistic conservatism. The anti-rationalistic movement found its spokesman in Rode, whose searching criticisms of contemporary culture were assembled in the two volumes of essays entitled *Regenerationen i vort Aandsliv* (*The Regeneration of our Spiritual Life,* 1923) and *Det sjælelige Gennembrud* (*The Spiritual Breakthrough,* 1928). In his critical essays Rode tried to assay the ultimate values of human existence as they had been expressed in literature, and to contrast the nostalgic literature of searching with the self-satisfied literature of philosophical materialism. In the realm of the novel, a pronounced anti-rationalism is to be observed here and there later, above all in the work of J. ANKER LARSEN (1874–1957), whose widely-read *De Vises Sten* (*The Philosopher's Stone*, 1923)[1] has an unmistakable mystic, spiritualistic tendency.

The critical reaction, however, found its foremost representative not in the mystic Helge Rode but in the rationalistic incisive thinker, outspoken individualist, and consistent nationalist, HARALD NIELSEN (1879–1957). Throughout his long life Harald Nielsen was a stormy petrel, but he has continued to voice his independent and—in a literal sense of the word—reactionary opinions, which very often have run counter to popular taste. In his earliest volumes of literary criticism he made his position most clear. Although he accepted realism, he rejected Brandes and all that Brandes stood for. He admired men like the Norwegian Bjørnstjerne Bjørnson—men who stood for traditional national concepts and men of integrity, for whom the individual meant less than an entire people and the soul more than the body. Nielsen has remained almost completely isolated in Danish literature. The criticism which he represents, although a living force, has remained only an undercurrent, perhaps because it is increasingly negative rather than positive, quite possibly a very necessary destruction but without an adequate constructive compensation.

His role as a literary critic diminished over the years, as his interest in political, economic, and social questions increased. From a keen analyst of the values of a national and virile literature, he slowly became a nationalist who represented the extreme or Hegelian right in Denmark. His first volume of essays, *Moderne Litteratur* (1904), had been preceded by several incisive articles, the first of which, on Johannes V. Jensen, was published when Nielsen was only 21 years old. From the beginning of his career, Harald Nielsen's position was clear-cut as an aesthetician who understood the material and psychological demands of a technological society in which domestic peace and progress depended on a well-disciplined and traditional, if undemocratic, society.

Harald Nielsen's own taste in literature, as it is expressed in his countless essays and criticisms, has never been one with that of the avant-garde; it can rather be identified with the taste of conservative, bourgeois Den-

1 Translated into English (New York and London, 1924), Dutch, German, Polish, Czech, Finnish, and Swedish. Anker Larsen's other books have also enjoyed considerable popularity abroad; three have appeared in English translation: *Martha and Mary*. Translated by Arthur G. Chater, New York, London, 1926; *A Stranger in Paradise* (Danish title: *Sognet, som vokser ind i Himmelen*). Translated by Ruth Castberg Jordan. New York, 1929; London, 1930; and *With the Door Open. My Experience.* (Danish title: *For aaben dør*). Translated by Erwin and Pleasaunce von Gaisberg, New York; London, 1931.

mark. He has been the courageous speaker for the stratum of society that was skeptical of a highly individualized aestheticism and skeptical of literature which lost sight of traditional values and which would solve the world's problems by projection of socialistic or psychological principles and methods. In many ways, therefore, his unchanging conservative position and judgment of literature is more typical of the status of literature in Denmark in the first decades of the twentieth century than the more striking contemporary original and experimental imaginative and critical literature.

Harald Nielsen's literary ideals were realized in poetry by VALDEMAR RØRDAM and in prose by JAKOB KNUDSEN, writers who represent a nationalist reaction against Brandesian internationalism and who belonged politically and socially to the extreme Right in Danish society. The work of Rørdam (1872–1946) stands in contrast to the introspective poetry of a Johannes Jørgensen. On the whole, Rørdam was to the poetry of the so-called lyrical reaction of the nineties what Jakob Knudsen was to Jens Peter Jacobsen—an antithesis. Rørdam's verse is not characterized by the metrical freedom or radical originality of his contemporary Johannes V. Jensen. He is, rather, a traditionalist in form and content; in many ways he hearkens back to the poetry of Oehlenschläger and Oehlenschläger's school. His attitude was that of a reactionary and a conservative, even when he seemed to be unconventional. Rørdam's vigor is suggestive of Holger Drachmann, although to be sure not of Drachmann as an iconoclast. Nor was Rørdam as unpredictable as Drachmann. He was a careful writer and a gifted lyrist whose work is characterized by the well-turned phrase. He was an especially able writer of objective, or to coin a phrase, projective poetry. He has often been compared with Rudyard Kipling, and it is noteworthy that Rørdam himself translated some of Kipling into Danish. Like Kipling, he was manly and nationalistic. He was as near a sword rattler and a drum beater as any writer can be in militarily impotent Denmark. An example is provided by the stirring lines of "Danmark i tusind Aar" ("Denmark, a thousand years"), one of his best known poems, which has enjoyed great popularity because of a musical setting by Carl Nielsen.[1] Incidentally, Rørdam, again like Kipling, traveled in the Far East. A drama, *Buddha* (1925) was an outgrowth of his Oriental experiences.

---

1 CARL NIELSEN (1865–1931), the distinguished Danish composer, also proved himself to be an able writer, principally in his autobiography *Min fynske Barndom* (*My Childhood on Funen,* 1927), a brief selection from which is contained in *Contemporary Danish Short Stories,* Copenhagen, 1957.

Rørdam was not without some affinity with his more famous Norwegian contemporary Knut Hamsun, as was reflected in his passing admiration for the reactionary, disciplinary, militaristic, and totalitarian elements of National Socialism during the German-Russian conflict of the Second World War. Rørdam was an example of the extreme Right made poetically articulate; he was proof that effective and aesthetically acceptable modern poetry need be neither progressive, liberal, nor eccentric. It is of interest to note that Kaj Munk, writing in 1940, stated that if the Danes were to ask for the Nobel Prize, it would be for Valdemar Rørdam.

Rørdam's production was large. Among his works in verse three titles take precedence: *Den gamle Kaptajn* (*The Old Captain,* 1906–07), which was apparently meant to be a Danish equivalent of the nineteenth-century Finnish-Swedish poet Runeberg's *Fänrik Ståls Sägner*; *Luft og Land* (*Air and Land,* 1910), which contains some of Rørdam's choicest poetry; and *Afrodites Boldspil* (*Aphrodite's Ballgame,* 1920). He also wrote several prose works and plays and was an able translator from English, Polish, and Russian.

While the world was forsaking time-tested ideas and ideals, and while this movement or that was agitating for the new pedagogy, the new political theory, the new psychology, and the new freedom, JAKOB KNUDSEN (1858–1917) had the courage to raise his voice in protest and to defend discipline rather than progressive schooling, a class system rather than socialism, obedience rather than psychological analysis, and responsibility rather than license. It is not altogether just to label Jakob Knudsen a regionalist, but it is true that his novels helped regional literature acquire a firm footing. Knudsen was a prosaic reactionary, but he was a man of principle. Virile, matter-of-fact, blunt, he was a moral preacher rather than a poet; he was no aesthete. Like the "old clergyman" in his novel by that title (*Den gamle Præst,* 1899), Jakob Knudsen was not afraid to criticize adversely whenever criticism was needed, and if need be, to make enemies for the sake of an inward conviction. There was in him a touch of Ibsen and in particular of Ibsen's strong-willed and idealistic "Enemy of the People," Dr. Stockmann, despite the fact that Ibsen was one with the new times, whereas Jakob Knudsen stood squarely against the current of modernism. Although he was himself a severe critic of nineteenth-century Grundtvigianism, Knudsen reminds us not a little of the great Danish cleric, poet, and seer for whom that movement is named.

There is no doubt about the type of man that Jakob Knudsen admired;

throughout his work he agitated for manliness, sincerity, and inflexibility. As Carl Roos has pointed out, subjectivity was truth for Jakob Knudsen as it was for Søren Kierkegaard. In Knudsen's opinion, the results of a man's philosophical thinking were worth fighting for, whether they represented absolutes or not. He was a vociferous Christian, but his Christianity was of a practical bent, independent of any modern system of flabby ethics. His sympathies were obviously with Pastor Carlsbierg— the old clergyman—when Carlsbierg was trying to protect a man from being prosecuted for what might be deemed justifiable manslaughter. Jakob Knudsen was skeptical of the great enthusiasm for foreign ideals that had been engendered by Brandes. To exchange indigenous for foreign culture meant to him a loss of many values. Knudsen was especially cool to new ideas if their virtue was principally that they were "different." An intense concern with the upbringing of the individual is found in many of his works; it is most clearly expressed in the novel *Lærer Urup* (*Teacher Urup*, 1909). His ability to portray human beings and his deep and sympathetic understanding of men who, like himself, were conscious of their goals and true to themselves, are felicitously united in the longer novel *Sind* (*Temper*, 1903), which together with his collection of regionalist short stories entitled *Jyder* (*Jutlanders*, 1915–17), will probably come to be looked upon as their author's lasting contribution to Danish literature.[1]

The conservatism and regionalism of Jakob Knudsen was extended and developed in the work of the much younger THORKILD GRAVLUND (1879–1939), who, of all Danish writers, was the most conscious of national and regional values. An ultra-conservative, Gravlund objected both to the radicalism and internationalism of Brandes and to the social inclinations of the regionalists Jeppe Aakjær and Johan Skjoldborg. In his novels, and first and foremost in the trilogy *Sognet* (*The Parish*, 1915–18), Gravlund made a plea for the solidity and traditions of rural Danish life. The novels complement his several studies of the Danish psyche, which he believed he was able to define and portray in its various local differences. The persons in *Sognet* represent various districts in Denmark, even to the extent of speaking in their several native dialects. Gravlund contrasted new radical ideas with the established practices of rural Denmark, to the advantage of the latter. For Gravlund, the rural parish was the ideal community, in which the very real inter-relationship of individ-

1 "Indomitability," translated by V. Elizabeth Balfour-Browne, is contained in *Contemporary Danish Short Stories,* Copenhagen, 1957.

*Sophus Claussen reading to Helge Rode (left) and the artist,
J. F. Willumsen, 1915.*

MARTIN ANDERSEN NEXO
Painting by August Torsleff, 1913.

uals underlay the course of events. Life itself was shown in its elemental
dependence on the soil. Unlike Jakob Knudsen or Jeppe Aakjær, however, Gravlund did not advocate any special reforms but rather the acknowledgment of a social balance which he felt to be threatened both by the
philosophy of individualism and the growth of socialism (i.e., social
democracy).

In the Jutlander JEPPE AAKJÆR (1866–1930), regional literature became
one with the literature of social consciousness and therewith had a foot
both in the camp which reacted against Georg Brandes and the camp
which accepted him. In reading Aakjær we perceive that both regional
and social literature are in part quite independent of Brandes in their
historical origins and *raison d'être,* just as they are in part dependent on
Brandes' program of making problems a matter of literary debate.

Like Henrik Pontoppidan and Martin Andersen Nexø, Aakjær was
early identified with the folk high school and its cultivation of folk-
tradition. In contrast to these two contemporaries, Aakjær remained an
advocate of regionalism after leaving the pious world of the folk high
school movement. While he advanced from conservative Grundtvigianism to a radical social and religious standpoint—he was at one time
imprisoned for blasphemy—he differed from many writers of the Left in
the early twentieth century in that he did not ally himself with partisan
political movements and did not acquire a cut-and-dried political philosophy. His most important prose work is the novel *Vredens Børn, Et
Tyendes Saga (Children of Wrath, a Hired-Man's Saga,* 1904), which makes
a plea for the betterment of living and working conditions for farm
laborers, a plea akin to that which was to be made by Martin Andersen
Nexø for urban laborers in *Pelle Erobreren. Vredens Børn* is not a subtle
book. One indignation is piled upon another; the author has marshaled
a host of injustices against the farm laborer and allowed his hero Per to
be subjected to them all. *Vredens Børn* holds forth no bright hope for the
future; Per gradually finds every road in Denmark blocked to him so
that his only alternative is emigration to America. The cry of injustice
rises from every page and consequently makes the book somewhat crass,
but the fact remains that Aakjær could rouse and anger his readers and
therewith achieve his didactic ends by literary means. Together with
similar criticism from other pens wielded by socially conscious writers,
Aakjær's merciless criticism of the well-to-do farmers who were all-too-
willing to exploit the downtrodden has alleviated a weakness in the
Danish social system. Aakjær spoke in a way which roused the conservative agricultural population, if not to action, at least to a recognition of

intolerable conditions. There is no doubt that *Vredens Børn* has done its part to help the lot of the farmhand in Denmark.

Aakjær was a curious combination, for he was a significant poet as well as a leading exponent of regional literature and an agitator to boot. Much of what Aakjær wrote was in dialect, but for him there was nothing incongruous about treating contemporary social questions in dialect. His prose could tremble with indignation, but in contrast to many social reformers, Aakjær was also an able writer of verse. He was widely known and beloved because of his poetry, especially the poems contained in the collection *Rugens Sange* (*Songs of the Rye,* 1906 and several times augmented). Aakjær, having experienced the enlightened and sophisticated ways of the Danish capital, returned to rustic life no longer naïve but sentimental in both the popular and philosophical sense of the word. The most casual perusal of the titles of his poems suggests his propensity for the idyllic: farmer's song, signs of spring, the glassy river. In reading his poetry, one is reminded of his slightly older American contemporary James Whitcomb Riley.

Aakjær is of particular interest to the English-speaking world as the Danish translator of Robert Burns. He was an enthusiastic admirer of the Scot's poetry. As he felt that Burns could not be properly reproduced in standard Danish, he attempted to recreate the flavor of Burn's dialect in the speech of Jutland. Gifted poet that he was, Aakjær's unusual translations are very creditable. Much of his own poetry of agitation is of slighter aesthetic import, although one sentimental ballad in this category, "Jens Vejmand," is among the most widely known Danish poems today by virtue of its having been set to music (by Carl Nielsen) and having become a modern folk song. His bucolic and nostalgic poetry is easy to understand. It is full of associations for Denmark's agriculturally minded population; it is alive with tenderness and fervor; and it frequently possesses a haunting rhythm. Aakjær's poetry promises to outlive his prose.[1]

The work of JOHAN SKJOLDBORG (1861–1936), like that of Aakjær, is of a complex nature. Like Aakjær, but in contrast to Gravlund, Skjoldborg was something of an agitator and a reformer, who wished to improve the lot of the hired hand and the freeholder. Again like Aakjær, Skjoldborg was a poet as well as a prose writer. Some of Skjoldborg's poems have been set to music and at least one, "Naar Vinteren rinder i

---

1 Translations of Aakjær's poetry into English are scattered. Seven poems in Danish and English are contained in *The Jutland Wind and other verse from the Danish peninsula...* by R. P. Keigwin, Oxford, 1944.

Grøft og i Grav" ("The Song of the Smallholder," 1897) has become nearly as popular as Aakjær's "Jens Vejmand."[1]

The tenant farmer and the smallholder found a friend and champion in Skjoldborg, whose novels, like those of the reactionary Gravlund, still are read in folk high school circles. As a novelist, Skjoldborg was rather artless. He wrote in a straightforward, sentimental, and dramatic fashion that partook of no subtlety, a fact which may account for the appeal of his prose to the common man. The so-called saga of the small-holder, *En Stridsmand* (*A Fighter*, 1896), which is his principal prose work, was originally published at the author's own expense after he had tried in vain to find a publisher, but it immediately won a large audience and has since gone through several editions. The plot of the novel is banal enough, but is supported by the ethical content which permeates Skjoldborg's writing.

HARALD BERGSTEDT (born 1877) carried on the tradition of regional literature as a provincial liberal in his volumes of verse entitled *Sange fra Provinsen* (*Songs from the Provinces*, 1913–21). Bergstedt, also a social agitator, but possessed neither of a brilliant nor stable mind, was able to infuse the hearty spirit of the small town and the countryside into his verse, which is not without a pastoral flavor. Like Valdemar Rørdam, Bergstedt is responsible for the waning of his own popularity because of his attitude toward the German occupation during World War II. While in retrospect the critic can see how Bergstedt and Rørdam in Denmark, like Knut Hamsun in Norway, might have sympathized with the ideas of National Socialism and have come to accept the Occupation, he nevertheless feels uneasy about a poet's subjugation of art to political force. Bergstedt's poetry has been identified, although possibly unjustly so, with divers political causes. As a consequence, his work is viewed today in a rather dubious light, although the popularity and influence of the *Sange fra Provinsen* are indisputable.

An early writer of regional literature with little social or political bias was MARIE BREGENDAHL (1867–1940), who was at one time married to Jeppe Aakjær. Her books are unusual in being descriptive and pictorial but not didactic. Whereas Jeppe Aakjær and Thorkild Gravlund were agitating in favor of certain political and social ideas, and protesting injustices and malpractices against the common man in rural areas, Marie Bregendahl endeavored to portray the common people without caricature and with deep sympathy. Her most powerful book is *En Dødsnat*

---

1 Also translated by Keigwin, *ibid.*

14*

(*A Night of Death,* 1912),[1] but her principal contribution to Danish literature is, however, the *Billeder af Sødalsfolkenes Liv (Pictures from the Life of the People of Sødal),* originally published in seven volumes (1914–23). These stories maintain a nice balance between the popular-sentimental novel and social problem literature, a fact which reflects the intellectual origins of their authoress in the work of Ibsen and Grundtvig, or more specifically, in Ibsen's later dramas and the folk high school.

We observe that a regional literature arose from a synthesis of the national critical reaction to Brandes and the social consciousness of the late nineteenth century. As the years went by, a regional literature in which social criticism early was implicit established itself as a genre separate from the literature of the Left, the literature of social protest. In Gravlund and in Jakob Knudsen, insofar as the latter is a regionalist, regionalism is identified with the Right. And the leading figure of the literary Left in Denmark, MARTIN ANDERSEN NEXØ (1869–1954), received his intellectual awakening not through socialist agitation or as the result of Brandes' influence, but through the Grundtvigian folk high school; his stay at two folk high schools was a decisive experience. Like Henrik Pontoppidan, he was for a short time a teacher at a folk high school, and like Pontoppidan, his early works suggest regionalism as well as incipient social criticism. It was not until after his travels in Spain and Italy that Andersen Nexø identified himself once and for all with the proletariat and chose to depict the impoverished, the men and women that God forgot. Whereas, in the last analysis, Pontoppidan became an introspective writer who stressed the necessity of a philosophy of life, and of knowing and being one's self, Martin Andersen Nexø came to be the champion of social revolution and the poet of social indignation. He did not cease to depict the lot of those oppressed; he was a writer whose sympathy lay with the lowliest, and he came to equate poverty with innate goodness.

Andersen Nexø's social message, the very obvious "tendentiousness" of his novels, beclouds the fact that he was a great artist. He was capable of instilling his own indignation into his readers; and our sympathies go out to his proletarian and human heroes and heroines. He learned much from Henrik Pontoppidan, although his language is far more salted with provincialisms than is Pontoppidan's academically classical Danish. It is noteworthy that he dedicated his principal work, *Pelle Erobreren (Pelle the Conqueror,* 1906–10), "to the master, Henrik Pontoppidan." But the two

---

1 Translated by Margery Blanchard, New York, 1931.

authors did not share a common philosophy. Pontoppidan, although a protagonist of social consciousness in his earlier works, was of a conservative and patriotic turn of mind and was conscious that man's salvation lay within man's mind, whereas Andersen Nexø adhered to the conviction that the well-ordered materialistic and internationalist society, conceived in the spirit of Marx, is the way to the Golden Age. Nexø and Pontoppidan took their stands, each in his way, against those currents which they defined as "romantic." For Andersen Nexø the old values of church and state and home were false, if they led to a disregard of the daily needs of the common man. His thinking was anthropocentric. For him it was enough to solve the material problems of this life without undertaking to debate abstractions, much less the question of a future life.

It was with *Pelle* that he established the genre of the proletarian novel. His novel has been widely read, translated, and imitated.[1] Four decades after the publication of *Pelle,* many writers in Denmark and abroad are conscious of Martin Andersen Nexø, but the epigoni and the imitators do not have his gift for portraying scenes and people with sympathy and touching understanding. There are few more moving figures in world literature than old Father Lasse and his little son Pelle during their years on the island of Bornholm. The social oppression that Andersen Nexø makes his readers sense through the persons of Lasse and Pelle is so severe that the effect borders on sentimentality.

Pelle is a novel of development (German: *Entwicklungsroman*) but without a conclusion. It is a sort of working man's *Wilhelm Meister* without the *Wanderjahre*. We follow the course of Pelle's life: first his humble lot on a Bornholm farm, then his years as a shoemaker's apprentice, then his lowly existence as a worker in Copenhagen, and finally the awakening of his intellectual and social consciousness, an awakening which leads him into the organized labor movement of the day and makes of him a radical social democrat and a labor leader who directs the general strike in Denmark in the nineties. At this point in the fourth volume of the series, Pelle is unjustly arrested and imprisoned. When he has served his term, he is no longer the militant labor leader. As a human being he now has a great lesson to learn in love and forgiveness. Andersen Nexø has increased the effectiveness of *Pelle* many times by giving Pelle not only moral strength and admirable characteristics but also common weaknesses and failings. Upon his release from prison Pelle finds one more

1 Translated into English by Jessie Muir and Bernard Miall, I-IV, London, 1913–16; New York, 1913–17. Repr. 1917, 1930.

child in his home than when he left, and he is quick to accuse his wife of the very conduct of which he himself was guilty.

Pelle ends on an optimistic and altruistic but at the same time a very curious note. Pelle is concerned with a coöperative housing project. Walking with his friend Morten, who is the author's *alter ego,* Pelle discusses his own fundamental good luck. Morten states that he is going to write a book about Pelle, as an example of "the naked man... (who is) going to take over the future." Pelle is skeptical and thinks that such a tale with a happy ending will not appeal to workers, but Morten replies:

> They will snatch at it, and weep with delight and pride at finding themselves in it. Perhaps they will name their children after it out of pure gratitude.

The novel breaks off at this point and one is left with Morten—or Andersen Nexø himself, as you will—prepared to write the very novel one has just read.

Many years later, in 1945, after Andersen Nexø had become an outspoken apologist for Communism, there appeared a sequel to *Pelle, Morten hin Røde (Morten the Red),* in which the main figure is the same Morten who was identified as the author of Pelle. In contrast to Pelle, Morten has remained true to the revolution, while Pelle compromised himself in trying to adjust himself to bourgeois society by accepting a governmental position and taking a non-revolutionary attitude. To the true believer in the revolution therefore, Pelle is discredited, and the far less attractive agitator Morten carries on in the faith. It is as if Martin Andersen Nexø were discrediting his own early achievement, or as if he felt pangs of conscience for having let Pelle compromise the revolution. In the years between *Pelle Erobreren* and *Morten hin Røde,* Andersen Nexø showed himself to be a friend of the revolution and an admirer of the Soviet experiment. A book on his travels in the Soviet Union after the First World War is entitled *Mod Dagningen* (*Towards the Dawn,* 1923).

From 1917 to 1921 Andersen Nexø published his second masterpiece, the five-volume novel *Ditte Menneskebarn* (*Ditte, Child of Man*) which depicts the life of an oppressed and essentially good woman, Ditte, who is a sort of female Pelle, from her birth out of wedlock until her early death at the age of 25.[1] In this short life span, Ditte has experienced more of the world and been in more difficult situations than is the lot of most human beings. From her childhood on she is the symbol of love and

---

1 Translated into English by A.G.Chater, Richard Thirsk, and Asta and Rowland Kenney in three parts, with the titles *Ditte. Girl Alive, Ditte. Daughter of Man,* and *Ditte. Towards the Stars.* New York, 1920–22; London, 1920–23. Repr. New York, 1931.

self-sacrifice. Her goodness is rewarded by ingratitude, deception, and seduction, although for a brief period her life is brightened by her friendship with a proletarian author living in Copenhagen, whom the reader probably should identify with Andersen Nexø himself. Especially noteworthy is the poetic, almost lyrical-mystical, manner in which Andersen Nexø prepares the reader for Ditte's story at the beginning of the book and takes leave of Ditte in an epilogue which likens the life of an individual to a star:

> Every second a human soul is born into the world. A new flame is lit, a star which perhaps may come to shine with unusual beauty, which in any case has its own unseen spectrum. A new being, fated, perhaps, to bestow genius, perhaps beauty, around it, kisses the earth; the unseen becomes flesh and blood. No human being is a repetition of another, nor is any ever reproduced; each new being is like a comet which only once in all eternity touches the path of the earth, and for a brief time takes its luminous way over it—a luminous body between two eternities of darkness. No doubt there is joy amongst human beings for every newly lit soul! And, no doubt they will stand round the cradle with questioning eyes, wondering what this new one will bring forth. Alas, a human being is no star, bringing fame to him who discovers and records it! More often, it is a parasite which comes upon peaceful and unsuspecting people, sneaking itself into the world—through months of purgatory. God help it, if into the bargain it has not its papers in order.

If it is the ability to create pictures and metaphors which make a poet, then Martin Andersen Nexø, for all his social agitation, was indeed a poet, as the above passage attests.

A third novel, *Midt i en Jærntid* (*In an Age of Iron,* translated into English as *In God's Land*),[1] published in 1929, depicts the well-to-do farmer, his relations to the political currents of the times and the agricultural inflation brought about by the First World War. Andersen Nexø also published several volumes of short stories. In the thirties, he made a contribution to Danish literature with his memoirs, which, together with *Pelle,* augur to secure his fame. Originally published in several volumes, 1932–39, the memoirs have been collected in two volumes as *Erindringer (Reminiscences).*[2] They are written with much of the same warm feeling and keen sense of social indignation as was *Pelle,* but without the didactic tendency required by so-called socialist realism. One is struck by the many parallels between Andersen Nexø's early life and that of his hero Pelle.

1 Translated by Thomas Seltzer, New York, 1933.

2 The first two parts of the reminiscences, translated by J.B.C.Watkins, were published as *Under the Open Sky,* New York, 1938.

Politically speaking, the literary Left has changed its physiognomy during the past eighty years, but the common bond of the social problem as subject-matter remains. Brandes wanted problems to be debated, and his contemporaries had conceived Ibsen as the foremost representative of a literature of social and moral debate. That Ibsen's deep-rooted philosophical convictions were overlooked or misinterpreted is beside the point here. As time passed, new problems were exchanged for old. From the more abstract questions of freedom and faith, discussion shifted to questions of practical social justice. It is curious that the literature which fulfilled Brandes' demand that problems be made a matter of debate was not the literature inspired directly by Brandes but inspired by forces apparently independent of him, forces which are closely allied to the emancipation of the Danish farmer in the nineteenth century: Grundtvigianism, nationalism, regionalism. The fundamentally aristocratic Brandes and the conservative nationalist Grundtvig can be said to have fathered a proletarian brood, for the mood of the writers who continued to make "problems a matter of debate" became more and more one of social indignation and revolt.

One direct ancestor of the newer literature of social protest is to be found in the products of Brandes' inner circle of the seventies: Holger Drachmann's early poem "Engelske Socialister," which was cited in the previous chapter. Many years passed, however, before the mood of Drachmann's fiery poem began to permeate Danish literature. The early literature of social consciousness was on the whole evoked by a sympathetic humanitarianism rather than by political radicalism.

In considering the development of problem literature in Denmark from the seventies onward, one must not forget that the social and socialistic doctrines that made themselves felt in Europe since the revolution of 1848 and the advent of Marxism have been the moulding forces of the literary Left. Especially since the Russian revolution, the extreme Left has been particularly conscious of what once was termed "the great Russian experiment", and no small percentage of its writers, including its dean, Martin Andersen Nexø, turned to Communism after the First World War.

As Danish literature gravitated toward the special interests of the several groups of writers mentioned above, the naturalism proclaimed by Brandes was supplanted either by symbolism, or introspection, or by a concern with social or psychological problems, or by the delineation of national and regional peculiarities. The turn away from many of the ideas associated with the young Brandes brought forth an inevitable counter-reaction which heralded a second wave of materialistic thinking and aroused to a renewed consciousness of heredity and milieu. This counter-reaction is embodied in JOHANNES V. JENSEN (1873–1950).

It was as a writer of tales that the young Johannes V. Jensen showed himself to be the consummate artist. He himself called his genre "the myth." In form brief, in essence a moving and most frequently a pathetic tale, Johannes V. Jensen's "myth" is the interpretation of an abstraction. Jensen's tales fall into three groups: The tales from the Himmerland, the tales from his travels in the Far East, and the other tales published under the recurrent title *Myter (Myths)*. *Himmerlandsfolk (People of the Himmerland,* 1898), the first of three collections of tales from the Himmerland, continued by *Nye Himmerlandshistorier, (New Tales from Himmerland,* 1904), and *Himmerlandshistorier. Tredie Samling,* 1910, gave promise of a new and forceful regional literature, but while Jensen was conscious of his Jutland heritage and believed in the ability of Jutland to revivify Danish culture, his art transcended the strictures of regional literature. Jensen was portraying human existence before a Jutland background. Compare, for example, the tales "Tre og Tredive Aar" ("Thirty-three Years"), "Jenes," and "Cecil," in which three pathetic life stories are narrated, but not without humor.[1] In a way Johannes V. Jensen may be said to be carrying on the tradition of Steen Steensen Blicher in giving realistic glimpses into life in Jutland. Incidentally, he is the author of a poetic apotheosis of Blicher, which contains these lines:

> He accepted rain and sun; he walked on *soil*.
> For him no idle concept, fathers' toil.
> He sought out treasures in the flouted nook.
> He registered the Jute in Denmark's book.

Written with greater pathos are the *Singaporenoveller (Singapore Stories)* of 1907 (later included among the "Exotic Tales"). As the author of these tales from the Far East, Johannes V. Jensen has earned the appellation Denmark's Kipling. With sympathy and understanding he has depicted life in the Orient, and in particular the subtle racial conflict between white men and Orientals, especially in the tales "Moderen" ("The Mother") and "Olivia Marianne." Here too he writes not without humor, as for example in "A Koy."[2] The exotic tales were later absorbed into the

---

1 "Cecil," translated by Lydia Cranfield, appeared in *The Norseman,* 1948, pp. 123–29; "Ann and the Cow," translated by Victor Folke Nelson, in *Denmark's Best Stories,* New York, 1928.

2 "Olivia Marianne," translated by C. A. Bodelsen, was published in the *London Mercury,* 1926, pp. 585–88.

revised collection of *Myter* so that their identification with the "myth" is indisputable.

There are several collections of tales and prose pieces originally published under the title of *Myter* (*Myths,* 1907, 1908, 1910, 1912, 1924); *Aarbog 1916 (Yearbook 1916)* and *Aarbog 1917* also contain "myths." It is not much amiss to speak of Jensen's myth as a twentieth-century fairy tale, i.e., *Eventyr*. "The myth is my form of the *Eventyr*," Johannes V. Jensen wrote in an article on "the myth as an art form." It was "in part dictated by the subject matter, which permitted concentrated treatment." "The form is my own. At first I wrote without being influenced by H. C. Andersen . . . but a continuation of the *Eventyr* in the spirit of Andersen, in an altered form, is conceivable." As different as Hans Christian Andersen and Johannes V. Jensen were from one another as personalities, they had several common characteristics: both were admirers of technological progress, both were ardent travelers and exploited their travels, and both were well received as novelists, although their tales have won them greater critical acclaim. The comparison is rather misleading; for what would Andersen have thought of Jensen's later production? Jensen's tales do not share the optimism or the pious mood characteristic of Andersen's writing, nor was Jensen a friend of the supernatural or a believer in divine goodness and ultimate good fortune. Of the elements which moulded him, and they may be represented by the names of Darwin, Walt Whitman, Kipling, and Bjørnson, there are not many traces of the grand master of the *Eventyr*.

It is more difficult to attempt to categorize the "myths" of Johannes V. Jensen than the tales of Andersen. Some myths tell of experiences in nature; others were generated by the author's travels; some are pure phantasy; others are recollections from childhood; and despite Jensen's acknowledged agnosticism, some border on the mystical. Jensen himself attempted a definition:

> Leave out the plot, concentrate on those short flashes of the essence of things that illumine man and time, and you have the myth... They are not short stories in the ordinary sense of the word, nor fairy tales; they have something of the essay and something of the quality of a musical theme, an attempt to focus the essence of life in a dream.[1]

Suffice it here to mention a few of the many "myths" contained in the first collection, published in 1907. "Knokkelmanden" ("The Bony Man"), identified by the author as the first of his myths, is a tale of life and death

---

1 Cf. Aage Marcus, "Johannes V. Jensen," in *The American-Scandinavian Review*, XX, 1932, p. 342f.

conceived symbolically in the figures of a music hall singer and a clown, a dying seaman and a baying hound. "Det gamle Ur" ("The old Clock") is both a personification and an attempt to capture a fleeting and nostalgic mood. "Majnat" ("May Night") relates a fantastic, inexplicable experience in the open and leaves the reader puzzled as to the author's intent. "Edderkoppen" ("The Spider") is a humorous tale bordering on the didacticism of Carl Ewald but distinguished by an inimically ironic ending. "Fusijama," finally, which closes the first collection of myths, is a religious confession of a non-believer.[1]

The various volumes of Jensen's *Myter* contain tales essentially the same in conception and execution as the tales from the Himmerland and the Far East, but some of the so-called myths are not imaginative tales at all but *causeries* and descriptive passages, as for example "Nordens Foraar" ("Scandinavian Spring") or "Lyse Nætter" ("Light Nights"). The genre of the myth was real enough in the hands of Johannes V. Jensen and while we may accept his definition, the fact remains that for Jensen himself, "myth" was also a convenient, elastic term which might be applied to any self-sufficient bit of prose from his pen.

Among his other early works, the historical trilogy *Kongens Fald* (*The Fall of the King,* 1900–01) is outstanding.[2] It is a delineation of life in the sixteenth century, and the tensions which obtained then, rather than a fictional biography of King Christian II of Denmark, who is nominally the leading character of the novel. The reader's attention is drawn more to a certain Michael Thøgersen, who in later life became the deposed king's companion and confidant, than to the king. In its conscientious attempt to penetrate into the minds of men who lived in the sixteenth century, and to portray in detail the life and times of a few historical or semi-historical figures, *Kongens Fald* is unlike Jensen's other works. But it has its measure of the fantastic that serves to distinguish it from the contemporary naturalistic novel.

Madame d'Ora (1904) and its sequel *Hjulet* (*The Wheel,* 1905) were a result of their author's sojourn in the United States. Although these novels have been widely read in Denmark, they leave something to be desired when judged critically; they seem to capitulate to the public's demand for dramatic effects. Madame d'Ora is secretly married to a famous scientist who is interested in spiritualism. Her scientist-husband

1 Translated by Elias Bredsdorff in *Life and Letters,* vol. 53, No. 117, 1947, pp. 112–3. Reprinted in *Contemporary Danish Short Stories,* Copenhagen, 1957.

2 Translated by Patrick Kirwan and Per Federspiel, London, New York, 1933. Repr. London, 1934; 1935.

is duped into believing that he has seen spirits in his own laboratory and into confessing a murder he has not committed. He shoots Madame d'Ora after she has been scratched by a broken test tube that happens to contain the bacteria of hydrophobia. *Hjulet* is of interest because of the lengthy translations into Danish from the poetry of Walt Whitman which are found towards the beginning of the book. But Whitman and the concept of progress and power symbolized by the wheel, to which allusions are made at the beginning and the end of the novel and which give the book its title, have nothing to do with the grotesque narrative that revolves about a homosexual religious swindler who provokes a general strike in Chicago and is subsequently murdered by the lover of the daughter of Chicago's wealthiest man. The characters in the novel, several of which appeared in *Madame d'Ora,* are exaggerated to the point of being preposterous. The narrative technique is that of the murder mystery. Johannes V. Jensen appears to have been on a literary by-path in his so-called American novels.

Johannes V. Jensen had written a number of significant books prior to 1906. The publication of his *Digte (Poems)* in that year may nevertheless be looked upon as epochal and as symbolic of new form in poetry, of the arrival of a new materialistic ethos, and of a synthesis of Brandesian thinking with the new century's penchant for abstractions. The verse, original in expression and content, protested the sentiments of the last decade of the nineteenth century. Jensen was not only a contradiction of the lyrical reaction of the nineties, but a contradiction of introspective aestheticism and degeneration. He exuded an enthusiasm made up of admiration for indigenous culture, primitive nature, physical force, and technological progress. "H. C. Andersen was the first in his time who took the natural sciences to be more than news; he saw poetry in the first railroads," wrote Jensen; and we are given to understand that the commentator was the Hans Christian Andersen of his own time. He too was a believer in "poetry's California"; he too was a journalist and an innovator.

One of Johannes V. Jensen's most important poems is entitled "Memphis Station."[1] In stark prose-poetry worthy of Walt Whitman, it contains reflections made in a railway station at Memphis, Tennessee. Who before in Scandinavian poetry had felt the rhythm of a locomotive and been able to express in verse the surroundings of the new everyday? Who had seen poetry in a sandwich? Who but Johannes V. Jensen could make his reader feel with him (in the poem "Ved Frokosten"—"At Lunch"):

---

1 Translated, with other poems by Jensen, in *A Book of Danish Verse,* 1922.

Now I'm well off.
There are 4 blooming sandwiches in front of me.
First I eat one with egg and herring.
O, the suspicion of sulphur dioxide and the
    iodine from the ocean's seaweed forests!
Then I sink my teeth in a young and solid piece
    of roast meat,
And here the flavor is fuller, if I say nothing.
The rolled sausage's bouquet of sheep and of
    oily machinery, weaving mills, increases
    my well-being.
The cheese binds together the spirit of
    putrefaction and burning love in my heart.

The so-called realists had not written like this. Was Johannes V. Jensen then not a realist or was he perhaps a real realist? To quibble about literary labels is idle. We shall refrain from applying the terms realist or romanticist to Johannes V. Jensen. His descriptions, which at first glance seem to be impressionistic and photographic, are also interpretative. Upon closer examination, the reader observes that he favors the myth, understood in the word's broadest sense. The nucleus of one of his stories is often an abstraction that he makes tangible. Yet, he was the embodiment of a counter-reaction against the symbolist poets.

Much of Johannes V. Jensen's poetry is virile and rough-hewn. It sometimes suggests the rhythm and resounding alliteration of Old Norse poetry. In fact, Jensen occasionally imitated Old Norse alliterative patterns, as for example in his poem "Til 'Den lange Rejse'" ("To 'The Long Journey'") and "Den nordiske Kvinde" ("The Scandinavian Woman"). His affinity for Old Norse literature also led him to undertake a translation of Egils Saga from the Icelandic and to edit a modern version of the Old Icelandic sagas in Danish translation.

From every page of Johannes V. Jensen's poetry and prose it is apparent that he, in contrast to so many of his contemporaries, was not searching for a life philosophy. He had one. He was content with this life. For him there was but one existence, the worldly existence in which we are participating. Jensen believed we must try to understand life and our fellow men, to understand our origins, and to strive for better material conditions. His attitude can only be called agnostic. His ethical rôle was that of the interpreter of men and events. He was a Darwinian, but a half-cocked, delayed-action Darwinian. Tenuous concepts of race and blood were fundamental to his thinking; were he not a great writer, he might deserve the appellation of charlatan. What he admired was in his own estimation Northern, Germanic, and Gothic, and he included in this category Rembrandt, Victor Hugo, Maupassant, Taine, Baudelaire,—and Columbus! What he did not admire was what he considered Southern, Romance, and Gallic. His thinking was not far removed from the racial mysticism of National Socialism, although he tried sternly to disassociate himself from the opprobrium of German racialism in the 1930's.

The sextet of novels with the common title *Den lange Rejse* (*The Long Journey,* originally published as *Det tabte Land, The Lost Land,* 1919, *Bræen, Fire and Ice,* 1908, *Norne-Gæst,* 1919, *Cimbrernes Tog, The Trek of the Cimbrians,* 1922, *Skibet, The Ship,* 1912, and *Christofer Columbus,* 1921) is Jensen's best known work, and with good reason.[1] Drawing on his fertile imagination and his abilities as an amateur anthropologist, he has made the history of man in northern Europe come alive and seem plausible, if in an oversimplified form; at the same time he has told a fascinating tale. There is nothing "real"—if by real is meant factual—about his narrative; it is the product of a poetic fantasy; and yet in the last analysis it rests upon the Darwinian theory. Here as elsewhere, he has consciously created a myth. His story of the rise of man from the most primitive times to the discovery of America by Columbus is a plausible incarnation of the past. In his hands, the Darwinian theory has become poetry, symbol, and myth. Jensen is capable of great syntheses and synopses. Artistically, *Den lange Rejse* does not reach the height of the author's *Eksotiske Noveller (Exotic Tales)* or *Himmerlandshistorier (Tales from the Himmerland)*, but it is his most ambitious accomplishment and his most widely read work. It is also the work which has permitted the freest play of his fantasy. In *Den lange Rejse,* he has symbolically depicted man's development, step by step, in the light of the Darwinian theory. Columbus, a figure that exerted a great attraction upon him, he interprets at the conclusion of the series of novels as the fulfillment of the Northern peoples' longing for the lost world of earliest times, and the result of the "long journey" from prehistorical to modern times. Christopher Columbus "created a new world from his *Weltschmerz*," Jensen wrote in an early poem. The figures in the various volumes of the series are to be viewed as types rather than as individuals, types which symbolize the cultural and technical progress of millennia, much like the figures in an anthropological museum.

Johannes V. Jensen expressed his dilettante anthropological opinions

1 *The Long Journey,* translated by A. G. Chater, London, 1922–24, New York, 1923–24, repr. New York, 1933 and 1945, does not include a translation of *Skibet.*

in a number of theoretical works, notably the collections of essays entitled *Den gotiske Renaissance* (*The Gothic Renaissance*, 1901) and *Den nye Verden* (*The New World*, 1907), and the postscript to *Den lange Rejse*, entitled *Æstetik og Udvikling* (*Aesthetics and Development*, 1923). The two volumes *Dyrenes Forvandling* (*The Metamorphosis of Animals*, 1927) and *Aandens Stadier* (*Stages of the Spirit*, 1928) constitute a counterpart to *Den lange Rejse* "in everyday and narrative form," as Johannes V. Jensen himself put it. Jensen also drew the parallel between his work and that of H. G. Wells and suggested that *Dyrenes Forvandling* was "an easily understood textbook about the evolution from animal to human being." Both books contributed to a popular understanding of the anthropologist's and ethnographer's standpoint and agitated for the theories of evolution and the survival of the fittest. "Nature does not strive toward equality," is the concluding sentence of *Aandens Stadier*. Both books are an expression of the spirited conviction with which Jensen was imbued upon viewing Fusijama for the first time and which evoked the sketch bearing the name of the Japanese mountain. While *Dyrenes Forvandling* contains reflections on the evolution of *homo sapiens, Aandens Stadier* is an attempt to define the stages in the spiritual development of man.

Jensen was a narrator rather than a thinker. The intrinsic value of his anthropological essays is very slight; nevertheless they meant much to a younger generation at the time they appeared in the late twenties. What is more, they provide a key to Jensen's world of ideas.

A spirit kindred to Johannes V. Jensen, but at the same time reminiscent of Jens Peter Jacobsen a generation before, is found in KNUD HJORTØ (1869–1931), who had little sympathy with the so-called lyrical reaction of the nineties. Hjortø was a many-sided author. Like Jensen, he was both the interpreter of a regional milieu and, in a novel entitled *Den gule Krønike,* the creator of a fabulous world myth; but he did not achieve a popularity comparable to Jensen's. In a trio of novels, *Støv og Stjærner* (*Dust and Stars*, 1904), *To Verdener* (*Two Worlds*, 1905), and *Hans Raaskov* (1906), which, together with *Folk* (1903), are his most widely-read works, Hjortø depicted male characters comparable to Jacobsen's Niels Lyhne and the conflict between men "without a center and the self-possessed women to which they were attracted. The early novel, *Folk,* recently (1954) reprinted in a large edition, treats village life and in particular the rôle of gossip in a small community. Unlike Jensen's *Den lange Rejse,* which is simple and lucid, and which draws parallels from the realm of common experience, Hjortø's *Den gule Krønike* (*The Yellow Chronicle,* 1923) requires a blind acceptance of the author's myth and demands

the reader's concentrated attention. That Hjortø was more psychologically inclined than Johannes V. Jensen, may be observed in the autobiographical novel *Hans Heilums Nat* (*Hans Heilum's Night,* 1924), a work
which suggest the stream-of-consciousness technique. As a psychological
novelist, Hjortø assumes a place in Danish literature between Jens Peter
Jacobsen and Hans Christian Branner.

Jensen's spiritual affinity with the poetry of longing and with the
literary traditions of an earlier age is reflected in the work of his disciple
LUDVIG HOLSTEIN (1864–1943). In comparing Holstein's verse with the
several essays which he wrote about Johannes V. Jensen, one is surprised
to find such an ardent admirer of Jensen in a gentle poet and nature lover.
Holstein himself explained, "Fantasy was a dethroned monarch when
Johannes V. Jensen stepped into literature. It is not the least of his contributions that he again gave fantasy its place in the sun." The remark is both
a declaration of faith on the part of Holstein and an incisive appreciation
of Johannes V. Jensen's abstract contribution to literature. Jensen is
interpreted to have been reacting not primarily against a *fin-de-siècle* attitude, but against the demise of imaginative literature. The bond between
Jensen and Holstein was cemented in their common preoccupation with
the phenomena of the natural world, their admiration of life-giving fer-
tility, their rationalistic awe of the endless complexity of the cosmos, and
their philosophical materialism. In Holstein there was something of the
rustic simplicity of Jeppe Aakjær and the distant, idyllic quality of his
Swedish contemporary Erik Axel Karlfeldt; there are memorial verses to
both poets from Holstein's pen. Holstein was above all the interpreter of
the Danish flora. His most frequently cited poem is "Den hvide Hyacinth"—"the white hyacinth," and the mere titles of some of the collections of his poems are further indicative of his bias: *Løv* (*Foliage,* 1915),
Mos og Muld (*Moss and Humus,* 1917), *Æbletid* (*Apple Time,* 1920).

A basic objective materialism as well as dilettantism in anthropology,
both characteristic of Johannes V. Jensen, are met with again in the work
of the individualistic and rustic THØGER LARSEN (1875–1928). Larsen,
Johannes V. Jensen, Jeppe Aakjær, and Johan Skjoldborg were the leading figures of the so-called Jutland movement in Danish literature at the
turn of the century. Actually we may speak of a movement only insofar
as certain ideas were common to the writers concerned, for there was
neither an organization nor a periodical about which the Jutlanders
could rally.

Thøger Larsen was an able poet, whose basic poetic concept was the
myth in the more usual sense of the word. Larsen's poetry is overwhelm-

JOHANNES V. JENSEN
c. *1930.*

JOHANNES JØRGENSEN
Drawing by Gerda Ploug Sarp.

GUSTAV WIED
Drawing by P. S. Krøyer

JEPPE AAKJÆR
Drawing by Achton Friis.

ingly descriptive; it lacks the immediacy of the lyrical experience. His subjects are chiefly natural phenomena: the seasons, the soil, the times of the day, the north wind, a winter storm. He is imbued with a feeling of the transience of the individual human life, of the vastness of the universe, and of the reality of physical existence. True to himself, he made no effort to imitate the sophistication of many of his contemporaries and was content to be provincial. He was nevertheless viewed as a member of the *avant garde*.

Larsen's taste and literary affinities become apparent if we examine the periodical *Atlantis,* which he published during the 1920's. In the first numbers of the periodical we note especially his own translations from Walt Whitman, together with poems by Sophus Claussen, Otto Gelsted, and the young Paul la Cour. As a disciple, the editor addressed Johannes V. Jensen in a poem which includes the lines:

> You came from a long journey
> And gave us the lost world.

Lyrical reaction and nationalism, regionalism, social criticism, and materialism—these are convenient labels which may be applied in order to try to make Danish literature up to the First World War historically intelligible. While one or more of these terms can be applied to almost all Danish writers, there are, however, at least two significant writers who cannot readily be categorized: Gustav Wied and Harald Kidde. Wied was a satirist and Kidde an introspective novelist. Aside from a general intellectual inheritance from the Brandesian school, they had nothing in common, but together they marked the end of an era, for neither survived the war years.

GUSTAV WIED (1858–1914) was the reincarnation of poetic irony, of the ironic mood that had made itself felt in literature in the thirties and forties and whose witty exponent had been Johan Ludvig Heiberg. He was, however, more than an ironic humorist; beneath the smiling surface of his work there lay both bitterness and sorrow. His own mask concealed a Danish satyr for whom all masks fall and for whom nothing is holy. He was a connecting link between Herman Bang and the twentieth-century Danish humorist Robert Storm Petersen; indeed, he was a friend of both. He was a Bang with humor and a "Storm P." who rubbed salt in wounds. He was a tragic clown. He hated all sham and all hypocrisy. He was a rational satirist who looked life in the face, and finally did not find it worth living.

Wied has a thrice-secured place in Danish literature as the author of a series of sadly and bitterly humorous sketches, above all *Silhuetter* (*Sil-houettes*, 1891) and *Barnlige Sjæle* (*Childish Souls*, 1893); as the author of a series of the so-called satyr-dramas which were meant to be read rather than to be played; and of the comedy *Thummelumsen* (1901). *Skærmydsler* (*Skirmishes*, 1901), which is not typical of Wied's dramas in his own private genre of the "satyr play," has transcended the inherent difficulties of performance, to become one of the successes of the Royal Theater.[1] His critique of life and the *leitmotif* of all his work are to be found in *Dansemus* (*Dancing Mice*, 1905), a long "satyr play," original in its execution, and in the dramatic quartet *Adel, Gejstlighed, Borger og Bonde* (*Nobility, Clergy, Burgher, and Peasant*, 1897). In his novels, which may be said to be aesthetically less significant than his plays and short stories, Wied usually assumes the rôle of a misanthropic and cynical humorist. Although somewhat drawn out, the novels are easy reading and have retained considerable popularity because of their anecdotal qualities: the unexpected situations which Wied was able to invent and the devastatingly ironical comments, both relevant and irrelevant to the narrative proper, which he scattered throughout a prose work. *Livsens Ondskab* (*Life's Malice*, 1899) and its sequel, the more loosely constructed *Knagsted* (1902), are peopled with grotesque characters. The title character of both works, Knagsted, or "life's malice," is a diligent collector of commas:

Ewald: The Fishermen: 27,335. The Death of Balder: 45,860. The Brutal Claqueurs: 39,022. I am only collecting *Danish* authors, you understand. One has to be a specialist. And it would be impossible to cope with the others anyway! And when I am through with Ewald, he continued, then I'll add him up. That really is the most fun! You know, Holberg amounts to six millions! But you have to be awfully careful; it's so annoying when the results are different the second time.

The pessimistic novel *Slægten* (*Kin*, 1898) is Wied's most serious attempt in the genre. Its theme, not uncommon in the contemporary novel, is the degeneration of a family; Wied has intertwined the fate of the family in question with that of an erotically possessed clergyman.

The unfinished autobiography, *Digt og Virkelighed* (*Poetry and Reality*) is an important complement to his works; it is a distillation of the humor and pathos found in his other writings. In the autobiography, Wied speaks of himself as schizophrenic; he writes that from adolescence on-

---

1 A story, "Children of Men," translated by Hanna Astrup Larsen, was published in *The American-Scandinavian Review*, 1915, pp. 281–84, and reprinted both in *Denmark's Best Stories*, New York, 1928, and in *Scandinavian Short Stories* (Penguin Books, 403), 1943. "A Bohemian," translated by J.B.C. Watkins appeared in *The American-Scandinavian Review*, 1944, pp. 50–54. —One of Wied's most successful plays, 2×2=5, translated by Ernest Boyd and Holger Koppel, was published in New York in 1923.

wards, "I felt and still feel that my ego is divided into two egos, myself and the other, so that any time I run into trouble 'the other' takes care of the matter and says: 'of what importance is it to you?' and I feel relieved."

Wied enjoyed being an iconoclast. There was an air of the sensational about him, but he was not without a concealed or possibly subconscious moral purpose. Like other social satirists, he roused his readers and hearers to the recognition of humbug, sham, and hypocrisy. One of his earliest stories, "De Unge og De Gamle" ("The Young and The Old," published in a newspaper in 1891, revised and republished in 1893), brought Wied into conflict with the law, and he was ultimately imprisoned for two weeks for the portrayal of a scene from childhood which, far from being the lascivious or offensive story that it was considered by the court, reveals him to have had an unusual understanding for the naïveté of the child and the suppressed desires of the middle-aged unmarried woman.

The various aspects of his genius are reflected in *Dansemus,* in which the dancing mice are of course symbolical of life itself. Like the other satyr plays, it is a mixture of drama and prose, the ostensible stage directions being essential to an understanding of the story. As in Bang's novels, there are several interwoven motifs. The form of Wied's drama is as untraditional as was Wied himself. The scenes are not divided into acts, and they are often impressionistic and anecdotal rather than dramatic in essence. Nor is the style uniform throughout the work; it changes as the meter might change in a series of connected poems. There is no single plot in *Dansemus,* but Wied's *pointe* is clear enough. The play concludes with an ironic remark in the stage directions: "he knows that the drama is a lie, that in reality the affair had just the opposite ending... but that is the greatness of a literary work!... poetry's function is to do away with reality and lift the child of man high above the filth of life on earth and right into the refulgent ideals' spring-cleaned heaven!"

The sharpness of Wied's wit has often been elucidated by pointing to a few of his unforgettable and unexpected lines. One of the most unexpected is the parenthesis following a stage direction which seems to be serious enough: "and at the top of the broad stone stairs stands father Mackeprang and watches his little rascal and his laughter resounds in the courtyard...

"The sun shines, the sky is blue. Dogs are barking, cows are mooing, horses neighing, and tomorrow is the harvest festival. It is a wonderful holiday! (H. C. Andersen)."

15*

What a blow! What irony! The apparent enthusiasm for an idyllic situation is nothing but a satirical parody of Hans Christian Andersen's style and optimism. At first reading one is not certain whether to laugh or be offended—and then one smiles. That is precisely the reaction that Wied wanted. It is the same over and over again in Wied's work; he cannot resist making a devastating remark.

Just as Wied's work satirized the illusions of everyday life, his death by his own hand symbolized the tragic bankruptcy of an era of progress and optimism.

The novels of HARALD KIDDE (1878–1918) hearken back to the eighties and are a synthesis of elements to be found in the works of Herman Bang, Jens Peter Jacobsen, and Vilhelm Topsøe. Although a preoccupation with the weak and degenerate is common to Herman Bang and Harald Kidde, the latter is, from the standpoint of ethical content and of form, very different from the former. They have a common point of origin in their choice of subject matter, but their prose technique is unrelated. And whereas Bang was content to portray hopelessness, Kidde sounded an optimistic note and contrasted positive with negative attitudes. By the depth of his psychological understanding, Kidde suggests Jens Peter Jacobsen and Vilhelm Topsøe. He was however a more introspective, pious, and tender writer than either Jacobsen or Topsøe.

In Harald Kidde's two principal works, *Aage og Else* (1902–03) and *Helten* (*The Hero,* 1912), the leading characters, respectively Tue Tavsen and Clemens Bek, are apparent failures. Neither is virile. Both receive the moral help of strong women, Tue of Lull Wedén, and Bek of Lucie Camrath. Tue Tavsen in *Aage og Else* is lost in melancholy; he is unable to overcome the power of the dead. Clemens Bek is a representative of familial decadence who is nevertheless a "hero" in the eyes of the author, and consequently of the reader, for having been able to subjugate himself to a life of service and to live by the force of his pietistic Christian faith.

In *Aage og Else,* Kidde portrays in the autobiographically tinged Tue Tavsen an egoistic person whose inability to disassociate himself from recollections of the deceased members of his family is actually self-sympathy. We are given to understand that Tue's antagonist and fiancée, Lull Wedén, is the granddaughter of a German philosopher who is the equivalent of Nietzsche; she defends Nietzschean thinking and tries to rouse Tue to life. The parallel with the Danish folk song which gives the book its title, and in which the dead Aage visits the living Else, is frequently drawn. (Incidentally the motif of "Aage and Else" also appears in Kidde's

Helten). Lull, like Else, is unable to call her beloved back to life. Time and again Lull must use all her powers to overcome Tue's introspection. Her struggle to bring Tue to a realization of Nietzschean values and to instill in him an enthusiasm for life seems several times to approach success, but each time Tue relapses into the melancholia of which he himself is not fully aware, since he believes that a compromise between his way of life and that of Lull can be achieved. When the first goal in their life together has been reached, and they are admitted as university students, Lull comes to the sad realization that Tue's melancholy nature is essential to his being and that it would never be possible for him to live according to the ethics to which she subscribes. Tue cannot escape the bonds that his birth and childhood experiences laid upon him. Aage is of the dead.

In many ways *Aage og Else* is a powerful and fascinating book, but it has its weaknesses. It is very long and has many false cadences. Kidde wrote with the patience and some of the philosophy of Kierkegaard. In a note to the second edition, Kidde's widow stated that Kidde, had he lived, doubtless would have revised and shortened this, his first major prose work. The emotional life which Kidde ascribes to his youthful leading characters seems improbably precocious. Similarly, it is incredible that Tue could be so frigid towards his fiancée, and that she would be willing to put up with his coldness for so long.

Helten, while the story of the defeat, is at the same time the story of a Christian victory. There can be little doubt that Kidde wanted to establish Clemens Bek as the protagonist of a sincere and living Christianity and to point out what a real Christian was like. Born in a house of prostitution, the illegitimate child of a nobleman, Bek is reared by a German pietist who sets the course of Bek's humble life. Bek flees the worldliness of Copenhagen and his own feelings to become an elementary schoolteacher on an island inhabited by fantasts in the waters between Jutland and Zealand. The story of Bek's life in poverty and faith is narrated to the island's new physician, whose eyes are opened to the sham in his own life and who thereby is given a goal for life. An example of Kidde's mastery of pathos, which reaches expression on nearly every page of *Helten,* may be found in the short story "Obolen" ("The Obol").[1] A key word to the emotions of his pathetic characters is *rædsel*—terror, i.e., trepidation.

---

1 Translated in *The Norseman,* vol. XIII. 1955, pp. 275-8—"The Lost Son," translated by V. Elizabeth Balfour-Browne, is contained in *Contemporary Danish Prose,* Copenhagen, 1958.

Aside from the amazingly reliable cultural-historical foundation which he was able to give his works, Kidde possessed a peculiar ability to express the inexpressible, as it were, to formulate the thousand thoughts and fears which are composite in the life of the individual soul. He was able to capture in flight the vibrations of an individual existence and to put into words the constant struggle which goes on in the human mind before decisions are made or even before a state of indecision is reached.

In 1904 Johannes Jørgensen prophesied that *Aage og Else* would be one of the books in Danish literature that "would be studied through the ages." His prophecy may well come true, for Kidde's novels are being read more and more and have been several times republished since his death.

Of the Danish writers from the beginning of the twentieth century, none was more widely read abroad than KAREN MICHAËLIS (1872–1950), by virtue of a novel which acquired international fame: *Den farlige Alder* (*The Dangerous Age*, 1910).[1] The book, which has been translated into twenty languages, was a herald of the introspective and analytical psychological novels inspired by Freudian thought that came to the fore some score of years later. It is neither shocking nor sensational, but has value as a human document which pertains to a very real and important problem: In diary form, *Den farlige Alder* tells of the mental agony of a woman in her forties who finds divorce and solitude the only solution of the psychic difficulties which plague her.

In Denmark, Karen Michaëlis is esteemed not so much for her novels as for the several volumes of her memoirs, originally published as *Træet paa Godt og Ondt* (*The Tree of Good and Evil*, 1924–30) and revised as *Vidunderlige Verden* (*Wonderful World*, 1948–49).[2] Her understanding of the psyche of the little girl, as evidenced in the memoirs, is unsurpassed at least in Danish literature.

A more sophisticated woman writer, EDITH RODE (1879–1956), the wife of the poet and critic Helge Rode, had a relatively large audience for many years, primarily as a writer of short stories, but also as a facile lyrist. Her tales, recollections, and verse demonstrate a penetrating understanding of everyday happening by a distinctly female psyche.[3] Probably more than any other member of her sex in Denmark, she was a

---

1 The English translation, by Beatrice Marshall, was first published in New York, 1911; London, 1912.

2 In collaboration with Lenore Sorsby, Karin Michaëlis also wrote a volume of memoirs in English entitled *Little Troll,* New York, 1946.

3 The humorous short story, "The Eternal Adorer" was published in *The Norseman,* 1950, pp. 344–46.

woman's writer. Were one of her many works to be selected as her best, it would be the second edition of her poems *(Digte)*, published in 1933, which contain lyrical reflections on the seasons and on commonplace events.

Still another writer who is a complete anomaly deserves mention here, FREDERIK POULSEN (1876–1950), known for many years as the director of the Carlsberg Glyptotek in Copenhagen. He was not primarily a literary figure, since his life work was in the field of classical art and archaeology. In addition to publishing distinguished studies in those fields, however, Poulsen was also an imaginative writer and a traveling journalist of no mean ability. His *forte* was the anecdotal tale. Even in his most widely-read novel, *Under hellenisk Himmel (Under Greek Skies,* 1908), Poulsen merely linked together, by the device of a central character, a series of short stories and travel sketches inspired by his own experiences and observations while working and traveling in Greece. Insofar, the novel is reminiscent of Vilhelm Bergsøe's earlier *Fra Piazza del Popolo,* which strung together a series of experiences, some real and more imaginary, of the Scandinavian colony in Rome. It was not until Frederik Poulsen confined himself to the anecdote and the sketch that he won an established, if detached, position in Danish belles-lettres. There are several collections and many editions of his stories and sketches.[1]

In the literary physiognomy of Denmark, there was a change of a negative nature around the year 1900. Norwegian writers gradually ceased to play an important rôle in Danish literature. Ibsen, Bjørnson, and Lie had been a living part of the Danish literature in the second half of the nineteenth century, but when those three older Norwegian writers disappeared from the scene, there was no new Norwegian movement making itself felt in Copenhagen. Only Knut Hamsun continued to be an important adjunct of Danish literature. The proud imprint of the Gyldendal publishing company, "Kjøbenhavn og Kristiania," came to mean less and less, and after the First World War, the literary union of Denmark and Norway, which had so long outlasted political separation and increasing cultural differences, was dissolved. Even the Norwegian branch of the firm of Gyldendal was established as an independent publishing house in Norway. Danes and Norwegians became less aware of their respective contemporary authors and, true to the spirit of the age, each literature became more self-sufficient, and fewer eyes saw beyond the national boundaries. In recent years, the Dano-Norwegian language

[1] A single volume has been translated into English: *Travels and Sketches,* London, 1923.

in Norway has changed under the impact of the "Landsmål" (or "New Norwegian") movement, which since 1848 has been trying to establish a Norwegian language based on Norwegian dialects and independent of Danish. Works by prominent Norwegian authors writing in the revised Dano-Norwegian have been "translated" into Danish, and similarly, Danish works are now put into Norwegian. Books written in Landsmål itself have never been readily accessible to readers of Danish, and the slight extra effort required for a Dane to read Dano-Norwegian literature is enough to make the general sale of that literature impracticable in Denmark.

The loss of Norwegian literature written in Danish and published in Denmark was in part compensated by the tendency of Icelandic writers to employ Danish as their medium. In the next chapter we shall have occasion to discuss the work of the best-known Icelandic writers of Danish, Gunnar Gunnarsson and Guðmundur Kamban, but mention should be made here of a drama by the Icelandic playwright JÓHANN SIGURJÓNSSON (1880–1919) entitled *Bjærg-Ejvind og hans Hustru (Eyvind of the Hills),* which was originally published in Copenhagen in 1911 and was translated and played abroad.[1] Sigurjónsson's melodramatic piece about lovers who sacrificed all for freedom was the most widely read drama published in Danish in the twentieth century, prior to the work of Kaj Munk in the thirties.

The general picture of Danish literature from the years of the "Breakthrough" until the First World War is clear, although the more recent the literature, the less well-defined it seems. Trends which date from the beginning of the twentieth century, if not back to the seventies, carry over into the twenties and thirties. The literature of social problems is the clearest case in point. To understand the twenties and thirties however, it is necessary to reflect on the chronological sequence of world events and to consider the impact of the First World War on Danish life and thought.

---

1 Cf. *Modern Icelandic Plays*: *Eyvind of the Hills, The Hraun Farm*. Translated by Henninge Krohn Schanche. New York, 1916.

CHAPTER XIII

A Disillusioned Generation

The outbreak of World War I was a great shock to intellectual Denmark as well as to the rest of the civilized world. The faithful, whether they were Christians, rationalists, intellectuals, or pacifists, saw their ideals cast down and trod upon after 1914. The era of peace which had begun at the conclusion of the Franco-Prussian war in 1871—incidentally, the same year as the young Dr. Brandes' first lectures at the University of Copenhagen—was at an end. Contrary to hopes and expectations, the technological advances of the new materialism had led not to a better world but to armed conflict and physical destruction. The war brought about a realignment of ideas, for whatever a man's faith might have been up to 1914, it was rocked by the war. The apparent security of systematic belief had turned out to be a delusion. Some thinkers subsequently became reactionaries, others became revolutionaries, and still others cynics. Directly or indirectly, all these conversions found expression in Danish literature.

As elsewhere in the Western world, the post-bellum era seemed chaotic, unfettered, and materialistic. This did not mean that the older generation ceased to exist or to write, but simply that younger writers who were skeptical of the *status quo* began to make their voices heard.

Many of the younger critical minds made a concerted effort to influence public opinion by rallying around new periodicals. Although short-lived, some of the new critical magazines of the twenties were not only representative of the times but influential in directing the course of contemporary Danish culture. To the established organs of public opinion like *Tilskueren (The Spectator)* which had been appearing since 1884, and *Gads danske Magasin,* which (as the continuation of *Dansk Tidsskrift*) was even older, was added a spate of aggressive new journals which advocated a variety of literary, artistic, and political panaceas for the world's ills.

The materialism and the regionalism of the pre-war literary generation were represented by the short-lived periodicals *Forum* (1923) and *Atlantis*

(1923–25), edited and written mostly by Johannes V. Jensen and Thøger Larsen, respectively.

In his periodical *Sirius* (1924–25), Otto Gelsted and his contributors upheld a rationalistic-materialistic standpoint, and defended the poetry of Tom Kristensen and Fredrik Nygaard, the art criticism of Poul Henningsen, and the theories of Johannes V. Jensen. For the few months during which the periodical appeared, Gelsted made a serious effort to assess the international literary scene, and published articles on Henri Barbusse, Joseph Conrad, and Thomas Hardy, among others.

A group of younger, academic poets, inspired by a new aestheticism, assembled around the journal *Klinte* (*Corn-Cockle*, 1920–21), which gained no great response from the reading public. Revived in 1925 as *Vild Hvede (Wild Wheat)*, it was carried on into the fifties under the able eclectic guidance of its self-sacrificing editor, the short story writer and poet Viggo F. Møller. It is still being published, although now under the title *Hvedekorn (Grains of Wheat)* and under different editorship. The periodical has championed no specific school of thought or aesthetic standpoint, but has served as a medium for younger writers of energy and promise. Fulfilling the indispensible rôle of the "little magazine," it has enabled several lyrists and prose writers who since have proven their worth to reach the small but critical group of readers who often predetermine an author's literary standing.

The periodicals whose influence was most keenly felt were of the radical, tempestuous, or left-wing type. From 1917 to 1920, *Klingen (The Blade)* focused attention on new directions in art. Later in the twenties the socialist and communist philosophies found intellectual expression in the internationally oriented *Clarté* (1926–27) and in the Scandinavian edition of *Monde* (1929–31) respectively. During the late twenties, as Sven Møller Kristensen has pointed out, the new iconoclastic materialism was articulated especially in the architectural *Kritisk Revy (Critical Review,* 1926–28), with which the name of the critic, inventor, and architect, Poul Henningsen (son of the novelist Agnes Henningsen) was closely associated. The critical and independent attitude of *Kritisk Revy* is succinctly expressed in a verse by Otto Gelsted which appeared in a number of that periodical:

> Should I eat the national
> Or the religious hay?

The national and the religious ideals were the patent answers of an older generation, and they failed to still the skepticism and longing of the disillusioned younger generation which was seeking newer or more substantial standards. Youth was then as now imbued with a desire to be creative and original.

It is possible, indeed it has become the fashion, to speak of an era between the two World Wars, although the validity of such a temporal category has yet conclusively to be demonstrated in cultural history. It is probably nearer to the truth to say that poets and thinkers in Denmark only reflected the unrest and violence and the shattering of ideals in Europe during and after World War I, while in World War II the Danes experienced war and its concomitant horrors, tragedies, and disappointments at first hand.

As a neutral, Denmark reaped commercial benefits from World War I. Because there were good markets to the west and south, a host of Danish importers and exporters soon acquired wealth. Even the farmer had his share of what in Danish was referred to as "goulash." His dairy products were in great demand, and retail prices rose sharply, while the costs of production increased only moderately. The devil-may-care attitude in some younger post-war writers can be understood only if one bears in mind the fundamental disharmony of destruction and good times which the war years brought. The golden harvest is represented in literature by the so-called Americanized, whisky-drinking writers. Chief among them were Tom Kristensen, Emil Bønnelycke, and Fredrik Nygaard, poets who were conscious of Walt Whitman and his doctrine that all of existence was worthy of poetic consideration. Their work has acquired several epithets: cynical, materialistic, and hard-boiled.

"I love everything that happens and everything that will happen," EMIL BØNNELYCKE (1893–1953) wrote in his series of impressionistic but sentimental prose poems entitled *Asfaltens Sange (Songs of the Asphalt, 1918)*, which voice a reckless admiration for technology. In the same volume he remarked—doubtless in order to shock his readers who may be assumed to have revered the work of the nineteenth-century Danish poet: "I love a match more than a poem by Christian Winther."

The disillusioned generation of intellectual revolt had as its foremost representative TOM KRISTENSEN (born 1893). In one of his early poems, "Landet Atlantis" ("Atlantis"), which appeared in the radical periodical *Nye Tanker (New Ideas)* in March, 1920, he cried out, "the world has become chaotic anew," and coined the shocking simile, "as beautiful as a bombarded railway station / is our youth, our force, our wild ideas." The poem concluded:

> In chaos I lift my rifle
> to take aim at the star of beauty.

His first volume of verse, *Fribytterdrømme* (*Dreams of a Freebooter,* 1920), struck a responsive chord and at once made him a spokesman for his generation and an archetype of the poetic unrest of the twenties. His poetry is a synthesis of the radical and bold metaphors and symbols of Sophus Claussen and the vibrant materialism of Johannes V. Jensen. In *Fribytterdrømme,* and in a second collection of poems entitled *Paafugle-fjeren* (*The Peacock Feather,* 1922) which he wrote during a voyage to the Far East, the poet was driven by his appetite for the exotic, for crass experiences and brilliant colors. He loved the names of foreign ports, but he was later to declare that it was Knut Hamsun's fault that he did. The first stanza of a poem "Ringen" ("The Ring") in *Fribytterdrømme* begins:

> Port Said and Colombo
> Penang, Singapore
> and Saigon, Hongkong, Yokohama!

and other stanzas invoke Honolulu, 'Frisco, Chicago, New York, and Baltimore. The exhilaration which Kristensen derived from his experience in the Far East, in Spain, and in France, coupled with his familiarity with modern American literature, was the essence of his youthful inspiration. Despite his explicit radicalism, his verse forms are remarkably simple and traditional. His ethic is very different from that of his sedate and more critical contemporary Jacob Paludan, who also essayed the New World but found it wanting, and who despaired to see the values of European culture, acquired and tried by many generations, exchanged for the papier-mâché ideals of the devotees of the dollar, the bar, and the automobile. The subsequent bankruptcy of the post-war materialistic philosophy was pictured in Kristensen's retrospective novel *Hærværk* (*Havoc,* 1930)[1], which is not without autobiographical elements. Like Kristensen, the major character in the novel in a literary critic of a Copenhagen daily newspaper. He spends much of his time drinking in cafés; he is confronted with anarchism and Catholicism as the alternative ways out of hopeless nihilism. The book is a series of crass situations, the sum of which is nil. Its leading characters know only chaos and destruction and apparently must experience devastation as the first stage in achieving a standpoint. As a novel, *Hærværk* is a monument to the twenties, a lost decade.

Tom Kristensen has continued to exemplify "the generation that was

1 English translation by Carl Malmberg, published by the University of Wisconsin Press, 1968.

to stumble at the start" (Paludan's phrase) by wavering between conflicting ideologies. He has leaned now to the Left and now to the Right, but never has he been the protagonist of a particular social or political philosophy. In this respect he differs greatly from many other young writers who emerged from the war years, who were associated with the Left, and who were reticent neither in accepting nor expressing social and political ideas, dogmas, and criticism.

Kristensen and Bønnelycke and some few other writers, notably FREDRIK NYGAARD (1897–1958) in his *Europaskitser* (*European Sketches,* 1919), wrote a materialistic poetry which had its roots in the earlier work of Johannes V. Jensen and which had received its poetic inspiration to no small extent from the work of Walt Whitman, who had been introduced into Danish literature through the medium of Johannes V. Jensen's translations in the grotesque novel *Hjulet (The Wheel)* in 1905. The young writers were carried away by Whitman's free rhythms and his enthusiasm for the world of material things. "Everything is beautiful" was the phrase which reverberated in Bønnelycke's poetry of asphalt, streets, and machinery; but Tom Kristensen soon repudiated the seductive phrase (as is evident from his critique of contemporary poetry published in 1925). Kristensen, *et al.,* were indeed representative of the times, but they were by no means the only poets of note in the early twenties. A complementary parallel was provided by their contemporary HANS HARTVIG SEEDORFF PEDERSEN (born 1892), who made his debut in 1915. Seedorff was closer to the tradition of wine, women, and song than were any of the other younger writers of the twenties. His was an optimistic voice in a world of recklessness and despair. The verse of his youth, although it evinces an awareness of Johannes V. Jensen, was inspired by Eros and wanderlust. The biological-historical problems of the naturalists, the ethical problems of the philosophers, and the social problems of the literary Left were not for his canvas. His verses have a spiritual affinity with the songs of the eighteenth-century Swedish poet C. M. Bellman and the lighter poems of the nineteenth-century Swedish poet Gustaf Fröding. The bright and spirited poetry of Seedorff's youth made him one of the most popular modern Danish poets. In his later years, however, Seedorff has been a sort of laureate on state occasions. He has also had a severe attack of propriety. His melodiousness and merry youthfulness have been replaced by a kind of pseudo-profundity. The youthful radical has become an old conservative, a development which is by no means unusual. Bønnelycke, once singer of the asphalt, became religious in his later years, and as a poet he had progressively less to say.

Seedorff has kept his voice, however; he was able to lift it to encourage his countrymen during the Occupation in World War II.

The poetry of Tom Kristensen, Emil Bønnelycke, Fredrik Nygaard, and the early Seedorff has often been called expressionistic. While the validity of this term has been questioned (and nowhere more incisively than in Tom Kristensen's own analysis of contemporary poetry which appeared in the Danish periodical *Tilskueren* in 1925), it is of interest to the student of European literature that the label "expressionism" also was applied to Danish literature as a whole by some critics at the end of the First World War.

Not all the young postwar poets were associated with the direction loosely identified as expressionistic. The most courageous of the disillusioned, JENS AUGUST SCHADE (born 1903), was much too concerned with the libertarian concept of freedom to toy with stylistic idiosyncrasy. A social critic and an iconoclast, Schade is as much a thorn in the side of a Marxist as he is in the side of a Victorian. He has always been too independent and too little of a partisan or even a disciplinarian to be confined by any set doctrines. Schade tries to break down arbitrary barriers, to remove repressions established by prudery and convention, and to lift a bubbling hymn of praise to the human being as he is in nature—his erotic impulses included. There is no doubt that Schade has taken a leaf from Walt Whitman's book. He not only shares Whitman's familiarity with otherwise veiled aspects of existence, but also Whitman's egocentricity.

"Do you know the bright poet, Schade,"

he asks in one of his poems that is typical of his egocentric writing. Schade, like Whitman, tries to be himself, starting from the marrow and working outward. He tries to throw off the yokes and bonds which family, tradition, and society have placed upon contemporary man. Church and state are his bane, but he is far from being a revolutionary, for he is fundamentally incapable of political association. He is rather an anarchist. In Freudian terminology, he has succeeded in freeing himself from his repressions and frustrations; but this success has been a self-conscious one, and Schade is a self-conscious poet. He is something of a *poseur*. He enjoys being looked upon as the bad boy of Danish literature, but the fact that he is acceptable actually lessens his influence in Danish literature today. He means to shock his contemporaries; but the squeamish contemporaries of two decades ago have been replaced by a generation mentally insulated against the sort of shock Schade can provide.

While Schade may seem preoccupied with the erotic element, it would be incorrect to consider his preoccupation psychopathic. He is the will-fully uninhibited radical who tries to give human love as much dignity as other necessary functions of life and to look the fact in the face that, stripped of the tabus of the past, sex provides clean, normal, exhilarating, and satisfying experiences. Schade feels that only when one loves is one really one's self; then all artificial barriers are broken down. Love is worth immortalizing in art: that is the conviction which is formulated in much of Schade's poetry and in the several novels he has written.

It is an anomaly that Schade, the iconoclast, has written a popular work which may well grace the shelves of the prude and the timid, namely *Sjov i Danmark (Sjov in Denmark)*, originally published in 1928. The book comprises a series of poems in an easy, humorous, and satirical vein, poems which tell, with digressions, the life story of an average Dane named Sjov (the name means "fun" and is presumably supposed also to suggest the name Schade to our minds). Sjov tries to break away from the burdens of the bourgeois tradition but is a failure as a student and as a lover; his attempt at revolution is ludicrous, and his effort to commit suicide is similarly unsuccessful. By implication, *Sjov i Danmark* contains much criticism of the established order, but it is such good-natured if satirical criticism that the effect of Schade's biting wit is pleasantly dulled.

Schade has inspired imitators and poetic plagiarists, but they have generally been crude where he has been clever. Nor have they established the rapport with a larger public which Schade has been able to maintain without compromising himself.

Of the several poets of the twenties, Tom Kristensen far more than Schade was the writer who came to symbolize the radical wing of the new generation. His counterpole was the outstanding Danish prose writer of the years around 1930, JACOB PALUDAN (born 1896). Tom Kristensen and Jacob Paludan are both important creative writers, and leading literary critics and translators as well. They have therefore exerted a threefold influence on their times. It is possible that Tom Kristensen has in the long run been more influential as a critic than as a poet; he has for many years reviewed books for the Copenhagen daily *Politiken* (which, it will be remembered, was founded as a radical newspaper by Brandes' followers). The lasting value of his criticism is apparent if one examines the two volumes of his selected book reviews and literary essays which have been published since the Second World War. As a translator, he has been zealous and energetic. Among the many novels which he has put into Danish can be mentioned works by Theodore Dreiser, D. H. Lawrence, and James T. Farrell.

Jacob Paludan is the leading literary critic of the conservative newspaper *Dagens Nyheder* (formerly *Nationaltidende*), and the editor of a widely-sold series of books which popularize arts and letters ("Hasselbalchs Kulturbibliotek"). Of the several books he has translated into Danish, the most notable is Sinclar Lewis' *Dodsworth*. His foremost contribution, however, is his novels.

Jacob Paludan was the antithesis of Tom Kristensen and the new materialism in the twenties. Paludan has been consistent in his philosophy of life, although he has become more tolerant of the civilization of the New World as it has grown more conservative in recent years. In essence, he is a social critic in the same way that Henrik Pontoppidan was a social critic. He has castigated contemporary weaknesses and pointed to the tenuous philosophy of the times as the cause of both social degeneration and moral collapse. He belongs to the critical Right, which would preserve and revivify rather than destroy and create anew. Paludan would retain old values, while Kristensen and the many writers who are more akin to Kristensen have tried to seek new values. While Kristensen and Emil Bønnelycke were discovering the poetry of asphalt, cement, and the locomotive, Paludan clung to the humanistic tradition and sympathized with belief in the supernatural. Kristensen was drawn to the exotic and the distant, to the Orient and the New World. Paludan's first-hand impressions of the New World were overwhelmingly negative. Kristensen was the apostle of American postwar literature in Denmark, of the works of Faulkner, Hemingway, Caldwell, and others. This literature Paludan rejected. Kristensen was international; Paludan was supra-national. Between them stood the other members of "the generation that stumbled at the start."

From the standpoint not only of ethics, but also of form, Paludan was a traditionalist or a renewer. While the new novel was almost by definition destroying formalistic prose, Paludan hearkened back to the dignified style of a previous generation, to the careful diction of the prose-poet, to the epic structure of the early nineteenth-century European novel. While many writers who won spontaneous applause in the twenties are today outmoded, Paludan gives promise of becoming a modern classic. He is an artist and a stylist who has had something to say. What he has written represents no effusion of the spirit of the times; it bespeaks the craftsmanship of the author and the union of idea and epic form. As a novelist, Paludan is strongly reminiscent of Henrik Pontoppidan in *Lykke-Per* and

KAJ MUNK

KAREN BLIXEN

MARTIN A. HANSEN

PAUL LA COUR

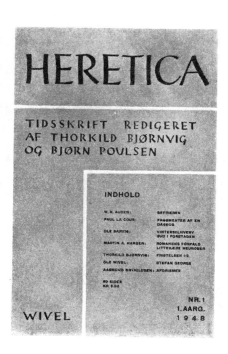

HERETICA

TIDSSKRIFT REDIGERET AF THORKILD BJØRNVIG OG BJØRN POULSEN

INDHOLD

W. H. AUDEN:	BEFRIEREN
PAUL LA COUR:	FRAGMENTER AF EN DAGBOG
OLE SARVIG:	VINTERSOLHVERV GUD I FORSTADEN
MARTIN A. HANSEN:	ROMANENS FORFALD LITTERÆRE NEUROSER
THORKILD BJØRNVIG:	FINSTELSEN 1-3
OLE WIVEL:	STEFAN GEORGE
AASMUND BRYNILDSEN:	AFORISMER

90 SIDER
KR. 3.50

NR. 1
1. AARG.
1948

WIVEL

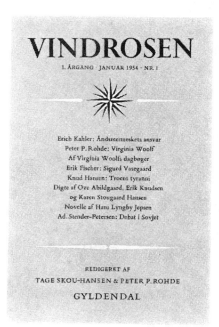

VINDROSEN

1. ÅRGANG · JANUAR 1954 · NR. 1

Erich Kahler: Åndsmenneskets ansvar
Peter P. Rohde: Virginia Woolf
Af Virginia Woolfs dagbøger
Erik Fischer: Sigurd Vasegaard
Knud Hansen: Troens tyranni
Digte af Ove Abildgaard, Erik Knudsen
og Karen Stougaard Hansen
Novelle af Hans Lyngby Jepsen
Ad. Stender-Petersen: Debat i Sovjet

REDIGERET AF
TAGE SKOU-HANSEN & PETER P. ROHDE

GYLDENDAL

HVEDEKORN

Ungermann.

Nr. 1   Januar   1952

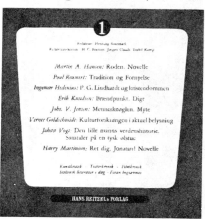

Litteratur Kunst Videnskab

PERSPEKTIV

1

Redaktør: Henning Fonsmark
Redaktionskomité: H. C. Branner, Jørgen Claudi, Ineke Kemp

Martin A. Hansen: Roden. Novelle
Poul Reumert: Tradition og Fornyelse
Ingemar Hedenius: P. G. Lindhardt og kristendommen
Erik Knudsen: Brændpunkt. Digt
Johs. V. Jensen: Menneskeøglen. Myte
Verner Goldschmidt: Kulturforskningen i aktuel belysning
Johan Vogt: Den lille manns verdenshistorie.
Samtaler på en tysk ølstue
Harry Martinson: Ret dig, Jonatan! Novelle

Kunstkronik · Teaterkronik · Filmkronik
Italiensk litteratur i dag · Foran Ingmarson

HANS REITZELs FORLAG

Literary periodicals published since World War II.

De Dødes Rige. Like Pontoppidan, Paludan is not only a critic but a chronicler of his own times. Paludan's rise as a novelist was slow but steady,
through the publication of *De vestlige Veje (The Western Roads,* 1922),
Søgelys (Searchlight, 1923), *En Vinter lang (One Winter long,* 1924), *Fugle
omkring Fyret (Birds Around the Lighthouse,* 1925),[1] and *Markerne modnes
(The Fields Ripen,* 1927). Of these novels the last-named is the most
successful. Born of post-war pessimism and critical of the times, it is not
without crude effects; but it reflects the sensitivity and emotionalism of
its author, the keenness of his feelings, and his penchant for descriptions
of nature. In its entirety the plot is scarcely credible, but as one reads the
novel it does not seem exaggerated.

Paludan's epic ability culminated in *Jørgen Stein* (1932–33)[2], which is a
monumental novel in modern Danish literary history and an impressive
and comprehensive study of life in Denmark between the two World
Wars. The wartime situation itself and its consequences were portrayed
many times in the Danish literature of the twenties and thirties, but
nowhere more forcefully or with greater penetration and incisiveness
than in *Jørgen Stein.*

Jørgen Stein, the novel's central character, is Paludan's symbol of the
"generation that was to stumble at the start," the generation that entered
adult life contemporaneously with the outbreak of World War I and the
consequent weakening of the traditional values in European society.
Jørgen Stein is also a symbol of degeneration and decadence. He does
not have the innate strength to overcome the difficulties he encounters.
The son of a government official in Jutland and the heir to the traditions
of many generations of Danish clergymen and public servants, he aban-
dons his cultural heritage only to stumble aimlessly through life. Without
a personal philosophy and lacking perseverance, he exerts his efforts first
in one direction and then in another; their sum and substance is slight
and ephemeral. He has good intentions but poor judgment. His faulty
judgment is characterized by his choice, at a crucial moment, of a modern,
emancipated woman instead of the faithful and conservative woman—
Nanna, his Gretchen—who really loves him and is his good and guiding
spirit. In love as in life, Jørgen Stein has never learned Ibsen's lesson: be
yourself. He tries rather to adapt himself to a series of friends who seem to
be pursuing specific goals. He takes refuge in his memories, and time and
again flees from the strictures and demands of daily life in Copenhagen
by returning to the scenes of his childhood. At the end of the narrative,

---

1 English translation by Grace Isabel Colbron. New York and London, 1928.
2 English translation by Carl Malmberg published by the University of Wisconsin Press,
1966.

he has become a smallholder, has married a matter-of-fact country lass, and is looking forward to the birth of his first child; but although there is the possibility of his finding meaning in some of man's oldest traditions and responsibilities, we are given to understand that Jørgen Stein has not really found a pattern within himself.

The debility and spiritual bankruptcy of the postwar era is the subject of Paludan's other novels as well as of *Jørgen Stein*. Symbolical is the title of the early novel *Søgelys*—"Searchlight." In his first novels, Paludan made a concerted effort to portray and to discredit the new times and the artificiality of postwar life, but those novels did not achieve their purpose as well as the more reflective, subtle, and philosophically inclined *Jørgen Stein*. Let it be said, finally, that Paludan is no mere social chronicler; he is a fine stylist who possesses an astounding ingenuity in coining phrases pregnant with association and connotation and in insinuating the precise nature of his mood into the mind of his reader.

Since *Jørgen Stein,* Paludan has published several volumes of essays.[1] He seems to have changed his literary rôle from being a critic and imaginative chronicler of his times to that of a reflective and sensitive essayist. Some of his essays are contemplative and introspective; others evince his appreciation of nature—as for example the collection *Han gik Ture* (*He Took Walks,* 1949). Two collections of his articles pertain to spiritualism, a subject to which he has been drawn because of his reaction against materialism—the materialism championed by one of the writers who impressed him most, Johannes V. Jensen.

The turbulence of the postwar era—of the generation represented by Tom Kristensen and Jacob Paludan—also produced the unpolished humanist NIS PETERSEN (1897–1943), who is known to the English-speaking world as the author of a remarkable historical novel entitled *The Street of the Sandalmakers* (*Sandalmagernes Gade,* 1931).[2] He wrote one other novel, *Spildt Mælk* (*Spilt Milk,* 1934),[3] which depicts the internal struggles and rebellion in postwar Ireland, and also several volumes of short stories and of verse.

The essence of Nis Petersen, the ideas which lie behind his prose and poetry, can be deduced from the novel *Sandalmagernes Gade.* The story is set in Rome during the reign of Marcus Aurelius. The time and place

1 Two essays, translated by Lydia Cranfield, have appeared in *The Norseman*: "Conversation and Company," in vol. IX, 1951, pp. 45–51, and "Chickens" in vol. XV, 1957, pp. 64–8.

2 Translated by Elizabeth Sprigge and Claude Napier. London; New York 1933. Repr. London, 1934.

3 Translated by Claude Napier. London; Toronto, 1935.

were chosen apparently because Nis Petersen felt them to provide parallels to conditions in his own country as he saw them. It was not a matter of re-creating the past as an historian, but rather of making the point that people then were much the same as people today and that the historical patina which time has laid upon past events must be disassociated from the events themselves. Petersen was well-read, if not formally highly educated, and he doubtless could have avoided anachronisms and even achieved greater historical detail had he wished; but he did not lose his touch with the common man. It is not too much to say that Petersen's novel was a contribution to the establishment of the new historical novel which neither burdens the reader with historical detail nor views a past age as the subject for melodramatic exploitation, but which makes an effort imaginatively to recreate the past.

Nis Petersen's position as a writer of Danish verse grows more secure with the passage of time. Although popular interest has dwelt principally on the bizarre aspects of his unstable life rather than on his serious literary efforts, Danish critical opinion elevates him above most of his contemporaries because of the quality of his poetry. Eclectic to the point of virtuousity, Nis Petersen was basically a traditionalist in his handling of meter. His penchant for rhythm was so strong that it often made his poetry verge on doggerel. The lilting, ballad-like nature of the poetry and a gruff, manly tone overlie a pervasive sentimentality and a profound sympathy with man sacrificed to Mars and Mammon. Petersen's philanthropic attitude found its most insistent expression in the poem "Elsker du Mennesket?" ("Do you love man?") in the first volume of his verse to be published, *Nattens Pibere* (*Night Pipets*, 1926) and in the prophetic "Brændende Europa" ("Europe Aflame") in the second collection, *En Drift Vers* (*A Drove of Verses*, 1933).

Nis Petersen's lamentation did not constitute a jeremiad: "No tears, no weeping from fear, no stillborn cry," as he was later to write in a poem about "the god of the sated," contained in *Til en Dronning* (*To a Queen*, 1935). In other poems, Petersen struck a different, optimistic and very nearly roguish note. Noteworthy is "Foraar ved Mariager Fjord" ("Spring at Mariager Fjord") in *Nattens Pibere*.[1]

The many poets of the twenties and thirties have dwindled in importance, and the rôles of the various journals or cliques with which they were associated are now of historical rather than aesthetic significance. The poets who have continued to interest succeeding generations of

[1] The translated poems, "Spring at Mariager Fjord," "Do you love man?" and "Europe Aflame" are found in *20th Century Scandinavian Verse*, Copenhagen, 1950, pp. 65 ff.

16*

readers were not, in general, closely affiliated with the literary schools. A few individualistic poets deserve special mention.

The young PAUL LA COUR (1902–56), who was later to become the spokesman for the aesthetically and metaphysically inclined poets of the forties, published three small collections of verse in the early twenties. His early poems are word pictures rather than philosophical reflections and are clearly the outgrowth of la Cour's interest in painting, particularly in the work of Henri Matisse (one volume of la Cour's verse is called *Matisse Bogen—The Matisse Book,* 1924). Nature and Eros are la Cour's subjects. In his later poems, he became more reminiscent, introspective, and abstract; his early motifs were augmented by memories of the First World War and the poet's childhood. In his early verse la Cour acknowledged his indebtedness to Johannes V. Jensen; the poem which gives the collection *Regn over Verden (Rain on the World,* 1933) its name is dedicated to Jensen. Another poem is dedicated to Jensen's disciple Ludvig Holstein, whom the early la Cour must be said to resemble more than Johannes V. Jensen; their verse is imbued with sensitivity toward nature and Eros, and at the same time is more melodious than the verse of Jensen. By 1938 a change had come over Paul la Cour; the motto of his introspective and pessimistic *Alt kræver jeg (I demand All)* published that year, was taken from Rilke, a fact which symbolized a change in both ethical standpoint and aesthetic attitude. During the Second World War la Cour was silent, and when he did begin to publish again, in 1946, he became the leading aesthetician for a younger generation of Danish poets, as we shall have occasion to discuss below.

PER LANGE (born 1901), a master of chiseled and lapidary verse, established himself as the leading neo-classicist in Danish literature with *Kaos og Stjærnen (Chaos and the Star)* in 1926. His position is that of a philosophical aesthete, an intellectual aristocrat, and a careful artist. While he has written little, his exquisite verse assures him a lasting place among Danish poets. The skepticism and humanism that pervade his work are suggested by the ironical poem "Kirken" ("The Church"), which ridicules men who "would make God their captive and built a trap vast and dark" but who, after "filling their edifice with music and sweet song" kneeled in the darkness, fearing His coming—and subsequently breathed a prayer of thanks when the awful God passed by and did not enter.

Easier verse which found many readers appeared in *Kosmiske Sange (Cosmic Songs,* 1928) by JOHANNES WULFF (born 1902), who also achieved popularity because of a light-hearted novel of young love, entitled *O, Ungdom (O, Youth,* 1929). SIGFRED PEDERSEN (born 1903) is worthy of mention as an unusually facile writer of humorous verse. His best known volume of poems is entitled *Nye og sørgelige Viser* (*New and Sad Songs,* 1933).

The current of social criticism which we identified in the foregoing chapter both with the regional literature at the turn of the century and the radicalism which stemmed from the Brandesian era and which found its leading exponent in Martin Andersen Nexø, was swelled by the war and its aftermath. Social criticism was far more vocal and more timely than the pregnant aesthetic literature which was primarily concerned with the artistic and which had Paul la Cour as its courier. Inflation, unemployment, and human exploitation were wounds in the flesh of society, while the transformation of social mores made thinking men more critical and subsequently more articulate.

Social criticism became the dominant note in the literary chorus after a brief swell of expressionistic materialism at the end of the war. The criticism was by no means all Marxist. The novels of Jacob Paludan bespoke a conservative reaction to the social changes wrought by the war, but Paludan's criticism, like that of many another writer, was not merely concerned with the changes in traditional values and standards. It was imbued with a deeper fear that life itself was meaningless and that hope was futile. This attitude, which approached the nihilism of a Tom Kristensen, suggests a bond between the extremes in postwar Danish literature and between seemingly carefree materialism and perturbed social consciousness.

Most of the literature of the twenties and thirties was conscious of social and economic problems. It was also predominantly a prose literature, although the Left had two outstanding spokesmen in the lyrical genre, Otto Gelsted and Harald Herdal. And they are the two lyrists of the literature of social protest who have been able to retain an audience. The poetry of OTTO GELSTED (1888–1968) is a remarkable combination of propagandistic socialist realism and tender emotion. On the one hand Gelsted is the social critic of "Reklameskibet" ("The Advertising Ship") contained in *Jomfru Gloriant* (1923), a poem that makes us wince with its cutting criticism of modern sham[1]. On the other hand he is the author of such moving verse as the lullaby "Til en ung Mor" ("To a Young Mother") with its choice diction and traditional metrical and rhythmic pattern. Here and there in his more traditional verse, he reveals his goal to be the utopian commonweal. In recent years Otto Gelsted's poetry

1 An English version, "The Show Boat," by R. P. Keigwin appeared in *Life and Letters,* vol. 53, no. 117, 1947, pp. 147–49. Repr. in *20th Century Scandinavian Poetry,* Copenhagen, 1950, pp. 52ff.

has more and more expressed social convictions, as he has taken his stand with the extreme Left.

The Left found one of its unswervingly partisan writers in HARALD HERDAL (born 1900), who, in his verse, short stories, and novels, has endeavored to speak for the inarticulate, the impoverished of Copenhagen: The young apprentice, the working mother, the unemployed laborer—in short, men and women who thirst for new and happy experiences. It is Herdal's strength to be able to paint in simple words vivid pictures from proletarian life. In Herdal there smoulders a resentment against the well-to-do, and against the leisure class. In one of his poems he even speaks of his hatred of social oppressors. For him there is only one salvation, through the religio-political faith of Communism.

In some of the many social novels which were published in the two decades following the war, there emerged a new manner of telling a story in the so-called collective novel. There was no leading character or "hero," but rather a relatively large number of characters that were of equal importance in the narrative. The protagonist of the collective novel in Danish literature was HANS KIRK (born 1898), whose *Fiskerne* (*The Fishermen,* 1928) has given its author a secure place in modern Danish literature. *Fiskerne* is both a sociological and psychological study of a colony of pietistic fishermen in Jutland. With incisiveness and objectivity, Kirk depicts the lives of sincere simple folk who are puritanical fanatics. While Kirk never shares the belief of his fishermen characters, he is capable of sympathetic understanding of a fervent, if misguided, religious zeal. His impartial presentation is more surprising in view of the fact that he is one of the faithful adherents of Communism in Denmark. His social consciousness has presumably inspired his political thinking rather than vice versa. His art is certainly "socialist realism" and is free of any tinge of the fantastic or the exotic.

Fiskerne is an unusually successful "collective" novel. All the members of the five families that make up the community of believers are of equal importance as characters in the book. The fishermen are pietists, who belong to the so-called "Inner Mission" wing of the Danish state church, and who bring their strict, ascetic faith into a Grundtvigian community and gradually, against odds, force their way of life upon their surroundings. Yet they actually lose in their struggle, for several individuals among them cannot overcome the natural desires of the flesh which the pietists condemn as the work of the devil. A father and stepdaughter commit fornication; and a girl sent out into the world returns to bear an illegitimate child. The first pair is overcome by remorse and welcomes death, but the girl Tabita is in her simple way a refutation and negation of the pietistic ideal, for she follows her heart and forsakes the austere faith of the fishermen, loves her child, and rejoices in the thought of marriage with her lover. Here the books ends. We are very subtly led to the conclusion that the religious philosophy of the pietists is a contradiction of the world of nature.

A similar collective novel, dealing with day laborers *(Daglejerne)* was published by Kirk in 1936, but neither it nor his several other novels have been felt by critics to possess the forcefulness and pathos of *Fiskerne,* which may be said to embody elements of the art of Pontoppidan and Andersen Nexø.

The ethical antithesis of Hans Kirk's *Fiskerne* is the series of novels by ERIK BERTELSEN (born 1898) about life in the Harboør area of Jutland from about 1860 onwards. The first of the novels, *Dagen bryder frem (Daybreak)* which was published in 1937, introduced the reader to a sentimental world where joys and tragedies are experienced by fundamentally honest, God-fearing folk who nevertheless are not infrequently weak and wayward. In his effort to depict the patternlessness of daily life, Bertelsen has employed the technique of the anecdote, although without attempting humor. Like Thorkild Gravlund, he has also made considerable use of dialect in order to achieve a local flavor.

The conscious contrast to Hans Kirk's novel is apparent in Bertelsen's depiction of pietism ("Inner Mission") among the fisherfolk. Whereas Kirk's reader was supposed to conclude that the pietistic movement was abnormal and would negate the driving force in the life of human beings, Bertelsen's reader is meant to draw the inference that pietism is a positive good, an anchor on the troubled sea of life, and a stabilizing force in lives that otherwise would be meaningless. Although the ethos of the novels is rather superficial, there is no doubt that Bertelsen's work transcends much of the regional literature of Denmark. His later books are not stereotyped and have demonstrated that he cannot be dismissed as merely another regionalist.

Social criticism of an unusually broad and sweeping nature is expressed in the works of KNUTH BECKER (born 1893), who is first and foremost the author of a series of semi-autobiographical novels about "Kai Gøtsche." The series began with *Det daglige Brød (Daily Bread)* in 1932 and now fills nine of eleven planned volumes. *Marianne,* the first part of the final trilogy, *Et Kors af Brosten (A Cross of Cobblestones),* appeared in 1956. Becker uses his subject as a device to express indignation at conditions which obtain in the family, in church and school, and in daily life in town and country. In *Det daglige Brød* he portrays the unwanted child, who is misunderstood by his parents and his environment, who is persecuted by adults that have forgotten the dream-world of their own childhood and the child's need for love, sympathy, and above all phantasy.[1] Becker, who must in part be speaking from personal experience, gives us to understand that Kaj is the victim of his milieu, if not of his unenviable heredity, and that Kaj is not evil at heart, despite the incredibly poor judgment which, even for a child, he consistently shows. The reader soon comes to feel that no matter what the situation, Kaj will be abused or will make the wrong decision. In the later novels of the series, Kai is the victim of an inhuman educational system, of military conscription, etc. Not until *Marianne* is there sounded an optimistic note. Institutions and conditions which arouse Becker's righteous wrath are adversely criticized by implication. It must be said, however, that Becker is overzealous in letting his hero suffer such a great number of injustices. Like Andersen Nexø in *Pelle Erobreren*, Becker has tended to overstate his case by having a single character suffer so much social injustice and degradation, though there can be no doubt that he is justified in laying bare deplorable conditions. His social criticism *in extenso* is the product neither of a fanatical nor a disgruntled mind and, like the work of Andersen Nexø, Becker's novels have not been without an effect on the Danish social conscience. Incidentally, there has been a gradual change in Becker's style as the series has progressed. He has paid less and less attention to conventional punctuation and the distinctions between direct and indirect discourse, and has fused objective narration with impressions and reactions in the minds of his several characters.

The twenties and thirties saw the publication of a relatively large number of novels which endeavored not to interpret and chastise as did the books of Henrik Pontoppidan, Martin Andersen Nexø, and Hans Kirk—to mention outstanding examples of Danish novelists who followed the path suggested by Brandes—but to paint a drab picture of drab everyday life. The subject matter of this new kind of prose narrative spilled over into drama and into verse as well. Street scenes and offices, the unemployed man and the self-effacing proletarian commanded much attention, if for no other reason than that such subjects had not previously been exploited in literature. For once, writers were not forced to employ an exciting plot and could glory in the colorless. The reading public was in a mood to accept the new realism, with its representations of the futility

---

1 Chapter 20 of *Det daglige Brød*, translated by J. F. S. Pearce, is included in *Contemporary Danish Short Prose*, Copenhagen, 1958.

of human existence. Nevertheless, the authors of the new realism cannot be called completely pessimistic. In the most depressing situations there is hope or the shadow of a promise of good fortune, perhaps just that modicum of hope which is essential to mechanical, modern, soulless existence.

Among the Danish writers of the novel which in its way chronicles the times but is ever concerned with psychological problems, LECK FISCHER (1904–56) is the most durable and MOGENS KLITGAARD (1906–45) and KNUD SØNDERBY (1909–66) are the most readable. The majority of Leck Fischer's works are even in content and quality; Klitgaard was more erratic. Fischer is noteworthy because he never was a partisan writer. Many of his generation have fallen by the wayside or found peace in some patent or partisan solution of the world's problems. Fischer agitates for no social or political philosophy, but in his prose helps carry on the grand tradition of objective writing which dates back to the late eighteenth century in the history of European literature. In this respect, he may be compared with Jacob Paludan. In reading *Det maa gerne blive Mandag* (*Monday May as well Come*, 1934), Fischer's most popular book, we are not conscious of any didactic intent. The author is content to portray a milieu and to delineate life as he has observed it. Far from being models for a new social order, Fischer's characters generally are individuals who lead grey and lonesome lives, who do not enjoy the blessings of a rich intellectual life, and who have not or cannot achieve a communion with their fellow men. Leck Fischer's most ambitious work is the trilogy *Leif den Lykkelige* (*Leif the Lucky*, 1928–29, revised edition 1935), which follows the fate of two childhood friends in their mature years and stresses the feeling of lonesomeness and lack of achievement that besets both characters, the one extroverted and outwardly successful, the other sensitive and timorous. The prize-winning novel *En Kvinde paa Fyrre* (*A Woman of Forty*, 1940), which suggests Karin Michaëlis' earlier successful novel about "the dangerous age," is a subtle portrayal of psychic difficulties which trouble a woman during the menopause, who, although having acquired a place in the business world, is nevertheless alone. Curious to note, the book is written in the first person.

Although he has been compared with both writers, Fischer is no more a Hans Kirk than he is a Henrik Pontoppidan. His principal concern in his works is the familial problem. The relations of child to parent, husband to wife, and brother to sister, interest him particularly. His treatment of marriage and family life is not banal; he is, rather, true to life. Fischer is a dramatist as well as a novelist and is remarkable as a master of dramatic economy. Like Ibsen, he is able to interweave the fates of several characters and round out plot and action so that there are no loose ends. Of his several plays, the best known is *Barnet* (*The Child*, 1936), which combines a double tragedy of lovers who take recourse to an abortionist and a married couple whose curse is childlessness.

Mogens Klitgaard, who died before reaching 40, is not as easy to characterize as Leck Fischer, for Klitgaard wrote not only proletarian novels—*Der sidder en Mand i en Sporvogn* (*A Man is Sitting in the Streetcar*, 1937), *Gud mildner Luften for de klippede Faar* (*God Tempers the Wind to the Shorn Lamb*, 1938)—but also two easily-read historical novels: *De røde Fjer* (*The Red Feathers*, 1940), and *Ballade paa Nytorv* (*Trouble at Newmarket*, 1940). He was more of a psychologist than Leck Fischer. His appealing and semi-autobiographical narrative in *Gud mildner Luften* was no mere series of external events in the life of a little man, but an analysis of character by means of a tale about outward experiences. *Der sidder en Mand i en Sporvogn* is, however, as typical of the sub-genre of the social novel of the 1930's as is Fischer's *Det maa gerne blive Mandag*. In fact, it is easy to draw parallels between the two books.

In the realm of the historical novel, Mogens Klitgaard evinced considerable originality. In an unassuming way, he is, with Nis Petersen, a protagonist of the modern historical novel. One wonders how his talent might have developed, had his life not been cut short. He is analytical, ironical, and humorous, with a flair for the dramatic situation in everyday life and its psychological implications. He has no difficulty in holding the attention of his readers. Klitgaard is also a connecting link between the social criticism which pulsed through the literature of the early thirties and the psychological portrayal which was to be the predominant characteristic of the prose of the forties.

The psychological novel of social consciousness, as distinguished from the novel of psychological analysis, was best represented in the thirties by works of Knud Sønderby—who later was to win a lasting reputation as an essayist—and in addition by the early novels of Martin A. Hansen. Sønderby's novel *To Mennesker mødes* (*Two People Meet*, 1932) delineates the ramifications that result from a chance meeting of a man and a woman who are lonely and describes the casual course of events which gradually leads to a dissolution of their relationship. The title of the book is a succinct summary of the plot and the narrative. The novel was to some extent a picture of the times, although not to the same degree as Sønderby's previous novel *Midt i en Jazztid* (*In the Middle of a Jazz Age*, 1931), which more resembled Hemingway.

In 1936 Sønderby published a novel of family life, *En Kvinde er over-flødig (A Woman too Many)* which in ethos, although not in action, suggests Leck Fischer's later novel about the woman of forty. In 1942 Sønderby rewrote his novel into a play that was given successfully at the Royal Theater. The central figure of the novel (and play), the Widow Tang, is obsessed by a desire to play a rôle in the lives of her mature children in order to overcome the realization that she is superfluous and that she has nothing intellectually to offer her children. She succeeds only in making them miserable and allowing herself to suffer from selfish delusions of martyrdom.

MARTIN A. HANSEN (1909–55), who by 1950 was to become Denmark's leading novelist, made his debut as an author with a type of literature which displayed only one of his many sides. His first novel, *Nu opgiver han (Now He Gives Up,* 1935), was apparently but another of the many pessimistic novels of the 1930's which dealt with social problems of the day. It superimposed upon a clash between two generations the attempt to introduce a new agrarian philosophy into the life of a farming community. A sequel, *Kolonien (The Colony,* 1937), told of the failure of agrarian communism in practice. Although Hansen's two early novels seem very different from the books he wrote in the 1940's, they are no more different than the later works are from each other. *Nu opgiver han* and its sequel are easier reading and demand less of the reader's imagination than do the more recent novels, but a comparison of them with the later novels and essays (discussed in Chapter XV) shows Hansen to have been imbued with certain fixed philosophical convictions since the beginning of his literary career.

The regional novel which had made a promising start early in the century found only a few devotees as the tide of internationalism rose in the twenties. Although Thorkild Gravlund and Marie Bregendahl continued to write, the key note in Danish prose fiction was socialistic and very nearly Marxian until the psychological narrative became preponderant in the late thirties. The three principal representatives of a new regional literature in the twenties were very different from one another: Erik Bertelsen, Erling Kristensen, and Johannes Buchholtz. Bertelsen, whose work has been discussed above, was a regionalist in the same sense as Thorkild Gravlund. He depicted rural life in an idealized way and was an apologist for the *status quo.*

ERLING KRISTENSEN (born 1893) took it upon himself to refute some of theses of Danish regionalists and to cast a clear cold light on the oft-idealized Danish agriculturalist. He was primarily concerned with the motives for men's actions. He has portrayed the "pillars" of an agricultural community in a fashion similar to Ibsen's in *The Pillars of Society* half a century before, first and foremost in *Støtten* (*The Memorial Stone,* 1927), the subtitle of which identifies the book both as a psychological study and a novel. Like Ibsen, Erling Kristensen delivers a sort of lay sermon, a parable that suggests weaknesses in every man. He reminds his readers that it is very easy to salve our consciences and to justify actions which, were they performed by others, we would be quick to condemn. Kristensen does not damn an entire social system nor any class of persons *per se*. For him, as for Ibsen, the rottenness of society lies in the inability of the individual to be true to himself and to accept responsibility for what he has done in the past.

There can be no doubt that Erling Kristensen wanted to deal a death blow to the sentimental and naïvely written idylls of rural life. At the same time, however, he wanted to lay bare the half-conscious motivations of human action in modern society. The pillar of society in *Støtten,* Mads Staadal by name, is a grasping man and a crafty man and a small man who is infinitely inconsiderate and selfish, and who can rationalize and excuse his own misdeeds even in the face of death. He has no other god than personal gain, for which everything can be sacrificed—honor, his wife, an innocent man. To be sure, there is a bit of conscience which plagues him in the form of the local clergyman who stresses retribution and perdition, but Mads changes to another parish where attendance at church conveniently increases his social prestige. Among the men and women of the community which knows Mads best, he actually commands respect for his cunning. The novel ends on a bitterly ironical note. The Grundtvigian school-teacher suggests a memorial stone be erected to Mads as a representative of the men "whose strong shoulders... bear the world."

JOHANNES BUCHHOLTZ (1882–1940) was the foremost portrayer of Danish village life in the twentieth century. He has been widely read both at home and abroad; a half dozen of his novels have been translated into English. His books, while not profound, are sufficiently complex and well-written to command attention from readers of several strata of society. The fantast Egholm in Buchholtz's two first successful novels, *Egholms Gud* (*Egholm's God,* 1915) and *Clara van Haags Mirakler* (*The Miracles of Clara van Haag,* 1916) is a kind of Hjalmar Ekdal, a photographer and would-be inventor (and again like Ibsen's character, with a daughter named Hedvig).[1] The tragic and touching figure of Egholm—

1 *Egholm and his God.* Translated by W. W. Worster. London, 1921. New York, 1922.—*The Miracles of Clara van Haag.* Translated by W. W. Worster. London; New York, 1922.

who is said to have been modelled after the author's father—stands out against the contrasting unimaginative and uninspiring life of a small town. A later novel, *Frank Dovers Ansigt* (*Frank Dover's Face*, 1933), whose main character was modelled upon a man whom Buchholtz knew, is written in the style of memoirs.[1] In fact, it is difficult for the reader to believe that the book is not the autobiography of a raconteur. The appeal of Buchholtz's work lies to a large extent in the unusual and unexpected into which he immerses his semi-historical characters; Frank Dover was dear to Buchholtz because he was a real person who had lived an adventurous life salted with the unexpected.[2]

Unlike the older Jakob Knudsen or Sophus Bauditz, Buchholtz does not try to idealize country life or to agitate for any particular personal philosophy. He is able to see the humor in everyday life as well as the element of stark tragedy in the life of a mere villager. He attempts neither a psychological analysis nor detailed philosophizing. His novels and short stories carry on the tradition of the story-teller who is able to entertain by depicting the actions and interrelationships of human beings as he envisages them, without feeling the necessity of giving fictitious action a happy ending.

A forceful regional literature was published in Danish by members of a complementary corps of Icelandic writers who enriched Danish literature during the first half of the twentieth century. Several Icelanders, notably Gunnar Gunnarsson and Guðmundur Kamban, chose Danish as their medium in order to gain a hearing in literary circles outside Iceland. Iceland, like the Faeroes, was a small cultural entity whose fate had been bound to that of Denmark since the Kalmar Union at the end of the fourteenth century. Supporting a population of fishermen and farmers, Iceland was highly literate—it is the most literate nation in the world today—and intellectually productive, but was very nearly isolated because of its geographical location and its unfamiliar language. Classical Icelandic literature from the Middle Ages was relatively well known, but the richness of modern Icelandic literature remained hidden until Gunnar Gunnarsson, Jóhan Sigurjónsson, and a few other Icelanders attracted world-wide attention when they employed Danish (or Norwegian in the case of Kristmann Guðmundsson) as their literary medium, spoke directly

---

1 The novel and its sequel, *Frank Dover og den lille Kvinde*, 1934, were translated by Eugene Gay-Tifft as *The Saga of Frank Dover*. New York, 1938; London, 1939.

2 The other novels by Buchholtz which have appeared in English are *Secret Arrows*, (Danish title: *De smaa Pile*), translated by Paula Wiking, London, 1934, and *Susanne*, translated by Edwin Bjorkman, New York 1933; London, 1934.

to larger audiences and thereby attracted translators. As a consequence of the attention which they evoked, Icelandic writers today can employ their native Icelandic and hope to be heard in the community of letters.

Although they wrote in Danish, Gunnar Gunnarsson and Guðmundur Kamban, like the earlier Jón Sigurjónsson, were principally concerned with life in Iceland, and theirs is really a contribution to Icelandic literature in a related tongue. Nevertheless, they have played a rôle on the Danish Parnassus and they cannot be overlooked in the history of Danish literature.

GUNNAR GUNNARSSON (born 1889) has been especially well-received and widely read in Denmark, which was his home from 1905 to 1939, when he returned to Iceland. His fame rests on two series of novels: *Borgslægtens Historie* (*The History of the People at Borg*, 1912–14)[1] and *Kirken paa Bjerget* (*The Church on the Hill*, 1923–28),[2] both of which portray Iceland and Icelandic life in a vigorous and original way without that affectation of saga-style which is noticeable in certain other modern Scandinavian writers. Gunnarsson also has written historical novels, among them *Edbrødre* (*The Sworn Brothers*, 1918), which is based on early Icelandic history;[3] and *Jón Arason* (1930), the gripping story of the life of Iceland's heroic last Catholic bishop.

Kirken paa Bjerget is Gunnarsson's *magnum opus*. It comprises five autobiographical novels which on the one hand depict the Icelandic scene, the people of Iceland and their customs, and on the other give insight into the mind of a child. The first two volumes are remarkable in that they portray the world through the eyes of a child from his fourth to tenth years. In order to accomplish his narrative purpose, Gunnarsson has necessarily drawn almost entirely on his own memories of childhood in Iceland. The novels are full of fantasy, without being fantastic, and draw extensively on many superstitions which even today are widely accepted in Iceland. While Gunnar Gunnarsson is perhaps a fulfillment of the demand for a national literature which has its roots in a national culture without being chauvinistic, he is in the last analysis dealing with universal situations and therefore makes an appeal to readers whether or not they have any knowledge of Iceland or particular interest in Iceland. In contrast to Knut Hamsun or Henrik Pontoppidan or even his younger

---

1 Translated into English as *Guest the One-Eyed,* by W.W.Worster. New York, 1922.

2 Translated by Evelyn Ramsden as *Ships in the Sky,* Indianapolis; London, 1938, repr. London, 1939; and *The Night and the Dream,* Indianapolis; London, 1938, repr. London, 1940.

3 Translated by C. Field and W. Emmé. New York, 1921.

countryman Halldór Laxness (who writes in Icelandic), Gunnar Gunnarsson is expressing no special or ethical philosophy. Neither dogmatic nor didactic, he is a story-teller whose poetic ability and imaginative powers assure his writings their place in world literature. He moves his readers by his powers of description and his portrayal of character rather than by rousing the emotions by delineating deplorable social conditions (as does Halldór Laxness) or by agitating for a philosophical conviction.[1]

GUÐMUNDUR KAMBAN (1888–1945) was frequently a social critic, but his great work was an historical novel about seventeenth-century Iceland: *Skálholt* (the title is a place name), published in four volumes 1930–32. Like *Skálholt*, Kamban's other historical novel, *Jeg ser et stort skønt Land* (*I See a Wondrous Land*, 1936) was published in both English and German translation.[2]

In the history of literature, Kamban has a place as a dramatist. *Hadda Padda,* published both in Danish and Icelandic in 1914 (and translated into English in 1917), won him immediate acclaim, although the drama can scarcely withstand the critical test of time.[2] The strong-willed Hadda makes away with herself in a melodramatic fashion after her fiancé has declared his love for her sister. The ethical content of the piece suffers at the expense of the dramatic effects, most of which are achieved through the technique of teichoscopy, i. e., action off-stage reported to the audience as it happens. After his first success, Kamban spent some time in the United States, and a number of his works, notably the ethically interrelated plays *Marmor* (*Marble*, 1918) and *Vi Mordere* (*We Murderers*, 1920) are laid there. *Marmor* is a moving defense of the struggle for judicial reform on the part of a leading American jurist; it was Kamban's greatest stage success. In its delineation of rising conflict between the two main characters, *Vi Mordere* asks by implication whether the murdered cannot on occasion be the guilty party in a murder. *De arabiske Telte* (*The Arabian Tents,* 1921) is a superior and more sophisticated work. A comedy of manners, it boxes the compass of marital infidelity and divorce in making the point that "every person's views are only a defense of his actions." This satirical play, which is not without considerable humor, is

1 Other works by Gunnarson which have appeared in English are *Seven Days' Darkness* (Danish title: *Salige er de enfoldige*), translated by Roberts Tapley, New York, 1930, London, 1931; *The Good Shepherd (Advent)*, translated by Kenneth C. Kaufman, Indianapolis, 1940; and *Trylla and other Small Fry* (*Trylle og andet Smaakram*), translated by Evelyn Ramsden, London, 1947.

2 *I See a Wondrous Land.* New York; London, 1938, repr. London, 1939.—*The Virgin of Skalholt,* translated by Evelyn Ramsden. Boston, 1935; London, 1936, 1937.

3 *Hadda Padda.* Translated by Sadie Luise Peller. New York, 1917.

remarkable for its use of mimicry to replace dialogue. Like many another twentieth-century playwright, Kamban relegates a partial explanation of the characters and their thoughts to the stage directions and therewith makes the play difficult to stage and hinders the actor's communication of the dramatist's intent and meaning, although of course without lessening the effectiveness of the drama when read.

Aside from the plays written by Icelanders in Danish, the rôle of the drama in the decade after the war was slight.

A single Danish play dealt directly with World War I: The once very influential *Ingen* (*Nobody*, 1920) by SVEND BORBERG (1888–1947). Writing from a psychological and very nearly a psychoanalytical standpoint, Borberg employed the familiar theme of the soldier thought dead, who returns home to find his wife enamored of another man. The full effect of Borberg's play is achieved by means suggestive of the various *Amphitryon* dramas. The soldier who returns is unrecognizable, while the other man—the stranger—resembles the soldier's former self. The wife is attracted both to the stranger and to the husband whom she does not recognize. The result of this tense situation is that the stranger kills the soldier's wife; the soldier, who is in a sense partially the stranger, and therewith his former self, takes the guilt of the crime upon himself. Borberg's other plays, similarly psychologically colored, do not possess the dramatic qualities of *Ingen*. Borberg's star has been eclipsed in Denmark since the Second World War because of his sympathies for National Socialism.

There were a few other dramatic attempts in the twenties which attest a growing interest in the psyche. The most unusual was SVEN CLAUSEN's fantastic *Nævningen* (*The Juryman*, 1929, written in collaboration with Peter Grove), which takes place in the mind of a groceryman named Sapiens. Clausen (born 1893) demonstrated himself to be an imaginative dramatist, but only one of his plays, *Kivfuglen (The Bird of Contention)*, has been successful on the stage.[1]

Although the drama seemed to be the least promising genre in the 1920's, the seed of a new drama which was to be the most influential of genres in the Danish literature during the next decade had already been planted. As early as 1925, Kaj Munk, who was to become the most controversial Danish author of the next twenty years, had already written one of his most effective dramas *(Ordet—The Word)*, but it was neither published nor played until 1932.

---

1 Translated by Peter and Ann Thornton in *Contemporary Danish Plays*, Copenhagen, 1955.

To recapitulate: The literature of the twenties and early thirties constituted in the first instance prose which dealt with social problems, and in the second instance lyrics in which a materialistic view of life predominated. In both genres there was relatively little experimentation with form; the means of expression were on the whole traditional. Other genres and sub-genres had a few devotees. Gunnar Gunnarsson kept the regional novel at a high level. Nis Petersen gave the historical novel new life. Only Paul la Cour, Per Lange and a few other poets cultivated *l'art pour l'art*.

CHAPTER XIV

Art vs. the Social Conscience

By the middle thirties, Danish literature had acquired some predominant characteristics which served to distinguish it from the post-war literature that was considered in the foregoing chapter. The drama once more became a vigorous genre, for the first time since the demise of Ibsen, Bjørnson, and Strindberg. Furthermore, the pacifist conviction among socially conscious writers began to be replaced by an "activist" philosophy, i.e., by the conviction that words, action, and if necessary, force must be used to combat the fascism which had established itself first in Italy, then in Germany, and finally in Spain, and which was believed to have a so-called Fifth Column in other European countries, including Denmark. It was also characteristic of the literature of the decade that prose writing on the whole began to veer away from the depiction of social evils toward an interpretive treatment of psychological problems. Specifically stressed was the lasting effect of a given situation on the individual's psyche rather than the temporary effects on his physical or even mental well-being. Freud was becoming more important than Marx as a prophet.

From the ashes of the naturalistic drama arose a new synthetic drama that transcended the experimentalism of the first two decades of the twentieth century and was both naturalistic and symbolic. With regard to form and technique it was in part a reaction against Ibsen and his imitators and in part an extension of the experimental drama in Germany, Italy, and elsewhere during the twenties. While the new drama gave evidence of learning from the psychology of Freud and Jung, it was not primarily a psychological drama.

Nor was it one with the literature of social consciousness; it was more artistic and more subtle than the socially inclined prose works which have been treated in chapter XIII. It frequently contained an emotional appeal. One might say that it was the insistence of the appeal which had made the use of dramatic form inevitable.

The three dramatists who gave new life to the Danish stage were Kaj Munk, Kjeld Abell, and Carl Erik Soya. Of the three, Munk was the traditionalist and Abell the experimentalist, while Soya was a satirical observer who is technically less easy to classify. Munk learned from Shakespeare, Ibsen, and Strindberg; and Abell from the European expressionists; Soya received his inspiration from Gustav Wied. Politically, they represented Right, Left, and Center. Early in their careers Munk dealt with abstract problems; Abell criticized the *status quo*; and Soya satirized human foibles. As the political situation in Europe grew more and more tense, however, all three dramatists turned their attention to contemporary problems; and the German occupation of Denmark finally confronted each of them with questions of the day which demanded immediate answers.

KAJ MUNK (1898–1944) was the most influential Danish dramatist of the first half of the twentieth century, but no critic would offer to write a favorable blanket criticism of his dramatic production. Friends of the theater are not wholly in agreement as to which dramas by Kaj Munk will stand the test of time. Nor can he conveniently be put into any literary category; that he was a Christian moralist makes him unusual. By profession, Kaj Munk was a clergyman, the pastor of a poor Jutland parish, but he was as unusual as a clergyman as he was a dramatist. The sermon and the drama were for him means of ethical expression, and he frequently employed a shock-effect in both sermon and drama. He was no mere didacticist. He wanted to shake his audience or his congregation and make its members think, but he was not preaching any patent message or moral. He was aware of contemporary world problems, and a number of his plays can be looked upon as commentaries on current events. For Munk, the aesthetic quality of the play was secondary to the idea, and it was primarily because of the dominance of ideas in his plays that he made his mark on contemporary drama. He was no great stylist and possessed little self-criticism. The apotheosis which followed his murder by minions of the German occupational forces in January 1944 was of no lasting significance in the history of literature, and today we are able to disassociate the name of Kaj Munk from the aura of martyrdom.

While some of his plays alluded to contemporary persons and events—*Sejren (The Victory,* 1936) to Mussolini and the Ethiopian war, *Han sidder ved Smeltediglen (He sits at the Melting-Pot,* 1938) to Hitler and the persecution of the Jews, and *Niels Ebbesen* (1942) to the German occupation in Denmark—the first of the two or three plays which seem to promise Kaj Munk a lasting place in literature was without such allusions, even though it takes place in the present and suggests religious tensions in Denmark. This play was *Ordet (The Word),* written in 1925 but first pub-

lished and staged in 1932,[1] four years after Kaj Munk's drama *En Idealist*
(An Idealist) had been a fiasco on the stage of the Royal Theater in Copenhagen. It has frequently been 'pointed out that *Ordet* was written as a
counterpart to Bjørnstjerne Bjørnson's *Over Evne (Beyond Our Power,* 1883
–95), and was the Danish clergyman's reply to the great Norwegian poet-
agitator.[2]

The dramatic kernel of *The Word* is the non-rational, non-scientific possibility of a resurrection—of the time when, so to speak, "the brick falls
upwards," and man transcends the limits of his rational knowledge. In
The Word Munk depicts adherents of two wings of the Danish state church,
the one Grundtvigian and the other pietistic, as finding a synthesis through
love and faith. To a Dane the contrast between Grundtvigianism and
pietism (the latter represented by the "Inner Mission" society) is full of
meaning, but foreign readers need have no knowledge of Danish secta-
rianism in order to appreciate *The Word*. The human problem and its non-
rational solution is not peculiar to a national culture. The miraculous
word which causes the resurrection is spoken by the fool, the naïve soul
—a young man who has lost his mind as a result of a great tragedy in his
own life. In making such an individual responsible for the miracle of the
drama, Kaj Munk has incidentally protected himself against rationalist
objection. Kaj Munk was himself of the rationalist persuasion, but he
understood how to make use of theatrical effects on the stage and to
leave a question in the mind of his audience—to express skepticism toward
the skeptics, as it were.

The plot of the drama is the basic, sure-fire tragic situation of young
lovers who are kept from one another by their feuding families. The
popular appeal of this situation is enhanced by letting the events take
place in a rural area whose sturdy inhabitants are an easy prey to caricature. Some of the lines in the drama overreach themselves in order to
shock or surprise the audience and to create tension and suspense. An
example is the sharp contrast of reports on the birth of a child, not to
mention the dead woman's rising from her bier. In *The Word,* as in several
other dramas, Kaj Munk verged on the overdramatic. He was indeed a
melodramatic rather than a reflective playwright. Yet in *The Word,* the use

1 It was first staged with the title *I Begyndelsen var Ordet—In the Beginning was the Word*.

2 *Five Plays by Kaj Munk*. Translated from the Danish by R. P. Keigwin, New York, London,
1953, contains the following: *Herod the King, The Word, Cant, He sits at the Melting-Pot,* and
Before Cannæ. A translation of *Niels Ebbesen,* by Keigwin, is included in *Scandinavian Plays of
the Twentieth Century. Second Series*. New York, 1944. Both volumes published by The American–Scandinavian Foundation.

of dramatic effects is not so excessive as to be offensive, whereas in some later dramas, Munk was tempted to exceed the boundaries which aesthetic judgment usually sets.

Next to *The Word, An Idealist* is Munk's most powerful play, despite the fact that it was a failure at the Royal Theater in 1928.[1] With incision and understanding, Munk delineates Herod's reasons for being a totalitarian and for appearing to be the incarnation of evil; but he does not make the audience sympathize with the tyrant. In *An Idealist* Munk appealed to the public's acceptance of the familiar when he chose a Biblical theme. In *Cant* (1931) he similarly employed an historical figure which enjoys a special place in the popular fancy, Henry VIII, and in addition he wrote in an easy style, incredible as it may seem—for the play is in blank verse. With *Cant,* which has been called the most Shakespearean of his dramas, Kaj Munk first attained popularity and general success. That he did was remarkable, for as Kaj Munk's cousin, Nis Petersen, pointed out, the play makes use neither of tension nor explosions nor surprises. It is, rather, a dramatic exegesis of the English word which Munk employed as a title. The pillars of state—both civil officials and churchmen—sway first one way and then the other to follow Henry's outrageously hypocritical arguments, the sum and substance of which is the desire first to marry Ann Boleyn and then to get rid of her; that a human life is at stake is skillfully overlooked. Nowhere did Kaj Munk demonstrate his mastery of dialogue and his ability to write ironically more clearly than in *Cant.* Considering the play in retrospect we adjudge it to be a condemnation of the philosophy that might makes right, and of the unuttered conviction that insincerity may be justified by false logic, by cant. The message in Kaj Munk's drama was minted for everyman, and was not meant as a commentary on the contemporary political situation.

Before World War II, Munk was the most controversial figure in Danish literature; during the German occupation he became a mouthpiece of Danish resistance and independence. His many poems, born of the moment's pressure, aroused the Danes against the aggressor, though they have little aesthetic value. The play *Niels Ebbesen* was an obvious allegory of the contemporary situation (1942) and was officially suppressed, although it was circulated clandestinely. As in the other dramas, Kaj Munk here showed himself to have been in agreement with the conservative Danish novelist Jakob Knudsen's belief that force and violence sometimes are justifiable. In the last analysis, Kaj Munk may be said to

---

1 It was successfully played at the Royal Theater a decade later.

have shared the philosophy of life which Jakob Knudsen had formulated around the turn of the century.

Much has been made of the anti-democratic attitude which Kaj Munk had in common not only with Jakob Knudsen but with the older Georg Brandes, of his belief in the use of force, and of his averred admiration for dictators. Judging him on the basis of the ethical message of *Han sidder ved Smeltediglen (He sits at the Melting-Pot)* and *Niels Ebbesen,* the point seems to have been overstressed. It is true that Munk was preoccupied with strong men—Herod, Mussolini, and Hitler among others—and that he was apparently to some degree sympathetic with fascist political theory; yet he was clearly aware of the evils of totalitarianism. The strong men who are the leading characters in his dramas do not excite our admiration. It was not by chance or because of opportunism that Kaj Munk became a most outspoken critic of the Germans after they subjugated Denmark in 1940.

From the standpoint of literary criticism, Kaj Munk's political persuasion is of little consequence. It was Kaj Munk's achievement that he reëstablished the drama as a leading literary genre not only in Denmark but in Scandinavia. Quite possibly he had more gifted contemporaries in the Norwegian Nordahl Grieg and the Swede Pär Lagerkvist, but it was around Kaj Munk that the discussion centered in the thirties. In him there was enough dramatic ability and self-contradiction to arouse both the critical and public tempers.

Whereas Kaj Munk was moved to write primarily to express ideas, KJELD ABELL (1901–61) was more concerned with the effectiveness of ideas presented from the stage. Munk was content to vary traditional dramatic patterns and did not feel called upon to employ new and striking devices, but Kjeld Abell was novel and original with regard to technique. He won the theatergoing public immediately and established his reputation with the so-called experimental drama *Melodien der blev væk (The Melody that Got Lost,* 1935).[1] The play was written with a great deal of satirical humor and was meaningful for every adult hearer. By the use of transparent but effective devices, some radical, some familiar, and some original, e.g., voices in the background, and impressionistically connotative scenes and masks, Abell holds the attention of his audience while he calls up scenes from the daily life of the little man, Larsen, and forcibly makes the point that every man must find a "melody" in his life, if life is to be more than mechanical existence. There is nothing abstruse

1 An English adaptation, by Frances Sinclair and Ronald Adam, was published in London, 1939.

about Kjeld Abell; his philosophy is sound and simple. He is able to get at the heart of practical matters without trying to balance philosophical abstractions. The apparent simplicity of his dramas is essential to his art.

Abell is a scenic innovator. He has dared to be original and to allow himself flights of fancy which become substance on the stage. Although he has been influenced by the cinema and writes to impart a message, he believes that the stage should not have a primarily photographic or elocutionary function but should be the visible bond between fantasy and reality. It is his conviction that "the theater... should always be the realm of phantasy for free thought." Art, for Abell, is privileged to be unconventional.

Abell's greatest success is *Anna Sophie Hedvig*, a drama about an insignificant, provincial schoolteacher who rebels against the injustices of a colleague and finally deliberately kills her.[1] The allegorical defense of the use of force against dictators is evident, and was unmistakable when the play appeared in 1939. Abell was here dealing with a serious ethical question which had immediate implications; his stand against totalitarianism was unequivocal.

The technique of dramatic narration in *Anna Sophie Hedvig* is the so-called flashback which has been extensively employed in the cinema. Within a conventional framework, Abell lets the story be told by episodes. The discussion during which the ethical problem of killing is debated in a Copenhagen drawing room at the beginning of the play, leads ultimately to the revelation that Anna Sophie Hedvig has committed a murder for the sake of peace and justice. The action is over when the drama begins, and the audience is at times twice removed from the action portrayed, for a housemaid is retelling Anna Sophie Hedvig's version of what happened at the school in Jutland. As in a film, there is no attempt to make the maid's testimony realistic. As she begins to speak, the actual events are presented on the stage, and she does not take up her rôle again until the end of the third act. The play ends symbolically with a transfiguration of the seedy provincial teacher-murderess. Together with a soldier (apparently a Spanish republican volunteer), Anna Sophie Hedvig stands before a firing squad. She says a bit clumsily to the soldier, "You fight for the future. When you died it is to make that possible... you know that it is of some use." The soldier, who represents the fight against political aggression and dictatorship in the big world, and Anna Sophie Hedvig, who repre-

1 English translation, by Hanna Astrup Larsen, in *Scandinavian Plays of the Twentieth Century, Second Series.* New York, 1944.

sents it in her small world, are not afraid of the consequences of their acts. "You don't sit still and content yourself with believing that there will come a time when it is wrong to kill..." These are Anna Sophie Hedvig's last words.

During World War II, Abell published two dramas which dealt in an abstract way with the German Occupation and in 1946 he summed up his opinion of Denmark's experiences during the occupation in the play *Silkeborg*. It has been suggested by several critics that Abell never quite fulfilled the promise which his early works gave.

The third dramatist, CARL ERIK SOYA (born 1896)—whose nom-de-plume is simply "Soya"—is a man of many ideas. He has written plays for both the stage and radio, as well as short stories, novels, aphorisms, and verse. Throughout his work, a psychological bent is apparent. He is the connecting link in the thirties between the theater and the school of psychologically inclined prose writers.

Soya's work is not without ethos, although it is a shifting ethos. His earliest works showed him to be a convinced naturalist; and the residual naturalist in Soya may be observed in an occasional use of obscene language and references in the later works. Thereafter, he became a psychological portraitist, and finally a reflective satirist who castigated the middle class and pondered the question of fate and predestination. All three facets of Soya are found in his gripping short story *Jeg kunde nemt ta' 100 Kroner* (*I could easily take 100 crowns*, 1931), which is a prose fore-runner of his play *30 Aars Henstand* (*Thirty Years' Reprieve*, 1944). A little clerk is beset with petty problems of existence which try his character. He finally succumbs to the very temptation which ultimately had brought imprisonment to his father. Free will or predestination? This is the prob-lem which forms the nucleus of several of Soya's later plays, notably his significant "play in six plays" entitled *Brudstykker af et Monster* (*Parts of a Pattern*, 1940), as well as *To Traade* (*Two Threads*, 1943),[1] *30 Aars Henstand*, and *Frit Valg* (*Free Choice*, 1948). Soya has since identified these four plays as his "tetralogy" and therewith suggested an association with Greek tragedy and the classical concept of fate. *Brudstykker af et Monster* reminds one of Thornton Wilder's *Bridge of San Luis Rey*, in its endeavor to find a pattern behind the apparent absence of cause in outward events. Although Soya tries to be an observer rather than a judge and accepts no theological explanation for the pattern of phenomena which he educes, his attitude is tangential to the metaphysical. It is expressed

1 English translation in *Contemporary Danish Plays*. Copenhagen, 1955.

in those words by Goethe which serve as the motto to *30 Aars Hen-stand*: "Denn alle Schuld rächt sich auf Erden"—all guilt is avenged on earth.

Even in his search for a life-pattern Soya can be humorous and satirical. This is best evidenced by the play *Frit Valg* (*Free Choice,* 1948), which has two conclusions. In one conclusion, honesty brings a series of tragedies. In the other, dishonesty on the part of one character seems to be the key to happiness for most of the other characters.

Soya has often been compared with Gustav Wied. They are indeed kindred spirits; it was Soya who founded the Gustav Wied Society in 1938. Like Wied, Soya is hard to classify because his satire is all-embracing. As cutting as Soya can be, as for example in his poignant allegory of the German occupation of Denmark entitled *En Gæst* (*A Guest,* 1941), he is a good-natured satirist. The best example of his humor is the earlier play *Chas* (1938), which pokes fun at the foibles of popular fancy, at journalism, and at sports enthusiasts. Soya's *Efter* (*Afterwards,* 1947), is a tragi-comic analysis of the ubiquitous human weakness for rationalization and at the same time the playwright's retrospective commentary on conditions during the Occupation. The principle characters in *Efter* have profiteered from the war and compromised themselves and their country. Now, afterwards, they are enjoying the bittersweet fruits of profiteering and they attempt to rationalize their past actions and excuse their current affluence.

More recently, Soya published a one acter, *Løve med Korset* (*The Lion with the Corset,* 1950), a witty dramatic exposition of the unsolved problem of cause and effect. The angel of peace is ill; undetermined is the cause of her illness, i. e., the cause of war. Three characters, identified as a romanticist, a materialist, and a psychologist, undertake to demonstrate by means of certain events from history interpreted in several ways where the origin of war is to be found. Whether they educe idealistic, economic or subconscious reasons, the ultimate cause is implied only to be hopelessly complex. Soya nevertheless leaves us with the impression that the psychologist has a convincing argument in demonstrating that Mr. Average Man and his family are so bored by the routine of daily life that war is a welcome change and stimulating experience. He suggests that the lion in man, i. e., the primitive subconscious, can be kept soothed, subdued or forgotten (or corsetted, to use Soya's original symbol) by stimulating motion pictures, stimulating plays, stimulating sports—by "play and phantasy, sports, films, dramas and novels" as a surrogate for war, as the psychologist, a good Aristotelian, pontificates. The angel of peace, if not cured by these *doctores,* can at least rise and walk in hope at the conclusion of the play.[1]

Soya has been especially successful in portraying the petit-bourgeois. While he is first and foremost a dramatist, his most widely-read work is the semi-autobiographical novel *Min Farmors Hus* (*My Grandmother's House*, 1943), a story of life in a petit-bourgeois home at the turn of the century, seen through the eyes of a five-year-old. The novel is written with imaginative understanding for the child's interpretation of an adult world. The scenes of the narrative are unforgettable because of their associative power, although it must be admitted that Soya taxes our credulity in having the grandmother commit a murder at the end of the book.

Soya caused a brief sensation by publishing a second autobiographical novel, *Sytten* (*Seventeen*, 1953–54)[2], which portrayed the difficulties of psychological and sexual adjustment that beset the adolescent. He wrote in as forthright and blunt a manner as presumably has been employed in world literature. The charges of pornography which at first were levelled against the book nevertheless soon ceased to be heard, and Danish readers on the whole came to accept *Sytten* almost as a handbook, as a scholarly critic humorously remarked when the book was republished in 1956.

Soya's use of concepts taken from the realm of Freudian psychology is more or less an adjunct to his satire in his plays, but the ventilation of psychological problems has been the intent of a series of other Danish writers, who had a forerunner in Karin Michaëlis, as the author of the above-mentioned *Den farlige Alder* (*The Dangerous Age*) in 1910.

Some of the outstanding novelists of the thirties who were given to psychological portrayal may by virtue of their subject matter also be considered regionalists and social critics. Two writers who in addition to Erling Kristensen gave psychological ethos to regional literature were Jørgen Nielsen and the Faeroese Jørgen-Frantz Jacobsen. Only since his premature death has JØRGEN NIELSEN (1902–45) received much critical acclaim, but he is now recognized as one of the more able Danish writers of the twenties and thirties. Besides a number of pessimistic and penetrating short stories, especially those in the collection *Lavt Land* (*Low Country,*

---

1 Technically the play is more striking than Soya's other dramas, for it makes use of stereoptikon and cinematic pictures in color to provide a continuously changing and symbolic background for the action and the ideas suggested by the three didacticists. The many stage directions are explanatory (e.g., "music as it sounds in Heaven") to such an extent that the full intent of Soya's wit can be appreciated only by the reader and not by the playgoer.

2 English translation by Carl Malmberg, New York: P. S. Eriksson, [1961].

1929), Nielsen wrote several novels, at least one of which, *En Kvinde ved Baalet* (*A Woman by the Bonfire,* 1933) attests his understanding of the psyche. Nielsen tells an everyday story without trying to exploit the dramatic possibilities of a situation. Here is life, not the way a philosopher or an idealist might plan it, but the way it is lived. Jørgen Nielsen had perhaps better insight into human beings than many a writer who perceives nuances and niceties which Nielsen either overlooked or omitted. In portraying men and women of flesh and blood, their incidental fates and petty anxieties, Nielsen was able to work on a background of rural life as realistic as any regional writer. We infer that Nielsen himself admired the straightforward, transparent existence of a farming community as opposed to the affectation and artificiality of sophisticated urban life.

Nielsen's first works were received simply as regional literature, but if they are considered to belong in that category, then regional literature is perceived to have acquired new substance. Like Johannes V. Jensen, Nielsen transcended the desire merely to represent Danish country life and the peculiar idyllic quality of the rural community after the fashion, say, of Thorkild Gravlund. He used regional figures because he was able to depict them as human beings whom he fully understood.

JØRGEN-FRANTZ JACOBSEN (1900–38) died before his only novel *Barbara* was published in 1938. A narrative of life in the Faeroes in the eighteenth century, *Barbara* is the more remarkable for being not a description of Faeroese life but a psychological study. Jacobsen's characters are neither puppets nor historical figures. To be sure, a great deal may be deduced about Faeroese life of the period from *Barbara,* but the novel can also be appreciated by a reader who is oblivious to its cleverly constructed historical background. This fact is remarkable, for Jacobsen was for a number of years the eloquent spokesman of the Faeroese cause in Denmark and wrote extensively on the question of Faeroese cultural independence, the use of the Faeroese language in Faeroese schools, and related matters. Even when Jacobsen was writing from his sickbed, he was as a novelist constantly the artist and psychologist. He created a remarkable woman, Barbara, who, though a polyandrist at heart, is such a child of nature that she evokes the sympathy of the reader.[1]

The tiny population of the Faeroes—less than 30,000 people—has contributed another writer of note to twentieth-century Danish literature: Jørgen-Frantz Jacobsen's friend WILLIAM HEINESEN (born 1900), who

---

[1] *Barbara.* Translated by Estrid Bannister, was published by Penguin Books in 1948.

combines social consciousness with psychological insight. Like the Icelanders Gunnarsson and Laxness, Jacobsen and Heinesen have acquired perspective by viewing their native land from abroad, that is, during sojourns in Denmark. Heinesen is a man of several talents. He had published several volumes of verse before he surprised Denmark with a series of novels which revealed both his socially critical attitude and his understanding of the human mind. Heinesen's novel *Noatun* won critical acclaim after it appeared in 1938.[1] *Den sorte Gryde (The Black Kettle,* 1949), a novel of sordid reality which dealt with the effect of the English occupation of the Faeroes during the Second World War and which technically is perhaps most closely related to Hans Kirk's *Fiskerne,* established his reputation among the reading public. He has since published a phantasy bordering on the allegorical, *De fortabte Spillemænd (The Lost Musicians,* 1950), which, although set in the Faeroes, is in no way dependent on a regional background for the development or effect of the narrative. In fact, a picture of the Faeroes scarcely emerges from Heinesen's novels, for as an imaginative writer Heinesen, like Jacobsen, is not primarily concerned with an inspection of regional culture.

In the novels of TOVE DITLEVSEN (born 1918) there is a fusion of social consciousness and psychoanalysis. She is the speaker for the child who has been hurt and for the young woman who has suffered because of her sex. In her prose and poetry she is often concerned with the sexual experience, its implications and its bitter and inescapable psychic results. Tove Ditlevsen has gone forth from the Copenhagen proletariat, and her writing shows the scars from her childhood. She is herself the hurt child and the young woman who has suffered. Sensitive and lyric by nature, she is at the same time delicate and forthright in her poetry, as, e.g., in the poems "Og der var en Nat" ("There was a Night"), from *Blinkende Lygter (Blinking Lamps,* 1947) and "En Kvindes Frygt" ("A Woman's Fear") from the second edition of *Pigesind* in 1944. She won immediate acclaim after publishing her first volume of poetry, *Pigesind (A Girl's Mind),* in 1939, a mature sequel to which appeared in 1955, *Kvindesind (A Woman's Mind).* She has gained a still wider audience with her prose works *Man gjorde et Barn Fortræd (A Child Was Hurt,* 1941) and *Barndommens Gade (Street of My Childhood,* 1943). She is particularly concerned with the long-range effects of childhood experiences on the life of the adolescent and the adult. Her social and psychological convictions are most easily discernible in *Man gjorde et Barn Fortræd,* where the life of a young woman is

1 Translated into English by Jan Noble as *Niels Peter.* London, 1940.

warped because of an undisclosed attack by a sexual pervert when she was a girl of nine. The barrier imposed by this experience is not broken down until the young woman confronts her childhood assailant eleven years later. Tove Ditlevsen's understanding of the mind of the adolescent is unusual, and her ability to portray fear and indecision at times suggests the penetrating psychological faculty of Harald Kidde, but her psychological thesis seems improbable and oversimplified. She is more convincing when she is less programmatic, as in *Barndommens Gade,* which is not dissimilar to the American Betty Smith's *A Tree Grows in Brooklyn. Barndommens Gade* takes a position somewhere between Andersen Nexø's *Pelle* and Soya's *Min Farmors Hus.* Andersen Nexø is, however, more of an agitator and Soya is more of a humorist than is Tove Ditlevsen. All three books just mentioned are autobiographical portrayals of life on certain social levels in Copenhagen; if one would discover how the the other half lives in contemporary Copenhagen, one had best read Tove Ditlevsen.

As an interpreter of the mind of a child, Tove Ditlevsen reminds one of H.C.Branner, although the social backgrounds which produced the two writers were very different. In her writings she is also more autobiographical and intensely personal than is Branner, although like him, she has been influenced by psychoanalytical thought.

H.C.BRANNER (1903–66) underwent a gradual growth until he is today regarded as one of the outstanding modern writers of Denmark. Contemporary criticism is nearly, if not entirely, in agreement regarding his talent. In retrospect we observe him to have been a psychological novelist in his early novels, but his penchant for psychoanalytic psychology did not become unmistakable until the publication of his short novel *Rytteren (The Riding Master)* in December 1949.[1] He later published a play in the same key: *Søskende (Siblings,* 1952).[2] His first novels were successful, but their substance and form are not essentially original. It was not until Branner published his collection of short stories, *Om lidt er vi borte (In a Little While We Are Gone,* 1939), that he identified himself with a particular style and a particular subject matter. A companion volume, similar in style and subject, *To Minutters Stilhed (Two Minutes of Silence),* followed in 1944. In his penetrating, moving, and somewhat sentimental prose, he is noteworthy as a portrayer of children and shows a sympathetic insight into the child's mind, the many irrational fears of childhood, and furthermore, the adults' world as it is viewed without comprehension

1 Translated by A. I. Roughton. London, 1951. Published as *The Mistress.* New York, 1953.

2 Translated into English as *The Judge,* by A. I. Roughton in *Contemporary Danish Plays.* Copenhagen, 1955.

through a child's eyes. At times he approaches the apparent naïveté of Hans Christian Andersen, but it is well to note that the naïveté is only apparent in both cases, although it is responsible for the impression which Branner, like Andersen, leaves upon many who read him superficially.

One of Branner's recurrent subjects is fear. Incidentally, the word fear served as the title of one of his stories (*Angst*, first separately published, 1947). It is fear of life and fear of unknown forces which drive the child to his death in *Barnet leger ved Stranden* (*The Child Playing on the Shore*, 1937), and which troubles young Børge in the novel *Historien om Børge* (*The Story of Børge*, 1942). Insecurity and fear compound the ethos of the short stories. To understand Branner's art one should examine a story like "Om lidt er vi borte" ("In a Little While We Are Gone")[1] from the collection bearing the same title. Branner can reproduce the petty fears of daily life and instill into his individual characters general and common characteristics contingent upon a general feeling of insecurity. He knows the timidity which afflicts the brave as well as the weak, the voluble as well as the inarticulate. He represents the hurt intellectual of the thirties and forties. The impersonal heartlessness of the world and the need for human charity are ever present in his prose. For him the great tragedy is a repetitious tragedy, the lack of understanding between human beings—parent and child, husband and wife, man and woman, brother and sister, employer and worker. He is a humanist. He writes of landscapes, objects, and animals only as they affect human existence. For him, the right of the individual to an independent, dignified existence is overwhelmingly important.

No small part of Branner's effectiveness may be ascribed to his stylistic simplicity. His lucid and uninvolved sentences are reminiscent of the spoken language. He favors the indirect quotation, the non-sequitur, and the prosaic metaphor. These are stylistic characteristics which he shares with writers of the so-called social realism, but Branner, in contrast to William Heinesen or Tove Ditlevsen, embodies no social doctrine in his works. Nor can he be identified with the political or the literary Left. His style does not represent an attempt to be naturalistic for the sake of a directed or didactic social pathos.

Starting with *Rytteren* (*The Riding Master*) in 1949, Branner put himself

---

1 Translated by Lida Siboni Hanson and Adda Gentry George in *The American-Scandinavian Review*, 1942, pp. 149–57. "A Child and a Mouse," from the same collection, translated by Evelyn Heepe, appeared in *Modern Danish Authors*, Copenhagen, 1946.—"The Three Musketeers," from *To Minutters Stilhed*, translated by A. I. Roughton, is found in *Contemporary Danish Prose*, Copenhagen, 1958.

in the front rank of Scandinavian writers who make use of Freudian symbolism and allegory. Whereas in the earlier works, his characters were motivated by irrational fear and were not moulded according to any predestined pattern, in the later works they are in the first instance the pawns of sexual desire, frustration, and perversion. Critical opinion, which united in praising Branner's early works and short stories, has been understandably divergent in assessing the more recent psychoanalytical studies, and especially the novel *Ingen kender Natten* (*Nobody Knows the Night*, 1955), which contains as unvarnished and unabashed references to perverted sexual symbolism as can be found in Danish and Scandinavian literature. It remains to be seen whether Branner's later works are first and foremost an expression of the humanist's disillusionment in mankind as its own destroyer during and after World War II or is simply the result of consistency in his attempt to penetrate the human psyche. On the surface at least, the latter explanation would seem to be the more plausible.

Another writer of psychological novels is AAGE DONS (born 1903), who, like H. C. Branner, seems to have no social axe to grind, and no didactic thesis to expound. His concern is the effect of experience and human relations upon the inner man, especially as that inner man develops through the years. This does not mean to say that Dons' novels are without action, but rather that the delineation of action is of much less importance to the author that the psychological effect of action or non-action. Dons first gained general critical approbation with *Soldaterbrønden* in 1936.[1] The novel has some elements in common with the literature of social criticism; the main character, Anna, is the product of a narrow religious upbringing which ultimately is the cause of her life's tragedy. On the other hand, Dons is not concerned with the background of childhood *per se,* but merely with the effect of the background on Anna and with the emotions and desires which necessarily are engendered in her and which subconsciously mould her life. Anna is first led into a clumsy love affair, then into a loveless marriage, and finally to murder—which is followed by remorse. Her every action nevertheless seems understandable and excusable. Dons's story is the more effective because the murder committed by Anna is not discovered and cannot lead to the catharsis granted by confession and repentance. Among Dons's more recent novels, *Den svundne Tid er ej forbi* (*The Past is Not Gone,* 1950) turns our attention to familial conditions and their effect on the growing child. The long-lasting

1 *The Soldier's Well.* Translated by Terence Shiel. London, 1940.

influence of the death as a child of one of the two brothers is a psychological *leitmotif* in the book.

In the genre of the lyric, Danish literature was split between *l'art pour l'art* and an activist philosophy in the twenties and thirties. The principal exponent of poetry as art was PAUL LA COUR (1902–56), a central figure in Danish poetry during the past two decades. It is not rash to prophesy that la Cour will retain a place in living Danish literature, if not for his poetry, at least for his reflective poetics entitled *Fragmenter af en Dagbog (Fragments of a Diary)*, published after the Second World War.

La Cour ventured not only into the realm of literature as a poet, novelist, and theorist, but also into painting both as a creative artist and an art critic. What is more, he demonstrated himself to be an able editor and translator. His affinity for Gallic culture is apparent in his translations of Cézanne's letters, of Baudelaire's criticism, and of Anouilh, Camus, and Giraudoux. He has also translated from the Spanish of García Lorca. As la Cour's critics regularly have pointed out, he is a successor to another great Francophile, the Danish symbolist Sophus Claussen. He is however more serious and less disjointed than was Claussen. Within Danish literature la Cour also owes a debt to Johannes V. Jensen's lyrical disciple Ludvig Holstein.

It has been aptly said that la Cour as the author of the volume of verse *Alt kræver jeg (I Demand All,* 1938) is the poetic equivalent of the author of *Jørgen Stein,* Jacob Paludan. Like Paludan, he is the sensitive intellectual who found no satisfaction in post bellum materialism, who was confronted by the catastrophe of war and beset by the concomitant and subsequent feelings of guilt and helplessness which the holocaust engendered. La Cour did not react to the times in a radical or unpredictable fashion. He was not tempted to throw culture and traditions overboard but tried rather to reëxamine the cultural heritage, presumably in an attempt to explain the sorry state of the world. He was concerned with the clarification of ideas rather than the search for new ideas. He was not willfully obscure and did not indulge in typographical vagaries. Although his verse is not always lucid, it partakes of a philosophical sincerity which has intellectual appeal. La Cour spoke to a relatively large audience, certainly relatively as large as any modern poet in England or the United States.

His general attitude toward the world is found *in nuce* in the title of a volume of selected poems published in 1942: *Mellem Sværdene (Between Swords)*. Here it is clearest to the reader that la Cour is conscious of an existence in crisis between two great world struggles, while he himself is a non-participant in the deciding battles. As for many of his generation,

the twenties and thirties of this century were for la Cour essentially the
years between the wars.

The poets of the thirties spasmodically experienced a deep-rooted
concern about the future, i.e., the political future of Europe. A poem
written in a mood of anxiety is Nis Petersen's prophetic "Brændende
Europa" ("Europe Aflame") from the year 1933. The poem which, six
years before the fateful September of 1939, specifically suggested the
coming of war to Poland and England, contains these lines:

> They put their hands on my knees
> – And look at me . . .
> Those small fine hands that must be shielded
> To be strong and supple
> On the day when they must aim the flame-throwers,
> Set off the mines and fire the torpedoes
> That shall scorch Europe.
>
> . . .
>
> Let us just once more
> Quarrel about whom to blame for the war.
> The little ones will listen in sad
> Forbearance . . .
>
> For they know
> –right through the torrent of words
> –that here
> –out of the pride, envy and hate
> In my terribly filthy mind
> War grows
> Like an ugly flower.[1])

There were more troubled voices as the Second World War approached.
When war finally came, mere anxiety ceased to be a predominant feeling,
and Danish poets became more positive in their assertions, more resolute
in their convictions and in their defiant attitude toward National Socialism in particular.

The activism to which Kjeld Abell exhorted his readers and hearers in
Anna Sophie Hedvig was heard also in the poetry of several young writers
during the Spanish civil war. The most prominent of these young poets
was GUSTAF MUNCH-PETERSEN (1911–38), who himself fell in Spain.
Politically he felt a responsibility to oppose totalitarianism and the forces

1 Translation by Martin Allwood and Helge Westerman.

18

which were destroying "the beautiful world that might be." He was the aesthetic protagonist and leading interpreter of an activist ideology during the thirties, and may be taken to symbolize the spirit of Danish poetry in that decade. Gustaf Munch-Petersen's verse is agitated by the strength of his convictions and by the necessity to break with the world of tradition into which he was born. The intensity of his belief, the unity of his life and poetry, led him to volunteer in the civil war in Spain. His poetry and the consciousness of his fate affected his contemporaries deeply; and his production, slight though it is in quantity, is of importance in understanding Danish poetry during the last twenty years.

Formally, Gustaf Munch-Petersen was among the avant-garde. He received considerable inspiration from the contemporary Swedish poetry which he knew well. The son of a Swedish mother and a Danish father, he himself wrote verse not only in Swedish and Danish but in English as well. His early poetry, with its loose metrics and forceful metaphors, is a high point of experimental poetry in Denmark. The impression, the single picture, lets the reader deduce the rationale of the poetry (as for example in his "Blod"—"Blood") rather than experience a logical sequence of ideas which would give a meaning in a traditionally rational way. His verse, like some of the poetry a decade before, has been called expressionistic, but there is an essential difference between the so-called expressionism of Tom Kristensen and his generation and that of Gustaf Munch-Petersen. Munch-Petersen used his metaphors and pictures in order to achieve an effect; and he spoke in anguish, uncertain of himself but sure of his ideal, uncertain of the word and the phrase, but obsessed by the picture that he would express. Consequently, compared to Tom Kristensen, he is relatively difficult to read.

Gustaf Munch-Petersen was one of the bolder poets of his generation, whose verse sometimes has been classified by the vague and scarcely complimentary term "surrealist." His poems are however different from what is taken to be surrealist poetry in the English-speaking world. There is no doubt about the meaning of his poems, even though they rely on a series of incomplete pictures or impressions to convey an idea. Like a number of his contemporaries, he simply released himself from the demands of traditional metrics and balanced verse. For example, in the same stanza his verses might contain from one to eight stresses. Gustaf Munch-Petersen, and therewith the poets who resemble or who have imitated him, are to be compared with those moderns who experiment with form without attempting to be fantastic or incomprehensible. Their poetry approaches prose, but is more effective than prose could be, not only because of a courageous use of figures of speech but also because of the mere visual pattern of poetry which forces the reader to read slowly and intensely.

Although attention was focused on the drama, literary efforts were rather equitably distributed in the genres of the novel and lyric poem as well as in the drama during the decade prior to the Second World War. A polarity in literature resulted from the dominance of two incompatible convictions: social consciousness which more and more was identified with an activist ideology, and a sincere belief in literature as art.

Beyond the usual and established literary sphere stands one writer whose work achieved prominence and recognition in the thirties and whose prestige has continued to increase: KAREN BLIXEN (1885–1962). Karen Blixen-Finecke, née Dinesen, does not belong to any parochial list of Danish authors. She belongs to English literature as much as to Danish, for she has herself written most of her works in English as well as Danish. Like many an eighteenth-century writer, she is an aristocratic member of the republic of letters and a citizen of the world, a fact which her pseudonyms reflect—Osceola, Isak Dinesen, Pierre Andrézel. She is a *grande dame,* but not of any old school. Anomalous as her position may be considered to have been in the thirties, she became the mark and symbol of a new literary school in Denmark by the end of the forties. As much as any other writer in Denmark today, she has inspired the anti-naturalistic current of the new aestheticism. Has she been a prime mover in the revolt against socio-philosophic literature and in the return to the formal, aesthetic standards which had been pushed aside since the reign of Johan Ludvig Heiberg? The literary historian a few decades hence may be able to give the answer and to delineate the relationship between the aristocratic phantasy of the Baroness Blixen and the more homely phantasy of Martin A. Hansen, who, until his death in 1955, was the spiritual leader of the literary right in contemporary Denmark.

A reader of *Seven Gothic Tales* (1934) and *Winter's Tales* (1942)[1] might well entertain the opinion that "Isak Dinesen" was the product of over-refinement and degeneration, so much are these fantastic stories concerned with the past and with material pleasures, so little do they seem to have any of the social consciousness which pervades much twentieth-century literature, and so far are they removed from the political implications of the present. The informed readers might also be puzzled at the great popularity which the tales have enjoyed both in Danish and

1 *Seven Gothic Tales* (Danish title: *Syv fantastiske Fortællinger*) was first published in English; *Winter's Tales* in Danish, as *Vintereventyr.*

English—for Karen Blixen has won the plaudits of the critics and the admiration and support of the reading public.

Seemingly incompatible with the fantastic literature of her pseudonyms, then, is the unique work, *Out of Africa* (Danish title: *Den afrikanske Farm,* 1937). The discrepancy between the literature of phantasy and the interpretation of primitive culture which comes from the same pen suggests the anomalous position of Karen Blixen in contemporary literature. There are nevertheless common denominators in her work: the keen powers of observation, a passion for adventure, and a concern with the past. Herself the daughter of a writer, Karen Blixen made her literary debut early in the century and prior to her marriage and her sojourn in Kenya. It was, however, not until her life as a coffee grower in Africa had come to an end that she published the work which at once projected her name on the international literary scene: *Seven Gothic Tales.* She therewith joined the ranks of the Danish authors who have lived and traveled abroad and who have returned to Denmark more articulate and richer in inspiration. Her return to the arts was successful, despite a personal philosophy and aesthetic taste at cross-currents to the popular canon.

The tales of this century's E. T. A. Hoffmann create for themselves a setting in which there is an interplay and expenditure of forces that apparently neither the reader nor the authoress can define or limit. The cause of action in a tale by Karen Blixen is often impenetrable, or if not that, then capable of being interpreted in various ways. It is frequently as if characters in the tales were being carried along by an invisible power, or as if some perverse Fate were thwarting the best of human intentions and designs. The persons in the tales seem real enough, despite the incredible situations in which they find themselves. They cannot explain why they act as they do—but in some cases, and notably in "Peter and Rosa" *(Winter's Tales)* a psychiatrist could account for the repressed Eros which drives the characters to their end.

An example of an unreal or imagined situation verging on madness in the mind of a character is found in "The Dreaming Child" *(Winter's Tales).* The supernatural is essential to "The Supper at Elsinore" *(Seven Gothic Tales),* where the major character is a shade, and in "The Monkey" (from the same collection) in which a metamorphosis from human being to animal to human being takes place.

In the "Consolatory Tale" in *Winter's Tales,* Karen Blixen lets a writer speak of his intent toward his readers. "I have laid a wager with Satan about the soul of my reader. I have marred his path and turned terrors upon him, caused him to ride on the wind and dissolved his substance, and when he waited for light there was darkness..." One wonders in how far his attitude may also be interpreted to be hers.

A reader of one of Karen Blixen's tales is not sure which of the many details so nicely presented are of direct significance to the dénouement. He finds himself going at a slower pace than he otherwise employs in reading imaginative literature, but with Karen Blixen's tales as with epic poetry, it is meaningless to read simply for the sake of plot, action, or character development. Karen Blixen's relish of detailed description, especially of scenes in nature (as, e.g., in "Peter and Rosa") may be part of a heritage from her father, A.W.Dinesen, the widely-read author of *Jagtbreve* (*Letters from the Hunt*, 1889–92, and many times reprinted), which he published under the pseudonym "Boganis."

As in much classical literature, it is not the absolute originality of motif but rather the treatment and interpretation of the motif that is of primary importance for Karen Blixen. The best example of her use of an already well-known story is "Sorrow Acre" *(Winter's Tales)* which is said to have been inspired by her reading of the Danish poet Paul la Cour's version of this modern folk tale (published in the periodical *Til-skueren* in 1931). "Sorrow Acre" is melodramatic and more sentimental than the other tales with its portrayal of a mother who is set to mow a vast field of rye single-handed in only one day, from sunrise to sunset, in order to save the life of her son—at the cost of her own. Yet here as elsewhere in Karen Blixen's imaginative writing, sustention of mood and suspense is quite as important as the narrative proper.

Karen Blixen is capable of writing an uncomplicated and exciting tale, as, e.g., "The Heroine" or "The Invincible Slave Owners" *(Winter's Tales)*, but her art seems more distinctive and the force of her favorite literary devices greater in "The Deluge at Norderney" and "The Roads around Pisa" *(Seven Gothic Tales)*, both of which suggest the tantalizing teleological problem of a metaphysical pattern in human existence.

In the last analysis, Karen Blixen's literary reputation probably derives from her noble and precise diction and from her ability to make her point fully without any visible haste or impatience. She has rarely been surpassed in patience and precision.

In the expository material which constitutes the bulk of *Out of Africa* there is nothing fantastic. Writing on the basis of her personal experiences and observations in Kenya, Karen Blixen (and in the Danish and later English editions without a pseudonym, as befits a report from her own life) is a sensitive and understanding interpreter of landscapes, animals, and people. She describes the psyche of the African native and recreates in the imagination of her Western readers the still-life and wild-life of an African farm. It is not strange that primitive Africa had such an appeal to Karen Blixen, for there in real life was the realm of the invisible and multiple forces which furnish the substratum for her tales. There, the actions of men, in this case the African natives and Indian immigrants, could be plumbed without ever reaching a solid bottom of rational and obvious motivation. Yet only in the section entitled "From an immigrant's notebook" do we find the fantast and narrator of the tales.

The strictures of a library's system of classification probably cause *Out of Africa* to be designated "description and travel," but such a label and categorical definition does this literary masterpiece an injustice. It is no more "description and travel" than is Thoreau's *Walden*. Karen Blixen's book comprises elements of autobiography, anthropology, poetry, and essay. It is the literary expression of a full life.

CHAPTER XV

A Need for Myth:
Danish Literature After 1940

The occupation of Denmark by German forces in April, 1940, made a much greater mark on Danish daily life and culture than had the coming of the Second World War in the autumn of 1939. While the shock of the Occupation and the emotions it engendered influenced much which was written after 1940, literature that dealt directly with the war and the Occupation was nevertheless of no great significance. The influence of the war was more subtle. Overnight the Occupation increased national consciousness and heightened the demand for symbols which could grant a kind of security in the face of material and political exigency. Just as the king became, even more than before, a visible emotive symbol of national unity and government, the metaphors of literature were employed with greater emotional effect. As a consequence, the Occupation contributed to the reëstablishment of the lyric as the predominant genre in Danish literature, after two decades during which interest had centered first in the social novel and then in the drama.

Oppressive wartime conditions helped establish common positive values and clear-cut goals for many elements of the population. The catastrophe was so great that the individual could share profound personal experiences with many of his fellow countrymen. As a result, in much that was published during the war years the imaginative writer assumed the rôle of a champion and at the same time a castigator of the nation, and a spokesman for the disheartened and the perplexed. The articulate found relatively large audiences and the poet many responsive readers. The trend which in the 1930's had seemed to indicate a separation of the poet from his potential readers was therewith reversed; and the cleft between the intellectual and the general public was diminished.

Since the Occupation was in part an emotional experience, we should not be surprised that it evoked so much verse. To be sure, the verse was often dominated by ideas to which the form was subordinate; but even though it had little aesthetic value, the inflammatory, nostalgic, and patriotic poetry written in such quantity during the Occupation brought

about an intensification of interest in literature and an increased awareness of the power of poetry. Not only was verse more penetrating than
prose; it was frequently the most practicable and effective way to vent
one's feelings. Poetry, transcending mere denotation, was able to say
what prose could not. Some poets were surprisingly outspoken in their
verse, as, e.g., POUL SØRENSEN (born 1906) in the collection of poems
entitled *April i Danmark* (*April in Denmark,* 1942).

Among the many poets who wrote during the war and who interpreted the feelings of a country fettered by a foreign occupying force,
none ranks higher than MORTEN NIELSEN, who met his death at the age
of 22 in 1944, as a result of his own participation in the organized Danish
movement of resistance to the German occupation. He is important not
as an agitator or a martyr but intrinsically as a poet and, like Gustaf
Munch-Petersen, as a symbol of his generation's desire for freedom. It is
still difficult to assess Morten Nielsen dispassionately, but this much is
certain: he was a young man who could voice in trenchant and well-
formed verse matters that were engaging the minds of his fellow-countrymen. He was able to interpret his own life philosophically and thus speak
for his own generation—the second to "stumble at the start" in the
twentieth century. In contrast to many contemporaries, he did not con-
centrate on the ephemeral. What concerned him were the emotional and
ethical aspects of human existence as affected by extant conditions. He
was obsessed by the feeling—and fear—that his life would be inadequate
and that the shadow of inevitable death which hung over the younger
generation of Danes, many of whom were members of groups actively
resisting the German occupation, would cut short his development as a
human being, as indeed it did. He spoke for a generation the members
of which were prevented from evolving along the idealistic and progressive lines which they cherished.

Morten Nielsen's verse is noticeably free from the signs of the inhibi-
tion and frustration which had plagued several preceding generations of
more constrained writers. Despite his tender years, Morten Nielsen was
a man of the world rather than a callow youth, but that did not make him
any less sincere or sensitive as a poet. It was his tragedy to have overcome
the restrictions of petit-bourgeois existence only to be confronted with
what seemed to be an insuperable political situation that could not be
resolved by reflection or philosophizing or by individual action. Morten
Nielsen and his generation were kept from realizing the "beautiful world
that might be" by the same forces which destroyed Gustaf Munch-Petersen, who coined the poignant and saddening phrase. Our awareness of

Morten Nielsen's tragic fate makes the concluding lines from his poem "Redegørelse" ("An Accounting") the more forceful,

> "everything is ended. And nothing
> is finished."

In contrast to most of the poetry of the Occupation, Nielsen's verse is still read in Denmark. A large edition of the collected poems was published ten years after his death.

Neither prose-fiction nor the drama produced many works of lasting value which can be labeled as war products. Aside from Kaj Munk's widely-read *Niels Ebbesen* (1942), which has been discussed in a previous chapter, there were no plays which dealt with contemporary conditions. Soya's post-war play *Efter* (*Afterwards*, 1947) considered ethical problems of the Occupation, but his wartime plays debated metaphysical and philosophical principles. Neither during nor after the war did Denmark produce a prose work inspired by the war which matched the calibre of the Norwegian novelist Sigurd Hoel's tense psychological and ethical study of the causes of collaboration, *Møte ved Milepelen* (*Meeting at the Milestone,* 1947), which passed judgment on Hoel's own generation that refused to accept the responsibilities it had incurred in youth. The Danish novel that most nearly approached Hoel's in ethical content was the first volume of the tetralogy *Drømmen og Virkeligheden* (*The Dream and Reality,* 1942), by MICHAEL TEJN (i.e., Mogens Klaehr, born 1911), which drew a critical picture of the empty idealist and contrasted him with the practical idealist—or realist—exemplified by a character who lost his life in the Irish civil war in 1920.

The prose written by members and friends of the resistance movement, while often allegorical, was generally didactic and functional. A notable exception is found in the moving diary and letters of the young KIM MALTHE-BRUUN, (1923–45), which were published posthumously under the title *Kim,* in 1945,[1] and which were eloquent evidence of the loss which Danish literature sustained by the death of some of Denmark's serious young men during the war.

Despite the impact of the Occupation, then, there was relatively little Danish literature concerned with the war. It was as if artistic endeavor could not be made subordinate to or even combined with the practical political demands of the moment. A purely generic or aesthetic consideration of Danish literature would scarcely acknowledge an era of war.

---

1 Translated by Gerry Bothmer, as *Heroic Heart.* New York, 1955.

For the literary historian, however, the war may be said to have established a kind of boundary between generations. At the close of the war a new group of writers whose names were unknown or as yet unheard in the thirties soon established themselves on the literary scene and in the consciousness of both the critics and the general public.

Characteristic of Danish literature after 1940 has been the ascendancy of a kind of supra-rationalism which superseded the nihilism evoked by the First World War and the socialistic materialism of the twenty years between the wars. The regression from the literature of social consciousness is best exemplified in the work of MARTIN A. HANSEN (1909–55), who was the most talented Danish prose writer to acquire fame during the war years. In the previous chapter his first two novels were mentioned as examples of literature that concerned itself with social problems. During and after the war he demonstrated the several facets of his ability as a writer. Today no living author has greater prestige in Denmark. That is the more remarkable since his later works possess a profundity, one might say a lack of simplicity and even lucidity in expression, that is uncommon in books which are sold in large numbers.

Although his canon is expansive, and he is not devoted to a single type of prose narrative, he has nevertheless subconsciously kept to certain recurrent themes: life in nature, an awareness of the roots of culture, and the importance of sincerity.

More than once Martin A. Hansen has been compared with Johannes V. Jensen. Several parallels may be pointed out: their lack of stylistic uniformity, their concern with folk culture, their preoccupation with myth, and their interest in the clash of tradition with the dynamics of contemporary society. Yet Hansen in many ways reacted against the older writer's philosophical materialism and literary naturalism. Johannes V. Jensen, although inclined to be sentimental, was always the rationalist, whereas Martin A. Hansen, who had a penchant for the fantastic, was not interested in finding some convenient rational or material explanation of phenomena.

The two novels which Hansen wrote during the war, *Jonatans Rejse* (*Jonathan's Journey,* 1941; revised edition, 1950) and *Lykkelige Kristoffer* (*Lucky Christopher,* 1945) won him critical acclaim. Denmark at once became aware that it possessed a new, original, and courageous author. Courageous is not too strong a term; it must have taken considerable self-confidence and fortitude to publish a book of such a highly imaginative nature as *Jonatans Rejse* at a time when the novel still was more or less expected to embody social realism.

In reading *Jonatans Rejse,* one is reminded of the ironic tales and extravagant imagery of the German authors E. T. A. Hoffmann and Jean Paul, who wrote over a century before. Jonathan, a smith, catches the devil in a metal flask and sets out to present his catch to the king. On his way he has a series of fantastic adventures and meets fantastic people. One might take the motif as belonging to an old fairy tale, were it not that the reader has an uneasy and growing feeling that the story is ultimately allegorical of conditions that obtain in the twentieth century. An example of the author's ironic, allegorical symbolism is the king's secret machine which permits him to see what persons are doing at a distance and to hear what they are saying, if only some possession of the person is placed within the apparatus. (The reader will remember that the story was written before the advent of popular television). The book also contains what may be interpreted as a subtle satire on Freudian psychology.

Lykkelige Kristoffer is a different kind of narrative, an historical novel which relates of events in the sixteenth century. Composed in strong rhythmic prose, the novel has a tendency toward dreamy recollection and *causerie.* The author's phantasy has nevertheless been limited by the historical material with which he worked, despite the freedom which he took with that material.

In 1950 Martin A. Hansen published still another novel, quite different from its predecessors: *Løgneren (The Liar)*[1]. It bears a marked resemblance to Harald Kidde's *Helten* (1912); like Kidde's novel, it is neither fantastic nor historical, but is psychological. It expresses in an obtuse way the author's philosophical and ethical convictions. Reflecting on the means employed in narrating the story, one is reminded of Kierkegaard's so-called indirect communication: the author's point is clear without ever having been made in so many words. Incidentally, Hansen's narrative was originally written for the Danish state radio; the unusual lucidity of the text may be ascribed to the fact that the story in its original form was designed for oral delivery.

Hansen's individuality of style and technique as a narrator are well demonstrated in "Midsommerfesten" ("Midsummer Festival"), one of the three short stories contained in the volume *Tornebusken (The Hawthorne Bush)* which appeared in 1946. In reading the story, one is struck first by the originality of the execution which is characteristic of each work by Hansen. In "Midsommerfesten" the author not only carries on a conversation with a reader; he tells a story which apparently is independent

1 Translated by John Jepson Egglishaw. London, 1954.

of the conversation, but which gradually merges into and fuses with the conversation in the consciousness of the reader. Again, it is as if Hansen were attempting Kierkegaard's indirect communication and as if the significance of the story lay in its very obtuseness. Exposition in the traditional sense of the word is not present. While some of his books, and notably his first novel, suggested the work of the older regionalist Thorkild Gravlund, the complexity of his canon and his love for abstractions seem very different from the qualities which we expect to find in popular national or regional literature. Indirectness of communication characterizes two volumes of individualistic essays entitled *Tanker i en Skorsten* (*Thoughts in a Chimney*, 1948) and *Leviathan* (1950), in which Martin A. Hansen perorated on cultural, ethical, and philosophical matters at the same time tangential and fundamental to his imaginative writing, as well as the anomalous *Orm og Tyr* (*Serpent and Bull*, 1952).[1]

Orm og Tyr is Martin A. Hansen's most remarkable and original book; it does not falls into any readily defined belletristic category. Most nearly in the style of an essay or *causerie*, it is a kind of interpretive history which tries to educe the essential character of religious belief in Denmark before and after the introduction of Christianity. It is a metaphorical and visionary, although retrospective work. Abstractly considered, *Orm og Tyr* is an attempt to comprehend the metaphysical motivations which, during the eras of heathendom and pre-Gothic Christianity, caused men to create what now are preserved as graves and runic inscriptions, churches, monuments, and ruins.

In *Orm og Tyr* Martin A. Hansen is a Christian apologist without being an apologist for Christian theology, dogma, or ecclesiastical practice. He is an apologist for faith. Axial in his dissertation are the Romanesque churches of Denmark in all their graphic simplicity. If his persuasion may be identified as neo-Romantic, his taste is not identical with that of the nineteenth-century enthusiasts for Scandinavian antiquity; for he looks askance at the later, Gothic architecture.

In reading *Orm og Tyr* (a slow process, for the book attests Hansen's large and in part unusual vocabulary, with a predilection for older glosses), one is inevitably struck by occasional similarities with some of the symbolic explanations given by Johannes V. Jensen in *Den lange Rejse*

1 Two of Hansen's short stories, translated by Lydia Cranfield, have appeared in *The Norseman*: "March Night," in vol. VIII, 1950, pp. 54–60, and "The Book," in vol. X, 1952, pp. 192–97. – "The Partridge," translated by Erik J. Friis, in *The American-Scandinavian Review*, 1955, pp. 383–86. – "The Birds," translated by R. P. Keigwin, is included in *Contemporary Danish Prose*, Copenhagen, 1958.

(The Long Journey), by the effort to achieve a flowing interpretation of primitive Scandinavian religion like that given by Vilhelm Grønbech (see below), and by a singular affinity for the Christian nationalism of N.F.S. Grundtvig. It would be no feat to demonstrate the author's awareness of Jensen, Grønbech, and Grundtvig, but it would be indefensible to assume that *Orm og Tyr* is merely a compound of elements extracted from the thought of these three distinguished countrymen. While the book contains an admixture of their thought with Hansen's, it may more justifiably be described as an original work inspired by the most pervasive intellectual synthesists that Denmark has produced. One could go even farther and point out parallels between Martin A. Hansen and Søren Kierkegaard, but Hansen's concept of the individual's dependence on a people and its national or local folk-culture puts him sharply at variance with Kierkegaard and calls to mind instead the writings of the Danish regionalist Thorkild Gravlund and in a broader sense the ideas of Herder and Grundtvig. If the mature Martin A. Hansen was in the final analysis a disciple and not a seer, then he was a modern disciple of Grundtvig.

The vividness of Hansen's constructive imagination is reminiscent of Johannes V. Jensen, with whom he shared the fundamental teleological assumption without however subscribing to the older writer's belief in evolution. For Martin A. Hansen there is a unity of past and present in the essential nature of the human being. In *Orm og Tyr*, it is as if he were projecting the reader into the past and declaring, this was our belief and although it is no longer our belief and cannot be so reëstablished, it might still be our belief.

Martin A. Hansen was not a historian in the academic sense of the word. He did not try to adduce new theories. Nor was he trying to popularize the research of scholars. His intention in *Orm og Tyr* was to inspire recognition of the past and reflection upon it and to inculcate reverence for the myth of an earlier age and the forms through which it was expressed.

Martin A. Hansen's convictions are representative of the dominant forces in Danish literature in the years since the Second World War. Although not primarily a poet, he identified himself with the members of the younger generation of Danish poets who were and are struggling with symbols and form, in order to achieve expression which will more nearly correspond to existence in the industrialized, atomized, and psychoanalyzed twentieth century and who, in his own words, have "arrived at the metaphysical through the use of reason."

A fundamental question which motivates not only the work of Martin A. Hansen, but of many of his contemporaries, lyrists as well as prose writers, is: What lies behind apparent reality? The self-satisfaction of naturalistic writing which portrayed rather than interpreted has been overtaken or perhaps transcended by a new literature that inclines toward the metaphysical and which seeks inspiration from writers and thinkers who look beyond the limits usually set by rationality.

It is perhaps unfair to take leave of imaginative prose literature without mentioning a number of other contemporary Danish writers who have established themselves as novelists of some promise; but it is idle to try to account for the many Danish writers who are currently plying their pens with some degree of virtuosity. If a list of names will serve any purpose, then several writers who have won plaudits from most Danish critics in recent years must be mentioned: HILMAR WULFF (born 1908), who carries on the tradition of social realism; HANS LYNGBY JEPSEN (born 1920), whose novels and short stories are of a psychological bent; ERIK AALBÆK JENSEN, (born 1923), whose novel *Dæmningen* (*The Dam,* 1952) has been acclaimed as a contribution to symbolic prose and has been as widely read as any serious post-war Danish novel; HANS JØRGEN LEMBOURN (born 1923), whose production hitherto has been highly variegated; and FINN GERDES (born 1914), who may be taken as representative of several talented contemporary Danish writers of short stories. It is apparent that many of the younger writers of prose have been inspired particularly by the novels and short stories of Ernest Hemingway.

A single younger Danish dramatist has made his mark since the Second World War: FINN METHLING (born 1917). He is able to manipulate the commonplace so that his audience is moved by the powers of association. The forty-minute dramatic monologue *Rejsen til de grønne skygger* (*Journey to the Green Shadows,* first played in 1952, published 1956) is a series of effectively interrelated scenes from the life of an average woman from birth to death. Methling is one of several dramatists who have written successfully for the Danish state radio. His *Sangen til Hanne* (*A Song for Hanne,* first broadcast in 1951, published 1953) evinces amusing originality of technique.

Much of the poetry of the years between the two World Wars had been either exotic and materialistic, or a product of the social conscience. These attributes were not predominant in the literature of the later forties and early fifties, when the resounding note was critical, symbolic, religious, or regional. The profound or labored metaphor had a renaissance, and the language of poetry came less and less to resemble the language of description and exposition. The charge of willful obscurity was subsequently raised against the younger poets; but they are not so obscure as to discourage readers from buying their poetry. Lyrists such as Erik Knudsen, Halfdan Rasmussen, Frank Jæger, and Ove Abildgaard, have a relatively large reading public. Though their verse, and the verse of their contemporaries, is often characterized by metaphorical abstractions and contrived symbols, the obfuscation of much modern and avant-garde poetry recently published in English is lacking. Nor have Danish poets (in contradistinction to a few of their Swedish contemporaries) indulged in much typographical experimentation.

ERIK KNUDSEN (born 1922) is an example of literary synthesis among the members of his generation. While he cannot be identified as a disciple or an imitator, one recognizes in his poetry the union of the Anglo-American conservative T. S. Eliot and the Danish Marxist Otto Gelsted. His first volume of poetry, *Dobbelte Dage* (*Double Days,* 1945), which appeared shortly after the conclusion of hostilities in World War II, gives a clear indication of Knudsen's literary antecedents. It contains poems addressed to Gustaf Munch-Petersen, Nordahl Grieg, and Morten Nielsen—all poets who had been sacrificed on the altar of Mars while striving to overcome the obstacles which kept them from the "beautiful world that might be." With them Knudsen felt a strong bond of sympathy, and it is not too far afield to designate him as Morten Nielsen's successor, so similar were their basic assumptions, as may be observed especially in Knudsen's poem "Mindreværd" ("Inferiority Complex").

Erik Knudsen's disillusionment and recognition of human folly was clearly expressed in the cycle of poems which constitute his second book, *Til en ukendt Gud* (*To an Unknown God,* 1947), in which he depicted his search for a faith to live by. He cries,

> I long for people who don't have polished sentences
> > hanging around their necks like pearls,
> People who stutter and use the simplest words . . . .

In another poem, "The World is a Madhouse," from the same collection, he observes,

> Once technology was an obedient little dog on a leash
> . . .
> Now it's a roaring lion, pulling us behind him.

Still more pointed is the poem which begins,

Is it you Einstein? Is it you Freud?
Who had knocked the bottom out of poetry
And showed us the poet as he is:
A little man with a wooden sword and a paper hat.

"O, psychologists," he concludes, "you have killed my old song and given me no new song to sing." Expressing the sentiments of the title of the collection, he declares further,

O, terrible knowledge–
I write neither for God nor men.
I write for myself,
To save my ego.

Knudsen's third collection of verse, *Blomsten og Sværdet* (*The Flower and the Sword*, 1949) represented a change of course. It is as if metaphysics had finally won over the skeptic, as evidenced by an optimism which permeates the first poem in the book, "Credo." He who loves, says Knudsen, shall have eternal life. Knudsen's more recent works have been more equivocal and without the inner unity of the poetry he published in the forties.

For all his serious verse, HALFDAN RASMUSSEN (born 1915) is read primarily as a humorist. Even in his first collection of poems, which bore the sober title *Soldat eller Menneske* (*Soldier or Human Being*, 1941), the humorous element in Rasmussen was irrepressible. Since 1951 he has published a series of volumes of humorous verse all entitled *Tosserier* (*Tomfoolery*) in which he gives free play to his sovereign wit and light-hearted originality. The serious poetry is unfeigned and straightforward. Halfdan Rasmussen is a proletarian poet, but he is a poet without a party or a program—unabashed, unpolished, and unfettered. He is a humanist as well as a humorist. He has achieved a wide audience for his poetry, but whether his poetry will outlive his claim to fame as a humorist is a matter of conjecture.[1]

FRANK JÆGER (born 1926) is worthy of mention as a widely read younger writer who is droll and witty. Since his first literary contribu-

1 More pronounced a humorist than Halfdan Rasmussen is PIET HEIN (born 1905) whose sophisticated verse, most frequently witty quatrains, is published under the pseudonym "Kumbel Kumbell," and enlivens the day for readers of the Copenhagen newspaper *Politiken*. The easy, rhyming verse of Piet Hein, with its predilection for strong metrical accent, reminds us of the pervading influence of Heine in the North. Piet Hein does not have as wide an appeal as did the late VIGGO BARFOED (1895–1948), whose daily poetic commentary on news items appeared for several years on the back page of the widely-distributed Danish newspaper *Berlingske Tidende*.

tions appeared in *Heretica,* it may be assumed that his serious verse is qualitatively as important as his humorous prose and poetry, but in the eyes of the reading public Jæger (the name means "hunter") is primarily the author of the prose sketches which make up *Den unge Jægers Lidelser (The Sufferings of the young Jæger,* 1953), the title of which parodies Goethe's *Werther.*

OVE ABILDGAARD (born 1916) demonstrated his poetic potential in the collection *Uglegylp (The Owl's Pellet)* in 1946 and has in his more recent verse spoken to an increasing audience. His poetry, while technically simple and traditional, frequently invites psychoanalytic inspection.

The lode stars of the new poetry have in the first instance been Rainer Maria Rilke, and to a lesser extent T. S. Eliot, Stefan George, W. H. Auden, and William Blake. A number of poets, as for example Per Lange, who has been mentioned above as belonging to a slightly older generation, and THORKILD BJØRNVIG (born 1918) and OLE WIVEL (born 1921), who belong to the youngest generation with a firmly established place in literature, seem not only to have read Rilke, but also to be striving to create Rilke-like metaphors and to achieve the same absolute originality of observation that is an essential characteristic of the German poet's work.

While Bjørnvig has published little verse of his own, he has distinguished himself as a translator of a volume of Rilke's profound and well-wrought poetry (1949). Bjørnvig's *Stjærnen bag Gavlen (The Star behind the Gable,* 1947) put Bjørnvig in the first rank of young Danish poets and at the same time made clear that the poet had found his inspiration in Rilke. In his second collection of verse, *Anubis* (1955) Bjørnvig demonstrated greater originality, although echoes of Rilke and of T. S. Eliot as well do not escape the careful reader. After the publication of *Anubis,* which, in contrast to much of the poetry written in the forties, was unequivocal and transparent without being simple or casual, Bjørnvig was hailed by the sexagenarian Tom Kristensen as the most significant Danish poet of the decade.

Rilke's impact upon Danish writers in the forties cannot be measured by the amount of his verse translated into Danish, for any Dane seriously interested in literature has a good command of literary German and is in a position to approach Rilke—or Stefan George—in the original. The average educated Dane knows English as well or better than German, but T. S. Eliot's poetry, presumably because of its impenetrability, has had a more limited appeal than Rilke's. A selection of Eliot's poetry (from *The Waste-Land* and other poems) was published in Danish translation in 1948. His Danish interpreters were not members of the younger generation of poets, but two of Eliot's contemporaries, Tom Kristensen and the gifted translator and literary causeur KAI FRIIS MØLLER (born 1888). The volume included an interpretive apologia by Kristensen.

Probably the strongest single influence on the younger generation came not from abroad nor from any imaginative writer but from the Danish philosopher and historian VILHELM GRØNBECH (1873–1948). To the reader familiar with Grønbech's style and with his generalities and paradoxes, there are many recognizable echoes in the prose essays of younger writers (and especially in the periodical *Heretica*). In particular, Grønbech's repeated statement that modern man is in need of a new myth struck a responsive chord. Time and again the spiritual hunger for a new myth is noticeable. Significant, for example, is Ole Wivel's remark that only the force of a myth could explain the experiences of the war years. Here is a key to the apparent lack of clarity in much modern poetry. Traditional forms and inherited ideas have not been adequate in the face of what repeatedly has been called the crisis of our time. The desire to be truly creative has led to a symbolism which sometimes is of such a personal nature that only the poet himself could know what he meant with his metaphor. The reality achieved by such poetry is, as one writer put it, "the isolated human being's reality." But isolation is the antithesis of the fellowship which a new myth should grant; and the new myth has yet to be achieved.

While Grønbech is only incidentally an imaginative writer, his position in Danish cultural history is too prominent that it can be overlooked in considering the background of contemporary Danish literature. A man of many gifts, he was successively a philologist, an organist, and a lecturer in English literature prior to his becoming professor of the history of religion in the University of Copenhagen. With his first great synthetic work, a study of the primitive religious concepts of the Germanic peoples,[1] Grønbech became an interpreter of the culture and cultural movements of the past. His interpretive explorations of the culture of classical and post-classical Greece, of mysticism, and of Christianity pointed a way out of the maze of factual knowledge which beset many young inquisitive and searching minds. The incisiveness and lucidity of his syntheses were almost seductively appealing in their intellectual emotionalism.

Grønbech was the great synthesist of twentieth-century Denmark, as

1 *Vor Folkeæt i Oldtiden,* I–IV, 1909–12; revised by the author and translated into English by William Worster as *The Culture of the Teutons,* London, 1931. *Religiose Strømninger i det nittende Aarhundrede* was published in English translation as *Religious Currents in the Nineteenth Century* by the University of Kansas Press, 1964.

Grundtvig and Kierkegaard had been the synthesists, seers, and prophets of nineteenth-century Denmark. His impact on younger contemporaries was scarcely less than that of Grundtvig on his contemporaries or of Kierkegaard on the growing community of his readers that arose after his death. Notable was Grønbech's interest in mysticism and the mystics of Europe and India which engendered a four-volume work (*Mystikere i Europa og Indien,* 1925–34) and in his study of William Blake (1934). He contributed much to an interpretation of the nineteenth century with his essay on the religious currents of that century (1922) and his study of Frederik Schlegel (1935). These and his many other works provided a generation with enlightenment and understanding about the culture and philosophies of the past and encouraged further synthetic thought about the primitive and metaphysical elements that are corporate in man's existence. Prior to his death Grønbech, with his colleague Professor Hal Koch, edited the periodical *Frie Ord* (*Free Words,* 1946–48), primarily an outlet that permitted Grønbech to speak on general topics of the day to an increasing audience.

The periodical *Heretica,* which was a spiritual fosterling of Grønbech, became the organ of the new, post-war literary direction, but not until 1948 did *Heretica* begin publication. In the interim the demand for literature in translation and for criticism of literature of the Allied nations was naturally great, and for several years the Danish book market was flooded with translations of English and American and to a lesser extent French books. It is a sign of the times that, according to a survey of Danish reading habits made in 1947, the most widely read authors in Denmark were American or English.

The demand for international literary orientation was met—aside from newspaper articles—by the periodical *Athenæum* (1946–49), which made a concerted effort to summarize the status of contemporary world literature in a spirit of internationalism that was tinged with Marxian thinking. *Athenæum* contained reviews of English, American, French, Swedish, and Soviet literature, and articles on several writers of international reputation such as Stefan Zweig and Thomas Wolfe, Jean-Paul Sartre, Jules Romains, Arthur Koestler, Cyril Connolly, and André Gide, William Saroyan, Henry Miller, and Alberto Moravia—some of whom were nearly unknown to the Danish reading public.

It was not until the end of the second volume of the periodical that the editor of *Athenæum,* Sven Møller Kristensen, stated an editorial policy: to provide a many-sided critical orientation in contemporary world literature—but in the very next issue (Winter 1949) it was announced that the periodical would pay more attention to Danish literature. It was as if the immediate function of the journal as a harbinger of the literature favored by the avant-garde throughout Europe had been fulfilled. At the same time, the leftist leaning of *Athenæum* became more pronounced. After two more issues it ceased publication, to be succeeded by the more partisan and progressively less influential *Dialog.*

The most important single contributor to *Athenæum* was the left-wing critic and poet Otto Gelsted, who was eulogized in the final number of the journal. And in the final number it was Gelsted who wrote *Athenæum's* concluding article on "Danish lyrics in crisis," in which he spoke out against the poetry of T. S. Eliot as the most frightening example of what he called "bibliothecal poetry." Yet it is indicative of the rôle Eliot played in the consciousness of post-war Danish poets that in a symposium about the common man and good literature, undertaken by *Athenæum,* the lyrists Paul la Cour and Erik Knudsen as well as the dramatist-novelist Leck Fischer all felt called upon to discuss the poetry of Eliot in their replies.

The literary situation had been unclear for a year or two after the war, i.e., until the political rapprochement dissolved which necessity and expediency had dictated. Then, with the establishment of *Heretica,* the die was cast. To be sure, *Heretica* (published 1948–53) did not speak for all the writers on the Danish Parnassus, but it represented a prevailing literary attitude and gave at least the semblance of unity to a group of younger writers. Though it made no extraordinary effort to win readers, *Heretica* nevertheless attracted a large number of subscribers, a fact which evidences the timeliness of the theses which were expounded and the questions which were debated in the periodical.

The writers who originally contributed to *Heretica* by no means formed a closed group, and they did not all even agree to continue to collaborate after the first few issues of the journal, but on the whole they had much in common. They were intensely concerned about poetic theory. They championed a return to the realm of aesthetics from the tangential areas of Marxian and Freudian thinking. They showed an affinity for the Existentialist direction in France. As loose as their association may have been, the members of the so-called *Heretica* group nevertheless represented the first concentrated efforts of an identifiable literary school in Denmark since the days of Johan Ludvig Heiberg a century before. And like the Heiberg school, the *Heretica* group stressed the aesthetic nature of literature. Literature was again to be art and not propaganda.

In answer to the criticism that *Heretica* inclined too much to the metaphysical, Martin A. Hansen wrote that the periodical had arrived at the metaphysical through the use of reason, therewith implying that the new school was progressive and transcendental rather than reactionary. He wanted to make the point clear that *Heretica* was not championing the irrational but seeking the reality behind apparent reality. For such a search the well-trodden paths simply would not suffice. In a similar vein, the publisher of *Heretica,* Ole Wivel, in referring with deference to the French Existentialist thinker Jean-Paul Sartre, said that "a new metaphysics was on the way."

It is not easy aesthetically to assess the enterprising publisher and poet Ole Wivel. Philosophically speaking, one may perhaps call him a neo-Christian, with roots in the work of the modern mystics, Rilke, William Blake, and Grundtvig. But his is a sophisticated and esoteric Christianity. He is clearly a member of the generation that felt the impact of Vilhelm Grønbech, but it is a matter of debate whether he has interpreted Grønbech correctly. Like not a few figures in the nineteenth century of whom Grønbech spoke and wrote, Wivel is searching for a new god. In Danish literature he is most closely associated with his friend, the late Martin A. Hansen, with whom he and the illustrator Sven Havsteen-Mikkelsen undertook many of the trips which were the genesis of Martin A. Hansen's *Orm og Tyr.* The same admiration for the Gothic church and the unity and strength of medieval religion which is found in Hansen is also present in Wivel's *Den skjulte Gud (The Hidden God,* 1952). The longing for an unknown god (which incidentally is also suggested by the title of Erik Knudsen's volume of verse *Til en ukendt Gud—To an Unknown God,* 1947) is also found in Wivel's most mature collection of verse, *Maanen (The Moon,* 1952). Wivel's earlier poetry, especially in *Jævndøgnselegier (Equinoctial Elegies,* 1949) contained a suggestion of T. S. Eliot; *I Fiskens Tegn (The Sign of the Fish,* 1948) was marked by mysticism, but *Maanen* is almost deceptively lucid.

An examination of the first few numbers of *Heretica* makes clear in what direction the periodical was moving and reveals its fundamentally exclusive and tendentious nature. The first number began with a poem by W. H. Auden (translated by Thorkild Bjørnvig); an advertisement for the Danish translation of Rilke's *Malte Laurids Brigge* was on the inside cover. There were two articles by Martin A. Hansen, one on the demise of the novel, the other on literary neuroses; an article on Stefan George by Ole Wivel; selections from Paul la Cour's informal poetics entitled *Fragmenter af en Dagbog (Fragments of a Diary)*; and poems by Bjørnvig and Ole Sarvig. The second number contained translations of poems by

Rilke, articles by Vilhelm Grønbech and Martin A. Hansen, and poems by Erik Knudsen and Frank Jæger. The third number included three articles on Vilhelm Grønbech in memoriam, by Ole Wivel, Thorkild Bjørnvig, and Martin A. Hansen.

Later numbers of *Heretica* brought articles about Morten Nielsen and a number of foreign poets: Yeats, Denis de Rougemont, Edith Södergran, Harry Martinson, Tarjei Vesaas, and Ernst Jünger—all writers who were and are the favorites of cliques of intellectuals, avant-gardistes, and esthetes throughout the Western world, and at the same time writers of stature who may be said to have left naturalism behind them and to be seeking in the realm of the aesthetic or the metaphysical. Not until the second volume of *Heretica* was there any obvious reflection of the war or a concern with the post-war situation *per se*.

The most important of the several considerations of poetry and of the place and function of the poet which were carried on in the columns of *Heretica* and which give the publication its eminent position in the literary consciousness of Denmark, were the above-mentioned "Fragments" of the poet Paul la Cour, that were expanded and published in book form the same year (1948). Despite his break with the editors, he represents the poetic attitude of the *Heretica* group, of which he had been a forerunner in the twenty years prior to the appearance of the periodical. After the Second World War, there was a new tone in his work. It was first expressed in the collection of poems entitled *Levende Vande (Living Waters)* in 1946. He was now concerned with the delineation and establishment of ultimate values, first and foremost the values of poetry.

In his aphoristic poetics, *Fragmenter af en Dagbog (Fragments of a Diary)*, to which the collection of poems entitled *Mellem Bark og Ved (Between Bark and Wood,* 1950) is a complement, la Cour is ever aware of the high calling of the poet, of the importance and dignity of the poem as a non-social, non-psychological phenomenon, and of the cultural need for the creative artist who has faith in the effectiveness of his art. The contents of *Fragmenter af en Dagbog* are suggested by a random selection of typical "fragments":

When you beautified your poem you killed it. When you impoverished it, that which was omitted became its wealth.

The deepest truth is metaphor. Touched by poetic logic.

The pinnacles of modern Scandinavian poetry–Fröding and Södergran, the great singers of sincerity.

You must not explore yourself. All exploration is cold and kills the poem. You must express yourself.

Poetry as we have it must be sacrificed in order to free poetry.

The "fragments" have from the first had a remarkable impact on younger Danish poets. One frequently hears echoes of Paul la Cour's lapidary and aphoristic style from the pages of the avant-garde organ *Hvedekorn (Grains of Wheat)*. La Cour inspired resoluteness and a renewed faith in the mission of poetry.

Philosophically partisan as it was, *Heretica* did not fail to arouse opposition. Many writers and critics found they could not accept the metaphysical persuasion espoused by the publication or could not agree with the political conservatism which it represented. They soon had an organ of expression in another periodical which, after the demise of *Athenæum* established itself as *Heretica's* antithesis: *Dialog* (1950 ff.). During its first year *Dialog* attracted independent minds and dissident elements from the *Heretica* group, notably *Heretica's* sage Paul la Cour and the younger poet Erik Knudsen, but *Dialog* soon championed the philosophy of socialist realism. The first volume, edited by Sven Møller Kristensen and Erik Knudsen, was an extension of *Athenæum* in spirit and principle. The first number contained poems by Paul la Cour and articles on Gustaf Munch-Petersen and Morten Nielsen. Despite a critique of dialectical materialism (by Erik Knudsen) in one number, however, it was clear by the end of the first volume that the new periodical was veering to the extreme Left. The second volume, starting after a hiatus of six months, had a new editorial board, a new format, and the announced policy of working for "peace, unity, liberalism, and better material and intellectual conditions." *Dialog* has subsequently remained oriented toward the Soviet Union. On the whole it has become an essentially partisan organ, to which few if any Danish writers of significance contribute. It thus evidences the tendency of Western intellectuals to disassociate themselves from organized Communism, as Communist prestige has diminished in the fifties. Incidentally, the literary prestige and influence of Communism in Denmark as elsewhere suffered its most serious reverse as a result of the suppression of the Hungarian revolt in November, 1956.

The political and social differences between Right and Left became more and more pronounced in literature during the years after the Second World War, so that most writers soon seemed to be affiliated with one of the two camps, and there was a schism caused by the clash of two political philosophies. In Denmark the main political camps can be identified roughly as the conservative and right-wing social democratic on the one side and the Marxist (including Communists and left-wing Socialists) on the other. Writers of both camps have had something of philosophical and political import to say, although their methods of communication, like their principles, have differed. There has been a general awareness of what often has been referred to as the "cultural crisis." Serious authors who incline to the psychological and metaphysical have respected the restrictions of literary forms and have employed the expository essay to express their convictions. Both Martin A. Hansen and H. C. Branner have written essays on social and intellectual problems tangential to the ideas that motivate their formal literary production. After disassociating himself first from *Heretica* and then from *Dialog*, Erik Knudsen (who is politically a socialist) tried to make clear his position between Right and Left in a volume of essays, *Galileis Kikkert* (*Galileo's Telescope*, 1952). If most authors have been conscious of the gap between poetry and reality, the members of the extreme Left have not. They have not hesitated definitely and consciously to agitate through literary media.

On the whole, the discussions of problems of the day in Danish periodical literature have been rather intramural, despite the great interest displayed in foreign literature at the conclusion of the war. The limitations of a national language have apparently been felt more strongly than before. References to Norwegian and Swedish contemporaries are frequent, but intellectual association with figures of international cultural importance is less frequent than, say, in Brandes' heyday or in the decade prior to the Second World War.

The clash between *Athenæum* (and later *Dialog*) and *Heretica* is indicative of the fact that since the Second World War the literary situation in Denmark is most conveniently and readily defined by an examination of literary periodicals, as was also the case in the years following World War I. To be sure, certain authors, like Paul la Cour and Martin A. Hansen, seem already to have made their mark and to have achieved a lasting place in literary annals, but in the case of many other authors, one does not find it easy to disengage the significant from the less significant, and it is only with a feeling of trepidation that a critic attempts to pass a lasting aesthetic judgment on contemporary writers of serious intent.

By 1950 the point had been reached where there seemed to be little demand for publications that represented neither Right nor Left, as the political tensions of the outside world became more clearly marked and exerted torsion on the Danish literary scene. Some non-partisan periodicals (notably *Gads danske Magasin*) ceased publication and for a time there remained only *Heretica* and *Dialog,* representing the extremes of meta-physical poetry and socialist realism. At this time the stock of the Left stood relatively high among liberal intellectuals, but as a consequence of events in the outside world and of the gyrations of Soviet Communism, the extreme Left had grown small by the mid-1950's, and the cultural rôle of its organ *Dialog* was slight, whereas the periodicals founded in the fifties seemed to be reaching large audiences. *Heretica,* which ceased publication in 1953, was soon replaced by the less esoteric *Vindrosen (The Compass,* 1954 ff.). The defunct *Gads danske Magasin* was resuscitated as *Det danske Magasin (The Danish Magazine,* 1953–1957) and was a conserva-tive organ for cultural debate. In 1953 *Perspektiv,* a new periodical of a general literary and political nature began publication. Four years later it absorbed *Det danske Magasin.*

Curiously enough it was *Vindrosen,* which was the outgrowth of the metaphysically inclined, right-wing *Heretica,* that became a forum for enlightened Marxism as well as for writers who bore the *Heretica* label. In *Vindrosen* the socially conscious Right and the intellectual Left have contracted an unusual *mariage de convenance.* Perhaps it would be more just and proper to say that *Vindrosen* represents an aesthetic, intellectual, and humanistic but not a political standpoint. While *Vindrosen* is first and foremost a literary organ, it nevertheless prints contributions of a general philosophical and political nature and therewith suggests the difficulty in trying to divorce belles-lettres from current events in restless, post-war Europe during an era of tension between East and West. Under the editorship of Peter P. Rohde and Tage Skou-Hansen, *Vindrosen* has print-ed contributions by Paul la Cour and a number of writers known from the pages of both *Heretica* and *Dialog.*

While *Vindrosen* is aesthetically and philosophically inclined and, despite its humanism, is nationally oriented, the more widely read *Perspektiv* is of a more international and general nature. *Perspektiv* identifies itself as a journal for "literature, art and science," and is a Danish complement to the English *Twentieth Century,* the American *Atlantic Monthly,* the Swedish *BLM,* and the Norwegian *Vinduet.* More than anything else, it too is a literary periodical, but it attempts to give its readers a general orientation not only in Danish and foreign literature, but also in matters of principle which concern both the outside world and Denmark. The first volumes of both *Perspektiv* and *Vindrosen* contained contributions by Martin A. Hansen and Erik Knudsen (who had at one time been editors of the right-wing *Heretica* and the left-wing *Dialog* respectively) and thus in-dicated the expansive nature of their editorial policy. In the first volume of *Perspektiv* are to be found articles by or about Graham Greene, Einstein, Anouilh, Vilhelm Grønbech, George Orwell, André Malraux, Cesare Pavese, Sigurd Hoel, and Herbert Read. *Perspektiv* has performed the Danish reading public a valuable service as a medium for the publication in Danish translation of foreign imaginative and critical writing. Danish writers are well represented in the pages of *Perspektiv*; but it may be termed a European periodical in the Danish language, whereas *Vindrosen* is more a repository for original contributions and an organ of the Danish avant-garde. The editorial policy of both periodicals and in particular the concern with cultural freedom and the freedom of expression suggests the position of the independent Copenhagen newspaper *Information* (founded as an organ of the Danish underground movement during World War II).

Characteristic of both periodicals is the quantity of graphic art which they reproduce, although neither is so vitally concerned with modern graphic art as either *Dialog* or the long-lived "little magazine" *Hvedekorn* (formerly *Vild Hvede*). The graphic art of *Dialog* is principally of an agitatorial nature. *Hvedekorn (Grains of Wheat)* publishes the work of younger artists. The other two periodicals generally reproduce the work of established artists. Collectively, the literary journals indicate the widespread Danish appreciation of and interest in illustrative art.

Such is the contemporary literary scene.

Judged by its contributions to international Western literature, Denmark has been prolific and productive during the first half of the twentieth century. Among the older generation of Danish writers, whose major contributions were made by the 1920's, Martin Andersen Nexø, Johannes V. Jensen, Henrik Pontoppidan, and Johannes Jørgensen spoke to large audiences abroad as well as at home, but with the exception of Andersen Nexø, relatively less in English-speaking countries than in Sweden and Norway, Germany, Russia, Poland, and Czechoslovakia, France and the Netherlands. Three Danes achieved the distinction of receiving the Nobel Prize in literature: Henrik Pontoppidan and Karl Gjellerup in 1917, and Johannes V. Jensen in 1944. Worthy of especial mention, finally, is the esteem which the critical works of Georg Brandes enjoyed at the beginning of the century.

Among European writers who achieved both a fixed place on Parnassus and who drew attention from abroad between the two great wars were the bilingual narrator Karen Blixen and the martyred playwright Kaj Munk. Karen Blixen's international reputation is to be sure far greater than Kaj Munk's. Her works have appeared in Norwegian, Swedish, Icelandic, and Finnish, German, French, and Dutch, as well as the original English and Danish, whereas Munk, although well represented in English and Swedish translation, has had only individual plays put into a few other languages (Icelandic, German, and Spanish).

Among somewhat younger writers who have published major works since the late thirties, Hans Christian Branner and Martin A. Hansen have each enjoyed international success principally because of individual works: Branner's *Rytteren (The Riding Master)* has appeared in English, Dutch, French, German, Swedish, and Norwegian translations; and Hansen's *Løgneren (The Liar)* has been translated into Norwegian and German, Dutch, English, French, and Finnish. The single novel *Barbara* of their Faroese contemporary Jørgen-Frantz Jacobsen (who died in 1938) has been even more widely read; it has appeared in Norwegian, Swedish, Icelandic, and Finnish, German, Dutch, English, French, and Italian. Individual works of Jacobsen's compatriot William Heinesen have also been translated into Swedish, Norwegian, and Icelandic, German and English.

Mentioned in the preceding paragraphs are twentieth-century Danish writers who have withstood the test of an international criticism and have demonstrated that their writing has intrinsic value by virtue of ethos and form, analysis and execution. Still other Danish writers have made contributions to international literature on a somewhat different plane and in a more popular vein. Books by Karin Michaëlis have been translated into a dozen or more languages, and books by J. Anker Larsen, widely known as the author of *The Philosopher's Stone,* into at least nine. Indeed, both writers are as well-known abroad as any of their literary countrymen except Hans Christian Andersen, Søren Kierkegaard, and Martin Andersen Nexø.

A few other Danish authors whose works have not been discussed above have been translated into several languages and won critical acceptance because of the original themes in their books. KNUD ANDERSEN (born 1890) has written convincingly of life at sea in a series of novels, several of which have been translated into German and English, Norwegian and Dutch, while individual novels have appeared in Czech, Finnish, and Italian. MARCUS LAUESEN (born 1907) is an interpreter of life along the Danish-German border; his *Og nu venter vi paa Skib (Waiting for a Ship,* 1931) has been translated into eight languages. SVEND FLEURON (1874–1966) has written tales about animals which have appeared in several languages but have enjoyed unusual popularity in German translation.

The erstwhile Arctic explorer PETER FREUCHEN (1886–1957) is known especially for his novel *Eskimo* (1934).

Although not contemporaries, some Danish authors from the past also belong to the living literature of the twentieth century both in Denmark and abroad. The popularity of Hans Christian Andersen is probably exceeded only by the Bible's in the Western world. Although not comparable with Andersen, Jens Peter Jacobsen, as the author of *Marie Grubbe* and *Niels Lyhne,* seems able to hold a firm place in the consciousness of litterateurs outside Denmark. More remarkable is the fact that three Danish writers have experienced a renaissance abroad in the last few decades, and notably in England and America. Søren Kierkegaard is the prime example. From the relative oblivion of national fame and German theological scholarship, he has been vaulted into an exalted and influential position in Western letters. The number of translations of his works into foreign languages (including Japanese) is legion. Ludvig Holberg's international reputation is not as spectacular, but it has continued to grow. Since 1940 many of his plays have appeared in new English, German, and French translations; *Niels Klim* has been republished in French; and a selection of his so-called "epistles" has been published in English. Steen Steensen Blicher, finally, although intimately associated with a national tradition from the early nineteenth century, was remarkably well received when a selection of his tales in English translation (with a foreword by Sigrid Undset) appeared in 1945.

Fate has dealt exceptionally harshly with contemporary Danish literature by removing from the scene many prominent and promising writers before they had passed or even reached their prime: Gustaf Munch-Petersen (died 1938), Nis Petersen (died 1943), Kaj Munk (died 1944), Morten Nielsen (died 1944), Martin A. Hansen (died 1955), Paul la Cour (died 1956), and Leck Fischer (died 1956). Denmark is much bereaved, but the living writers of stature, who will be treated in the following chapter, have received both inspiration and stimulus from their predecessors, as one senses in reading what has come from their pens. If Denmark today cannot boast of a new Holberg or Oehlenschläger, Kierkegaard or Grundtvig, Hans Christian Andersen or Frederik Paludan-Müller, Henrik Pontoppidan, Martin Andersen Nexø or Johannes V. Jensen, it nevertheless remains a highly literate country. To be sure, a literature cannot be judged by its past glories, but *noblesse oblige*; and Denmark continues to feel a deep responsibility toward literary traditions and toward authors of national significance and international reputation who made contributions to literature within the memory of man.

The awareness of literature in Denmark is widespread. A high level of general education, an extensive public library system, opportunities for adult education, the remarkable cultural function of the Danish newspaper, and the tradition of owning books all make for a large and receptive community of readers. Critical consciousness and a concern with literary problems is vigorous and insatiable; interest in literature published in the major languages is spirited.

The number of Danes who have published novels, stories, and poems is very large. A recent popular handbook[1] lists some 500 Danes (in a population of somewhat over four million) who have published two or more volumes of prose or poetry. The novel, the short story, and the lyric are widely cultivated genres in Denmark. There as elsewhere the novel is by far the most read genre, but the fact that a large quantity of verse both appears in periodicals and is separately published is noteworthy. If the drama is a stepchild in recent Danish literature, Danish interest in the drama is nevertheless vigorous. The Danish theater is international in spirit and is open to foreign impulses; contemporary French and American drama in particular has commanded much attention since World War II.

Contemporary Danish society respects individuality and self-expression and demonstrates its appreciation of literature by enlightened popular and state support of literature and other cultural endeavor. Denmark is —after Iceland—one of the leading nations of the world in the production per capita of books and periodicals. Although Danish writers, publishers, and booksellers are by no means satisfied with the place of the book in the public mind, to the foreign observer Denmark seems to uphold a rich humanistic tradition and to enjoy a high degree of literary culture.

---

1 *Vor tids hvem skrev hvad 1914–1955,* Copenhagen 1955.

CHAPTER XVI

Points of the Compass:
Recent Danish Literature

Compared with the new directions and the widespread conscious experimentation with poetic form which characterized intellectual ferment in other, contemporary Western literatures, post-war Danish literature remained noticeably conservative through the 1950's. In the 1960's, however, Danish literature assumed readily identifiable characteristics which showed a strong affinity with the progressive and even revolutionary tendencies dominant in several other literatures. These characteristics were not really new; nor did they belong to hitherto unknown cultural currents. There was, rather, a rapid and demonstrable shift in emphasis within Danish literature as it became more disposed to accept syntactical liberties and uninhibited naturalism, while it became more a part of European literature—and less a specifically Scandinavian phenomenon. Above all, Danish literature identified itself with the concept and ideal of "modernism," which had not previously been predominant in Northern Europe. It became a literature informed by the spirit of Gustav Munch-Petersen rather than of Martin A. Hansen. The shift in attitude was exemplified through the adoption by the hitherto more nationally oriented literary periodical *Vindrosen* of the editorial policy which had prevailed in the internationally oriented cultural organ *Perspektiv*. *Vindrosen*—"the compass"—indeed became the compass for the literary pathfinders of the 1960's; *Perspektiv* expired slowly, with a final volume published in fascicles between 1965 and 1969.

The key word of the 1960's was "modernism." There was an awareness of the concept on the part of imaginative writers, professional critics, and the reading public, although without an attendant realization that modernism is a general term which does not identify a school or even a particular kind of writing. Reduced to its simplest terms, modernist literature is non-retrospective and different from what has gone before. Answering his own rhetorical question, "what is modernism," the perceptive Danish critic TORBEN BROSTRØM (b. 1927) wrote in 1959 in *Vindrosen* (of which he was later to be co-editor, 1966–68) that it was "an effort to penetrate that which is human, and above all in those areas which have not previously been treated consciously by older writers." He noted further that the poet sought a language of form which corresponded to his cognition.

These attempts at definition, while necessarily imperfect and incomplete, are nevertheless indicative of what Danish criticism had in mind when referring to modernism. While every generation and every decade may be said to be in some ways different from the preceding generation or decade, there is not always the willful break with tradition which Danish modernism implied. The modernism of the 1960's in Danish literature could be called literary radicalism, devoid of naïveté. There was greater concern with form than with subject-matter and a cultivated awareness of the psychological and philological possibilities inherent in the word. Psychologically this meant a break with Freudian dogma; philologically, a tendency to word-play. With regard to form, literary radicalism encouraged abandoning the restrictions of syntax; with regard to substance, it tried to absolve society from bourgeois mores, both in the choice of subjects suitable for belletristic treatment and in greater freedom of expression in handling those subjects. Ultimately, it engendered an impersonal kind of poetic manifestation.

In attempting historically to find some point from which the growth of Danish modernism may be reckoned, one fastens on the early work of OLE SARVIG (b. 1921). From his debut in 1944 with *Grønne Digte (Green Poems)*, he tried to help create the myth which his generation so sorely wanted. In so doing, Sarvig served as a catalyst among young Danish writers for a decade. The boldness of his imagery in subsequent volumes of verse and his championship of the cause of modernism was reflected in the work of other young Danish poets. Sarvig's literary theses were reënforced by his own interest in the visual arts, an interest which led to the publication of criticism seeking to explain the relation between art and poetry, notably in his *Krisens Billedbog (Picture Book of the Crisis,* 1950; second, rev. ed., 1962*)*. Playing upon Kierkegaardian overtones, the neo-Christian Sarvig identified an aesthetic direction, a literary direction, and artistic direction in modernism. The third direction was, of course, to be viewed as the synthesis which could lead to a positive goal. Sarvig, along with other contemporaries, demonstrated parallels between poetic and artistic fancy on the one hand and actuality on the other, parallels which were substantiated by twentieth-century developments within the natural and physical sciences. That is to say, the creativity of the imagination proved to have a counterpart in actuality.

Curiously enough, Sarvig did not himself pursue the course of development which might have been prophesied for him in the early 1950's; instead, he subsequently wrote several popular novels. In fact, very few writers who dominated the literary scene in the early 1950's maintained a lasting position of importance. Writers who were well established and widely discussed around 1955 were still writing fifteen years later, to be sure, but their works, and especially their older works, had rather limited appeal to the critical and the general public. There were exceptions, first and foremost THORKILD BJØRNVIG, who published three new collections of verse, *Figur og Ild (Figure and Fire)*, *Vibrationer (Vibrations)*, and the more difficult but neo-classical *Ravnen (The Raven,* i.e., the constellation Corvus) in 1959, 1966, and 1968 respectively, and was able to complete a doctoral dissertation on the work of Martin A. Hansen in the interim (1964). JØRGEN GUSTAVA BRANDT (b. 1928), who made his debut in 1949 as a protégé of the group of writers associated with the periodical *Heretica,* has similarly proved to be more flexible and many-faceted than most of his contemporaries. Ever keen to create new images, and given to subtle satire, Brandt, who employed an impressionistic stream-of-consciousness technique in *Janushoved (Janus Head)* in 1962, returned to a more lucid, but more personal and introspective, style in the two collections of poems entitled *Ateliers* in 1966–67.

New names came quickly to the fore and caused a greater shift in attention than might ordinarily have been expected in so short a time. Members of a new generation that was soon to dominate the scene insistently drew attention to themselves, while the bonds which connected *Vindrosen* with its spiritual origins were dissolved. The reasons for this change were not merely literary and aesthetic. The younger generation looked in vain for the better society a wartime had envisaged; it showed pronounced disaffection toward a world order where there was such a great discrepancy between ideals and reality, where tensions mounted between East and West, and where the major powers continued to employ armed force (especially typified, toward the end of the decade, by the Vietnam War). The older writers who had searched in vain for a new myth had little appeal as spiritual leaders for a postwar generation which moved from disillusioned disengagement to aesthetic activism and political engagement. Indicative of the difference in mood between the end of the 1950's and the end of the 1960's is the kind of question which was debated in literary journals ten years apart. In the fall of 1957, *Perspektiv* printed a symposium on "the isolation of the artist." Ten years later the subject would scarcely have been raised: the youthful practitioners of art and literature did not feel isolated from the main currents of the time.

A noticeable feature of the Danish literary scene in the 1960's was the large amount of criticism written for public consumption both in periodicals and in book form, particularly on the subject of modernism in literature. Criticism was so pervasive that it must be said to have played a role within literature itself. A reader could not confront poetry or prose without some awareness of the critical discussion being carried on in magazines, daily newspapers, books, and over the radio. Consequently, it became increasingly difficult to be a naïve reader. The critics were themselves often imaginative writers, as in the case of several editors of *Vindrosen*. Other eloquent and analytical critics, of a more academic and theoretical persuasion (and notably Aage Henriksen and Johannes Fjord Jensen, who together established a new critical-pedagogical periodical, *Kritik,* in 1967), served as rallying points for young writers of both an imaginative and critical bent. Thus the 1960's can be identified as introspectively critical as well as modernist. The large amount of criticism which seems to have some lasting validity suggests a parallel with Georg Brandes' most active years.

The changes in Danish literature in the dozen years between 1957 and 1969 are best shown by a consideration of *Vindrosen,* the critical and literary organ which originally had superseded *Heretica* (see pp. 297ff.). As its editors changed, so too it changed spirit and contents. Prior to 1959 when two new stellar figures of Danish imaginative literature and criticism, VILLY SØRENSEN (b. 1929) and KLAUS RIFBJERG (b. 1931) took over as editors, the journal had already undergone a mutation and had acquired the international outlook and philosophical-aesthetic bias agreeable to the new editors. In 1958, *Vindrosen,* while still under the editorship of Tage Skou-Hansen and Peter P. Rohde, had performed the remarkable function of reviving Danish interest in German literature—an interest which had been dormant since World War II. The periodical printed not only Villy Sørensen's article about the German "Gruppe 47" but also translations of articles by Gottfried Benn, H. E. Holthusen, Karl Jaspers, and Ernst Jünger, short stories by Ilse Aichinger and Heinrich Böll, and verse by Benn and H. M. Enzensberger. A politically generated cultural prejudice was noticeably alleviated. The moving spirit behind the change was the young and politically irreproachable Villy Sørensen, who had made a serious study of German philosophy, had already translated Hermann Broch into Danish, and was later to write books on Nietzsche (1963) and Kafka (1968).

Sørensen soon established himself as one of the best critical minds in Denmark, when he published *Digtere og Dæmoner (Poets and Demons),* a series of philosophically charged essays about Danish and German literature, in 1959, and issued a collection of his journalistic writings 1959–1961,[1] *Hverken-Eller (Neither-Nor)*, in 1961. Even earlier, he was recognized as one of the country's most successful imaginative writers. His *Sære Historier (Unusual Stories,* 1953*)*[2] and *Ufarlige Historier (Harmless Stories,* 1955*)* are sophisticated, often whimsical tales with an admixture of the fantastic and even the grotesque. They eschew the common devices which are employed in contemporary literature for the sake of greater realism or for shock value. Sørensen consciously suggests that some of his tales are parallel to legends, and himself calls attention to similarities with Kafka (the first collection contains a "Kafka-Idyl."). He wants to engage the reader's imagination and he keeps interest high by prolonging the tension in the denouement, so that the reader is kept wondering how the situation which the author has created can possibly be resolved. Much of the action and dialogue, while arresting and entertaining, seems to be unmotivated, whereas in Sørensen's later creative writing, notably in *Formynderfortællinger (A Guardian's Tales,* 1964*)*, the philosopher is visible behind the story-teller and there is both a sense of serious motivation and symbolic meaning behind the narrative. Oddly enough, there is more relevance to everyday life and more of a realistic technique in the later tales, which—with the exception of "En Fremtidshistorie" ("A Story of the Future")—are set in the past, than the early tales which were set in the present. Sørensen's deliberately expository style, use of phantasy, and predilection for fortuitous circumstance are reminiscent of Karen Blixen. Viewed by itself, Villy Sørensen's imaginative writing seems to have little relation to the modernism which became the order of the day in Danish literature of the 1960's. Even with his editorial work—which includes an anthology of the writings of Marx and an edition of Kierkegaard's *Begrebet Angest*—Sørensen's production is not unusually large, but it has maintained a consistently high level and has been influential in moulding critical opinion among his contemporaries.

Klaus Rifbjerg's rise to literary fame was as spectacular as Villy Sørensen's. His debut was a collection of poems entitled *Under vejr med mig selv (Getting wind of myself)* in 1956 which a reviewer in *Vindrosen* called "awfully fresh and talented," a phrase that is applicable to much of Rifbjerg's production. This first volume of poems, which bore the subtitle

---

1 A second collection, *Mellem Fortid og Nutid (Between Past and Present)* was published in 1969.

2 Published in English as *Tiger in the Kitchen and other strange stories* tr. by Maureen Neiiendam. (New York: Abelard-Schuman [1957]).

"premature autobiography", contains many appealing and humorous metaphors and images. It gives the impression of wit and sarcasm and social criticism rather than of aesthetic experimentation. It also indicates a familiarity with Johannes V. Jensen's verse from the early years of the century—a suggestion which is emphasized and at the same time erotically transformed in the poem "Frokost" ("Lunch") in Rifbjerg's next book of verse, *Efterkrig (Postwar,* 1957*)*. Rifbjerg parochially identified himself with bourgeois Copenhagen in the early poems: he was writing primarily about life in the Danish capital for readers who shared that life. The intentionally limited horizon, albeit now extending to Denmark's borders, is still evident in the rather slapdash verse in *Fædrelandssange (Patriotic Songs)* from the year 1967. An example showing several characteristics of the early poetry is "Bedsteforældre" ("Grandparents"),[1] which concludes,

> I am a small share
> in an unknown future
> deposited in a bank of safety
> among old people
> who soon shall die.

The early Rifbjerg went in heavily for sexual allusions and was in general a daring or "angry" young man. While these traits are still noticeable in his short stories of the mid-1960's, his poetry transcended such prolonged erotic immaturity and became almost monumentally modernistic in the course of a few years. He began to group words without syntactic connectors, to abandon punctuation, to juxtapose the incongruous, and to create new word combinations which are not simply metaphors. The dependence on word association which is so essential to the lengthy poem *Camouflage* (1961) is suggested by a readily comprehensible and semi-humorous poem like "Det er blevet os pålagt" ("We have been called upon," first printed in *Vindrosen,* 1960) which begins, in Jens Nyholm's translation,

> We have been called upon
> by statistics
> in an average life
> to open a very great number of
> doors, tin cans,
> purses, wallets, checking accounts,
> to close a very great number of
> the same
> except tin cans.

1 English translation by Jens Nyholm in *The Literary Review* VIII (1964), p. 96.

With *Camouflage,* modernism and syntactical experimentation *à la* Joyce made its clearest impact on Danish literature. Rifbjerg had quickly established himself as a brilliant and promising writer, who could communicate his ideas and his images to the average reader and who was a leader of his own generation. He now elected to employ the psychologically extreme technique of depending almost entirely on the power of association rather than carrying on any sort of rational argument; he therewith risked his literary reputation and popularity by writing without the usual restraints of form and syntax. One could not say for sure whether he was showing the intrepidness of an explorer or the arrogance of the intellectually elite. In any case, despite a sharp division of opinion about the new work, Rifbjerg grew in stature by demonstrating a remarkable versatility.

In a series with the common title *Portræt (Portrait),* published two years later, Rifbjerg varied his technique by employing a sort of cinematographic impressionism and depending on the visual effect of the printed poem to help convey an idea. Essentially, Rifbjerg was giving a series of insights into human life at various stages of development: he provides a sequence of naturalistic-psychological situations depicted without inhibitions. He did exactly the same through a different medium in the volume of short stories *Og andre historier (And other stories)* published in 1964. (The title, which echoes Hans Christian Andersen, may possibly complement his co-editor, Villy Sørensen's *Unusual Stories* published eleven years previously). Like H. C. Branner a quarter of a century before him, Rifbjerg was able to write convincingly from the viewpoint of a child; in Rifbjerg, however, the viewpoint could change as the child *persona* grew older. There is a continued preoccupation with sexuality in Rifbjerg: puberty, perversion, and adultery provide a strong undercurrent in the stories, which, however, are told in a disarmingly naïve manner, consciously disregarding bourgeois prejudice and without a suggestion of indignation—as for example in "Frække Jensen" ("Bold Jensen"), the tale of a perverted radio repairman who used his shop to commit immoral acts with children and on whom the narrator himself informed. Almost an affectation in Rifbjerg's language is the tendency to use jargon, vulgarities, and the parlance of the street. While Rifbjerg can be psychologically complicated, as in the story "Peter Plys" ("Winnie the Pooh"), where erotic associations from childhood create a highly ambivalent emotional situation for an adult, most often he is not subtle. He plays upon human weaknesses, which are pictured in an exaggerated fashion. Rifbjerg's strength as a narrator is his willingness to dispense with unnecessary details but to emphasize those details—in themselves perhaps insignificant—which echo insistently in the minds of the characters and subsequently in the mind of the reader.

Rifbjerg has written in all major genres. His first novel, *Den kroniske Uskyld (Chronic innocence,* 1958*)*, which deals with the erotic problems of teenagers and a kind of short-circuit between two generations, was a popular success and has been several times reprinted. Four later novels have very different plots, although eroticism is common to them all. As a novelist Rifbjerg has not always been able to amalgate his linguistic virtuosity and his ability to create grotesquely humorous situations with convincing character portrayal. *Arkivet (The Archives,* 1967*)* is perhaps worthy of mention as a modern story about the white-collared little man who appeared so often in the literature of the 1930's; the novel concentrates on the trivial events of everyday life. Rifbjerg won greatest critical acclaim for *Anna (jeg) Anna (Anna—I—Anna,* 1969*)*, which portrays a woman with a psychopathic split personality—to make his point Rifbjerg has her speak sometimes in the first and sometimes in the third person—whose flight from a compulsion neurosis leads her into a series of dramatic, erotic, and brutal adventures in the company of a young fugitive from justice. Especially by building up tension and introducing the unexpected, Rifbjerg holds the attention of the reader from the beginning of the story, a morning in Karachi, to the abrupt end, a morning near the harbor of Copenhagen. Psychologically, Rifbjerg seems convincing although, rather illogically, everything is related in the present tense.

The two-act play *Hvad en mand har brug for (What a man needs,* 1966*)* is of interest because of its form. In substance a story of disillusionment in the same spirit as *Arkivet* and using some of the elements of Kjeld Abell's *The Melody that Got Lost,* it is strongly reminiscent of German Ludwig Tieck's *Der gestiefelte Kater* as well as Johan Ludvig Heiberg's *Julespøg og Nytaarsløjer,* both from the first half of the nineteenth century. The action shifts from stage "reality" to the play within the play, so that there is a confusion of reality and stage-acting.

As editors of *Vindrosen,* Villy Sørensen and Klaus Rifbjerg did not feel the limitations of any narrow horizon. In fact, in the first year of their collaboration, they set the tone for the 1960's by publishing imaginative prose by Samuel Beckett, Brendan Behan, and Alain Robbe-Grillet, articles by both French and German critics, as well as contributions by incisive Danish critics—Niels Barfoed, Thorkild Bjørnvig, and Torben Brostrøm—and imaginative writers—Ove Abildgaard, Ole Wivel, and,

again, Bjørnvig, among the established names, and several slightly younger but very promising talents such as Cecil Bødker, Jørgen Sonne,
and Jess Ørnsbo. All of these Danish writers soon proved themselves in
the tourney of popular and critical judgment and thus proved the vision
of the periodical's editors. Time and again *Vindrosen* brought foreign
literature—French, Spanish, Polish, English, German—to its readers,
but on the average it gave more space to domestic than to foreign talent.
Practically every Danish writer of the decade whose work might be discussed in a detailed appraisal of Danish literature made an appearance in
Vindrosen, from the octogenarian causeur, ALBERT DAM (b. 1880), whose
homely but serious reflections gained him an unexpectedly large audience
chiefly among middle-aged readers, to the radical young poetess CHAR-
LOTTE STRANDGAARD (b. 1944).

Toward the end of the decade the periodical showed an increase in
political awareness. In 1967 it published three articles on the Vietnam
War and devoted several pages to Greek poetry after the establishment
of a military junta in Greece. In taking leave of *Vindrosen* in 1968, Niels
Barfoed (who had been an editor since 1964) wrote that "the presentation
of a new Danish literature has had to make way for social and political
orientation, which of itself has supplanted literary-theoretical orientation." The trend toward social and political discussion became
clearer in 1969 with another change of editors. Primarily as a reflex of the
Vietnam War, but also because of the Russian occupation of Czechoslovakia 1968 and in response to various kinds of unrest both at home and
abroad, *Vindrosen* and Danish literature as a whole was indisputably
engagé by 1970.

The modernism which claimed so much attention in the 1960's is
identified by syntactical and even grammatical experimentation, by forced
but often non-metaphoric imagery frequently colored by sexual experience, and by the importance of word associations. Syntactical eccentricity
went to the limits of comprehensibility, so that some attempts to be linguistically creative can be called chaotic and absurd—although willfully
so. The most consistent practitioner of expression through syntactic chaos
was IVAN MALINOVSKI (b. 1926), who was a regular contributor to *Vindrosen* throughout the decade. He was originally inspired by Ole Sarvig but,
unlike Sarvig, continued to work with difficult imagery and to produce
modernistic verse in a probing, intense fashion. A notable example of
modernist poetry is Malinovski's collection *Galgenfrist (Respite at the
Gallows,* 1958), in which the first poem bears the portentous Latin title
"Disjecta membra." This unpunctuated poem consists of a series of dis-

jointed images which, taken in sequence, give the poem its meaning. The surrealistic effect—also achieved in other poems, such as "Tøbrud" ("Thaw")—is characteristic of Malinovski's entire production. His collection of verse *Vi skal leve som var der en fremtid og et håb (We must live as were there a future and a hope)*, published in 1969, suggests Malinovski's relationship to other currents in contemporary literature by using as a title a phrase coined by another poet, OLE BUNDGÅRD POVLSEN (b. 1918). Unlike Malinovski, Bundgård Povlsen employs clear imagery and syntax and draws from a broad spectrum of subject matter. His verse is more typical of the times with its fluctuation between willful objectivity and irrepressible subjectivity, seen in the retrospective collection significantly entitled *Tidsdigte (Poems of the Times)*, edited by Torben Brostrøm and published in 1967.

An example of the rapid transition from traditional lyric exposition to semi-incomprehensibility for the casual reader is the work of JESS ØRNSBO (b. 1932), an editor of *Vindrosen* 1964–65. His *Digte (Poems, 1960)* contained verse composed with normal syntax but full of striking metaphors with psychological overtones and prose poetry which depended on the pathos of common situations for its effects. There were also erotic images infused with ironic and suggestive humor, as in the lines, "And sex / like a dog / wants petting every day" ("og kønnet / som en hund / skal røres hver dag"). Only four years later, however, in the collection *Myter (Myths, 1964)*, Ørnsbo depended mainly on the effect of associations to communicate his ideas to the reader, while he intentionally destroyed traditional meaning by the use of bizarre images and juxtapositions. One might query, for example, what he had in mind when he coined such a phrase as "crazed rubber cyclops." In Ørnsbo as in numerous of his contemporaries, some words and phrases seem to have found their way to paper by virtue of sound association rather than as the adjunct of an abstract concept which the poet presumably wants to project. It would be incorrect to label this manner of writing as arbitrary, for it consciously endeavors to represent the reality which is the nervous maze of human perception.

Two other lyrists, both of whom may be called artistic modernists, JØRGEN SONNE (b. 1915) and PER HØJHOLT (b. 1928), represent predominantly an international and a national orientation respectively, although they have much in common formally. Sonne, who has translated widely and who admits a special indebtedness to English literature, is a master of sophisticated composition and is given to abstruse cultural allusions. Højholt, who originally established himself under the aegis of *Heretica,* evinced a satirical bent as well as a penchant for original observations in the three volumes of poetry he published in the 1960's. The mature and penetrating quality of his later verse may be illustrated by the line from *Poetens Hoved (The Poet's Head,* 1963): "Where everything confronts its own image, reality ceases." Both Sonne and Højholt, like several of their contemporaries, underwent a perceptible development in the 1960's toward a less metaphorically lucid poetry and a greater awareness of the possibilities of auditory effects.

A subsequent and tangential development of the modernism exemplified in Denmark by Malinovski and Rifbjerg is the current of "concrete" poetry which was slow to make headway in Denmark or to appear in *Vindrosen,* but which acquired sudden legitimation with the publication of VAGN STEEN's *Digte? (Poems?)* in 1964. Steen (b. 1928) and other writers who have used similar techniques represent a rapid movement away from the Freudian introspection which had made itself felt so strongly in Danish literature for decades as well as from the awkward experimentation with forms and language associated with modernism. Unlike the experimentors who depended primarily upon phonic effects and intellectual constructs, the concrete poets explore the possibilities of the word itself, play openly with language and—in a way like Baroque poets— stress the visual effect of the printed and written word. Steen is full of imaginative humor and has been able to engage the sympathetic attention of a large number of readers both old and young. His publications subsequent to *Digte?* are as much efforts to make the reader see the poetic potential of words, as to understand what Steen himself has done with them. Steen says bluntly that the poem no longer need be an emotional outpouring or the expression of the individual. His vantage point is that of the philologist.

Not all concretist poets have been as forthright as Steen. Some have depended more on the visual image itself than upon the word and could be called graphic artists rather than poets. Especially under the impact of concretism, however, Danish poetry in the late 1960's turned from metaphor and evolved a descriptive poetry which depends on realistic imagery, syntactical freedom, and word-play for its effect. In an incisive note to an anthology of contemporary verse, *Eksempler (Examples,* 1968), HANS-JØRGEN NIELSEN (b. 1941), himself a poet and critic, spoke for the younger generation of imaginative writers when he quoted the German philosopher Wittgenstein's remark that the limits of one's language are the limits of one's world. For contemporary poetry the sentiment may also be reversed.

The methods of concrete poetry, albeit much tempered by numerous other currents, reached a triumphant apex with the publication in 1969 of *Det (It)* by INGER CHRISTENSEN (b. 1935). This unusually long collection of texts printed both as massive prose and in verse form should be read neither *in toto* as a single dynamic work nor as a collection of individual poems. It must be considered as a collection of poetic texts in groups that are assimilable somewhat like Biblical books, as is suggested by the key word to the book's tripartite contents: *logos*. The reader is affected primarily by an impelling and rhythmic use of language in which the most pronounced rhetorical device is a kind of progressive, climactic anaphora that suggests a modern symphonic technique. Repetition, word play, parallelism, and irony seem more important than imagery *per se*. Inger Christensen's driving ethical concern with the essentials of human existence informs her work. Acidly critical, she is intrinsically the ironic castigator of human folly, although *Det* has been called—and probably correctly—a kind of modern Genesis.

Modernism is a broad concept; not all the poets who have won critical acceptance resemble the writers who have dominated the literary scene on the one hand or the concretists on the other. BENNY ANDERSEN (b. 1929) is such a poet, in whose work a dynamic movement is visible from the metaphorical, in *Kamera med Køkkenadgang (Camera with Kitchen Privileges, 1962)* to the only semi-metaphorical and descriptive, in *Den indre Bowlerhat (The Inner Derby, 1964)*. The descriptive, even enumerative, tendency suggested by some of Benny Andersen's perceptive verse is more pronounced in the work of POUL BORUM (b. 1934), whose impressionistic, rhymeless but alliterative poems nevertheless reflect the poet's own emotional experience. He seemed to be aware of Benny Andersen's ironic admonition, "it is indefensible to bring words into the world" ("Det er uforsvarligt at sætte ord i verden") when he himself wrote programmatically in *Rinkesten (Rolling Stone, 1964)*—a collection which ends with a poem in English by Wallace Stevens—"I will let my poem be like a deserted farm in the hills / unpeopled and without needs." Borum was advocating what Stevens called pure poetry and Rainer Maria Rilke, the *Ding-Gedicht*. As with the concretists, the word, like the visible object, was to have its own existence and not primarily to be an expression of emotion. In a versified note, "To the reader," at the conclusion of *Sang (Song, 1967)* Borum wrote,

I envisage a situation
where we on equal footing
could communicate to one another

> essential things
> And until then
> my words stand alone

The new *Ding-Gedicht* had a practitioner even earlier in the poetess CECIL BØDKER (b. 1927) whose verse combines such naïve charm and sophistication and is so pervaded with gentle humor that, were she to be judged by her poetry, she might seem disassociated from the modernism of the 1960's. Noteworthy examples of her early poetic style are "Adam's Rib," and "Vacation" from her first volume of verse, *Luseblomster (Dandelions, 1955)* and the "Ode to a Dead Cat" from her second, *Fygende Heste (Flying Horses, 1956).*[1] In simple language which is both metaphoric and descriptive and with a marked tendency toward personification, she asks such nostalgic questions as in the poem "Faceless,"

> September
> was it you who went
> freezing
> past my door
> with whey-tinged hands
> shamefully behind your back?

Cecil Bødker has the appeal of the young Tove Ditlevsen from two decades earlier, but her writing has less of the pathetic undertone which underlay (and still underlies) Tove Ditlevsen's writing.

Although Cecil Bødker's early poems were well received, her reputation grew measurably with the publication of her collection of short stories, *Øjet (The Eye, 1961)*. Whereas the drama had dominated Danish literature in the 1930's, poetry in the 1940's, and the novel in the late 1940's and early 1950's, the most succesful genre since the late 1950's has been the short story. Cecil Bødker is only one of several writers who first established themselves in other genres and who have subsequently written noteworthy short stories. Others are PETER SEEBERG (b. 1925), who won acclaim with his novel *Bipersonerne (Subordinate Characters, 1956)*, about involuntary laborers in wartime Berlin; POUL ØRUM (b. 1919) Denmark's most prolific novelist after 1953; TAGE SKOU-HANSEN (b. 1925), one of the original editors of *Vindrosen*, who made his mark early as author of two novels about the Occupation; and the poet Benny Andersen—not to mention the philosopher-critic Villy Sørensen and the all-round *littérateur* Klaus Rifbjerg, whose contributions to the genre have

---

1 These poems, tr. by George Schoolfield, are to be found in *The Literary Review* VIII (1964), pp. 115 ff.

been mentioned above. Generally speaking, collections of short stories by individual authors, as well as anthologies of short stories, have been more widely read in the 1960's than in the two or three previous decades. Villy Sørensen's first two volumes of short stories have both appeared as paperbacks and as such have been reprinted several times. A fourth edition of Klaus Rifbjerg's *Og andre historier* was published in 1967. *I morgen kommer paddehatteskyen (The mushroom cloud will come tomorrow)*, the collection of short stories with which PETER RONILD (b. 1928) made his debut in 1959, was reissued in 1966, the same year his second collection was published. Cecil Bødker's *Øjet* was reprinted in 1967 and 1969.

The title story from the collection *Øjet*[1] created effective new imagery and engaged the sympathetic attention of the reading public. It is at the same time stylistically creative and sociologically moving. The "eye" which impersonally views an eschatologically frightening situation speaks for a generation which cannot erase from its subconscious the possibility of destruction and chaos brought about by atomic warfare. There is to be sure no mention of the atomic bomb or other instruments of destruction and no apparent didactic intent which favors any political or even religious persuasion. The reader is nevertheless bound to share the concern and feeling of insecurity from which the story has sprung:

> "I'm the eye that saw; I have no use for any explanations. That the cause was this or that makes no difference, because what happened was the way it was, indisputable, a conjunction of circumstances which flowed into one another and could be seen.
> And which I could see."

The effect of the story, like much modernist verse, depends on the associations which it evokes, although there is no attempt to subvert exposition and syntax. As in later works, however, Cecil Bødker does demand from the reader an ability to combine elements of her narrative into a whole which she herself need not spell out. Like most of the other stories in *Øjet* the title story is not bound to place or time. Elements which would limit the lasting validity of the narrative situation have been avoided. Despite the eschatological quality of "Den yderste dag" ("Doomsday"), a boy's experience with a fox might have taken place at any point in history or prehistory where the essentials of the story were given: a natural catastrophe, a boy, a fox, and a dead bird. Only the passing

---

1 "The Eye" tr. by Walter Foote was published in *The Literary Review* VIII (1964), pp. 121–129 and reprinted in *Stories From The Literary Review*, Fairleigh Dickinson University Press, 1969, pp. 54–64.

mention of an automobile in another story, "Tyren" ("The Bull") associates it with the twentieth century.

One of the attributes of modernism especially noticeable in the short
story is an analytical and almost clinical interest in the psychic forces
responsible for individual, eccentric, and unusual responses to visible
as well as hidden stimuli. So common are such responses that one hesitates to identify them as matters of abnormal psychology, although not
a few subjects employed by writers who are attracted to psychic phenomena are indeed abnormal and even pathological by usual standards.

Imaginative writers like Cecil Bødker and Peter Seeberg, who evince
special perceptiveness for the psychic problem, are not satisfied merely
to address themselves to the eternally valid but somewhat bald subject
of sexual drives, but instead suggest other reasons for human action—and
depict some of the more subtle variations of Eros in daily life as well.

As the author of the collection *Eftersøgningen (The Search, 1962)*, Peter
Seeberg has shown himself as a master of the psychological sketch.
Unlike Cecil Bødker in her prose works, he is sometimes a humorist to
boot. Seeberg has a subtle comprehension of the demented mind, for
which he shows sympathetic understanding. He neither revels in depicting
sexual excesses nor passes a moral judgment. Rather, he shows the fine
line which separates apparently normal from distinctly abnormal behav-
ior—perhaps clearest in the story "Bulen" ("The Dent"),[1] originally
published in *Vindrosen* in 1961, in which a psychotic outburst and catharsis is evoked by a series of trivial annoyances culminating in the main
character's reaction to a scratched automobile fender. The subtlest story
in the collection is "Kapitulation," in which a man is suffering from a
psychosis that takes the outward form of trying in vain to remember
something. His wife's commonplace, that he will "figure it out in the
morning," far from quieting the storm, really serves to exclude a solution
of the problem.

SVEND ÅGE MADSEN (b. 1939) goes a step farther than Seeberg in drawing pictures of schizophrenia and insanity in his collection of short
stories *Otte gange orphan (Eight times orphan, 1965)*. Madsen shows profound insights into the psychopathic mind. He tries to write from the
standpoint of the egocentrically insane person while, at the same time,
he (like Seeberg) stays within the perimeter of the average man's realm
of daydreams and psychic aberration. He lets his readers sense a pattern
in the deranged mind and in the ideas, perverse though they may be, which

1 English tr. by Børge Gedsø Madsen in *The Literary Review* VIII (1964), pp. 47–53.

drive the psychopath to action. The narration is in the form of monologues, disrupted only by the introduction of a second person. Whereas in
his first novel, *Besøget (The Visit,* 1963*)*, his debt to certain literary
antecedents, notably Kafka and Beckett, was fairly clear, Madsen demonstrated an original and brilliant narrative technique in the first part of
his so-called "anti-novel," *Lystbilleder (Pictures of Pleasure,* 1964*) :* the
plot is told in a series of brief, impressionistic paragraphs in which words
are used repetitiously as in some modern poetry and in which the illusion
that the narrative seems to create is methodically destroyed time and
again in order to establish a thesis. For example: "A girl who was raped
in India. Or someplace like that. Yes, India will do." Verse-like imagery,
the contiguity of ideas and experiences, and the power of association create both fantastic and satirical situations. Madsen is modern, not in the
sense of the "modernism" which was so pervasive in the Danish literary
consciousness for a decade, but by writing in a new way—and a way
which would not have been used for publication by an earlier generation.

Still a different approach to psychological problems and the phenomenon of the weird in what seems to be the everyday world is met in the
short novels of ULLA RYUM (b. 1937). Her *Natsangersken (Songbird of the
Night,* 1963*)* and *Latterfuglen (Laughing Jackass,* 1965*)* have enjoyed popular success, although they do not satisfy the formula that would require
a reader somehow to be able to identify himself with a novel's main
character.

Between imaginative literature and history, finally, lies the new—and
enthusiastically received—sub-genre of the "documentary novel," which
has its Danish master in THORKILD HANSEN (b. 1927). This type of narrative, based on exacting scrutiny of source material and, where possible, an attempt to reëxperience the events which are recounted, must be
distinguished from the traditional historical novel in which the author
gives his imagination free play. Success with the documentary novel
depends on an ability to work within the strictures of historical evidence
and to eschew the melodramatic while nevertheless employing an imaginative style. Early associated with the contributors to *Heretica,* Hansen
gravitated via history and archeology toward the reinterpretation of half-
forgotten events of extraordinary human endeavor. His *Det lykkelige
Arabien (Arabia Felix,* 1962*)*[1] is an arresting and detailed portrayal of
the eighteenth-century Danish expedition to Arabia which is identified

---

1 *Arabia Felix, the Danish Expedition of 1761–1767,* tr. James & Kathleen McFarlane. New
York: Harper & Row; London: Collins, 1964.

with the name of its sole survivor, Carsten Niebuhr. In 1965 Hansen published a similar work about Jens Munk's seventeenth-century search for the Northwest Passage. After reporting on the Jens Munk Memorial Expedition with his archeological colleague Peter Seeberg, Hansen turned to the sordid story of the Danish slave trade, which he described in a moving trilogy: *Slavernes Kyst (The Slaves' Coast,* 1967), *Slavernes Skibe (The Slaves' Ships,* 1968), and *Slavernes Øer (The Slaves' Islands,* 1970). With their delineation of memorable human experiences, Hansen's books have won both critical and popular acclaim and have earned him a series of literary awards.

By 1970 the term "modernism" was no longer a label which sufficed to identify the most influential currents in Danish literature. One could speak, rather, of several qualities which were characteristic of the contemporary literary scene: the freedom to depict without inhibitions any and all events and conditions in human life on the psychic as well as the physical level and at least superficially a tendency toward graphic description of sexual behaviour; a renewed awareness of social and political responsibility on the part of the artist; the apperception of cultural movements which were not national in origin, an indifference toward traditional aesthetics, and a concomitant emphasis on the intrinsic value of auditory and visual symbols. Poetry and short stories were cultivated with somewhat more success than the novel and considerably more success than the drama—a genre which the newer media of radio and, particularly, television in part preëmpted, without, however, giving promise of creating works of lasting interest. The sharp rise in the cost of printing and publishing which accompanied economic inflation exerted a slightly negative effect on the position of the book in Danish culture, but the body politic continued, both directly and indirectly, its enlightened support of imaginative literature.

BIBLIOGRAPHICAL NOTE

Elias Bredsdorff, *Danish Literature in English Translation. A Bibliography.*
Copenhagen, 1950, is an indispensable reference work. The compiler has
endeavored to list not only all known translations of Danish poetry and
prose published through 1949 but also books and articles in English
about Danish literary subjects.

The following anthologies of Danish literature in translation are re-
commended to the reader who does not have a command of the Danish
language:
A Book of Danish Verse. Translated into the original meters by S.
Foster Damon and Robert Silliman Hillyer. Selected and annotated by
Oluf Friis. New York: The American-Scandinavian Foundation, 1922.
Denmark's Best Stories. An Introduction to Danish Fiction. A Selection of
Short Stories by Andersen, Blicher, Goldschmidt, Jacobsen, Schandorph,
Drachmann, Bang, Pontoppidan, Wied, Knudsen, Larsen, Skjoldborg,
Nexø, Jensen, Söiberg, Gunnarsson. Edited by Hanna Astrup Larsen.
New York: The American-Scandinavian Foundation [1928].
20th Century Scandinavian Poetry... General Editor, Martin S. Allwood.
Copenhagen: Gyldendal, 1950. Therein: pp. 31–105, Denmark. Edited
by Knud K. Mogensen. With an introduction by Harald Engberg.
Contemporary Danish Plays. An Anthology. [Introduction and supervi-
sion of translations by Elias Bredsdorff]. Copenhagen: Gyldendal, 1955.
Contemporary Danish Prose. [Supervision of translation by Elias Breds-
dorff]. Copenhagen: Gyldendal, 1958.
The Literary Review (Teaneck, New Jersey: Fairleigh Dickinson University) VIII:1. Denmark number. Fall 1964.

Anthology of Danish Literature. Bilingual edition. Edited by F. J. Billeskov Jansen and P. M. Mitchell. Carbondale & Edwardsville: Southern
Illinois University Press, 1971.

Some of the more important books and articles written in English about
Danish literature, including several titles which have appeared since the
publication of Bredsdorff's bibliography, are listed here.

ANCIENT LITERATURE

Axel Olrik, *Viking Civilization*. Revised after the author's death by Hans Ellekilde. New York: The American-Scandinavian Foundation, 1930.

Axel Olrik, *The Heroic Legends of Denmark*. Translated from the Danish and Revised in Collaboration with the author by Lee M. Hollander. New York: The American-Scandinavian Foundation, 1919.

G. Turville-Petre, *The Heroic Age of Scandinavia*. London: Hutchinson's University Library [1951].

THE BALLADS

A Book of Danish Ballads. Selected and With an Introduction by Axel Olrik. Translated by E. M. Smith-Dampier. New York: The American-Scandinavian Foundation, 1939; Oxford University Press, 1939.

Johannes C. H. R. Steenstrup, *The Mediaeval Popular Ballad*. Translated by Edward Godfrey Cox. Boston, 1914.

S. B. Hustvedt, *Ballad Criticism in Scandinavia and Great Britain during the Eighteenth Century*. New York: The American-Scandinavian Foundation, 1916.

W. P. Ker, "On the Danish Ballads I-II", in *Collected Essays of W. P. Ker*. Edited with an introduction by Charles Whibley. Vol. II. London, 1925.

S. B. Hustvedt, *Ballad Books and Ballad Men. Raids and Rescues in Britain, America, and the Scandinavian North since 1800*. Cambridge: Harvard University Press, 1930.

EIGHTEENTH-CENTURY LITERATURE

J. W. Eaton, *The German Influence in Danish Literature in the Eighteenth Century. The German Circle in Copenhagen 1750–1770*. Cambridge: University Press, 1929.

NINETEENTH-CENTURY LITERATURE

Edmund W. Gosse, "Four Danish Poets" (Grundtvig, Bødtcher, Hans Christian Andersen, Frederik Paludan-Müller), and "The Danish National Theatre," in *Studies in the Literature of Northern Europe*. London, 1879; repr. 1883. Republished in Gosse's *Northern Studies*. London, 1890.— An interesting complementary memoir is Gosse's *Two Visits to Denmark. 1872, 1874*. London, 1911.

MODERN POETRY

Oluf Friis, "Outlines of Danish Poetry from Oehlenschläger to

Johannes V. Jensen," in *Edda,* XXI, 1924, pp. 13–69. Complements *A Book of Danish Verse,* 1922.

HANS CHRISTIAN ANDERSEN

Georg Brandes, "Hans Christian Andersen," in *Creative Spirits of the Nineteenth Century.* Translated by Rasmus B. Anderson. New York, 1923; London, 1924. Originally published as *Eminent Authors.* New York, 1886.

Fredrik Böök, *Hans Christian Andersen. A Biography.* tr. George C. Schoolfield. University of Oklahoma Press, 1962.

Signe Toksvig, *The Life of Hans Christian Andersen.* London, 1933; New York, 1934.

A Book on the Danish Writer Hans Christian Andersen his Life and Work. Copenhagen, 1955. Contains contributions by Julius Bomholt, Svend Larsen, Paul V. Rubow, Erik Dal, and Cai M. Woel.

STEEN STEENSEN BLICHER

Sigrid Undset, introduction to *Twelve Stories* by Steen Steensen Blicher... New York: The American-Scandinavian Foundation, 1945; Oxford University Press, 1946.

N. F. S. GRUNDTVIG

P. G. Lindhardt, *Grundtvig. An Introduction.* London: S. P. C. K., 1951.

Hal Koch, *Grundtvig.* Translated from the Danish. With an Introduction and Notes by Llewellyn Jones. Antioch (Ohio), 1952.

Johannes Knudsen, *Danish Rebel: A Study of N. F. S. Grundtvig.* Philadelphia, 1955.

Ernest D. Nielsen, *N. F. S. Grundtvig: An American Study.* Rock Island (Illinois), 1955.

Note: *Grundtvig Studier,* published annually since 1948 by the Danish Grundtvig Society, includes English summaries of articles and reviews.

LUDVIG HOLBERG

Oscar James Campbell, *The Comedies of Holberg.* Cambridge: Harvard University Press, 1914.

"The Danish National Theater: Ludvig Holberg," in Henry Ten Eyck Perry, *Masters of Dramatic Comedy and their Social Times.* Cambridge, Mass.: Harvard University Press, 1939, pp. 199–235.

JENS PETER JACOBSEN

Alrik Gustafson, "Toward Decadence. Jens Peter Jacobsen," in *Six*

Scandinavian Novelists. New York: The American-Scandinavian Foundation, 1940; Oxford University Press, 1941. Repr. 1967.

SØREN KIERKEGAARD

Walter Lowrie, *Kierkegaard.* Oxford University Press, 1938.

Walter Lowrie, *A Short Life of Kierkegaard.* Princeton University Press, 1942; Oxford University Press, 1943, repr. 1965.

David F. Swenson, *Something about Kierkegaard.* Revised and enlarged edition. Edited by Lillian Marvin Swenson. Minneapolis (Minnesota), 1945.

Aage Henriksen, *Methods and Results of Kierkegaard Studies in Scandinavia. A Historical and Critical Survey.* Copenhagen: Ejnar Munksgaard, 1951.

Note: the number of articles which have been published in periodicals about Kierkegaard is enormous. Attention is called to the special issue of *Orbis litterarum* (X, 1-2), also separately published as *Symposion Kierkegaardianum,* which contains contributions in the major languages. Of interest to the student of literature is Aage Henriksen's "Kierkegaard's Reviews of Literature," pp. 75–83.

FREDERIK PALUDAN-MÜLLER

Georg Brandes, "Frederik Paludan-Müller," in *Creative Spirits of the Nineteenth Century.* New York, 1923; London, 1924.

KAREN BLIXEN ("ISAK DINESEN")

Eric O. Johannesson, *The World of Isak Dinesen.* University of Washington Press, 1961.

Robert W. Langbaum, *The Gayety of Vision. A Study of Isak Dinesen's Art.* New York: Random House [1965].

The standard histories of Danish literature are the following.

Carl S. Petersen and Vilhelm Andersen [and Richard Paulli], *Illustreret dansk Litteraturhistorie* I-IV, Copenhagen: Gyldendal, 1924–34. With valuable bibliographical supplements. An historical presentation which treats of literature in the broadest sense of the word, this work replaced P. Hansen, *Illustreret dansk Litteraturhistorie* I-III, Copenhagen, 1902, which was meant to supersede N. M. Petersen, *Bidrag til den danske Literaturs Historie* I-V, Copenhagen, 1868–72.

F. J. Billeskov Jansen, *Danmarks Digtekunst*. Copenhagen: Ejnar Munksgaard, 1944. In progress; volume III appeared in 1958. A generic and aesthetic study of Danish literature.

Oluf Friis, *Den danske Litteraturs Historie*. Copenhagen: H. Hirschsprungs Forlag, 1945. In progress. The first volume constitutes the most thorough study of Danish literature through the Age of the Reformation which has been written.

Sven Møller Kristensen, *Dansk Litteratur 1918–1952*. Sixth edition. Copenhagen: Ejnar Munksgaard, 1965. A detailed examination of the works of contemporary Danish writers. With a supplement on the years 1952–1964.

Dansk Litteratur Historie. By Gustav Albeck, F. J. Billeskov Jansen, Oluf Friis, Peter P. Rohde, Hakon Stangerup, Torben Brostrøm, and Jens Kistrup. General editor, P. H. Traustedt. I–IV. [Copenhagen:] Politikens Forlag, 1964–66.

Bio-bibliographical information about Danish writers of the first half of the twentieth century is to be found in *Dansk skønlitterært forfatterleksikon 1900–1950*. Ed. Svend Dahl, Ludvig Bramsen, Mogens Haugsted, Povl Engelstoft. I–III. Copenhagen: Grønholt Pedersen, 1959–64.

ON PRONOUNCING DANISH NAMES

The following rules are intended as a guide to an acceptable anglicized pronunciation of Danish names. They are not intended to produce a Danish pronunciation, which can be achieved only by exposure to the spoken language.

VOWELS. In accented syllables they may be given the following values:

    a as in *father*
    e as in *bed*
    i as in *machine*
    o as in *obey*
    u as in *rude*
    y (the equivalent of German *ü,* or the French *u* in *sur*)
    æ like the *a* in *acre* when long and
        like the *e* in *deck* when short
    ø (nearly the equivalent of German *ö*) like *u* in *burr*
    aa (å) like the *o* in *ford*

In unaccented syllables the values are similar, except that *e* is pronounced like the *e* in *father.*

DIPHTHONGS.

    au, av like *ou* in *house*
    ei, ej, aj, and *-eg* like *eye*
    oi, øj, øy like *oy* in *boy*

CONSONANTS. On the whole they are pronounced as in English. Note, however, the pronunciation of

    j like *y* in *yes*
        (*bj-* is therefore pronounced like the beginning of *beauty*).
    s and *z* like the *s* in *sick* (never as in *easy*)
    w like *v*
    ch like *k*
    d between vowels or after a vowel like the *th* in *this*
        (e. g., Wied, pron. *veeth*)

In certain positions, some consonants are usually silent:

 d after *n, l, r* and before *s* (e.g., Andersen, pron. *ahnnersen*;
  Kierkegaard, pron. *keerkagore*)

 g between vowels (e.g., Jæger, pron. *yayer*)

 h before *j* or *v* (e.g., Hjortø, pron. *yortö*)

 j after *k* or *g* (e.g., Gjellerup, pron. *gellerup*)

ACCENT. Generally the first syllable is accented, but names of non-Germanic origin ordinarily do not have the accent on the first syllable (e.g., Pontóppidan).

INDEX

OF AUTHORS, TRANSLATORS, AND TITLES

*

According to international usage, *æ (ä)* and *ø (ö)* are treated as *ae* and *oe*.

[333]